Implementing Augmentative
and Alternative Communication

Implementing Augmentative and Alternative Communication

Strategies for Learners with Severe Disabilities

WITHDRAWN

by

Joe Reichle, Ph.D.
Professor
Department of Communication Disorders
and
Training Director
Research and Training Center
on Community Living
University of Minnesota
Minneapolis

Jennifer York, Ph.D., P.T.
Assistant Professor
Department of Educational Psychology
and
Training Director
Institute on Community Integration
University of Minnesota
Minneapolis

and

Jeff Sigafoos, Ph.D.
Lecturer
Fred and Eleanor Schonell Special Education Research Centre
The University of Queensland
Brisbane, Australia

with invited contributors

·P·A·U·L·H·
BROOKES
PUBLISHING C°

Baltimore · London · Toronto · Sydney

Paul H. Brookes Publishing Co.
P.O. Box 10624
Baltimore, Maryland 21285–0624

Typeset by The Composing Room of Michigan, Inc., Grand Rapids, Michigan.
Manufactured in the United States of America by
The Maple Press Company, York, Pennsylvania.

Library of Congress Cataloging-in-Publication Data

Implementing augmentative and alternative communication : strategies for learners
with severe disabilities / edited by Joe Reichle, Jennifer York, and Jeff Sigafoos,
with invited contributors.
    p. cm.
Includes bibliographical references and index.
ISBN 1-55766-044-1
1. Communication devices for the disabled. 2. Mentally handicapped—Means
of communication. I. Reichle, Joe (Joe Ernest), 1951—   II. York,
Jennifer. III. Sigafoos, Jeff.
RC429.I46 1991
616.85′503—dc20   90–2139
                                              CIP

Contents

About the Authors

Joe Reichle, Ph.D., is Professor in the Department of Communication Disorders and Training Director of the Research and Training Center on Community Living at the University of Minnesota. He has published extensively on beginning augmentative and alternative communication systems for learners with severe disabilities. His other research interests include the development of positive interventions to replace excess behaviors, and improving service delivery for people with developmental disabilities. He is involved in preparing speech and language pathologists and special educators to meet the educational needs of learners with severe disabilities, and has provided technical assistance to educational agencies both in the United States and abroad. He serves on the editorial board of the *Journal of The Association for Persons with Severe Handicaps.*

Jennifer York, Ph.D., P.T., is Assistant Professor in the Department of Educational Psychology and Training Director of the Institute on Community Integration at the University of Minnesota. As an educator and physical therapist, she has worked directly and indirectly with children with severe and multiple disabilities for over 10 years. Most of her work has focused on the integration of students with severe disabilities into regular school and community environments, and on effective collaboration among members of the transdisciplinary team. She has published and consulted extensively throughout the United States and Canada on these topics. She serves on the editorial board of the *Journal of The Association for Persons with Severe Handicaps.*

Jeff Sigafoos, Ph.D., is Lecturer at the Fred and Eleanor Schonell Special Education Research Centre at The University of Queensland in Brisbane, Australia. His research interests include teaching augmentative communication skills to learners with severe disabilities, and the development of data-based educational plans. He has provided technical assistance to numerous human service agencies serving adults with developmental disabilities. He is a consulting editor for the Canadian journal, *Developmental Disabilities Bulletin.*

Also contributing to this volume are:

Paris DePaepe, M.S., Department of Educational Psychology, University of Minnesota, Minneapolis, Minnesota 55455

L. Scott Doss, Ph.D., Department of Communication Disorders, University of Minnesota, Minneapolis, Minnesota 55455

Anne Lindgren, M.A., Anoka-Hennepin Independent School District No. 11, Anoka, Minnesota 55303

Peggy Locke, Ph.D., Project Director, Department of Communication Disorders, University of Minnesota, Minneapolis, Minnesota 55455

Theresa Mustonen, M.A., Department of Educational Psychology, University of Minnesota, Minneapolis, Minnesota 55455

Laura Piché, M.A., Department of Communication Disorders, University of Minnesota, Minneapolis, Minnesota 55455

Marj Solbrack, M.A., Department of Communication Disorders, University of Minnesota, Minneapolis, Minnesota 55455

Gloria Wiemann, Ed.S., Occupational Therapist, Intermediate District 916, White Bear Lake, Minnesota 55110

Preface

THIS BOOK WAS written for students and professionals interested in serving people with severe and multiple disabilities. The information contained in this book reflects the fieldwork, applied research, and research synthesis of the contributors, who have extensive histories of working with teachers, paraprofessionals, therapists, and parents of learners with moderate or severe intellectual disabilities and who, for the most part, do not produce speech.

Although this book addresses both graphic and gestural modes of communication, the primary emphasis is on graphic augmentative communication systems that include photographs, line drawings, and product logos arranged on communication boards or in communication wallets. The book is unique in that it provides specific information about *how* to teach beginning communication skills to learners with severe disabilities of any age.

In the first chapter, we overview the scope of augmentative and alternative communication by providing an orientation to the major aspects of practice. This chapter describes what is meant by graphic and gestural communication modes. Chapter 2 outlines some of the major decisions that a program team must address in designing and implementing augmentative communication systems for individual learners. Chapter 3 emphasizes the importance of ensuring that augmentative and alternative communication systems are functional and have direct relevance to the needs of learners and their listeners. This chapter describes how the strategies used by educators to scrutinize the daily environments and activities encountered by each learner can be used to identify communicative utterances to teach that best correspond with the communication demands and opportunities of daily life.

Chapters 4, 5, 6, 7, and 8 describe communicative functions and interactive uses of language, and suggest intervention strategies. Chapter 4 defines the range of communicative functions that can be taught, including requesting, rejecting, providing information, and other social communicative functions. Chapters 5 and 6 examine procedures that can be implemented to teach an initial repertoire of requesting and rejecting, respectively. These two communicative functions have been selected for in-depth discussion because they have been described as initial programming priorities for providing learners with the greatest measure of control over their environments. Chapter 7 explores the area of teaching learners to engage in communicative exchanges using newly established communicative functions. Attention is given to aspects of initiating, maintaining, and terminating communicative interactions. Chapter 8 provides an in-depth discussion of the challenges involved in establishing spontaneous and generalized use of newly established communicative repertoires. The emphasis in this chapter is on considering generalization and spontaneity as issues to be addressed during acquisition rather than subsequently.

Chapters 9 and 10 provide a more detailed discussion of nitty-gritty instructional issues. Chapter 9 suggests specific procedures and considerations for establishing symbol discriminations. Chapter 10 provides an in-depth discussion of individual instructional prompts and systems of prompts that are often used to establish communicative repertoires.

Chapters 11, 12, and 13 address implementing communication intervention procedures with individuals who have particularly challenging needs. Chapter 11 addresses learners who may have learned that repertoires of aggression, self-injury, property destruction, and/or self-stimulatory behavior can be used communicatively to seek attention, goods, and services, or to escape or avoid undesired objects, people, and events. This chapter examines viable assessment and intervention strategies aimed at teaching socially acceptable communicative behavior to compete with unacceptable repertoires. Chapter 12 addresses learners with severe physical disabilities that significantly affect the communicative mode and selection techniques that can be implemented. This chapter is intended to acquaint the reader with motoric disabilities and positioning and handling strategies pertaining to establishing augmentative or alternative communication systems. Chapter 13 provides a detailed discussion of considerations and strategies for designing and implementing scanning modes of augmentative and alternative communication.

Chapter 14 presents a discussion of ways in which the graphic mode can be used as a nonintrusive prompt system with which the learner can engage in activities such as performing household chores, going shopping, and following picture recipes. These applications represent an area in which graphic mode applications can assist the learner in becoming more independent in daily life.

Several important topics have not been addressed in this book. For example, being able to understand language spoken by others is critical to being able to engage in conversation. There is also a growing literature suggesting that, at least for some learners, understanding communicative behavior serves as a facilitator of learning to produce communicative behavior. In this book we have chosen to discuss those aspects of communication with which we have the most experience and therefore feel most comfortable. Consequently, the reader may occasionally be subjected to our slightly narrowed viewpoints. For this we appreciate the reader's tolerance.

Acknowledgments

THE AUTHORS WISH to thank Dr. Robert Bruininks and others at the Institute on Community Integration who have generously supported the authors during the past several years. Additionally, our thanks go to the St. Paul Public Schools and the students whose photos are displayed throughout this book. Several colleagues, including Dr. Jim Halle, Dr. Janis Chadsey-Rusch, and their students, have provided useful feedback on draft chapters. Ms. Barbara Karni, production editor at Paul H. Brookes Publishing, has served as our one-person technical support group. Her patience, professionalism, and helpful guidance have made this book far more readable than it would have been without her. Finally, we would like to acknowledge William Keogh of the Center for Developmental Disabilities, University of Vermont. Approximately 12 years ago, Mr. Keogh served as colleague and mentor to the senior author. In this capacity he generously gave of his time and resources to provide on-the-job training to a fledging assistant professor. For his efforts, Professor Joe Reichle will forever be indebted.

Implementing Augmentative and Alternative Communication

1

An Overview of Augmentative and Alternative Communication Systems

Theresa Mustonen, Peggy Locke,
Joe Reichle, Marj Solbrack, and Anne Lindgren

FOR A VARIETY of reasons, many people are unable to communicate by speaking. When a person cannot speak or is unintelligible, his or her ability to convey information to others is severely limited. Interactions with family members, friends, caregivers, and people in the community may be frustrating for all involved. People whose speech is unintelligible or nonexistent often benefit from augmentative or alternative communication intervention. *Augmentative* communication refers to the use of aids or techniques that supplement existing vocal or verbal communication skills. *Alternative* communication refers to the communication methods used by a person without any vocal ability (Vanderheiden & Yoder, 1986).

The need for augmentative or alternative communication may result from a number of conditions. In many cases, the need for augmentative or alternative communication is permanent. People with developmental disabilities often exhibit delayed or disordered speech. When retardation is severe or profound, the ability to communicate through speech may be greatly impaired, necessitating the use of augmentative communication techniques. Autism may also necessitate an augmentative communication system. People with autism may benefit from being taught to communicate through the use of symbols, gestures, or signs. Sensory impairments (i.e., blindness and deafness) may also affect the development of vocal or verbal skills, predisposing a person with a sensory impairment to communication skill deficits (Siegel-Causey & Downing, 1987). The need for an augmentative communication system to supplement or replace speech may become even more critical when a person has multiple disabilities.

People who have suffered traumatic brain injury or stroke may also benefit from an augmentative or alternative communication system (Beukelman & Yorkston, 1989). Some diseases may result in a progressive degeneration of vocal mode capabilities. Multiple sclerosis, amyotrophic lateral sclerosis, and Parkinson's disease are acquired conditions that have progressive degenerative effects on speech ability.

In other cases, the need for augmentative or alternative communication may be temporary. For example, illnesses or injuries that require tracheostomy or intubation may cause a temporary inability to communicate vocally.

This book focuses on augmentative and alternative communication systems as they pertain to people with severe communication impairments that are related to severe or profound mental retardation or autism rather than illness or injury. The first part of this chapter provides an overview of graphic mode communication systems. Types of symbols, methods for displaying symbols (on electronic and non-electronic devices), and techniques for indicating the choice of a symbol (i.e., direct access, scanning, and encoding) are discussed. Special features of electronic communication systems are also examined. The second part of the chapter provides an overview of gestural mode communication. Characteristics of gestures and signs, idiosyncratic and conventional signs and gestures, and advantages and disadvantages of gestural mode communication are reviewed.

Many learners rely upon a combination of options both within and across communication modes. Vanderheiden and Lloyd (1986) elegantly stated the case for designing augmentative and alternative communication systems that use the best of graphic as well as gestural communication modes. As they put it ". . . the communication system for a disabled individual, therefore, should not consist of a single technique or aid, but rather a collection of techniques, aids, symbols and strategies that the individual can use interchangeably" (p. 52). Within the graphic mode, learners who primarily use an electronic communication system may also use a nonelectronic aid (e.g., in en-vironments demanding greater portability, or in environments such as the beach, in which electronic devices could be damaged). Across modes, a learner may use sign and gesture on some occasions, and a manual graphic aid in others (i.e., when a very explicit message must be communicated to a nonsigner). Use of more than one mode is examined in Chapter 2.

Lloyd and Fuller (1986) and Vanderheiden and Lloyd (1986) refer to symbols as encompassing a continuum that ranges from static to dynamic. According to Vanderheiden and Lloyd, *dynamic symbols* have their meanings conveyed by change, transition, and/or movement, and therefore cannot be considered permanent and enduring. *Static symbols* include graphic symbols and objects that are permanent and enduring. They do not have to be changed or moved in order to have their meaning conveyed. Given these definitions, it is easy to see why static symbols tend to be associated with communication boards and graphic mode systems, while dynamic symbols tend to be associated with gestural mode systems.

Although the terms "static" and "dynamic" are often used to refer to symbols, we have chosen to characterize symbols as being associated either with the graphic or the gestural mode, without reference to their dynamic and static characteristics.

A technique refers to the method used by the learner to select and display symbols. Graphic mode selection techniques include direct selection, in which the learner directly indicates a symbol from a display, and scanning, in which another person or an electronic cursor menus choices, allowing the learner to signal when the desired symbol appears. In the gestural mode, the interventionist must determine: 1) whether a gesture is produced using one or two hands, 2) how the hands are shaped to produce the gesture, 3) where in the signing space a sign is produced, and 4) whether movement of the hands/arms is required during the production of the gesture.

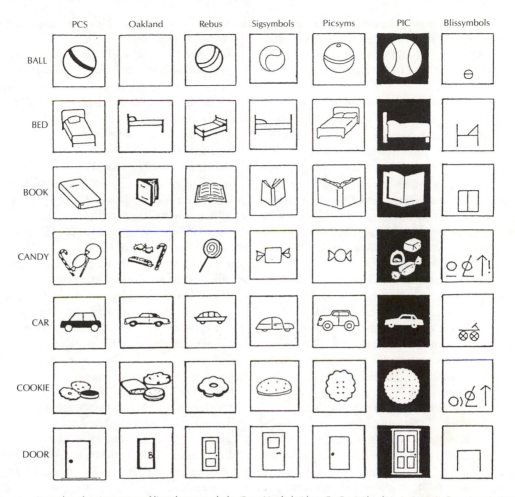

Figure 1.   Examples of various types of line-drawn symbols. (From Vanderheiden, G. C., & Lloyd, L. L. [1986]. Overview. In S.W. Blackstone [Ed.], *Augmentative communication: An introduction*. Rockville, MD: American Speech-Language-Hearing Association. Copyright © 1986 by American Speech-Language-Hearing Association; reprinted by permission).

GRAPHIC MODE COMMUNICATION

In graphic mode communication, two-dimensional or three-dimensional representations are used to symbolize objects and concepts. Symbols take a variety of forms.

Representational Symbols

Line Drawings

Line drawings may consist of detailed sketches or more crudely rendered outlines. Line drawings usually consist of black lines on a white background or white lines on a black background. A number of line-drawn symbols are available commercially (Figure 1).

One type of commonly used line drawing is called a rebus symbol (see Figure 1). The word *rebus* is derived from Latin, and is defined as a puzzle composed of words or syllables that appear in the form of pictures. Often, the rebuses used to represent words or parts of words resemble their referrants in sound. For instance, a drawing of an insect resembling a bee might be used to represent the verb *be*, since *bee* and *be* sound the same. Single pictures or combinations of pictures may be used as rebuses (Silverman, 1989).

Printed letters or syllables can be added gradually in order to introduce traditional orthography (printed letters, words, or phrases). For example, the word *candy* could be represented by a drawing of a can plus the letters "d" and "y." Over time, the symbols are removed as learners acquire skills in reading printed words. Rebuses have been used in teaching both children with and children without mental retardation to read (Woodcock, 1958, 1965; Woodcock, Clark, & Davies, 1968, 1969).

Rebus symbols can also be used with non-readers or with learners whose potential for acquiring reading skills is very limited. Rebuses are often used on communication display surfaces. The symbols can be used alone or in conjunction with printed words that enable literate communication partners to decipher messages quickly.

The most commonly used rebus symbols are the American Guidance Service Rebuses (Clark, Davies, & Woodcock, 1974; Clark & Woodcock, 1976; Woodcock, 1965; Woodcock et al., 1968). The *Standard Rebus Glossary* (Clark et al., 1974) contains over 800 different rebuses. Over 2,000 words are represented, consisting of single rebuses, combinations of rebuses, or rebuses combined with letters of the alphabet.

In addition to rebus symbols, a number of other graphic communication symbols are available commercially. *Picture Communication Symbols* (PCS and PCS Book II) are line-drawn symbols representing nouns, verbs, and adjectives (Johnson, 1981, 1985). PCS are available that consist of black lines on white paper, of black lines on colored stamps, and of stickers whose background color corresponds to the type of symbol (i.e., symbols on green back-

grounds are verbs, symbols on orange backgrounds are nouns).

Symbols from the *Oakland Schools Picture Dictionary* (Kirstein & Bernstein, 1981) consist of black lines on white backgrounds. The set consists of over 500 symbols, indexed alphabetically and by category. Half-inch, 1-inch, and 2-inch sizes are available.

Picsyms (Carlson, 1984) consist of over 1,800 black line-drawn symbols on white backgrounds, indexed alphabetically. Guidelines are provided for drawing additional symbols by using six-row by eight-column grids.

Sigsymbols (Creagan, 1982; Creagan & Lloyd, 1984) consist of black line drawings on white backgrounds. They can be pictographic, meaning that they represent words or ideas through pictures; or ideographic, meaning that ideas are represented through the use of characters or graphic symbols. The original sigsymbols were graphic representations of British Sign Language signs. They have since been developed from other sign systems as well (Vanderheiden & Lloyd, 1986).

Pictogram Ideogram Communication (PIC) symbols consist of 400 white-on-black symbols (Maharaj, 1980). Although they were designed in this manner to increase their visual saliency (Vanderheiden & Lloyd, 1986), research has not demonstrated a clear advantage of white-on-black images (Bloomberg, 1984; Blyden, 1989; Campbell & Lloyd, 1986; Meador, Rumbaugh, Tribble, & Thompson, 1984).

Blissymbols consist of black line drawings on white backgrounds. They were originally developed to serve as an international written language (Bliss, 1965). Blissymbols include symbols that are pictographic (i.e., words are represented visually through the use of outlines that suggest the referent), ideographic (i.e., abstract concepts are represented through shapes associated with the referent), or arbitrary (i.e., assigned to a particular line or configuration of lines). All these types of symbols are shown in

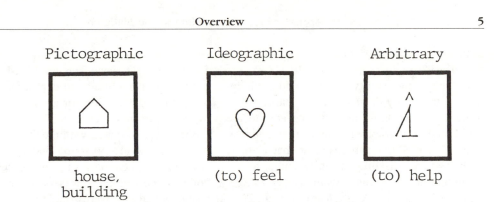

Figure 2. Examples of pictographic, ideographic, and arbitrary Blissymbols.

Figure 2. The set of symbols consists of approximately 100 meaning-based shapes (Silverman, 1989). These shapes can be used alone or in combination. Used alone, each symbol represents a general concept. By combining a symbol with another symbol or symbols, the meaning of the resulting symbol is modified. The meaning of a Blissymbol can be changed in other ways as well. For instance, adding a symbol representing a grammatical class (i.e., noun, verb, adverb, adjective) above the root symbol changes the meaning. Moving the position of a symbol in relation to other symbols, increasing or reducing the space between elements, using elements in a compound symbol more than once, and enlarging or reducing the size of a root symbol are other ways in which meaning can be changed. Other ways in which meaning can be changed include placing the symbol meaning "the opposite of" in front of a symbol; adding or superimposing meaning-based lines on a symbol; placing symbols used to designate tense, mood, or voice above a symbol; and using symbols that pluralize singular nouns (Silverman, 1989).

Photographs

As representations of real objects, clear photographs can be easy for learners and listeners to recognize. The context in which an item appears may affect its recognizability (e.g., a photograph of a sewing thimble may be recognized more readily if it is photographed next to a spool of thread and a threaded needle). Black and white or color photographs can be used on graphic communication systems. Mirenda and Locke (1989) found that color photographs were more easily recognized than black and white photographs.

Product Logos

Product logos can also be used as symbols. Learners may easily recognize logos of products with which they are very familiar. Color reproductions of product logos can be made, and reduced or enlarged as necessary.

Traditional Orthography

Printed letters, words, or phrases comprise another potential symbol set. Traditional orthography is desirable if both the users and their communication partners can read. Displays consisting of commonly used printed words, letters of the alphabet, and numerals can enable a learner to create an unlimited number of messages.

Traditional orthography may also be used in combination with other symbol sets. For example, the letter s can be added to a rebus symbol to form a plural (Silverman, 1989), or a printed name can be added to the Blissymbol for *man* to indicate a particular man (Vanderheiden & Lloyd, 1986).

Although the ability to read and spell increases the utility of this method, learners with limited reading skills may still be able to use traditional orthography to augment communication. Research has demonstrated that learners with moderate disabilities can be taught to discriminate among printed words (Dory & Zeaman, 1975; Sidman & Stoddard, 1967).

Lexigrams and Premack-Type Symbols

Lexigrams (Rumbaugh, 1977; Rumbaugh, Gell, & von Glaserfeld, 1973) and Premack-type symbols (Carrier, 1976; Carrier & Peak, 1975; Premack, 1970; Premack & Premack, 1974) are symbols that do not in any way resemble their referents. Lexigrams are two-dimensional symbols. They consist of 9 design elements that can be used alone or in combinations to produce 225 different lexigrams. Although they are highly abstract, these symbols may be easier to discriminate than letters (Romski, Sevcik, Pate, & Rumbaugh, 1985). Premack-type symbols are three-dimensional, ⅛-inch thick, plastic shapes. Carrier symbols are a type of Premack-type symbol designed for use with the Non-Speech Language Initiation Program (Carrier & Peak, 1975) for children with mental retardation. Originally designed as part of a computer-based language training system for use with primates, both lexigrams and Premack-type symbols were later used in teaching communication to people with mental retardation (Carrier, 1976; Romski, White, Millen, & Rumbaugh, 1984).

Tangible Symbols

Real Objects

Objects are sometimes used as symbols. This approach, which has been used by van Dijk (1966, 1967) and Stillman and Battle (1984) in their work with learners with dual sensory impairments, involves using an object typically as-

sociated with a person or activity as a symbol for the referent. For instance, a leash could be used to inform a blind and deaf teenager that it is time to take his dog for a walk. Real object symbols can be either very similar or identical to the item associated with the referent. Miranda and Locke (1989) found that among people with varying degrees of developmental disabilities, performance was nearly equal on a task in which they were asked to match identical and nonidentical objects to their referents.

Real objects that are closely associated with a referent can also be used as symbols. For example, a stapler might be used to represent a stapling work task, or a button similar in size and shape to the buttons on a learner's coat might be used to symbolize going for a walk outside.

Miniature Objects

Miniature objects can also be used as symbols. For example, a miniature coffee cup could be used to inform a worker that it is time for a coffee break. Since it may not always be possible to find miniature objects that are identical to real objects, replicas that bear a strong similarity to their referents may need to be substituted.

Little research has been done on the transparency (i.e., guessability) of miniature objects. Miranda and Locke (1989) compared the transparency of 11 different types of symbol sets and found that nonidentical miniatures were less easily recognized than nonidentical objects, color photographs, and black and white photographs by subjects with varying degrees of developmental disabilities. Landman and Schaeffler (1986) found that five children with cerebral palsy who were unable to identify pictures consistently could be taught to initiate requests using miniature objects attached to communication boards.

Parts of Objects

Parts of objects can also be used as symbols. For instance, instead of using a full-length straw to symbolize a juice box, a small section could be cut from the straw and attached to a communication board. Using portions of objects, rather than whole objects, results in a savings of space on a display surface, and improves the portability of a system. Instead of having to transport a bulky object from place to place, a learner must carry only a portion of the object that serves as a symbol for the referent.

Textured Symbols

Symbols can also be constructed by using textures that are either closely associated with a referent or arbitrarily assigned to represent the referent. Terry cloth fabric could be used to inform a learner of bath time, since washcloths and towels are made of terry cloth and are closely associated with bathing. Sandpaper could be assigned arbitrarily to symbolize a favorite cookie.

Differences among Symbols

Symbols used in graphic communication systems vary on several dimensions, including degree of iconicity, or how well a symbol suggests its referent; ease of acquisition, or how easy a symbol is to learn; and how well skills acquired during instruction are generalized to natural situations and maintained.

Iconicity refers to how easily the meaning of a symbol can be guessed. Symbols can be viewed along a continuum with regard to iconicity. At one end of this continuum are *transparent* symbols. A *transparent* symbol is one whose meaning is easily guessed. An example would be a PCS symbol of a cookie. *Translucent* symbols are not readily guessable without additional information. For example, a viewer unfamiliar with Picsyms might not be able to guess the meaning of the symbol for a cookie (see Figure 1). However, once informed that the symbol represented a kind of food, most viewers would be able to identify it correctly. At the other end of the spectrum are symbols whose meanings are not readily guessable, and whose

relationships to their referents are arbitrary. These symbols are sometimes described as *opaque*. The printed word *cookie*, for example, does not resemble a real cookie in any way. Figure 3 illustrates this continuum.

Several studies have attempted to measure the degree of transparency and/or translucency of various symbol sets. Musselwhite and Ruscello (1984) had groups of children and young adults guess the meaning of symbols from Blissymbol, Picsym, and Rebus systems. The meanings of Picsyms and Rebus symbols were found to be much easier to guess than the meanings of Blissymbols. These results were obtained even when symbols depicting verbs and adjectives were examined. Mizuko (1987) found that preschool children without disabilities found Picsyms easier to guess than Blissymbols. Picsyms representing verbs and adjectives were found to be less guessable than PCS.

Given these results, it might be reasonable to expect that photographs would be more iconic than line drawings (Chapman & Miller, 1980; Mirenda; 1985; Reichle & Yoder, 1985), but less iconic than miniature objects, parts of objects, or real objects. There are not, however, sufficient data to support such a hierarchy of iconicity. Indeed, it is possible that the relative size of a symbol has an important impact on its guessability. Miniature objects, for example, may be perceived as more abstract than is generally presumed simply because they are so much smaller than the corresponding real objects.

Another issue involves the ease with which symbols are acquired. Whereas transparency studies have focused primarily on the ease with which learners without disabilities guess the meaning of symbols, learnability studies have tended to focus on comparing how quickly learners with and without disabilities can be taught to discriminate among symbols in a variety of tasks (Clark, 1981; Ecklund & Reichle, 1987; Mizuko, 1987).

The results of learnability studies have been consistent with the results of guessability stud-

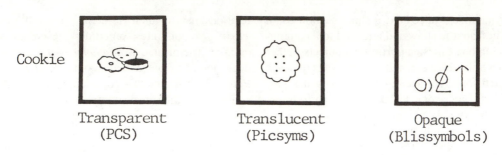

Figure 3.   The continuum of symbol iconicity ranges from transparent to opaque.

ies; that is, iconic symbols tend to be easier to learn and more consistently maintained and generalized. One of the first studies in this area was reported by Clark (1981). In this study, 36 preschool children without any apparent disabilities were asked to name Rebus symbols, Blissymbols, printed words, and abstract plastic symbols. The names for Rebus symbols were recalled more often than the names of Blissymbols. Blissymbols were recalled more often than abstract plastic symbols. For nonreading preschool children, naming printed words proved to be the most difficult task.

Results obtained by Ecklund and Reichle (1987) and Mizuko (1987) have been consistent with Clark's findings. In these studies, learners were asked to name displayed pictures and to select the correct symbol names using Rebus symbols, Picsyms, PCS, and Blissymbols. Performance with Blissymbols was worse than performance with the other symbol sets. These results, obtained with preschool children without disabilities, tend to confirm that the relationship between a symbol and the corresponding spoken word is more readily established with iconic symbols.

The relationship between symbol guessability and ease of acquisition has also been demonstrated among learners with developmental disabilities. Hurlbut, Iwata, and Green (1982) taught three learners with multiple disabilities to select the graphic symbol corresponding to a displayed object. Some objects were represented by iconic Rebus-like symbols;

others were represented by Blissymbols. All three learners acquired the object labels more rapidly when the corresponding symbols were iconic. Generalization of correct symbol selection to other similar objects, and maintenance of acquired responses were also superior. Mirenda and Locke (1989) found evidence for a hierarchy of symbol systems in an auditory match-to-sample task (i.e., the learner selects the symbol named by the experimenter). In this study, real objects produced the most correct responses, followed by photographs (color, then black and white), miniature objects, line drawings, and Blissymbols. The available evidence tends to suggest, therefore, that iconic symbols are more readily acquired by both learners with and learners without disabilities.

Another important issue is whether skills acquired during instruction will be maintained, and whether skills will generalize to use in other settings. While abstract symbols, such as printed words, many Blissymbols, and lexigrams, can be taught as part of a functional communication system (Romski, Sevcik, & Pate, 1988), for some learners it may prove more difficult and time consuming to do so. One reason that iconic symbols may be associated with positive intervention outcomes is that such symbols closely resemble the items they represent. In addition, symbols that look similar to objects are more frequently paired with those objects in the natural environment. The line drawing on a package of cookies will often look like the cookies contained within. The learner who frequently eats this type of cookie may, therefore, have had numerous opportunities to pair the package and the actual cookie. Such incidental pairings of symbol and object no doubt occur less frequently with abstract symbols.

As a general guiding principle, the selection of iconic symbols may facilitate acquisition, generalization, and maintenance of graphic mode communication systems. For learners who acquire the use of symbols easily, it may not be necessary to use iconic symbols. Abstract symbols may have their own advantages. It has frequently been suggested that Blissymbols can more readily be combined in sentence-like forms that replicate the ways in which grammatical speech can be used to create novel utterances. Moreover, printed words that usually accompany abstract symbols have the advantage of being immediately recognizable by most people in the community.

Nonelectronic Methods for Displaying Symbols

A learner who communicates graphically could carry all his or her symbols in a pocket. Over time, however, the symbols would get lost or worn out. Moreover, the learner would have to sort through the entire set to locate the needed symbol. For these reasons, various methods have been devised to store and display symbols. Symbols are often arranged on boards or cards, placed on blank pages within photo albums or books, or slipped into the clear plastic compartments of a credit card holder in a wallet.

Communication Boards

Communication boards are usually flat surfaces on which a matrix of two-dimensional symbols is affixed. The size of the board is determined by both the communicative needs and the physical limitations of the user. In some cases, the size of the wheelchair lap tray, which is commonly used as a mounting surface for a communication board, will determine the size of the communication board. For instance, an augmentative system user who spends much of his or her time in a wheelchair with a lap tray, but whose fine motor and visual skills are unimpaired might use a communication board consisting of a matrix of square symbols arranged on a 2′ x 2′ surface mounted on a wheelchair lap tray. A learner with impaired vision might need to have a smaller board with larger symbols. A learner whose motor skills limited his or her ability to reach might require an even smaller board so that all of the symbols could be reached.

Communication Books

Symbols can also be displayed on the pages of photo albums, or on notebook divider pages in three-ring binders. These methods allow numerous symbols to be stored, and can be advantageous for learners with large vocabularies. They also allow the arrangement of symbols by frequency of use, semantic category, or some other logical format. However, this type of display method can be bulky and awkward to transport.

Communication Wallets

Symbols can also be displayed in wallets (Figure 4). Lightweight, durable nylon or canvas wallets are often used. Symbols can be arranged on cards and inserted in the wallet's vinyl credit card sleeves. Alternatively, individual symbols can be backed with Velcro® and secured with Velcro -faced strips attached to the inner surfaces of the wallet. This allows displays to be modified for use in various environments. Wallets are easily portable, but do not allow a large number of symbols to be displayed at one time. Wallets are also easier to misplace than communication books or boards.

Selection Techniques

A learner who communicates through the use of graphic symbols must somehow indicate to a communication partner which symbol he or she

Figure 4.   A communication wallet.

is selecting. Learners with relatively unimpaired motor skills may simply point at the various symbols. However, learners with motor impairments may have difficulty using this method, and may have to rely on alternative techniques, in which their communication partner participates in selecting symbols. Various techniques for selecting symbols from the communication board, book, or wallet are available.

Direct Selection

In direct selection, the learner points to the desired symbol. This can be done by touching the symbol with a finger or a pointer (Figure 5). Learners with little or no voluntary movement of their arms or legs, but good head control are sometimes fitted with specially designed headgear in which a pointing device, such as a dowel rod or a light beam pointer, is attached to a head band (Figure 6).

Direct selection of symbols can also be accomplished in other ways. An elbow, toe, or heel can be used to point to a symbol. Gazing at a symbol for an extended period of time—called "eye pointing" or "eye gazing" (Eichler, 1973)—represents another direct select technique. Eye gaze works best when the learner has a large display surface with widely spaced symbols, since it may be difficult for the learner's communication partner to discern which symbol the learner is selecting if the board contains many small or closely spaced symbols. When eye gaze boards are constructed of clear plexiglass, as opposed to opaque materials, and the listener faces the learner with the eye gaze board between them, the listener can more easily discern the symbol a learner is selecting through eye gaze (Figure 7).

Direct selection of symbols, with or without the use of pointers, head sticks, or other as-

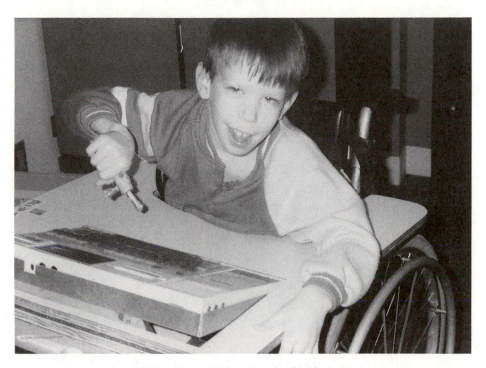

Figure 5.   Direct selection using a hand-held pointer.

sistive devices, is almost always the fastest selection method. If the learner has adequate control of voluntary movement, direct selection of symbols will probably be the preferred selection method. If the learner has severe motor impairments, another method for selecting symbols may need to be used either exclusively or in combination with direct selection.

Scanning

Scanning is often used by learners whose motor impairments preclude their use of a direct select technique. In a scanning technique, the learner is offered choices of available symbols, and indicates his or her choice by performing a predetermined signal that informs the listener that the desired symbol has been reached.

Manual Scanning Techniques   In manual scanning, a communication partner points to the available symbols. The learner indicates that the desired symbol has been menued by performing a predetermined discrete behavior. For instance, a learner could nod his or her head, or use a knee switch to ring a bell. (Chapter 12 addresses selecting a signaling response in learners with severe physical disabilities.)

Manual scanning is not limited to graphic mode communication, but can be used aurally with people who communicate vocally. Often, people with some verbal skills produce vocalizations that are not readily intelligible. For instance, Doug, an adult with severe mental retardation, approaches Mitch, a service provider at his group home, and asks what sounds to Mitch like "Sankday furday?" Mitch, who is new to the group home, looks puzzled and says, "What?" Doug repeats his question, only to be met with another request for clarification. Mitch then starts guessing at elements of the question by saying, "Furday. Do you mean *Fri-*

Figure 6.   Direct selection using a head-mounted light pointer.

day?" Doug shakes his head and repeats "Furday, furday." Mitch then asks "Oh, *Thursday*?" and Doug nods his head in affirmation. With part of the message deciphered, Mitch repeats "Sankday, sankday." "Do you mean *Saturday*?" Doug shakes his head. Mitch asks "Thursday? What's on Thursday?" Doug repeats "Sankday" in a questioning tone. Suddenly, Mitch realizes that Doug might be attempting to say "Thanksgiving Day," which was approaching. "Thanksgiving Day Thursday? Is that what you're asking?" he asks. Doug nods. Mitch responds "Yes, this Thursday is Thanksgiving Day." In this example, Mitch menued potential vocabulary choices by stating the alternatives, as opposed to offering graphic symbols.

Manual scanning may be a useful way to begin teaching use of an electronic scanning device. However, exclusive use of manual scanning can result in a learner becoming very dependent on a communication partner for initiating and maintaining interactions, since the learner cannot communicate unless the partner offers choices. Moreover, manual scanning is a relatively slow way of selecting symbols.

Electronic Scanning Techniques The symbol display surface on an electronic communication aid consists of a grid of small lights. On some devices, activating a switch causes a light or a series of lights to become illuminated. Once the switch is activated, the light, known as a cursor, begins to move across the display surface. When the cursor under a desired symbol is illuminated, the learner again touches the switch, thus stopping the moving cursor. On other devices, the learner must activate the switch each time he or she wants the cursor to advance across the display. Electronic scanning

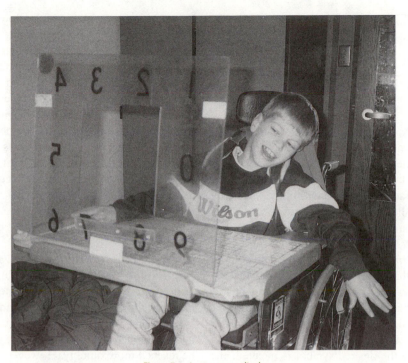

Figure 7. An eye gaze display.

significantly reduces the communicative burden on the learner's communicative partner, since the partner does not need to menu choices.

An important decision the interventionist must make for learners using the electronic scanning devices is the type of scanning pattern to use. Each of the scanning patterns is examined in the following sections.

Linear Scanning The simplest scanning pattern is *linear,* or *sequential,* scanning (Figure 8). With this technique, the cursor proceeds straight across the display surface, one symbol at a time until it reaches the end of a row. It then moves to the first symbol on the left in the next row.

Linear scanning has the advantage of being very predictable, and requires only a single response to activate or deactivate the cursor. A learner who uses this pattern may learn to return his or her gaze to the spot from which the cursor began its travels after making a selection, thus anticipating the next attempt. However, linear scanning can be the most time-consuming pattern of scanning to use. This slowness may be an advantage for some learners and a disadvantage for others. If a learner has difficulty performing the response required to stop the cursor, linear scanning combined with a slowly moving cursor may allow him or her enough time to anticipate and plan the motor movements for the required response. However, if the learner responds too late and misses the target, or fails to respond, he or she must wait until the cursor scans through the remainder of the array and starts over. A learner with the ability to follow a rapidly moving cursor and respond quickly may be able to use this technique efficiently.

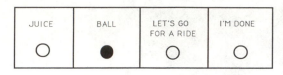

JUICE	BALL	LET'S GO FOR A RIDE	I'M DONE
○	●	○	○

Figure 8. A linear scanning display.

Circular Scanning Circular scanning follows the same principles as linear scanning, except that the cursor moves in a clockwise or counterclockwise direction around a circular display surface. Symbols are illuminated one by one, until the cursor reaches the desired symbol. An example of circular scanning is shown in Figure 9.

Row-Column Scanning In row-column scanning, the cursor usually begins at the top left corner of the board and moves downward. The learner produces a discrete response (e.g., nods his or her head) to select a row. The cursor then moves across the selected row from left to right. When the desired symbol is menued, the learner signals again to stop the cursor.

Group-Item Scanning Group-item scanning is similar to row-column scanning. A learner first selects a group of items, and then selects individual items within that group. Groups can be formed based on semantic categories, environments in which use occurs, or on any other logical division. If a manual scanning application is used, the communication partner can hold up the cards on which categorized symbols are affixed. When the card to which the desired symbol is attached is located, the learner signals his or her partner to begin pointing to each of the symbols on that card.

Page-Item Scanning and Page-Group-Item Scanning In page-item scanning, a page in an electronic or manual system is selected first, and then an item from that page is selected. In page-group-item scanning, first a page, then a group, and then an item is selected.

Directed Scanning In directed scanning, a directional control switch, such as a joystick, is used to determine the direction of the cursor.

Four-position joysticks, which allow a cursor to move up, down, left, and right, and eight-position joysticks, which permit diagonal movements as well, are available. Separate push button switches can also be used to control the direction of a cursor. An example of directed scanning using a joystick is shown in Figure 10.

Directed scanning gives the learner more control over the cursor, and also allows a learner to "back up" if he or she goes past the target. However, directed scanning also requires that a learner be able to engage in several discrete motor movements, or be able to reach and use several different switches that control the cursor.

Physical and Intellectual Demands* of *Scanning Techniques Row-column, group-item, page-item, and page-group-item scanning increase the efficiency of scanning systems. When fewer movements of the cursor are required to reach a desired symbol, symbols may be reached more quickly. However, these methods require that a learner be able to engage in a sequence of direct responses. For instance, to engage in row-column scanning, a learner must be able to recall or visually locate the row in

Figure 9. A circular scanning display.

Figure 10. Directed scanning with a joystick.

which an item is located, and to signal which row should be scanned. Then the learner must visually locate the item within that row, and respond again in order to select the desired item.

Group-item scanning and page-group-item scanning require that the learner complete an even longer chain of responses. To use group-item scanning, the learner must either quickly compare the alternatives within each group as the groups are being menued, or recall in which group a symbol is located. The items within the selected group must then be scanned, and a symbol selected.

Page-group-item scanning requires that a learner scan three times, first as pages are offered, then as groups on a selected page are offered, and finally as individual items within a group are offered.

Electronic Scanning Methods The main advantage of an electronic communication de-

vice for learners with significant motor disabilities is that symbols can be selected more efficiently. This is particularly true for electronic scanning. In order to scan, a learner must be able to activate the switch that controls the scanner. A learner's ability to use an electronic scanning device depends on whether or not he or she is able to perform at least one reliable, discrete, motor response. If a reliable response cannot be identified, it may be possible to identify a movement that the learner could be taught to control (see Chapter 12). Once an appropriate motor behavior has been identified, a scanning method for activating the switch must be selected. The scanning method selected must be compatible with the learner's discrete motor response, or the motor response targeted for instruction. Several scanning methods, including step element scanning; regular, or automatic scanning; and inverse scanning, are available (Blackstone, 1989).

In *step element scanning* the learner must activate the switch repeatedly to advance the cursor. Each time the switch is activated the cursor advances by one symbol.

A learner using *regular,* or *automatic, scanning* activates the switch to start the cursor. The cursor continues moving until the learner touches the switch again, which stops the cursor. To restart the cursor, the learner must reactivate the switch.

Inverse scanning requires a learner to maintain continuous contact with the switch in order to move the cursor. When the learner releases the switch, the cursor stops.

Types of Switches Microswitch technology has enabled many learners with severe motor disabilities to use augmentative communication aids. These switches fall into several categories (Burkhart, 1985).

Push Switches Push switches are activated by applying pressure to the switch. Most push switches require the application of continuous pressure to maintain switch activation. Release of pressure results in switch deactivation. Push switches can be activated by any body part and vary in sensitivity. Switches of this kind include push button, push plate, rocking, joystick, and pressure switches.

Air Pressure Switches Air pressure switches, also known as *pneumatic, bulb, air cushion,* or *squeeze* switches, are operated by changing the air pressure between the switch mechanism (called a *transducer*) and the contact surface. In one kind of air pressure switch, the learner grasps a bulb in his or her hand and squeezes it to activate and deactivate the switch. In another type of air pressure switch, called a *sip and puff switch,* the learner holds the end of a flexible tube between his or her lips and activates the switch by blowing into the tube and sucking air out of the tube. Use of a sip and puff switch requires that a learner have good control over his or her lips and breathing.

Leaf Switches Leaf switches consist of a plastic flap measuring approximately 1 inch wide and 6 inches long. The learner's movement out of a neutral position contacting the switch activates it. Leaf switches vary in the degree of movement needed for activation.

Mercury Switches Mercury switches are constructed from small plastic or glass sealed tubes that contain a small drop of mercury and two wire prongs. When the tube is in a position in which the mercury contacts both prongs simultaneously, the circuit is complete and the switch is on. When tilted out of that position, the mercury moves away from the prongs and deactivates the switch. Mercury switches are often delicate and difficult to mount so that learners with reflexive movement do not accidentally activate the switch.

Single Muscle Sensors A single muscle sensor, or P-switch, is a small disk attached to a part of the body and connected by a wire to a small control box. Movement of the disk sends a signal to the circuitry, which amplifies the current and enables an electronic component to activate switch closure. The sensitivity of the switch can be increased or decreased to detect a variety of movement. The P-switch allows even a very weak muscle movement to be used to control a communication device.

A combination of manual direct select and electronic scanning techniques may be useful for learners who have some direct select skills, but are unable to sustain the movements required for making selections for an extended period of time. Such learners may benefit from having a limited array of enlarged symbols consisting of important or frequently used symbols that must be reached quickly (e.g., "Help!"). This array could be combined with an array of small symbols that could be reached via a scanning technique, as shown in Figure 11.

In a second option, a learner who is unable to point to a single symbol on a communication board could be taught to use a modified form of group-item scanning. If the communication board were divided very clearly into several sections, the learner could more actively par-

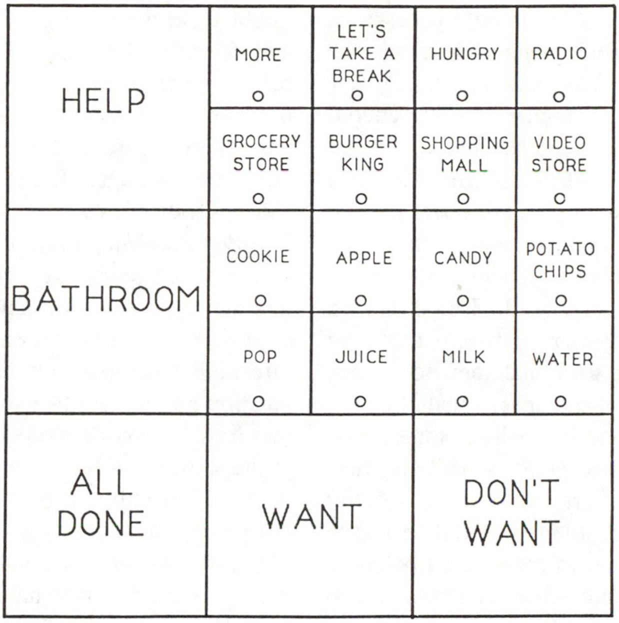

HELP	MORE ○	LET'S TAKE A BREAK ○	HUNGRY ○	RADIO ○
	GROCERY STORE ○	BURGER KING ○	SHOPPING MALL ○	VIDEO STORE ○
BATHROOM	COOKIE ○	APPLE ○	CANDY ○	POTATO CHIPS ○
	POP ○	JUICE ○	MILK ○	WATER ○
ALL DONE	WANT		DON'T WANT	

Figure 11.   Scanning overlay combined with enlarged symbols for direct selecting.

ticipate in a communicative interchange if he or she directly selected a section of the board, and then signaled his or her partner to begin manually scanning the items within the section. The same principles could be applied to page-group-item scanning methods.

Using Encoding with Scanning or Direct Selection

Encoding refers to the learner's use of multiple responses to select a single desired message from an array of available messages. It is used in a variety of ways in everyday situations. Maps, for example, use encoding to help users find locations. A taxi driver who wants to locate a particular street could randomly peruse a map of the city until she finds the street. A more efficient technique would be to scan the alphabetized listing of streets to find the desired street and corresponding code. A telephone that allows the user to program a symbol to represent frequently called numbers is another example of encoding. A waiter who records an order

for two bacon, lettuce, and tomato sandwiches on whole wheat bread by writing "2 BLT-WW" is also using encoding.

Encoding can be combined with either direct select or scanning techniques. Suppose a learner has a communication board made up of letters of the alphabet. She could combine the necessary letters to spell out the message "I want to watch the 'I Love Lucy' show." However, by combining *letter encoding* (i.e., abbreviations) and direct selection, the learner could point to the letters "W," "T," "V," and "L." Her communication partner, who has been apprised of the code or has available a listing of the codes and their meanings, is able to translate the message into "watch television—Lucy." In this case, the combination "WTV" stands for "watch television," and "L" is the code for the name of the television show. A learner who has a scanning device could use the same technique to *scan encode* a similar message. The only difference would be that the learner would electronically scan rather than point to the letters.

Manual scan letter encoding would necessitate a communication partner menuing letters as the learner signals his or her choices.

Number encoding is similar to letter encoding, except that numerals rather than letters are used to represent vocabulary. For example, each of a learner's vocabulary items could be assigned a numerical code. "Apple" might be coded with the number 7, "peanut butter sandwich" might bear the code 9. To ask for an apple and a peanut butter sandwich, a learner would simply point to 7 and then to 9. For learners with large vocabularies, vocabulary encoded with double and triple digits might pose special problems, since pointing to 7 and then to 9 could also be interpreted as a request for item number 79. This dilemma could be solved by teaching the learner to engage in a behavior that would signal listeners that the selection was complete. A learner could remove his or her hand from the switch after selecting 7 to indicate that a separate selection was upcoming, or maintain contact with the switch between activations when requesting the item assigned the code 79.

Alphanumeric encoding uses combinations of letters and numerals to represent vocabulary. For example, "A-1" might stand for apple, while "A-2" might mean apricot. Just as maps use alphanumeric encoding to help users find locations, this type of encoding can be used to direct communication partners to the location of a symbol on a board. A learner using alphanumeric encoding could direct select or scan to the letter "B" and the numeral "6" on the small directory to tell the listener he or she wanted the item represented by the symbol located at the intersection of column B and row 6.

Icon (symbol) encoding occurs when different symbols are combined to represent unique messages. Some electronic communication devices can be programmed so that selecting a certain combination of symbols yields a complete message. For example, pressing the symbols "question mark," "hamburger," and "French Fries"

might yield the message "May I have a burger and fries?" This type of encoding has been called *semantic compaction*. It allows a user to produce novel sentences from prestored words and phrases in addition to recalling programmed messages (Damper, 1986; Goossens', Elder, Caldwell, & Page, 1988).

Color encoding may be useful for learners who have difficulty distinguishing different letters and numerals, but have the ability to distinguish colors. In color encoding a learner can direct a listener to a particular area of a communication board, then to a specific symbol within that area. A color encoded board is configured in the same manner as a regular communication display. The difference is that squares are initially large and slightly separated from one another, or otherwise distinctively bordered. Each square is divided into halves, thirds, or quadrants, which are then assigned different background colors. By pointing to the large square, the learner can narrow the choice down to the symbols located within that square. Then, by pointing to a color card located within easy reach, the learner can indicate which of the symbols within that quadrant he or she is selecting. Hinderscheit and Reichle (1987) were successful in teaching a learner with severe intellectual delays to use direct color encoding.

Features of Electronic Communication Devices

Electronic communication aids offer a number of advantages to the augmentative or alternative communication system user. Most importantly, electronic aids reduce the user's communicative responsibilities. An electronic communication aid can allow the learner to produce a message that is far more sophisticated than the learner's own language skills. For example, contingent on touching a symbol representing a soft drink, an electronic aid could produce the phrase, "Gee, I'm thirsty. I'd like a medium Diet Cherry Coke."

Many electronic communication aids can

produce speech output. This is a significant advantage for both the speaker and the listener. In the classroom, for example, a teacher may ask, "Who wants to tell what he did last night?" With speech output, the learner may respond from his or her seat. The teacher need not move next to the learner, the learner need not look at the communication board, and a peer need not interpret for the learner. Speech output also allows the learner to communicate even if he or she does not have a listener's attention. In contrast, a learner using a nonelectronic communication aid must first produce a signaling response (e.g., loudly vocalize, activate an electronic buzzer) to obtain the listener's attention prior to selecting symbols.

A third advantage of an electronic communication aid is that it allows the learner to create a message that can be stored. For example, while at the zoo, a learner might want to create a message about something he sees. When he arrives home, he can quickly and efficiently display the message. More sophisticated augmentative system users may use their electronic communication aid as a portable lap-top computer, thus integrating the functions of communication aid and word processor.

Some learners are unable to use direct selection because they lack the ability to produce a usable selecting response. Such learners must use scanning techniques. As pointed out earlier, a scanning technique is usually much slower than a direct select technique. Some electronic communication aids clarify inferior selecting responses. For example, in an *electronic averaging option,* a learner might use a head pointer. To communicate, the learner aims the head pointer at a symbol. Some learners' aim may be imprecise. To compensate for this lack of precision, some devices can add increments of time during which the learner establishes contact with a particular symbol in a selection attempt. When cumulative contact time reaches a predetermined criterion, a symbol is electronically selected. This technique allows learners who

would otherwise have to scan to use a direct select technique.

Electronic communication aids are advantageous in that they can: 1) significantly lessen the communication burden on the listener, 2) offer spoken output, which allows the learner to communicate at a distance and without first obtaining a listener's attention, 3) store messages to be used in conversation or written text at a later time, and 4) clarify a qualitatively poor selection response.

Speech Output Electronic communication aids yield either synthesized or digitized speech output. *Synthesized speech* is produced by a device that converts preprogrammed mathematical information about vocal tract parameters into an audible reproduction of the human voice. Synthesized speech can be used in an application called *text-to-speech,* in which the user of a device constructs utterances from typed text input. This input is analyzed and converted to simulated phonetic information by a set of preprogrammed mathematical algorithms. Synthetic speech differs from natural speech in that it includes a limited number of the redundant cues that often enable a learner to discern meaning from natural speech even if intelligibility is low (Greenspan, Nusbaum, & Pisoni, 1985). Consequently, many synthesized speech applications are significantly less intelligible than speech. However, continued exposure generally results in improved listener understanding.

In *digitized speech,* sometimes referred to as *resynthesis* or *synthesis-by-analysis,* human speech waves are sampled at a rapid rate, and the acoustic information in the wave is stored digitally in a computer's memory. To reproduce the speech, information is retrieved from computer memory and converted to an understandable replication of the original signal. Because the output consists of processed human speech, it is nearly as intelligible as normal speech. Moreover, the natural prosody and other characteristics of the speaker's voice (e.g., age, sex, intonation) are maintained. A drawback is that the high quality of reproduction takes up much of the available computer memory, thus limiting the amount of storage space available for speech output. Moreover, digitized speech does not lend itself to text-to-speech applications.

Intelligibility of speech reflects the total amount of information available to and assimilated by the receiver of the intended message (Voiers, 1982). Damper (1984) proposed that for speech to be beneficial to a listener, it must be instantly intelligible to even a naive listener. Beukelman and Yorkston (1979) found that the ability to understand speakers with dysarthria (a speech production problem) deteriorated significantly when speech intelligibility fell to 81%.

Several recent studies (Hoover, Reichle, Van Tasell, & Cole, 1987; Logan, Pisoni, & Green, 1985; Mirenda & Beukelman, 1987, 1990) have tried to assess the intelligibility of synthetically generated speech. Results of these studies, summarized in Table 1, demonstrate that many speech synthesizers produce speech output that is below the 81% level of intelligibility suggested by Beukelman and Yorkston (1979) as the point at which listener understanding may significantly deteriorate. Intelligibility data suggest that certain types of output (e.g., Dec-Talk™, First Byte's Smooth Talker 3.0 Male™, Adaptive Communications' Real Voice™) are more intelligible than others (e.g., Street Electronics' Echo II™, VOTRAX™, First Byte's Smooth Talker 2.0 Male™). It also appears that intelligibility can be improved when sentences, as opposed to single words, comprise the output (Hoover et al., 1987; Mirenda & Beukelman, 1987, 1990).

Currently, VOTRAX™ and Echo™ are the most commonly used speech synthesis systems in augmentative communication applications (Mirenda & Beukelman, 1987). Data from several studies have demonstrated that speech output generated by these synthesizers is less intelligible and of lower quality than that produced by other synthesizers. If the 81% intelligibility level is accepted as a criterion for intelligibility,

the speech output of many currently available electronic communication devices could be judged unacceptable as a primary communication channel. Other problems also exist. On some devices, the volume controls may be difficult for the user to control, particularly if the user has impaired motor functioning. Distortion may also occur at higher volumes if an inferior speaker is used.

Although the output from speech synthesis devices is less intelligible than natural speech, its use in augmentative and alternative communication offers several advantages over systems without speech output. Learners who use devices with speech output have been found to be more dominant and in control of conversation than users of nonelectronic graphic displays (Buzolich, 1982, 1983). Moreover, conversations with users of augmentative devices with speech output were characterized by fewer communication breakdowns, fewer guesses or requests for clarification by communication partners, and increased interrupting by the augmentative user (Buzolich, 1982, 1983).

Speech output also allows a learner to gain the attention of a potential communication partner who is not in the learner's immediate vicinity or is not attending to the learner. It allows a learner to interact with people who cannot read or understand the meanings of the symbols on a learner's display surface. Speech output can also normalize interactions between speakers and listeners. Communication partners are able to communicate face-to-face rather than sit or stand side-by-side, since the learner's partner does not have to see the display surface. Communication partners are relieved of the burden of having to translate the symbols to which a learner points.

Visual Output of Electronic Communication Devices Many electronic communication devices with speech output also display messages visually. The user creates a novel utterance or selects a preprogrammed message, which appears on a screen built into the device. On some devices, it is necessary to issue an-

Table 1. Intelligibility of synthesized speech

Task	Synthesizers	Quality	Study
Identification of one syllable words	MITalk-79™, TSI prototype I™, DecTalk™, Infovox SA101™, Prose 3.0™, VOTRAX™, ECHO™	DecTalk™ most intelligible; VOTRAX and ECHO least intelligible	Logan, Pisoni, & Greene (1985)
Consonant-vowel-consonant words presented: a. in isolation b. preceded by the carrier phrase "Say the word _____." (i.e., low-probability condition) c. at the end of a redundantly cued sentence (i.e., high-probability condition)	ECHO II™, VOTRAX™	*Single words:* VOTRAX™ and ECHO II™ approximately equal (both below 22% intelligible) *Low probability and high probability conditions:* VOTRAX™ greater than ECHO II™	Hoover, Reichle, Van Tasell, & Cole (1987)
Identification of single words and sentences	ECHO II™, VOTRAX™, DecTalk™	*Single-word condition:* DecTalk™ most intelligible (59.6%–83.6%) ECHO II™ least intelligible (less than 40%) *Sentence condition:* DecTalk™ most intelligible (80.9%–96.7%) ECHO II™ ranged from 35.3% to 68.2%.	Mirenda & Beukelman (1987)
Identification of single words and sentences	SmoothTalker 2.0™ (male and female), SmoothTalker 3.0™ (male and female), Artic R65B™, VOTRAX™, Lightwriter™, RealVoice™	*Single-word condition:* SmoothTalker 3.0™ (male) and RealVoice™ most intelligible (45.43%–63.71%). Lightwriter™ and SmoothTalker 2.0™ (male) least intelligible (27.71%–42.57%). *Sentence condition:* SmoothTalker 3.0™ (male) and RealVoice™ ranged from 50.63% to 91.59%. Lightwriter™ and SmoothTalker 2.0™ (male) ranged from 41.90% to 72.54%.	Mirenda & Beukelman (1990)

other command for voice output. On others, visually displayed and spoken messages occur simultaneously. Visual displays are useful for communication partners, since they provide a means of clarifying the message if speech output is difficult to understand.

Visual output is displayed via a light-emitting diode (LED) or a liquid crystal display (LCD) surface. LCD displays require significantly less energy and drain less power on battery-operated devices than LED surfaces. However, LCD surfaces can be difficult to read under certain lighting conditions. LED displays are easier to read in environments where glare is a problem. Some manufacturers have attempted to overcome the problem of glare on LCD displays by allowing adjustments to be made in the viewing angle of the screen to compensate for variability in lighting.

In addition to visual displays, many devices have built-in printers, allowing spoken and/or displayed messages to be printed. Some devices can also be connected to peripheral printers, enabling the user to use the device as a word processor and produce permanent written products.

Other Features   Electronic aids allow a user access to a large number of messages that may be displayed on a single surface, as opposed to the multiple surfaces required by books or wallets. Multiword messages can also be stored under a single symbol, resulting in a savings of motor movements.

Some electronic aids may be easier to use than nonelectronic aids for learners with physical disabilities. For instance, if a learner has difficulty pointing and maintaining contact with a symbol, his or her finger may wander off the symbol before the listener can see which symbol the learner selected. Other learners may slide their fingers across several symbols before coming to rest on the desired symbol. Some devices compensate for these problems by a process called *electronic averaging*. Devices with this feature can be programmed so that speech output occurs after a prespecified length of contact with a symbol. In the first example, setting a short delay between pressure to a symbol and subsequent voice output would mean that a learner could touch a symbol for only a moment and still achieve speech output. In the second example, sustained contact would be required for output, thus eliminating the problem of output that results when other symbols are touched accidentally.

GESTURAL MODE COMMUNICATION

Human speech is often supplemented through the use of gestures. Most people use a rich variety of body movements and facial expressions when they speak. Sometimes learners with impaired or nonexistent vocal communication skills are taught to communicate through gestures. Gestural mode communication is generally used to supplement communication in other modes.

There is an extensive body of literature demonstrating success in teaching gestural mode production to learners with multiple disabilities and learners with autism (Barrera, Lobato-Barrera, & Sulzer-Azaroff, 1980; Cohen, 1981; Kleinert & Gast, 1982; Oliver & Halle, 1982; Reichle, Rogers, & Barrett, 1984; Shaeffer, Kollinzas, Musil, & McDowell, 1977). Koegel, Rincover, and Egel (1982) noted that the procedures that have proved most successful in teaching expressive gestures have been similar to procedures that proved effective in teaching expressive speech. In the first step, an object referent is made available and the teacher delivers a prompt to encourage the learner to produce the gesture that corresponds to the object. In the second step, the prompts are gradually faded. Finally, in the third step, a new item is introduced, and the first and second steps are recycled.

Guessability of Signs and Gestures

Fristoe and Lloyd (1977) proposed that the iconicity of signs and gestures makes them easier to acquire than spoken language. Doherty (1985) defined iconicity as comprised of translucency and transparency, terms which were defined earlier in this chapter. He reported that the literature shows that iconicity facilitates comprehension of the meanings of signs by learners with and learners without disabilities.

Another factor influencing sign acquisition involves the *concreteness* of a sign or gesture. A concrete sign is one whose referent is easily perceived through the senses, especially sight or touch. For example, "cup" is a very concrete sign, since one can easily see, touch, or imagine a cup. Other signs (e.g., "love") represent more abstract concepts, which are difficult to perceive via the senses.

Luftig and Lloyd (1981) determined that adults with normal hearing learned signs rated as highly translucent and highly concrete more easily than signs that were not highly translucent and concrete. Luftig, Lloyd, and Page (1982) compared the translucency and concreteness ratings of nouns and verbs. They found that verbs were rated significantly more translucent than nouns, but that nouns were rated as being more concrete than verbs. Page (1985) compared translucency ratings by adults, 4-year-olds, and 7-year-olds of nouns, verbs, and adjectives that frequently appear in initial lexicons of people with communicative impairments. They found that verbs were rated more translucent than nouns or adjectives by all age groups. Similar research by Luftig (1983) determined that learners with moderate to severe retardation acquired signs rated high in transparency faster than signs that were less transparent. The most difficult to learn signs were those that were rated low in both translucence and concreteness.

Motor Components of Signs and Gestures

Motor components of signs and gestures may significantly affect their learnability. The shape or shapes assumed by the hands, the orientation of the hand/arm to the learner's body, and the part of the body from which the sign or gesture is produced appear to influence acquisition (Doherty, 1985). Although the literature is somewhat limited, certain sign configurations appear to be easier to learn from the standpoint of motor requirements.

Contact Signs and Gestures Signs and gestures that require contact between both hands or between the hand and the body have been referred to as *contact signs* (Stremel-Campbell, Cantrell, & Halle, 1977). Several studies have reported that fewer teaching opportunities are required to teach contact signs to learners with severe disabilities (Stremel-Campbell et al., 1977; Thrasher & Bray, 1984). This finding has been explained by the fact that

tactile feedback received during sign formation facilitates acquisition. A related explanation is that the contact serves as a self-generated response prompt to the next step in producing the sign.

Signs and Gestures Requiring Symmetrical Movement Signs and gestures that require a symmetry of hand movement (particularly if moving to midline) of both hands may be somewhat easier to learn. Doherty (1985) suggested that this may be the case, since symmetrical movements to midline emerge very early in infants without disabilities. For example, Dennis, Reichle, Williams, and Vogelsberg (1982) reported that as early as 5 months of age infants begin moving both hands to midline to seize a crib mobile suspended above them.

Signs Produced within View Dennis et al. (1982) reported that signs produced within the learner's visual field may be easier to acquire than signs that incorporate movement that cannot be viewed directly by the learner while he or she is producing them. For example, some signs may be produced near the face, limiting the degree to which a learner can view his or her actions. Visible signs are believed to be easier to acquire because visual feedback is believed to help the learner approximate the sign.

Signs Requiring Single Movement Signs that require a single motor movement for production (e.g., the sign for "mine," which is formed by bringing the right hand toward the chest) place significantly fewer demands on the learner's ability to combine and integrate motor movement. Other signs require a chain of movements to be produced. The sign for "soft drink" is a good example. Figure 12 shows the formation of this sign. Each hand must form a different position. While one hand serves as a base (handshape as if holding a can) the second hand moves to the base hand. As the moving hand retracts, the handshape is changed. This particular sign requires a number of sequential steps to be produced in which location and handshape are altered. Each of the steps re-

Figure 12.   Hand positions assumed in the formation of the sign for a soft drink.

quired to produce this sign can be task analyzed. There is some evidence to support that
signs involving multiple steps may require more
teaching opportunities to establish than other
signs with fewer steps.

Levels of Gestures

Wundt (1973) described four levels of gesture,
including mime, demonstrative gestures, descriptive gestures, and symbolic gestures. Vanderheiden and Lloyd (1986) have defined each
of these levels as follows:

1. Mime: using the whole body in direct im-
    itation (as in acting)
2. Demonstrative gesturing: pointing or in-
    dexing, showing form and size, or display-
    ing an object
3. Descriptive gesturing: drawing in the air;
    shaping hands into three-dimensional rep-
    resentations; imitating the movement of a
    person, animal, or object; or using a sec-
    ondary trait (e.g., pushing up imaginary
    glasses to represent a person who often en-
    gages in that mannerism)
4. Symbolic gesturing: using culturally influ-
    enced gestures whose forms are essentially
    unrelated to their meaning (e.g., the thumbs
    up signal for good luck). Comprehension
    of symbolic gestures requires an ability to
    associate the gesture with its abstract
    meaning.

The discussion that follows focuses on demonstrative gesturing and symbolic gesturing,
which capture much of the early gestural behavior engaged in by children. Mime and descriptive gestures are easily integrated into a discussion of symbolic gesturing.

The most basic form of gestural communication involves body movements and vocalizations. Behaviors such as crying when uncom-
fortable or retreating when frightened or dis-
gusted are among the most primitive forms of
communication. Learners often engage in these
behaviors without intending to communicate.

Bates, Camaioni, and Volterra (1975) describe a sequence of communicative behavior
followed by infants. They define as *perlocutionary* the reflexive and voluntary behaviors
that are interpreted as having communicative
value and typically result in attention from others and the satisfaction of needs. Bates et al.
(1975) suggested that perlocutionary communication in infants is not produced for the benefit of a listener and occurs prior to intentional
communication. That is, although the infant is
not aware of the communicative value of his or
her acts, the caregiver responds to the behaviors
as though the infant were attempting to communicate through them. Slightly later, an *illocutionary* phase (Bates et al., 1975) is
characterized by the infant's growing use of behaviors produced with the intent of controlling
others. This phase involves the use of objects in

various ways (e.g., grasping objects, extending objects toward adults), immediate and delayed repetition of behaviors that previously resulted in positive reinforcement, and pointing to call another's attention to an object or event. The locutionary phase signals the emergence of words that are used as symbols. McLean and Snyder-McLean (1988) have suggested that the distinctions made by Bates et al. (1975) appear applicable to learners who experience severe and/or multiple disabilities.

Other investigators have proposed similar ways of looking at early communicative gestures of people with severe disabilities. Siegel-Causey and Downing (1987) used the term *nonsymbolic* to refer to the use of gestures, vocalizations, eye contact, facial expressions, and body movement used to communicate. Learners who use non-symbolic communication transmit messages using movements and behaviors. Siegel-Causey and Ernst (1989) differentiate nonsymbolic communication into nonintentional and intentional forms of communication. Nonintentional communication refers to reflexive or voluntary behaviors that are not used specifically to communicate, but are inferred by others to have meaning. In contrast, intentional nonsymbolic communication behaviors are behaviors a learner uses specifically to affect another's behavior.

Rowland and Stremel-Campbell (1987) use the terms *preintentional, intentional, presymbolic,* and *symbolic* to describe the sequence in which expressive communication behaviors develop in all learners. *Preintentional behaviors* are reflexes or involuntary reactions to stimuli. While the learner does not perform the behavior deliberately in order to affect another's behavior, these actions are often interpreted as being communicative. Intentional behaviors differ from preintentional behaviors in that the learner engages in these behaviors voluntarily. However, the learner does not engage in the behaviors to exert control over another's behavior, although these actions, like preintentional behaviors, are interpreted as communicative. During the non-conventional presymbolic stage, the learner becomes aware of the power his or her behavior can exert, and deliberately uses gestures, eye contact, and vocalizations for a variety of communicative functions.

Conventional presymbolic communication is characterized by the use of widely recognized gestures, with meanings agreed upon by others from the learner's culture. Conventional symbolic communication occurs when the learner demonstrates an ability to pair a symbol with a referent. At this stage, the learner is able to use highly recognizable and guessable gestures and symbols to represent objects found in the environment. Abstract symbolic communication involves the use of symbols that do not bear a direct relationship to their referents. This level is characterized by the use of single words or signs. Finally, formal symbolic communication emerges, during which time the learner produces multiword utterances according to grammatical rules.

McLean and Snyder-McLean (1988) described three levels of intentional communicative gestures that have been observed in people with severe disabilities. The first level, referred to as *primitive communication signaling behavior,* consists primarily of actions directed toward people and objects. This level includes behaviors such as reaching for an object, pulling away from stimuli, gesturing with objects, and tugging at another's hand or placing someone else's hand on an object. The second level of early communicative behavior, referred to as *conventionalized behavior,* includes gestures that are not accompanied by contact with an object or person. Examples of this type of behavior are pointing at objects or people, accompanying gestures with vocalizations, and occasionally producing a few manual signs or words in the presence of their referents. Referential communication is characterized by the use of five or more manual signs or words and numerous gestures used spontaneously and produced in the absence of their referents.

These descriptions of emerging gestures share many common features. Table 2 illustrates how various behaviors could be classified using each taxonomy. (Chapter 4 provides additional information that elaborates on descriptors used by McLean and Snyder-McLean [1988].)

Demonstrative Gesturing

A variety of examples of demonstrative gesturing emerges in an early repertoire of gestures performed by both children with and children without disabilities. Most instances of demonstrative gesturing fit a class of gestures referred to by McLean and Snyder-McLean (1988) as conventional communicative acts. Some of the more common demonstrative gestures are described below.

Pointing Pointing emerges in infants at about 9 months of age (Murphy & Messar, 1977), and refers to extension of the arm, hand, and/or finger. Frequency of pointing increases as the child matures, with 20- and 24-month-old children pointing more frequently than 9- and 14-month-old infants (Murphy, 1978). At first, pointing may be used by the child in examining interesting objects, sounds, and events (Bates et al., 1975). Early pointing behaviors are not used to attract attention. However, as the child matures, pointing is used to attract adult attention, and can be used to request objects or activities. Pointing to request may stem from the young child's behavior of trying to reach for and grasp objects in the environment. If the object is out of reach, the child may stretch out his or her arms and whine, then look at the nearby parent. An attentive parent will move the object within reach or give it to the child. If this occurs several times, the child may learn that reaching for an object that is out of reach and whining usually results in being given the item. The child learns that whining may not be necessary if the adult is being attentive, but that it is necessary

to indicate which item is desired by pointing to it.

In addition to pointing in order to request, a child may point to comment on the existence of an object or to call it to the attention of someone else. If such behavior is reinforced consistently, its frequency is likely to increase.

Experience with people with severe and/or multiple disabilities suggests that research on development of people without disabilities is applicable. Even among people with severe disabilities, there is a long-term propensity to produce more often those behaviors that have resulted in the procurement of objects or attention. (For intervention strategies that can be derived from the developmental research, see Chapter 5).

Gestures Involving Objects Showing, offering, and giving an object to another person are also forms of gestural communication and may be performed in order to obtain items, activities, and attention, or to request to leave an activity. These behaviors emerge sometime after infants begin accepting offered objects, which occurs at about 8 months of age. If an adult is standing several feet from an infant and extends an object, the infant will generally extend an arm toward the object. The adult will usually respond by placing the object in the child's hand. *Showing behavior* usually emerges after the child has begun to accept offered items. In this routine, the child approaches an adult while holding an object. When the adult establishes eye contact with the child, the child extends his or her arm to the adult so that the object is clearly visible. Often the adult will interpret the child's approach and arm extension as an intent to give the object. However, at this stage, the child will often retract his or her arm if the adult attempts to take the object (Bates et al., 1975). Later, the child will extend the object and wait until the other person takes the object. At about age 1, the child will actively seek out an adult while holding an object of interest and offer

Table 2. Taxonomies of communicative behaviors

Behavior	Bates, Camainoi, & Volterra (1975)	Siegel-Causey & Downing (1987) / Siegel-Causey & Ernst (1989)	Rowland & Stremel-Campbell (1987)	McLean & Snyder-McLean (1988)
Change in posture	Perlocutionary	Nonsymbolic (nonintentional)	Intentional	Primitive
Cry, goo, gurgle	Perlocutionary	Nonsymbolic (nonintentional)	Intentional	Primitive
Pull away from stimulus (nonreflexive)	Perlocutionary	Nonsymbolic (intentional)	Nonconventional/presymbolic	Primitive
Smile	Perlocutionary	Nonsymbolic (intentional)	Intentional	Primitive
Use of an object to request an item or more of an item	Illocutionary	Nonsymbolic (intentional)	Nonconventional/presymbolic	Primitive
Push away object, person	Illocutionary	Nonsymbolic (intentional)	Conventional/presymbolic	Conventionalized
Head shake (yes/no)	Illocutionary	Nonsymbolic (intentional)	Conventional/presymbolic	Conventionalized
Pointing at objects/people	Illocutionary	Nonsymbolic (intentional)	Conventionalized	Conventionalized
Consistent vocalizations	Locutionary	Nonsymbolic (intentional)	Concrete	Conventionalized
Multiword utterances, multisign/symbol use	Locutionary	—	Formal	Referential

the object to the adult. If the adult does not accept the object, the child may place it in the adult's lap and return for it sometime later.

The routines of showing, offering, and giving are important interpersonal skills that result in obtaining objects and attention. Further sophistication of these routines will allow the child to control the behavior of others in the environment. For example, a young child may take an empty bottle off the countertop and hand it to her father in order to communicate a request for more juice. In the same way, a person with severe disabilities may go to the hall closet, remove both his own and a caregiver's coat, and hand the person the coat in order to request a walk outside.

Touching Others　　Touching another person can also serve communicative functions. A small child may tug on his father's arm and lead him to the door to bring him to the sandbox. Touches, such as hugs or pats on the back or the hand can be used to express affection, or to encourage, compliment, or comfort someone. Over time, behaviors such as these may be shaped into less intrusive demonstrative gestures, such as pointing. A history may develop in which a child reaches for the adult's clothes and pulls the adult toward an area of interest. Eventually, the adult comes to anticipate this event and responds before the child actually touches him or her. As the history becomes well established, the child learns that simply moving in the direction of the adult while extending his arm (constituting a gross pointing gesture) is sufficient to result in the adult's attention.

Head Nodding　　Head movement is another behavior that may develop as a result of shaping. The side to side movement of the head to indicate "no" often appears to serve a communicative function before the child uses it intentionally. For example, a child may try to avoid the second spoonful of a bad tasting food item by turning his or her head away from the oncoming spoon. If he or she successfully avoids the spoon, the adult may attempt to get the child

to take another bite by moving the spoon in front of the child's mouth and saying, "Want another bite?" The child may again repeat the head turn, this time the other way. The adult may decide the child has eaten enough and terminate the meal, or move on to a different food item. In this example, side to side head turning is reinforced by a withdrawal of the bad tasting food item. A negative reinforcement paradigm is operating in which engaging in a particular behavior results in the cessation of an aversive stimulus.

Head nodding in affirmation could be shaped in a similar manner. For example, a young girl with severe physical disabilities eats while seated in her wheelchair. Her mother heeds the occupational therapist's advice to work on independent head control during feeding by encouraging the child to hold her chin level rather than allowing her head to roll back. The mother offers the child a spoonful of food at midline, holding it just below her daughter's mouth so that the child must tilt her head forward and down to reach the spoon. The mother says, "Want another bite?" and praises her daughter whenever she moves her head downward toward the spoon. Occasionally she says, "Show me you want another bite" and "Yes, you want another bite!" to encourage her daughter to continue eating. The head nod to indicate "yes" is thus shaped in the same way that the "no" head shake was formed.

Idiosyncratic Behaviors Used as Symbolic Gestures

Sometimes, gestures have communicative value for the person who uses them and for those familiar with the learner, but are not likely to be understood by strangers. For example, Ben, a 55-year-old man with severe mental retardation, uses many idiosyncratic gestures. He recently moved from an institution to a group home in a rural area and spends some of his free time paging through outdoor magazines and field guides to birds, animals, and flowers, and going for walks around his new home. Shortly after he moved to the group home, Ben observed a rabbit sitting under a shrub. He grasped a staff member's arm, led her to the window, and pointed to the rabbit, which was wiggling its ears. Ben rested his hand against the side of his head, extended his index finger, then moved it back and forth in imitation of the rabbit's ear movement. The staff member smiled, nodded approvingly, and said "Yes, the rabbit is wiggling its ears." In this instance, Ben was using descriptive gesturing.

Conventional Gestures: Sign Languages and Sign Systems

Hamre-Nietupski et al. (1977) enumerated the commonly used and generally understood gestures that were used in communicating with learners with severe mental retardation. The logic for such collections of gestures, called *gestural symbol sets,* were believed to be highly recognizable in the community, portable, and quick to produce. Fiocca (1981) found that 77% of the signs in Hamre-Nietupski's list were identified successfully by people serving people with severe disabilities.

Perhaps the best known gestural symbol set was developed by Skelly (1979). This collection of gestures, called *Amer-Ind,* is based upon "hand talk" used by American Indians. Amer-Ind was originally reported to be above 80% guessable (Skelly, 1979; Skelly, Schinsky, Smith, & Fust, 1974). More recent literature reported by Vanderheiden and Lloyd (1986) suggests that guessability (transparency) may be closer to 50%.

Although Amer-Ind is probably the most prevalent gestural set used by persons with severe disabilities, Doherty, Karlin, and Lloyd (1982) reported that the "generally understood gestures" of Hamre-Nietupski et al. (1977) were more guessable than a sample of gestures comprising Amer-Ind.

Signs are used frequently in language intervention programs with people with mental retardation (Bonvillian & Orlansky, 1984; Fristoe & Lloyd, 1978). Sign languages have their own vocabulary, syntax, and grammar, and are independent of the native spoken language of the country in which they originate (Vanderheiden & Lloyd, 1986). Sign languages developed in a country-specific manner. There are British, Chinese, French, Japanese, Korean, Swedish, and a host of other sign languages associated with different spoken languages. Vanderheiden and Lloyd (1986) reported that only 10%–15% of signs across these languages are similar.

Gestuno is an international sign language developed by the Unification of Signs Commission of the World Federation of the Deaf. Gestuno Signs were selected from American Sign Language and a number of other sign languages. Vanderheiden and Lloyd (1986) question the utility of using Gestuno with learners with severe disabilities, recommending instead that Gestuno be used as ". . . a valuable resource for signs and gestures. . ." (p. 78).

Unlike sign languages, *sign systems* attempt to retain the word meaning and word-order aspects of a particular language. For example, Signing Exact English attempts to adhere to the syntactic and morphological rules of English. Sign systems allow for an easier translation between sign and spoken or written sentences in a particular language. Vanderheiden and Lloyd (1986) have referred to such sign systems involving the English language as manually coded English, or pedagogical signs. Typically, manually coded English is reported to be produced slightly slower than spoken English or American Sign Language.

Advantages of Gestural Communication

Unlike the graphic mode user, the learner who uses gestural communication does not have to "get ready" to communicate. Because there is no device to switch on, wallet to remove and open, or pages to turn, gestural communication is also faster. It requires the use of no assorted paraphernalia, such as wallets, notebooks, carrying cases, or prosthetic devices, to assist in selecting a symbol, making it the most portable type of system.

Another advantage is that the meanings of some gestures can be easily guessed. A gesture to signify the act of cutting with a scissors might consist of extending the index finger and middle finger while holding the flexed ring finger and little finger against the palm with the thumb, then repeatedly aducting and abducting the index finger in imitation of opening and closing a pair of scissors. Because the gesture so closely resembles the action of cutting, it is easily guessable.

Gestures have the advantage over speech of being able to be produced more slowly. Being able to slow down components of a sign may make signs easier to learn than speech or symbols. Finally, signs and gestures permit the interventionist to use a host of prompting techniques that do not require the learner to be able to imitate.

Disadvantages of Gestural Communication

Primitive gestural forms (McLean & Snyder-McLean, 1988; Rowland & Stremel-Campbell, 1987; Seigel-Causey & Guess, 1989) have received much attention. Interpretation of a learner's early, somewhat idiosyncratic gestures may be problematic. Although it may be possible to shape some of these rudimentary gestures (e.g., pulling away from undesired items) into conventional gestures or signs, it may be difficult to do so with others, thus leaving the learner dependent on his or her listener.

Another potential drawback of teaching gestural mode communication is that in order for optimal acquisition to occur, the learner's communication partners should be at least as competent in the system as the learner. The learner's communication partners should be committed to using the mode throughout the day in both expressive and receptive exchanges with the learner (Bryen & Joyce, 1986). Bryen, Goldman, and Quinlisk-Gill (1988) found that parents and teachers of a group of students with severe disabilities who were being taught signs had more limited sign repertoires than speech and language therapists. Since parents and teachers have more daily contact with learners than do speech and language therapists, their lack of competence in sign production may limit a learner's progress. This potential drawback points to the importance of teaching those people with whom a learner regularly interacts to use the selected system. A related disadvantage of the gestural mode is that many of the learner's potential communication partners may not understand the various gestures or signs used by the learner.

The lack of a permanent display is another disadvantage of gestural communication. A learner with a vocabulary of 150 signs must be able to recall and produce each sign from memory. In contrast, a graphic mode user has a display of symbols available. Furthermore, symbols can be color coded or arranged by semantic category or by the environment in which they are used, making it easier for a learner to narrow down the page or area of the display in which a particular symbol is located. This is not an option with gestures.

Gestural communication may impose limits on a learner's ability to request specific items. A learner may be able to request a particular class of item, such as a cracker or a cola. However, unless a learner can be taught to finger spell, requesting a specific type or brand of cracker or cola may be difficult. This is particularly important with learners who exhibit very limited preferences.

Circumstances Favoring the Use of Gestures

If a learner already uses a number of natural gestures that are easily interpreted by strangers, it is usually a good idea to allow him or her to continue to use those gestures. It may also be possible to make a learner's natural or idiosyncratic gestures more easily understood by others by teaching the learner to chain a more guessable gesture to the original gesture. For example, a learner who requests a drink by pursing his lips could be taught to follow lip pursing by raising an imaginary glass to his lips.

In cases where a learner frequently engages in excess behavior in order to escape a situation, it may be desirable to teach a gesture as a means of rejecting items or activities. A gesture can be produced rapidly, whereas use of a rejection symbol requires that a learner pull a wallet out of his or her pocket, or open a communication book, find the reject symbol, and point to it. If the learner becomes aggressive or self-injurious when confronted with demands, it may be beneficial to provide him or her with a more rapid means of communicating dissatisfaction. (This topic is addressed in greater detail in Chapter 11).

Gestural mode communication may also be called for when a learner's communication partners are sometimes out of close proximity. For example, a learner with multiple disabilities works in an office stapling fliers. He is a graphic mode user, and has no way of communicating with his supervisor when she is across the room. Consequently, when his stapler runs out of staples, he must wait until a staff person notices the situation and fills the stapler. This situation could have been avoided if the learner had been taught to produce a gesture (waving his hand in the air, pointing to the stapler) to request assistance.

INTEGRATING THE USE OF VOCAL, GESTURAL, AND GRAPHIC MODES

Recent surveys of speech and language pathologists and special educators have suggested that augmentative and alternative communication systems are becoming more prevalent for learners with severe developmental disabilities (Fristoe & Lloyd, 1978; Goodman, Wilson, & Bornstein, 1978; Matas, Mathy-Laikko, Beukelman, & Legresley, 1985). The gestural mode is used more often than the graphic mode (Bryen & Joyce, 1985). No doubt the reason for this prevalence is due in part to tradition—signs have long been successfully acquired by learners with severe disabilities.

The authors believe that all modes of communication that can be functional for a particular learner should be used. The concurrent use of vocal, gestural, and graphic modes can be achieved in a number of different types of combinations.

Simultaneous Mode

A number of studies has addressed the utility of teaching communication in more than one mode simultaneously. Most of the work that has been done has documented the successful implementation of gestural and vocal mode intervention programs (Barrera et al., 1980; Brady & Smouse, 1978). Barrera et al. (1980) found a combined gestural and vocal mode intervention to be effective in establishing production more than either mode taught alone. Brady and Smouse (1978) showed multiple mode intervention to be superior to single mode intervention in establishing an initial repertoire of comprehension skills. However, other investigators have reported that when vocal and gestural mode are combined, learners with childhood autism may be more apt to attend to the gestural component than the vocal component (Carr, Binkoff, Kologinsky, & Eddy, 1978). Other investigators have suggested that the successfulness of simultaneous mode use may depend on whether the learner has mastered generalized imitation at the point of intervention (Carr & Dores, 1981; Carr, Pridal, & Dores, 1984; Remington & Clarke, 1983).

Mixed Mode

Keogh and Reichle (1985) speculated that some learners may benefit from a communication system in which some vocabulary items are taught in one mode while different vocabulary items are taught in another mode. Specific vocabulary items are assigned to a particular mode after the interventionist carefully scrutinizes the communicative demands of the learner's environment. (Ecological inventories used to scrutinize communicative demands are examined in Chapter 3.) Some vocabulary may be able to be represented with highly guessable gestures. Other vocabulary, such as V-8℗ Tomato Juice, may require a level of specificity that can be achieved easily only through the use of product logos. Proponents of mixed mode systems suggest that use of a mixed mode allows the learner and the interventionist to take advantage of the best features of both gestural and graphic modes. At the same time, this option does not rule out representing vocabulary in both gestural and graphic modes at some later point.

Duplicated Mode

Proponents of the duplicated mode believe that a learner should be able to represent the same vocabulary in both the graphic and the gestural mode. They argue that it is difficult to assign vocabulary to a particular mode, since communicative production depends on the situation in which vocabulary is used. That is, a learner with duplicate vocabulary in gestural and graphic modes who wishes to communicate thirst on a playground would probably find it easier to gesture than to take a communication wallet out and locate the symbol. However, when interacting with a babysitter unfamiliar with the learner's gestural system, a request for a drink of water might be better communicated through the use of a graphic symbol.

The introduction of duplicated mode vocabulary often occurs sequentially. That is, a learner may have acquired a significant repertoire of signs and gestures while residing in an institutional setting. Upon moving into the community, the learner is no longer able to rely on signs and gestures, since few people in the community sign. As a result, some of the signs in the learner's repertoire must be duplicated.

SUMMARY

People without disabilities supplement their messages by using gestures, facial expressions, eye gaze, and vocal inflections and intonations. At times, these nonverbal methods may be used to replace speech entirely.

The person with a disability that causes a severe communication impairment may need to rely almost exclusively on the use of the augmentative and alternative modes introduced in this chapter. Succeeding chapters cover assessment of a learner's existing communicative behaviors, selection of communicative skills to teach, and design of interventions to teach targeted communication skills. Replacing excess behavior with functional communication and strategies for teaching communication skills to learners with severe disabilities are also discussed.

The chapters that follow are based on the premise that everyone, regardless of the level of physical or cognitive impairment, possesses at least a rudimentary means of communication and has the potential for acquiring additional skills. The challenge facing special educators is how to provide learners with functional means of communicating their basic needs and desires, and to strive continually to improve the learner's communicative skills.

REFERENCES

Barrera, R.D., Lobato-Barrera, D., & Sulzer-Azaroff, E. (1980). A simultaneous treatment comparison of three expressive language training programs with a mute autistic child. *Journal of Autism and Developmental Disorders, 10,* 21–37.

Bates, E., Camaioni, L., & Volterra V. (1975). The

acquisition of performatives prior to speech. *Merrill-Palmer Quarterly, 21*(3), 205–226.

Beukelman, D.R., & Yorkston, K.M. (1979). The relationship between information transfer and speech intelligibility of dysarthric speakers. *Journal of Communication Disorders, 12*, 189–196.

Beukelman, D.R., & Yorkston, K.M. (1989). Augmentative and alternative communication application for persons with severe acquired communication disorders: An introduction. *Augmentative and Alternative Communication, 5*, 42–48.

Blackstone, S.W. (1989). Visual scanning: What's it all about? *Augmentative Communication News, 2*(4), 1–8.

Bliss, C. (1965). *Semantography*. Sydney, Australia: Semantography Publications.

Bloomberg, E. (1984). *The comparative translucency of initial lexical items represented by five graphic symbol systems*. Unpublished master's thesis, Purdue University, West Lafayette, IN.

Blyden, A.E. (1989). Survival word acquisition in mentally retarded adolescents with multihandicaps: Effects of color—revised stimulus materials. *Journal of Special Education, 22*(4), 493–501.

Bonvillian, J.D., & Orlansky, M.D. (1984). Sign language acquisition: Early steps. *Communication Outlook, 6*(1), 10–12.

Brady, D.O., & Smouse, A.D. (1978). A simultaneous comparison of three methods for language training with an autistic child: An experimental single case analysis. *Journal of Autism and Childhood Schizophrenia, 8*, 271–279.

Bryen, D.N., Goldman, A.S., & Quinlisk-Gill, S. (1988). Sign language with students with severe/profound mental retardation: How effective is it? *Education and Training in Mental Retardation, 23* (2), 129–137.

Bryen, D.N., & Joyce, D.G. (1985). Language intervention with the severely handicapped: A decade of research. *Journal of Special Education, 19*(1), 7–39.

Bryen, D.N., & Joyce, D.G. (1986). Sign language and the severely handicapped. *Journal of Special Education, 20*(2), 183–194.

Burkhart, L.J. (1985). *Homemade battery powered toys and educational devices for severely handicapped children*. College Park, MD: Linda J. Burkhart, P.O. Box 793.

Buzolich, M.J. (1982). *Interaction analysis of adult augmented communicators: A pilot study*. Unpublished manuscript, University of California, San Francisco.

Buzolich, M.J. (1983). *Interaction analysis of augmented and normal adult communicators*. Un-published doctoral dissertation, University of California, San Francisco.

Campbell, A., & Lloyd, L. (1986). *Graphic symbols and symbol systems: What research and clinical practice tell us*. Paper presented at the Conference of the American Association on Mental Deficiency, Denver.

Carlson, F. (1984). *Picsyms categorical dictionary*. Lawrence, KS: Baggeboda Press.

Carr, E.G., Binkoff, J. A., Kologinsky, E., & Eddy, M. (1978). Acquisition of sign language by autistic children: Expressive labeling. *Journal of Applied Behavior Analysis, 11*, 489–501.

Carr, E.G., & Dores, P.A. (1981). Patterns of language acquisition following simultaneous communication with autistic children. *Analysis and intervention in developmental disabilities, 1*, 347–361.

Carr, E.G., Pridal, C., & Dores, P.A. (1984). Speech versus sign comprehension in autistic children: Analysis and prediction. *Journal of Experimental Child Psychology, 37*(3), 587–597.

Carrier, J., Jr. (1976). Application of a nonspeech language system with the severely language handicapped. In L. Lloyd (Ed.), *Communication assessment and intervention strategies* (pp. 523–547). Baltimore: University Park Press.

Carrier, J., Jr., & Peak, T. (1975). *Non-slip: Non-speech language initiation program*. Lawrence, KS: H & H Enterprises.

Chapman, R., & Miller, J. (1980). Analyzing language and communication in the child. In R.L. Schiefelbusch (Ed.), *Nonspeech language and communication: Analysis and intervention* (pp. 159–196). Baltimore: University Park Press.

Clark, C.R. (1981). Learning words using traditional orthography and the symbols of Rebus, Bliss, and Carrier. *Journal of Speech and Hearing Disorders, 46*, 191–196.

Clark, C.R., Davies, C.D., & Woodcock, R.W. (1974). *Standard rebus glossary*. Circle Pines, MN: American Guidance Service.

Clark, C.R., & Woodcock, R. (1976). Graphic systems of communication. In L. Lloyd (Ed.), *Communication assessment and intervention strategies* (pp. 549–605). Baltimore: University Park Press.

Cohen, M. (1981). Development of language behavior in an autistic child using total communication. *Exceptional Children, 47*, 374–379.

Creagan, A. (1982). *Sigsymbol dictionary*. Hatfield, Herts., England: A. Creagan, 76 Wood Close.

Creagan, A., & Lloyd, L. (1984). Sigsymbols: Graphic symbols conceptually linked with manual signs. *Proceedings of the Third International Con-*

ference on Augmentative and Alternative Communication (p. 44). Cambridge: MIT Press.

Damper, R.I. (1984). Speech technology and the disabled. In J.N. Holmes (Ed.), Proceedings of the First International Conference on Speech Technology (pp. 135–143). Amsterdam: IFS and North-Holland.

Damper, R.I. (1986). Rapid message composition for large vocabulary speech output aids: A review of the possibilities. Augmentative and Alternative Communication, 2(4), 152–159.

Dennis, R., Reichle, J., Williams. W., & Vogelsberg, T. (1982). Motoric factors influencing the selection of vocabulary for sign production programs. Journal of The Association for the Severe Handicapped, 7, 20–33.

Doherty, J.E. (1985). The effects of sign characteristics on sign acquisition and retention: An integrative review of the literature. Augmentative and Alternative Communication, 1(3), 108–121.

Doherty, J.E., Karlin, G., & Lloyd, L. (1982). Establishing the transparency of two gestural systems by mentally retarded adults. Paper presented at the annual meeting of the American Speech-Language-Hearing Association, Toronto.

Dorry, G.W., & Zeaman, D. (1975). Teaching a simple reading vocabulary to retarded children: Effectiveness of fading and nonfading procedures. American Journal of Mental Deficiency, 76(6), 711–716.

Ecklund, S., & Reichle, J. (1987). A comparison of normal children's ability to recall symbols from two logographic systems. Language, Speech, and Hearing Services in the Schools, 18(1), 34–40.

Eichler, J.H. (1973). Instruction for the ETRAN eye signaling system. Ridgefield, CT: Jack H. Eichler.

Fiocca, G. (1981). Generally understood gestures: An approach to communication for persons with severe language impairments. Unpublished master's thesis, University of Illinois, Urbana-Champaign.

Fristoe, M., & Lloyd, L. (1977). The use of manual communication with the retarded. Paper presented at the tenth annual Gatlinburg Conference on Research in Mental Retardation, Gatlinburg, TN.

Fristoe, M., & Lloyd, L.L. (1978). A survey of the use of nonspeech systems with the severely communication impaired. Mental Retardation, 16(2), 99–103.

Goodman, L., Wilson, P.S., & Bornstein, H. (1978). Results of a national survey of sign language programs in special education. Mental Retardation, 6, 104–106.

Goossens', C.A., Elder, P.S., Caldwell, M.A., &

Page, J.L. (1988). Long range planning: A continuum of semantic compaction overlays. Proceedings of the Third Annual Minispeak Conference (pp. 1–24). Anaheim, CA.

Greenspan, S., Nusbaum, H., & Pisoni, D. (1985). Perception of synthetic speech generation by rule: Effects of training and attentional limitations. Research on Speech Perception (Progress Report No. 11). Bloomington, IN: Indiana University.

Hamre-Nietupski, S., Stoll, A., Holtz, K., Fullerton, P., Flottum-Ryan, M., & Brown, L. (1977). Curricular strategies for teaching nonverbal communication skills to verbal and nonverbal severely handicapped students. In L. Brown, J. Nietupski, S. Lyon, S. Hamre-Nietupski, T. Crowner, & L. Gruenewald (Eds.), Curricular strategies for teaching functional object use, nonverbal communication, problem solving and mealtime skills to severely handicapped students (Vol. 8, Part 1, pp. 94–250). Madison, WI: Madison Metropolitan School District.

Hinderscheit, L.R., & Reichle, J. (1987). Teaching direct select color encoding to an adolescent with multiple handicaps. Augmentative and Alternative Communication, 3(3), 137–142.

Hoover, J., Reichle, J., Van Tasell, D., & Cole, D. (1987). The intelligibility of synthesized speech: Echo II versus Votrax. Journal of Speech and Hearing Research, 30, 425–431.

Hurlbut, B.I., Iwata, B.A., & Green, J.D. (1982). Nonvocal language acquisition in adolescents with severe physical disabilities: Blissymbol versus iconic stimulus formats. Journal of Applied Behavior Analysis, 15, 241–258.

Johnson, R. (1981). The picture communication symbols. Salana Beach, CA: Mayer-Johnson.

Johnson, R. (1985). The picture communication symbols: Book II. Salana Beach, CA: Mayer-Johnson.

Keogh, W.J., & Reichle, J. (1985). Communication intervention for the "difficult-to-teach" severely handicapped. In S.F. Warren & A.K. Rogers-Warren (Eds.), Teaching functional language (pp. 157–194). Austin, TX: PRO-ED.

Kirstein, I.J., & Bernstein, C. (1981). Oakland schools picture dictionary. Pontiac, MI: Oakland Schools Communication Enhancement Center.

Kleinert, H.L., & Gast, D.L. (1982). Teaching a multihandicapped adult manual signs using a constant time delay procedure. Journal of The Association for the Severely Handicapped, 6(4), 25–32.

Koegel, R.L., Rincover, A., & Egel, A.L. (1982). Educating and understanding autistic children. Boston: College-Hill Press.

Landman, C., & Schaeffler, C. (1986). Object communication boards. *Communication Outlook, 8* (1), 7–8.

Lloyd, L.L., & Fuller, D.R. (1986). Toward an augmentative and alternative communication symbol taxonomy: A proposed superordinate classification. *Augmentative and Alternative Communication, 2*(4), 165–171.

Logan, J., Pisoni, D., & Greene, B. (1985). Measuring the segmental intelligibility of synthetic speech: Results from eight text-to-speech systems. *Research on Speech Perception (Progress Report No. 11).* Bloomington, IN: Indiana University.

Luftig, R.L. (1983). Translucency of sign and concreteness of gloss in the manual sign learning of moderately/severely mentally retarded students. *American Journal of Mental Deficiency, 88*(3), 279–286.

Luftig, R.L., & Lloyd, L.L. (1981). Manual sign translucency and referential concreteness in the learning of signs. *Sign Language Studies, 30,* 49–60.

Luftig, B.L., Lloyd, L.L., & Page, J.L. (1982). Ratings of sign translucency and gloss concreteness of two grammatical classes of signs. *Sign Language Studies, 37,* 305–343.

Maharaj, S. (1980). *Pictogram ideogram communication.* Regina, Canada: The George Reed Foundation for the Handicapped.

Matas, J., Mathy-Laikko, P., Beukelman, D., & Legresley, K. (1985). Identifying the nonspeaking population: A demographic study. *Augmentative and Alternative Communication, 1*(1), 17–31.

McLean, J.E., & Snyder-McLean, L. (1988). Application of pragmatics to severely mentally retarded children and youth. In R. L. Schiefelbusch & L.L. Lloyd (Eds.), *Language perspectives: Acquisition, retardation, and intervention* (pp. 255–288). Austin, TX: PRO-ED.

Meador, D., Rumbaugh, D., Tribble, M., & Thompson, S. (1984). Facilitating visual discrimination learning of moderately and severely mentally retarded children through illumination of stimuli. *American Journal of Mental Deficiency, 89,* 313–316.

Mirenda, P. (1985). Designing pictoral communication systems for physically able-bodied students with severe handicaps. *Augmentative and Alternative Communication, 1*(2), 58–64.

Mirenda, P., & Beukelman, D.R. (1987). A comparison of speech synthesis intelligibility with listeners from three age groups. *Augmentative and Alternative Communication, 3*(3), 120–128.

Mirenda, P., & Beukelman, D.R. (1990). A comparison of intelligibility among natural speech and seven speech synthesizers with listeners from three age groups. *Augmentative and Alternative Communication, 6*(1), 61–68.

Mirenda, P., & Locke, P.A. (1989). A comparison of symbol transparency in nonspeaking persons with intellectual disabilities. *Journal of Speech and Hearing Disorders, 54,* 131–140.

Mizuko, M.I. (1987). Transparency and ease of learning symbols represented by Blissymbols, PCS, and Picsyms. *Augmentative and Alternative Communication, 3*(3), 129–136.

Murphy, C.M. (1978). Pointing in the context of a shared activity. *Child Development, 49,* 371–380.

Murphy, C.M., & Messar, D. (1977). Mothers, infants, and pointing: A study of gesture. In H.R. Shaffer (Ed.), *Studies in mother-infant interaction* (pp. 325–354). New York: Academic Press.

Musselwhite, C.R., & Ruscello, D.M. (1984). Transparency of three communication symbol systems. *Journal of Speech and Hearing Research, 27,* 436–443.

Oliver, C., & Halle, J. (1982). Language training in the everyday environment: Teaching functional sign use to a retarded child. *Journal of The Association for the Severely Handicapped, 8,* 50–62.

Page, J. (1985). Relative translucency of ASL signs representing three semantic classes. *Journal of Speech and Hearing Disorders, 50,* 241–247.

Premack, D. (1970). A functional analysis of language. *Journal of Experimental Analysis of Behavior, 14,* 107–125.

Premack, D., & Premack, A. (1974). Teaching visual language to apes and language deficient persons. In R. Schiefelbusch & L. Lloyd (Eds.), *Language perspectives: Acquisition, retardation, and intervention* (pp. 347–376). Baltimore: University Park Press.

Reichle, J., Rogers, N., & Barrett, C. (1984). Establishing pragmatic discriminations among the communicative functions of requesting, rejecting, and commenting in an adolescent. *Journal of The Association for Persons with Severe Handicaps, 9,* 31–36.

Reichle, J., & Yoder, D.E. (1985). Communication board use in severely handicapped learners. *Language, Speech, and Hearing Services in Schools, 16,* 146–167.

Remington, B., & Clark, S. (1983). Acquisition of expressive signing by autistic children: An evaluation of the relative effects of simultaneous communication and sing-along training. *Journal of Applied Behavior Analysis, 16,* 315–328.

Romski, M.A., Sevcik, R.A., & Pate, J.L. (1988). Establishment of symbolic communication in persons with severe mental retardation. *Journal of Speech and Hearing Disorders, 53,* 94–107.

Romski, M., Sevcik, R., Pate, J., & Rumbaugh, D. (1985). Discrimination of lexigrams and traditional orthography by nonspeaking severely retarded persons. *American Journal of Mental Deficiency, 90,* 185–189.

Romski, M., White, R., Millen, C., & Rumbaugh, D. (1984). Effects of computer-keyboard teaching on the symbolic communication of severely retarded persons: Five case studies. *Psychological Record, 34,* 39–54.

Rowland, C., & Stremel-Campbell, K. (1987). Share and share alike: Conventional gestures to emergent language for learners with sensory impairments. In L. Goetz, D. Guess, & K. Stremel-Campbell (Eds.), *Innovative program design for individuals with dual sensory impairments* (pp. 49–75). Baltimore: Paul H. Brookes Publishing Co.

Rumbaugh, D. (Ed.). (1977). *Language learning by a chimpanzee: The Lana project.* New York: Academic Press.

Rumbaugh, D., Gell, T., & von Glaserfeld, E. (1973). Reading and sentence completion by a chimpanzee (Pan). *Science, 82,* 731–733.

Schaeffer, B., Kollinzas, G., Musil, A., & McDowell, P. (1977). Spontaneous verbal language for autistic children through signed speech. *Sign Language Studies, 17,* 287–328.

Sidman, M., & Stoddard, L.T. (1967). The effectiveness of fading in programming a simultaneous form discrimination for retarded children. *Journal of the Experimental Analysis of Behavior, 6,* 1–27.

Siegel-Causey, E., & Downing, J. (1987). Nonsymbolic communication development: Theoretical concepts and educational strategies. In L. Goetz, D. Guess, & K. Stremel-Campbell (Eds.), *Innovative program design for individuals with dual sensory impairments* (pp. 15–48). Baltimore: Paul H. Brookes Publishing Co.

Siegel-Causey, E., & Ernst, B. (1989). Theoretical orientation and research in non-symbolic development. In E. Siegel-Causey & D. Guess, *Enhancing nonsymbolic communication interactions among learners with severe disabilities* (pp. 17–51). Baltimore: Paul H. Brookes Publishing Co.

Siegel-Causey, E., & Guess, D. (1989). *Enhancing nonsymbolic communication interactions among learners with severe disabilities.* Baltimore: Paul H. Brookes Publishing Co.

Silverman, F.H. (1989). *Communication for the speechless.* Englewood Cliffs, NJ: Prentice-Hall.

Skelly, M. (1979). *Amer-Ind gestural code based on universal American Indian hand talk.* New York: Elsevier.

Skelly, M., Schinsky, L., Smith, R., & Fust, R. (1974). American Indian Sign (AMERIND) as a facilitator of verbalization for the oral verbal apraxic. *Journal of Speech and Hearing Disorders, 39,* 445–466.

Stillman, R., & Battle, C.W. (1984). Developing prelanguage communication in the severely handicapped: An interpretation of the van Dijk method. *Seminars in Speech and Language, 5* (3), 159–170.

Stremel-Campbell, K. Cantrell, D., & Halle, J. (1977). Manual signing as a language system and as a speech initiator for the nonverbal severely handicapped student. In E. Sontag (Ed.), *Educational programming for the severely and profoundly handicapped* (pp. 335–347). Reston, VA: Council for Exceptional Children.

Thrasher, K., & Bray, N. (1984). *Effects of iconicity, taction and training technique on the initial acquisition of manual signing by the mentally retarded.* Paper presented at the 17th annual Gatlinburg Conference on Research in Mental Retardation, Gatlinburg, TN.

Vanderheiden, G.C., & Lloyd, L.L. (1986). Communication Systems and their Components. In S.W. Blackstone (Ed.), *Augmentative communication: An introduction* (pp. 49–161). Rockville, MD: American Speech–Language–Hearing Association.

Vanderheiden, G.C., & Yoder, D.E. (1986). Overview. In S.W. Blackstone (Ed.), *Augmentative communication: An introduction* (pp. 1–28). Rockville, MD: American Speech–Language–Hearing Association.

van Dijk, J. (1966). The first steps of the deaf-blind children towards language. *International Journal for the Education of the Blind, 15,* 112–114.

van Dijk, J. (1967). The non-verbal deaf blind child and his world: His growth towards the world of symbols. *Proceedings of The Jaaverslag Institute voor Doven, 1964–1967* (pp. 73–110). Sint-Michielsgestel, The Netherlands: Institute for the Deaf.

Voiers, W.D. (1982, March). Some thoughts on the standardization of psychological measures of speech intelligibility and quality. In D. Pallet (Chair), *Workshop on Standardization for Speech I/O Technology* (pp. 177–181.) Gaithersburg, MD: Institute for Computer Sciences and Technology, National Bureau of Standards.

Woodcock, R.W. (1958). An experimental test for remedial readers. *Journal of Educational Psychology, 49,* 23–27.

Woodcock, R.W. (Ed.). (1965). *The rebus reading series*. Nashville: George Peabody College, Institute on Mental Retardation and Intellectual Development.

Woodcock, R.W., Clark, C.R., & Davies, C.O. (1968). *The Peabody rebus reading program*. Circle Pines, MN: American Guidance Service.

Woodcock, R.W., Clark, C.R., & Davies, C.O. (1969). *The Peabody rebus reading program teacher's guide*. Circle Pines, MN: American Guidance Service.

Wundt, W. (1973). *The language of gestures*. The Hague: Mouton.

2

Defining the Decisions Involved in Designing and Implementing Augmentative and Alternative Communication Systems

Joe Reichle

DESIGNING AND IMPLEMENTING augmentative or alternative communication systems for learners with severe disabilities requires teamwork. The composition of the team will depend upon the learner's personal support network, his or her physical and mental abilities, and a range of logistical factors, such as availability of personnel and the array of environments and activities the learner encounters daily.

Once the team has been assembled, it must begin to gather the information required to match the learner with the optimal augmentative or alternative communication system available. This is a crucial task. The purpose of this chapter is to identify the decisions that must be made in establishing and monitoring an augmentative or alternative communication program for a learner with severe disabilities (Figure 1). The chapter also serves as an overview of many of the proceeding chapters.

What questions need to be answered in matching a learner with a system?

1. What reasons does the learner have to communicate?
2. How does the learner currently meet communication obligations and opportunities?
3. Which communicative intents and vocabulary should be taught to enable the learner to meet communicative obligations and opportunities?
4. Which communication mode or modes (vocal, gestural, graphic) best match the learner's communication needs and abilities?
5. What decisions must be made for getting started in the graphic mode?
6. What decisions must be made for getting started in the gestural mode?

Some interventionists believe that two related issues must also be addressed, namely: 1) is the

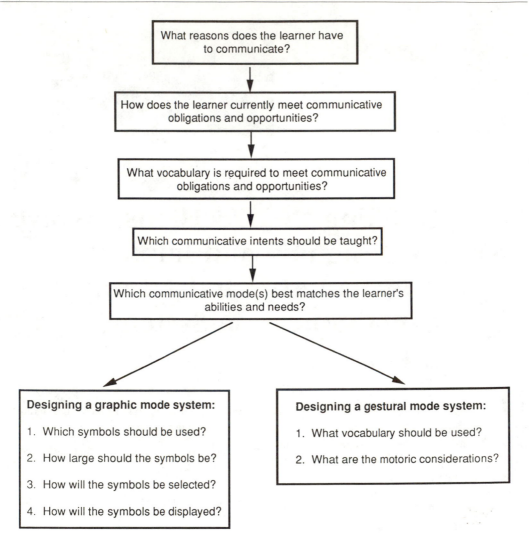

Figure 1.   Decisions involved in designing augmentative or alternative communication systems.

learner cognitively capable of using an augmentative or alternative communication system, and 2) has the learner been sufficiently unsuccessful in the vocal mode to warrant intervention in the gestural and/or graphic mode? The position taken in this book is that there are no cognitive prerequisites to communication, and that it is appropriate to implement alternative communication concurrently with vocal mode instruction. These issues are examined in the following sections.

ARE THERE COGNITIVE PREREQUISITES TO IMPLEMENTING AN AUGMENTATIVE OR ALTERNATIVE COMMUNICATION SYSTEM?

Rice (1983) has stated that "there is a detectable sense of frustration regarding the elusiveness of cognition and its role in language impairment and the remediation process" (p. 347). There appear to be no conclusive data to support the conclusion that certain cognitive behaviors must be in place before an initial repertoire of communicative behavior can be implemented. The fact that certain communicative skills and cognitive skills emerge concurrently may represent a causal relationship, may be coincidence, or may be due to some underlying source common to both communication and cognition. Despite this lack of evidence, some interventionists persist in demanding cognitive prerequisites. As a result, a learner may be forced to learn inappropriate and nonfunctional series of tasks aimed at teaching presumed cognitive prerequisites, or a learner may be prohibited from receiving any communication instruction at all.

Some specifications of cognitive prerequisites that have been posited in augmentative communication decision rules are vague (Reichle & Karlan, 1988). For example, Shane and Bashir (1980) concluded that unless a learner's level of functioning is commensurate with that of a 12-month-old, the learner is "probably not at an appropriate age for communication prosthesis, even one made out of the most iconic materials" (p. 315).

Several more specific classes of cognitive milestones that have been described as cognitive prerequisites to successful communication intervention are examined in the following sections. Some of these cognitive milestones are simply not necessary to beginning an initial communicative repertoire, while others are important, but can be incorporated into the intervention protocol.

Means–End

Much of the debate over cognitive prerequisites has focused on the issue of intentionality, or *means–end*. Means–end refers to how learners obtain objects, activities, and/or attention. Specifically, it refers to the coordination of methods to achieve a planned goal. During early development of means–end, the method must be an inherent part of the ongoing action sequence (e.g., looking at a desired object, reaching for

the object). Later, means–end procedures become more sophisticated, in that the learner will temporarily divert his or her attention from the end in order to devise a means to achieve the end (e.g., a learner may move to another part of the room in order to fetch a chair in order to place the chair near a counter, climb the chair, and reach the cookies). Communicatively, around 1 year of age, children without disabilities begin to attract adults' attention and to vocalize in an effort to obtain attention, goods, and/or services. This newly discovered skill of *social agency* represents a special instance of means–end behavior that emerges in most children between approximately 12 and 18 months of age (Piagetian sensorimotor stage 5). It allows the learner to begin using adults as tools with which to achieve desired goals. Many professionals argue that until the learner is capable of seeking out a listener and obtaining the listener's attention, truly interactive behavior cannot take place. Many decision rules about when to establish augmentative communication skills have thus identified social agency as a prerequisite. There is no evidence to support this view, however.

Reichle and Yoder (1985) reported that children who were functioning below normal levels on the Uzgiris-Hunt scales at 12 months acquired discriminative use of black and white graphic symbols. McIntire (1974) described the acquisition of an initial repertoire of sign by an 8-month-old child. Stillman, Alymer, and Vandivort (1983) taught learners with profound disabilities to use signals to obtain access to specific gross motor activities. These signals consisted of abbreviated forms of the action, idiosyncratic gestures, or actual manual signs. These communicative behaviors were used to initiate activities, to request recurrence, to redirect to another activity, and to terminate activities.

The signaling behavior engaged in by the learners in the Stillman et al. (1983) study was not used conditionally as a function of listener presence. That is, given the proper context, the learners produced their signal whether or not a listener was present. As Reichle and Karlan (1988) have stated, "even though these handicapped individuals did not recognize the role of the audience and, therefore, would not be considered to have 'intentional' communication, they did demonstrate an ability to learn a contextually relevant action (signal) to control some aspect of the activity (the goal)" (p. 328).

The rationale used by those who endorse mastery of means–end as a prerequisite to communication intervention seems to be rooted in results of studies that have shown that the ability to use means that are independent of the end goal appears to be correlated strongly with prelinguistic communicative acts as well as initial single-word utterances in children without disabilities (Bates, Benigni, Bretherton, Camioni, & Volterra, 1979). The relevance of means–end to the acquisition of intentional communicative behavior seems to lie in the conditions necessary for learners to exercise intentional control over other people in their environment. Rice (1983) has stated that "the communicative behaviors of very young children can be regarded as *interactive* in nature, instead of being driven solely by a child's cognitive accomplishments" (p. 348). If this is true, it should be possible to teach communicative repertoires by response shaping as a result of successive interactions between the child and the caregiver, without specifying a particular level of means–end as a prerequisite.

Similarly one can conceptualize communication as involving two separate instances of discrimination. First, the learner must match a symbol to a given object or event. Second, the learner must come to learn that producing that symbol will be useful only when a listener is attending. These skills can be taught either concurrently or sequentially. There is little evidence to suggest whether a concurrent or sequential approach is more efficient. It is clear, however, that there are instructional options that do not require mastery of means–end behavior prior to the initiation of an augmentative or alternative communication program.

Imitation

Although means–end seems to receive the most attention as a cognitive prerequisite to the establishment of an augmentative or alternative communication system, imitation has also been cited as a prerequisite. The basis for this point of view seems to be the literature on vocal mode communication of children without disabilities.

Many communication intervention programs rely exclusively on the vocal mode to teach communication production skills. Approximation of spoken words can be taught by reinforcing successfully better approximations (*response shaping*) and/or response prompting strategies. As a rule, response shaping is a tedious and time-consuming procedure because the learner must discover the correct sound based only on the teacher's reinforcement of successively better approximations when they occur. Although some sounds require movements outside the mouth (e.g., lip closure for "m," lip rounding for "o") that can be physically guided, it is generally accepted that learners who are able to imitate vocal models proceed much more quickly in vocal mode intervention programs than learners who cannot. Consequently, vocal imitation has come to be considered by many as being very important in learning to produce language.

Similar reasoning was applied to the importance of motor imitation as a prerequisite for gestural mode intervention. Although imitation is probably the most straightforward method of acquiring new forms of vocal mode communication, it is not necessarily the quickest route to acquiring vocabulary in the gestural and graphic modes, where a number of other response prompts, including physical prompting, can be used.

Object Permanence

Object permanency is often cited as a cognitive

prerequisite to communication intervention. Ault (1977) defined object permanency as ". . . the knowledge that objects continue to exist even where one is not perceiving them . . ." (p. 36). Perhaps the best way to characterize object permanency is to say that when a learner has this construct, he or she realizes that "out of sight does not mean out of mind." Attaining knowledge of object permanency allows infants to free themselves from the perceived environment to consider events that are not visible and/or not immediately present. Developmentally based descriptions of object permanency have focused on the child's acquisition of visual pursuit and searching skills.

For some time, interventionists have assumed that object permanency was critical in the acquisition of both communicative comprehension and production (Bricker & Bricker, 1974; Kent, 1974; Owens & House, 1984). Other investigators, such as Bloom (1970), noted that children did not appear to talk about things other than those immediately present until they were about to master the concept of object permanency.

A number of investigators (Bates et al., 1979; Corrigan, 1976; Ingram, 1974; Miller, Chapman, Branston, & Reichle, 1980) have searched for critical links between language acquisition and object permanency and have, for the most part, failed to establish object permanence as a prerequisite, although a few investigators (Moore, Clark, Mail, Rajotte, & Stoel-Gannon, 1977) have found significant correlations between object permanency and language acquisition.

Object permanency among learners with severe disabilities has received limited attention. Typically, tasks used to evaluate the extent to which a learner displays object permanency have involved the use of a *displacement task*. That is, an item that was visible is hidden. Illmer, Rynders, Sinclair, and Helfrich (1981) found that motor abilities significantly affect children's performance in object permanency

tasks. Furthermore, there is some evidence to suggest that performance in object permanency tasks varies significantly as a function of the power of the reinforcer.

One reason a learner might have difficulty demonstrating object permanence might be his or her inability to retrieve vocabulary. For example, a graphic mode learner whose entire vocabulary is not displayed may be unable to retrieve vocabulary from memory that could be used in a given situation.

Another communicative disadvantage that may face the learner with a less than complete grasp of object permanency involves the ability to communicate about objects and events that may not be immediately available to the learner. For example, a learner may request a soft drink only when he or she sees one. Nevertheless, although the ability to represent and communicate about displaced referents is clearly important, it may not be critical in order to begin to establish an initial communicative repertoire. Children between 12 and 18 months, for example, rarely mention displaced referents.

IS VOCAL MODE FAILURE A PREREQUISITE TO IMPLEMENTING AN AUGMENTATIVE COMMUNICATION SYSTEM?

Decision rules described by Chapman and Miller (1980), and Shane (1980) establish certain deficits a learner must display in order to be a candidate for an augmentative or alternative communication system.

Alpert (1980) pointed out some of the risks in using decision rule strategies such as those proposed by Chapman and Miller (1980) and Shane and Bashir (1980), especially with children (such as those with autism) who have normal hearing and the physiological capacity for producing speech. For such children,

. . . alternative nonspeech intervention will be attempted only after the child has persistently failed to learn functional vocal behavior. This is unfortunate, for not only does the child remain without a means of communicating during the entire training period, but as the child gets older, the probability that he will acquire functional communication skills may be reduced. (Alpert, 1980, p. 401)

The bulk of the available literature suggests that implementing a gestural or graphic system does not decrease, impair, or impinge on the acquisition of vocal mode skills. In fact, there is some evidence to suggest that, in some cases, implementing a graphic or gestural system may actually facilitate the comprehension and/or production of spoken communication. Barrera, Lobato-Barrera, and Sulzer-Azaroff (1980) reported that teaching speech and signs was more efficient than teaching signs alone in establishing an initial repertoire of communication among learners with autism. Brady and Smouse (1978) reported a similar outcome in their efforts to teach receptive vocabulary to learners with autism. Carr, Pridal, and Dores (1984) and Remington and Clarke (1983) reported that with learners who could already verbally imitate, combined speech and sign input facilitated speech comprehension.

This evidence suggests that in some instances, an augmentative communication system may serve to facilitate the acquisition of vocal mode skills. No data suggest that the implementation of augmentative communication jeopardized vocal mode progression. Consequently, there seems little reason to consider gestural or graphic modes exclusively in learners who fail to vocalize.

In order to design and implement an augmentative or alternative communication system, many decisions must be made by the team of professionals, paraprofessionals, and parents who serve the learner. The remainder of this chapter examines some of the most critical decisions.

WHAT REASONS DOES THE LEARNER HAVE TO COMMUNICATE?

Most leading interventionists believe that a beginning communication repertoire should provide the learner with a systematic method of exerting control over his or her environment. For most learners, being able to obtain desired objects, activities, and attention (requesting) and escaping and avoiding undesired objects, activities, and attention (rejecting) represent important reasons to communicate.

The primary basis for the selection of initial communicative intents and vocabulary should be the ecological analysis. The team must identify communicative intents and specific vocabulary that are relevant for each learner. (A process for conducting an ecological inventory to determine communicative functions and vocabulary is described in Chapter 3. The range of communicative intents that can be selected for instruction is discussed in Chapter 4.)

Some environments, activities, and situations demand communicative behavior from the learner. For example, when a learner is asked if he wants ice cream or cookies for dessert, a communication demand is presented to which the learner is obligated to respond. Other situations represent opportunities to communicate but carry no requirement to do so. For example, while a learner is sitting with classmates during lunch he or she may interact socially with classmates, but need not do so.

In addition to identifying intervention targets for the learner, an ecological inventory may also serve as the basis for identifying intervention targets for those who interact with the learner. For example, adults who interact with users of augmentative systems often overuse yes/no questions. These interactions are problematic for several reasons. First, they place the learner in the role of a responder (Light, Collier, & Parnes, 1985). The learner is taught to wait until a specific question is asked before responding. As a result, users of augmentative or alternative systems tend to be poor initiators of interactions (Light et al., 1985). Another adverse consequence of the overuse of yes/no questions is the limited vocabulary it demands. An ecological inventory can be used to identify naturally occurring opportunities in which people in the learner's environment can routinely replace yes/no questions with different forms. For example, during a break at work, a learner's coworker might ask, "What kind of pop do you want?" instead of "Do you want Diet Pepsi™?"

HOW DOES THE LEARNER CURRENTLY MEET COMMUNICATION OBLIGATIONS AND OPPORTUNITIES?

Several strategies that learners may employ in response to communicative opportunities and obligations may be problematic. First, the learner may fail to respond at all. Reichle, York, and Eynon (1989) described some learners as engaging in very passive behavior. These learners either showed no interest in their environments or were able to participate in the environment without engaging in communicative behavior. This condition has been referred to as *learned helplessness* (Guess, Benson, & Siegel-Causey, 1985). Other learners may attempt to communicate, but do so using either idiosyncratic or excess behavior. (Chapter 11 addresses strategies that can be used to replace excess behavior with socially acceptable communication. Chapters 5, 6, 7, and 8 address strategies that can be used to establish an initial communicative repertoire for learners who engage in little communicative behavior.)

A learner's use of communicative behavior may depend on the expectations of the listener. For example, if a communication partner says, "Gee, it's sunny outside," the learner is not obligated to respond. However, if the partner says, "What's your name?" there is an obligation to respond. Several investigators have reported that learners with severe communicative deficits who use augmentative communication systems typically respond only to utterances that require responses. This phenomenon has been documented in literature describing the interaction between users of augmentative and alternative communication systems and their vocal mode communicative partners (Harris, 1978; Light et al., 1985).

Failure to take advantage of communicative opportunities may occur for a variety of reasons. In some cases, the learner may fail to recognize unprompted communicative opportunities. Interventionists often report that such learners lack spontaneity. (This issue is addressed in Chapter 8.) In other instances, the user of an augmentative or alternative system may fully recognize an opportunity to communicate, but may find the effort required to do so to be excessive. (Chapter 7 addresses this issue.)

WHICH COMMUNICATIVE INTENTS SHOULD BE TAUGHT?

The ecological inventory results in the identification of specific communication obligations and opportunities. With these identified, the interventionist can begin to determine specific intents and vocabulary that can be used to meet demands and opportunities.

If the learner fails to engage in any responsive communicative behavior, the interventionist can begin to establish a communication program without having to replace an inefficient communicative repertoire. If the learner engages in some communicative behavior, the interventionist must determine whether existing behavior is: 1) understandable to people not familiar with the learner, 2) socially acceptable, and 3) not already part of an existing repertoire of perseverative or otherwise inappropriate behavior. If the behavior is guessable and socially acceptable, the interventionist may choose to strengthen the behavior by reinforcing it and, over time, shaping it into a nonvarying form. If the behavior does not meet these criteria, the interventionist may choose to replace it with a more acceptable or efficient form.

Selecting initial communicative intents is complicated by the fact that the communicative intents that are most important to the learner may not be most important to the interventionist. For example, the learner might be interested in having some ice cream (requesting an object) while the interventionist might be more interested in teaching the learner to request assistance when he needs help buttoning his jeans. It is important to address both the learner's and the listener's needs in selecting an initial repertoire of communicative intents.

WHICH COMMUNICATIVE MODES BEST MATCH THE LEARNER'S ABILITIES AND COMMUNICATIVE NEEDS?

The various modes of augmentative and alternative communication systems—vocal, gestural, and graphic—were reviewed in Chapter 1. There are advantages and disadvantages to each mode. Many learners will learn to use a combination of vocalizations, gestures, and graphic symbols to meet their communicative needs. Determining which mode to use for which communicative intents and vocabulary will depend on numerous factors.

One of the most important factors is the demands of the environments in which the learner will function. Some environments lend themselves well to a particular mode. For example, ordering at a fast food restaurant is well suited to use of a graphic mode communication wallet. The learner is able to formulate the order while sitting at a booth away from the ordering line. With Velcro™-backed symbols and corresponding Velcro™ backing on the pages of the communication wallet, the learner can display all the items he or she wants to order on one page. When the learner reaches the head of the line, he or she need only hold up the wallet and show the display. Another advantage of using a wallet in this situation is that wallets are used commonly in such environments, and thus appear natural.

Certain communicative intents may be better suited to particular modes. For example, in teaching a generalized rejecting response as a replacement for aggression, it may be important that the learner produce the rejecting response quickly and in such a way that it can be seen at a distance (so that the listener can be warned before coming close enough to be the target of aggression). The gestural mode allows both of these advantages providing the gesture selected is highly guessable.

Comparing Performance in Different Modes Sequentially

Alpert (1980) identified a training/assessment procedure for determining the optimal nonspeech mode to use with children with autism. The procedure involves teaching specific language responses in two nonspeech modes. This strategy might be thought of as a process for generating performance baselines in learning alternative language skills (i.e., signing and graphics). By comparing the respective acquisition rates between the baselines, the interventionist should be able to identify a single mode as preferable.

Rather than specifying an arbitrarily imposed failure criterion using one communication mode prior to initiating another mode, Alpert (1980) suggested implementing both graphic and gestural modes and observing learner performance on each. Either the learner would demonstrate superior performance in one of the modes (in which case that mode would be selected) or the learner would perform equally well or poorly in both modes (in which case the selection of a mode would be arbitrary).

Although a sequential selection strategy may be useful, there are potential disadvantages. Sequential selection strategy may delay the learner's acquisition of communicative skills if the mode to be sampled second proves to be the mode of choice. Additionally, a sequential sampling strategy presumes that there is one best mode. Certain environments may more readily accommodate a particular augmentative mode. Consequently, many learners may benefit from the concurrent use of several different communication modes. That is, some environments might more readily support the use of sign while others may readily support the use of graphic symbols. If a concurrent sampling could be achieved, any potential superiority of one augmentative system over another might become obvious at an earlier point. Moreover, although learner performance is critical, other criteria specific to the learner's environment can be considered (e.g., communicative demands of the learner's environments).

Alpert's (1980) strategy of establishing performance baselines in the selection of augmentative systems is appealing in that it allows a decision to be based on data regarding the learner's acquisition performance in each mode. At question, however, is the advantage of using a strategy in which modes are sampled one at a time.

Comparing Performance in Different Modes Concurrently

Establishing concurrent performance baselines involves establishing intervention programs in both the gestural and graphic modes concurrently. This concurrent implementation can be achieved in several ways. In one strategy, the interventionist teaches a sign or gesture and a graphic symbol for each vocabulary item. In a second strategy, vocabulary is assigned initially to a single mode. Consequently, some vocabulary is communicated with signs or gestures while other vocabulary is communicated with graphic symbols.

Concurrently sampling potential augmentative or alternative communication modes offers several distinct advantages over a sequential sampling procedure. First, a learner need not fail in one mode before another is sampled. Data on more than one mode are collected from the inception of the intervention process. Second, and perhaps more importantly, concurrent sampling procedures offer an opportunity to match particular communicative environments or situations with the optimal mode. The following sections provide a more explicit explanation of each of several strategies that may be implemented to establish concurrent sampling procedures. Subsequently, a description of how

instruction is implemented in more than one augmentative mode is provided.

Teaching the Same Vocabulary in Each Mode   Teaching the same vocabulary in two different modes has two potential advantages. First, the learner can use gestures with people who sign and graphic symbols with people who do not. Second, gestures can be used when it would be difficult or impossible to use a graphic display (e.g., in a swimming pool). Reichle and Ward (1985) taught a 13-year-old learner with autism to use signs to communicate with people familiar with signs, and a communication board to communicate with strangers. The learner was taught to present a message card to a prospective communication partner reading, "I am unable to speak. Do you use sign language?" Selection of a mode was based on the listener's reply. Reichle and Ward (1985) reasoned that with listeners who understand signs, the gestural mode was efficient. However, since few people in the community understand signs, the extra time required to teach the learner the discriminative use of a communication board was worth the effort.

Teaching the same vocabulary concurrently in more than one mode may have several disadvantages. Learning a graphic symbol as well as a sign, gesture, or spoken word to represent a single object or activity may create a problem when precise cues specifying which response form to use are lacking. The learner may become confused by the fact that on some occasions gestures are used and on other occasions graphic symbols are used. Perhaps more importantly, it can be argued that because the repertoires of learners with severe disabilities are already delayed significantly, it would make more sense to introduce the greatest number of different vocabulary rather than duplicating symbols for a single vocabulary item in each of two modes. In effect, teaching several different communicative symbols for the same referent may be analogous to teaching a learner to be bilingual before he or she has mastered a single language.

Teaching Different Vocabulary in Each Mode Assigning different vocabulary to gestural and graphic modes represents an effort to capitalize on the advantages and minimize the weaknesses of each mode without requiring the learner to learn two representations for each vocabulary item. Using different vocabulary in each mode requires the interventionist to scrutinize the communicative obligations and opportunities in the learner's environment and the learner's ability to learn to select gestural and graphic symbols.

In Chapter 1, mixed mode augmentative and alternative communication was described in which different vocabulary was assigned to each mode used. With learners who have severe disabilities, this option affords the greatest flexibility in designing an augmentative or alternative communication system. By teaching each vocabulary item in only one mode, the number of different vocabulary introduced is maximized. At the same time, the long-term option of also teaching the learner to use a second mode to represent a particular vocabulary item is not forfeited.

Distinguishing between Concurrent Sampling and Total Communication

There is an important distinction between the sampling strategies that have been described and the traditional notion of *total communication,* or the *simultaneous method.* Although Moores (1974) pointed out that there are different interpretations of total and simultaneous communication, it is generally accepted that both are characterized by the concurrent presentation of vocal and at least one augmentative mode to represent a vocabulary item. The basis for advocating total communication is that such an approach may maximize the probability of learning successes with low-functioning learners (Hopper & Helmick, 1977). Thus, the operative principle in total communication is the concurrent presentation of speech and sign, gestures, or graphics. There is growing evidence

that the concurrent presentation of two or more communication modes may be most helpful under certain conditions. Carr and Dores (1981) and Remington and Clarke (1983) reported that among learners with autism who were provided with sign plus verbal input, those who acquired communicative behavior in both modes were verbally imitative at the outset of intervention, that is, they were able to attend to and use a verbal model as a response prompt. Correspondingly, a learner who could not imitate verbally, acquired sign but not verbal behavior. These data suggest that total communication in communication production intervention is most likely to succeed when the learner is able to attend to and act upon each type of event presented as a discriminative stimulus.

How Is Instruction Implemented in More Than One Augmentative Mode?

Concurrent implementation of both graphic and gestural modes begins by scrutinizing the communicative obligations and opportunities available in the learner's environment. Chapter 3 examines strategies that may be implemented to make these determinations.

Once intervention opportunities and obligations have been defined, the vocabulary and corresponding communicative intents can be identified. In matching the specific mode to the targeted communicative event, it is important for the interventionist to ask some critical questions:

1. Is speed a critical aspect of communicating in the identified situations?
2. Is there a guessable gesture that is sufficiently explicit to communicate the targeted message?
3. Does the utterance targeted require a great deal of specificity (e.g., small chocolate mocha shake)?
4. Could the mode that is chosen to represent specific vocabulary be used with equal efficiency in other communicative situations that the learner will encounter?

Some communicative obligations and opportunities will lend themselves best to a graphic mode application (e.g., asking for help in finding artichoke hearts in a grocery store). In other communicative contexts (e.g., greeting a peer, rejecting an unpreferred food item) the gestural mode will represent a better choice because of its speed and portability. For some vocabulary, the most efficient long-term strategy may be to use both a graphic and a gestural symbol (e.g., "hamburger" could be signed at home, but displayed graphically at a fast food restaurant.

Mastering the differential use of two different modes to represent the same vocabulary item is enormously challenging for learners with severe disabilities. For that reason, wherever possible a single mode should be selected for instruction.

DESIGNING A GRAPHIC MODE SYSTEM

A number of decisions confront the interventionist designing a graphic mode communication system. The most important of these include:

1. What type of symbols will be used?
2. How large will the symbols be?
3. How will the learner select the symbols?
4. How will the symbols be displayed?

All of these questions must be addressed early in the intervention process. Each of these areas is examined in the following sections.

What Type of Symbols Should Be Used?

A number of different symbol options exist, including: traditional orthography (written words), pictures, photographs, product logos, line drawings, miniaturized objects, and actual objects. In general, the more a symbol directly resembles the item it is intended to represent, the easier it is to learn. However, Reichle and Yoder (1985) demonstrated that learners who were unable to discriminate among less abstract symbols (color photographs) were taught to recognize more abstract symbols (line drawings), thus suggesting that appropriate symbol options should be determined individually by assessing the learner's ability to match symbols to their referents.

Hurlbut, Iwata, and Green (1982) compared symbol selections taught as object names in iconic symbol and Blissymbol formats. For all three participants, each having severe and multiple disabilities, the more iconic symbols were more easily acquired, generalized, and maintained.

Another study (Welch & Pear, 1980) found that real objects were more easily recognized than either photographs or picture cards from the Peabody Picture Vocabulary Test. In this study, comparisons were made sequentially in an ABC design replicated across four learners. When taught with real objects, three of four learners showed better generalization of vocabulary used to provide information in the natural environment. Trials to criterion, however, were not appreciably different for any of the three symbol formats.

These comparative studies of different symbol systems generally argue in favor of using symbols that are the most guessable. However, every learner has a unique personal history that may override this general guiding principle. For example, one learner with whom the author worked did as well discriminating among line drawings as he did discriminating among color photographs. This was puzzling until the learner's mother related that for the previous 3 years she had used line drawings of specific toys to indicate the contents of various plastic storage containers. Over the course of several years, this learner had had thousands of teaching opportunities in matching line drawings to real referents, and had become a generalized line drawing matcher. It is imperative, therefore, to determine the most appropriate symbol system for each learner individually.

It is easy to implement several distinctly different symbol formats at the inception of a graphic mode intervention program. Product logos can be used to represent snack items, such as candy bars, soft drinks, and potato chips. Items that do not typically come in product packages can be represented by color photographs, black and white photographs, or line drawings.

The goal of such a procedure is not necessarily to select a single "best" symbol type. Instead, in those instances in which there are choices among methods of representation, the interventionist can, over time, compare performance empirically. Moreover, when data obtained through a sampling procedure suggest that a learner will experience difficulty using a particular symbol, the interventionist can be prepared to address the potential problems that might arise. For example, sometimes color photographs and product logos are more difficult to recognize than black and white line drawings. Occasionally a learner will use the color of a symbol as the basis for discriminating it from other symbols. Unfortunately, when another symbol sharing the same color is introduced, the learner may have tremendous difficulty discriminating between the two symbols. Obviously, this problem is less likely to occur with black and white photographs. Other learners may have difficulty distinguishing line drawings but be able to discriminate between product logos (e.g., Snickers™ and Milky Way™ bars).

Several measures can be used to evaluate learner performance on each of several symbol types. The number of teaching opportunities required for a learner to master symbols represents an important consideration. Additionally, spontaneous use of symbols is often of great concern and can be measured by examining the frequency of nonprompted responses to a particular symbol. Other important aspects of generalization for the interventionist to consider include being able to use vocabulary with a variety of different persons in a host of different environments. Additionally, it is important that the learner's use of newly established vocabulary endure over time.

Clearly, the use of a particular type of symbol can influence the success or failure of the learner's augmentative or alternative communication system. Careful selection is critical. Some learners may have such great visual impairment that two-dimensional symbols cannot be used. In these instances, textured symbols cannot be used. (Chapter 1 examines the use of real objects and textured symbols.)

How Large Should the Symbols Be?

The size of the symbols used in a graphic mode display is determined largely by the learner's visual acuity and (in the case of a direct selection technique) the precision of his or her pointing skills. Visual impairments are common in learners with severe and/or multiple disabilities (Cress et al., 1981).

How Will the Learner Select the Symbols?

In designing an augmentative or alternative communication system, the interventionist must decide which selecting technique—direct selection or scanning—the learner will use. Direct select techniques are usually quicker and place less of a communicative burden on the listener. Unfortunately, some learners have upper extremity motor impairments that preclude the use of a direct select technique. For such learners, a scanning technique may be more efficient. (Chapter 13 examines the range of scanning options.)

Although most learners use either direct selection or scanning, some learners use both techniques. For example, certain vocabulary (e.g., "help") may need to be reached quickly. The learner may want to have a few important symbols displayed so that they may be selected directly. Other, less frequently used symbols may be smaller and reached via a scanning technique.

To use a direct select technique, a learner must have adequate visual acuity and be physically capable of a selecting response, such as pointing. Initially, the interventionist must determine whether the learner can select a symbol clearly when symbols are displayed side by side. If the learner is unable to do so in such a way that a naive listener could understand which symbol had been selected, the symbols must be moved apart until there is sufficient distance between symbols that the learner's selection is clear. Initially, a matrix of blank squares the same size as the smallest symbol is constructed. A single symbol is presented randomly at different locations within the matrix. Care is taken to present the symbol in a range of positions (e.g., center, extreme left, top, bottom). If the learner's pointing skills are not sufficiently precise, the individual squares of the matrix are separated so that the space between squares increases (Figure 2). Eventually, the spaces should be sufficiently far apart so that the learner can unambiguously select a symbol.

Another technique for improving the discriminability of the learner's selection is to provide the learner with an orthotic or prosthetic aid, such as a plastic pointer. In other instances, repositioning the learner or the communication aid will improve the precision of symbol selection.

Once it has been determined that a learner will rely upon a scanning technique, a myriad of other issues arises. One or more of the various types of scanning strategies described in Chapter 1 must be selected. A signaling response must be chosen. These questions are addressed in depth in Chapter 13.

How Will the Symbols Be Displayed?

With the symbols and selection methods identified, a series of related questions emerges. What type of device (e.g., board, wallet, cards, book) should house the symbols? How should the symbols be arranged within a page and across a page?

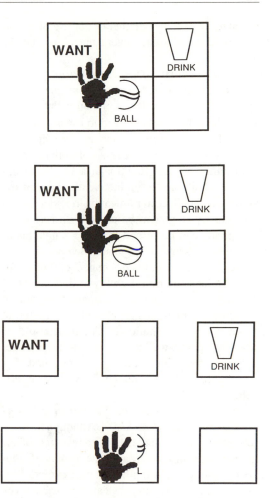

Figure 2. Symbol matrices. Increased spacing between symbols allows for discrete pointing.

Wallets and purses are desirable aids, because they are commonly used by many people and thus do not draw attention to the user. Trifold or bifold wallets can be used. Trifold wallets provide greater space for symbol displays but are thicker and therefore fit more tightly in a learner's pocket. Bifold wallets are thinner, but provide less surface area on which to display symbols. In addition to providing a storage location for symbols, wallets function as a location to keep important personal items and money. In order to determine whether or not use of a wallet would be efficient, several questions must be addressed.

Can the Learner Handle a Wallet? Many wallets are difficult to open unless one hand is used to hold the wallet down on a flat surface while the other hand is used to touch a desired symbol. It is thus important to determine whether the learner has the use of both hands. If both hands are not functional, a variety of options is available to the interventionist. For example, a small communication booklet bound together by rings can be used. With ring binders, pages can be turned to with a single hand.

Another issue is whether a learner can remove a wallet from his or her pocket. For learners who lack the motor ability to do so, several options are available. For example, a portion of the learner's back pocket could be sewn shut to make the pocket shallower. A handle could be attached to the wallet to make it easier to retrieve. The wallet could also be attached to a retractable keychain attached to the learner's belt.

How Should Pages Be Turned in a Portable Communication Aid? Although they are compact, wallets have the disadvantage of allowing little surface area for the display of symbols. However, although each page provides little space, many pages can be used. The interventionist must determine whether the learner is able to or can learn to turn pages. An occupational therapist can usually assess a learner's page turning ability. The occupational therapist also may have helpful suggestions for modifying the pages of the wallet for making them easier to turn. For example, flexible pages may allow the learner to use a palmer grasp, wrinkling the page slightly but turning it nevertheless. Other options involve displaying pages in a "fan array," as shown in Figure 3, rather than in a traditional book page array. The fan array allows the learner to place the wallet on a surface and slide his or her palm across the array of open pages.

Figure 3.   A fan array allows the learner to place the wallet on a surface and slide his or her palm across the array of "pages."

How Should the Learner Search for a Symbol? Being able to turn pages and knowing that pages must be turned to locate a desired symbol are different skills that effect use of a multipage display. For example, Reichle and Brown (1986) described a learner who was unable to search systematically across a multipage array to locate a target symbol. During a baseline period the learner was required to retrieve his communication wallet from his pocket, open it, and scan the pages to match a symbol to a real object held by the interventionist. A correct response was scored if: 1) the learner located the symbol on the first page, or 2) the learner turned the page if the appropriate match was not on the first page and continued to turn pages until the correct match was completed. Reichle and Brown (1986) suggested that symbols be dispersed across pages in a multipage array relatively early in the intervention process, since learners may otherwise become so accustomed to the rule that there is always a correct symbol on the display in front of them that they become confused when a target symbol is moved to another page.

DESIGNING A GESTURAL MODE SYSTEM

In Chapter 1, the gestural mode was shown to be portable and quick but less desirable than other modes because of: 1) the small number of listeners who understand gestures, 2) the lack of a constant display of the available repertoire, and 3) the need for a certain level of motor competency to articulate signs.

Because of the limitations of the gestural mode, it is rarely adopted as the exclusive mode of communication for learners with severe and/or multiple disabilities. Rather, it is used to supplement a learner's graphic and vocal mode system. Occasionally, the gestural mode is used as the only mode of communication. For example, a highly aggressive learner might use a communication wallet or board as a weapon, thus ruling out use of the graphic mode. Such instances are rare, however, and in most cases gestural communication supplements other modes.

Establishing a mixed mode system of augmentative communication skills is highly efficient. To use multiple modes, the interventionist must address a number of issues pertaining to instruction in the gestural mode. The following sections address some of the more important ones.

What Vocabulary Should Be Taught?

Most investigators agree that learners who use a combination of communicative modes tend to select symbols that are the easiest to produce (Light et al., 1985). There is evidence to suggest that some gestures may be easier to acquire because they are somewhat guessable to the learner. That is, some signs and gestures resemble a referent or an action commonly used with a referent. For example, the sign for "eat" resembles the movements the learner would use in eating. Finally, communicative effort can be considered from the listener's perspective. That is, the easier the speaker is to understand, the greater the likelihood that the listener will wish to interact communicatively with the speaker in the future. Each of the areas just outlined will be addressed.

Selecting Guessable Gestures   The guessability of signs and gestures is very important to the listener, since very few people understand signs, and fewer than 20% of signs in ASL and slightly less than 50% of gestures in a system such as Amer-Ind are guessable. Consequently, it is very important to select gestures and signs that maximize the possibility of clear communication between learner and listener. Guessable signs are also easier for learners to acquire.

The ecological inventory, examined in Chapter 3, represents the first step in selecting vocabulary. Once communicative obligations and opportunities have been identified, the interventionist may carefully evaluate each one to determine if there is a guessable gesture that could be used in the situations identified. If no gesture is associated with the situation, a guessable sign can be sought.

In Chapter 1, the terms *transparency* and *translucency* were introduced. Translucency affects the ease with which a sign or gesture is acquired. While highly translucent signs may be somewhat easier to learn than more opaque signs, translucency will be of little benefit to a listener in the community. Transparency, however, is of great importance in determining the general public's ability to decipher signs and gestures. Perhaps the best way to gauge the transparency of a sign is to use the gestures being considered for instruction in the natural environments in which the learner will use them. If the gesture is understood by people in that environment, then it is sufficiently transparent to be effective. If the gesture is not understood, the interventionist must decide whether to change the gesture or explain its meaning to the listener. For example, the clerk at a local convenience store may have been in his position for 2 years, during which time he frequently met a particular learner. It might be worthwhile for the interventionist to explain the learner's gestures to this clerk, so that the learner would be able to shop at this store. Several important caveats are warranted. First, should either the learner or the clerk move, the learner's communication system in this environment will be jeopardized until a new clerk becomes familiar with the learner's repertoire. Second, not all listeners will be willing to become familiar with the learner's gestures. Even if reasonably translucent symbols are selected, signing may place a significant enough communicative demand on the perspective listener that he or she may avoid interacting with the learner.

Identifying translucent signs is somewhat less straightforward than identifying transparent signs. One strategy is to present signs or gestures to prospective listeners. As each sign is presented, its meaning is explained to the listener. The signs are then shown again. Those that are the most translucent should be most easily recalled.

It is important to place the role of sign guessability in selecting an initial repertoire of signs and gestures in the proper perspective. First, much of the available data on translucency involved learners without cognitive disabilities. The results may or may not apply to learners with disabilities. Second, although the translucency of a sign has been shown to influence the rate at which it is acquired, it may not be the single most important factor. The reinforcing value of an item might have a greater effect on the rate at which the corresponding gesture is acquired. That is, a candy bar represented by an opaque gesture might be more easily acquired than a highly guessable gesture for water.

Can the Learner Remember Signs Taught?   At first glance, it would seem that a learner's ability to remember signs would not be influenced by the mode of communication. Upon closer examination, however, it is clear that using a communication board is much like taking a multiple choice test, while signing is more like taking a fill in the blank test. In the graphic mode, the learner's entire vocabulary may be on display. In the gestural mode, the learner must remember the array of vocabulary.

The learner's ability to remember can be assessed in several ways. For example, suppose a learner sees his mother put away a bag of candy just before the family leaves the house. Upon returning home, he sees his sister eating some of the candy. If the learner retrieves the candy, he can be assumed to have remembered where his mother had put it. The learner's ability to remember affects his or her ability to use signs and gestures. Because there is no permanent symbol display, the learner may need to be reminded of appropriate gestures.

What Motor Capabilities Optimize the Use of the Gestural Mode?

Some learners have very severe upper extremity impairment that significantly affects their ability to produce the handshape or the hand/arm movement in space to form intelligible gestures. Consequently, the relationship between the learner's motor skills and the motor complexity of the signs and gestures targeted to teach has several important implications. First, unless signs and gestures can be articulated precisely, they may not have sufficient communicative value for individuals in the learner's environment. Second, even if the learner can articulate signs and gestures clearly, the effort required may not be sufficient for the learner consistently to produce them. Each of these issues is addressed in the following sections.

Dennis, Reichle, Williams, and Vogelsberg (1982) described three motor aspects of sign production: 1) prehension patterns (handshape), 2) bilateral/unilateral movement patterns, and 3) combined use patterns.

Prehension Patterns (Handshape)   How a learner moves his or her hand represents an important component in the development of children's discovery of the world and what they can and cannot accomplish with their hands. Prehension involves a gradual refinement of motor skills based on both stability of postural muscles and mobility of discrete body parts. Skilled hand use is further integrated with, and adapted to, tactile, visual, and proprioceptive cues from the environment. The development of major prehension patterns is well established by 18 months of age.

The ability to use discrete patterns of prehension is perhaps most closely correlated with the development of gross motor postures and movements. In children without disabilities, the progression from prone and supine posture of the newborn to infantile postures of sitting, creeping, and standing reflects the control of head, neck, shoulder, and trunk musculature. Control of this large muscle group is required to assume and maintain each of these antigravity positions and to move in them. This same development of head, neck, shoulder, and trunk musculature is necessary for the acquisition of progressively more discrete prehension patterns. Summaries and definitions of prehension in the developmental literature describe a relatively invariant progression of gross motor and prehension patterns as they develop through the first 12–18 months of life (Bobath & Bobath, 1967; Erhardt, 1975; Gesell, 1940; Halverson, 1973; Illingsworth, 1970; Sheridan, 1975). These patterns are described in Figure 4.

The initial neutral hand position shown in Figure 4 is a relaxed hand that involves no active prehension pattern. This pattern is used in the production of signs involving a simple touch, usually to another body part, such as in the sign for *hat,* in which the signer need only touch the top of the head with his or her fingers. Other voluntary grasp patterns are arranged sequentially as they are described in the literature of normal development. Figure 4, therefore, shows a hypothetical hierarchy of prehension patterns based on development in children without disabilities.

Two additional patterns that are not described in the development literature are listed in Figure 4. These patterns have been included because of their frequent occurrence in the hand patterns of manual signs. They include the crossed finger pattern, in which one finger, usually the mid-

dle, is crossed over another, usually the index (such as seen in the R hand); and the isolated little finger pointing pattern that occurs with inhibition of at least two other fingers (used to form the I hand).

Hand/Arm Movement Figure 5 presents the various hand movement patterns seen in children without disabilities. These children alternate between bilateral and unilateral arm movements as they acquire static postures and dynamic balance in new situations, such as sitting and standing. At each higher level of gross motor control, the demands of gravity become greater. Initially, children use both arms for support or balance in a new position, and the arms are not free for skilled hand use. As stability in each position is acquired, children can free one hand for an activity, while continuing to rely on the other for support. As head, trunk, and shoulder control improve further, children can free both hands for an activity. With both hands free, early bilateral mirror movements are seen in which both hands move identically, reflecting a degree of integration of two sides of the body. As rotation develops, one arm is used to cross midline, while compensatory movements are made with the rest of the body and other arm so that balance is maintained. Children can cross midline in sitting at 8–9 months, but may not be able to do so on all fours until 12–14 months.

As righting and equilibrium reactions improve in a given situation, children can manipulate objects at midline with each hand free to perform a different function. One hand may stabilize objects while the other manipulates them. Abell et al. (1978) describe this pattern as occurring at 12–18 months. When children no longer require object stabilization, they can actively manipulate an object or two different objects with both hands simultaneously. They can use two different grasps and handshapes and move both of them in an integrated manner.

The unilateral/bilateral hand use patterns in Figure 5 are arranged in a hypothetical hier-

Prehension Patterns	Age Level	Description	Illustration
0. Neutral hand	birth	Fingers relaxed, neither distinctly flexed nor strongly extended. Sign motion from arm rather than fingers.	
1. Squeeze	5 months	Fingers curled, no palm contact, raking or clawing pattern.	
2. Palmar	6 months	Fingers to palm.	
3. Thumb adduction	6-9 months	Adduction of the thumb so it touches the side of the hand or palm.	
4. Midposition of the forearm	8-9 months	Thumbs up, palms of hands face each other when forearms are rotated to midposition.	
5. Thumb abduction	9 months	Abduction of the thumb so that it is away from the side of the hand or palm.	
6. Wrist movements	9-10 months	Voluntary wrist flexion-extension, radial-ulnar deviation and rotary movements.	
7. Opposed grasp	10 months	Fingers approach or touch abducted thumb to grasp.	
8. Pointing radial finger	10 months	Isolated control of radial finger, usually the index finger, while at least one other finger is inhibited.	
9. Release	10 months	Exaggerated straightening or extending of the fingers.	
10. Full supination	12 months	Palm up position of hands with forearm rotation.	
11. Crossed finger	?	One digit crossed over another.	
12. Pointing ulnar finger	?	Isolated little finger pointing with inhibition of at least one other finger.	

Figure 4.   Developmental sequence of prehension patterns used in the production of signs. (From Dennis, R., Reichle, J., Williams, W., & Vogelsberg, T. [1982]. Motoric factors influencing the selection of vocabulary for sign production programs. *Journal of The Association for Persons with Severe Handicaps, 7*, 20–33; reprinted by permission).

archy based on the literature on development in children without disabilities. The last pattern shown is not described in this literature, but is included because of its frequent occurrence in manual sign language. Crossing midline, however, both unilaterally and bilaterally is described by Ayres (1975) and is used in the Southern California Test of Sensory Integra-

Unilateral/Bilateral	Age Level	Description	Illustration
1. Unilateral	4-6 months	Arm does not cross midline of body; the arm is used parallel to the body or at midline.	
2. Bilateral mirror movements	6 months	Two identical handshapes or movements; not crossing midline moving the same or opposite.	
3. Bilateral movements	7 months	Two different handshapes or movements; not crossing midline; moving the same or opposite.	
4. Unilateral across midline	8-11 months	One hand crosses midline of the body or face.	
5. Bilateral one base one mover	12-18 months	One hand is stable, while the other hand moves at midline. The two hand-shapes may be the same or different. One hand is the base and the other moves relative to that base.	
6. Bilateral both movers	18-24 months	Two different or similar handshapes at midline each moving.	
7. Bilateral crossing midline with two hands	?	Both hands cross the midline of the body or face.	

Figure 5.   Unilateral/bilateral movement patterns in the production of signs. (From Dennis, R., Reichle, J., Williams, W., & Vogelsberg, T. [1982]. Motoric factors influencing the selection of vocabulary for sign production programs. *Journal of The Association for Persons with Severe Handicaps, 7*, 20–33; reprinted by permission.)

tion. Ayres (1975) cites research that indicates that it is easier to cross midline on the body than the face. It is only presumed that it is more difficult to cross midline with two hands than it is with one.

Combining Prehension and Movement Patterns   Several additional factors affect the development of well-articulated sign production. These include signs that require different

beginning and ending handshapes and signs that involve combinations of successive actions.

Different Beginning and Ending Handshapes   The term *fluidity* has been used by Wilbur (1979) to refer to the learner's smooth transition from one handshape to another during the production of a sign. Although a number of investigators have described systems to categorize the type of fluidity (Friedman, 1976; Kegl

& Wilbur, 1976), no attempts have been made to document the effect of fluidity upon the learner's ability to acquire or use signs.

Combinations of Successive Actions Combining successive actions to produce a given sign requires learners to produce a sequenced chain of different motor behaviors. Examples are most clearly observed in the production of compound signs. Bellugi (1975) defined compound signs as signs that have two separate parts, each of which is a clearly identifiable word (e.g., baseball). Although there is information describing how these compound signs differ from separate individual production of each component sign (Bellugi & Klima, 1976), there is no information on the relative difficulty of using compound signs compared to noncompound signs.

These factors indicate that one should consider more than a learner's ability to perform isolated motor patterns required to produce a sign. It is important to consider motor planning—that is, the combinations and sequences of movement that comprise the fluid production of a gesture.

SUMMARY

This chapter summarizes many of the decisions that must be addressed in beginning an augmentative and alternative communication system. The position taken here is that augmentative and alternative systems can be implemented without requiring many of the cognitive prerequisites that have been described in the literature. Moreover, a learner need not prove that he or she is incapable of communicating vocally before an alternative mode is implemented. Graphic and gestural mode systems can be taught concurrently with vocal mode programs as part of a systematic plan aimed at preventing communicative deficits.

This chapter highlights many of the issues covered in depth in later chapters. It is possible that many decisions that must be addressed by the learner's team have not been examined. Unfortunately, the science of augmentative and alternative communication is still in its infancy. Decisions discussed in this chapter represent an effort to establish a more objective base from which the interventionist can operate.

REFERENCES

Alpert, C.L. (1980). Procedures for determining the optimal nonspeech mode with autistic children. In R.L. Schiefelbusch (Ed.), *Nonspeech language and communication: Analysis and intervention* (pp. 389–420). Baltimore: University Park Press.

Ault, R. (1977). *Children's cognitive development.* New York: Oxford University Press.

Ayers, J. (1975). Sensorimotor foundations of academic ability. In W.M. Cruickshank & D.P. Hallahan (Eds.), *Perceptual and learning disabilities in children (Vol. 2): Research and theory* (pp. 301–358). New York: Syracuse University Press.

Barrera, F.D., Lobato-Barrera, D., & Sulzer-Azaroff, E. (1980). A simultaneous treatment comparison of three expressive language training programs with a mute autistic child. *Journal of Autism and Developmental Disorders, 10,* 21–37.

Bates, E., Benigni, L., Bretherton, I., Camaioni, L.,

& Volterra, V. (1979). *The emergence of symbols: Cognition and communication in infancy.* New York: Academic Press.

Bellugi, U. (1975). *The process of compounding in American Sign Language.* Unpublished manuscript, Salk Institute for Biological Studies, La-Jolla, CA.

Bellugi, U., & Klima, E. (1976). Two faces of sign: Iconic and abstract. In S. Harnad, H. Steklis, & J. Lancester (Eds.), *Origins and evolution of language and speech.* New York: Academy of Science.

Bloom, L. (1970). *Language development: Structure and function in emerging grammars.* Cambridge: MIT Press.

Bobath, K., & Bobath, B. (1967). Neurodevelopmental treatment of cerebral palsy. *Physical Therapy, 47,* 1039–1041.

Brady, D.O., & Smouse, A.D. (1978). A simultaneous comparison of three methods of language training with an autistic child: An experimental single case analysis. *Journal of Autism and Childhood Schizophrenia, 8*, 271–279.

Bricker, I.U., & Bricker, D. (1974). An early language training strategy. In R. Schiefelbusch & L. Lloyd (Eds.), *Language perspectives: Acquisition retardation and intervention* (pp. 431–468). Baltimore: University Park Press.

Carr, E.G., & Dores, P.A. (1981). Patterns of language acquisition following simultaneous communication with autistic children. *Analysis and Intervention in Developmental Disabilities, 1*, 347–361.

Carr, E.G., Pridal, C., & Dores, P.A. (1984). Speech versus sign comprehension in autistic children: Analysis and prediction. *Journal of Experimental Child Psychology, 37*(3), 587–597.

Chapman, R., & Miller, J. (1980). Analyzing language and communication in the child. In R.L. Schiefelbusch (Ed.), *Nonspeech language and communication: Analysis and intervention* (pp. 159–196). Baltimore: University Park Press.

Corrigan, R. (1976, April). *The relationship between object permanence and language development: How much and how strong?* Paper presented at the Stanford Child Language Research Forum, Stanford University, Palo Alto, CA.

Cress, P.J., Spellman, C.R., DeBriere, T.J., Sizemore, A.C., Northam, J.K., & Johnson, J.L. (1981). Vision screening for persons with severe handicaps. *Journal of The Association for the Severely Handicapped, 6*(3), 41–50.

Dennis, R., Reichle, J., Williams, W., & Vogelsberg, T. (1982). Motoric factors influencing the selection of vocabulary for sign production programs. *Journal of The Association for Persons with Severe Handicaps, 7*, 20–33.

Erhardt, R.P. (1975). Sequential levels in development of prehension. *American Journal of Occupational Therapy, 10*, 592–597.

Friedman, L. (1976). *Phonology of a soundless language: Phonological structural structure of American sign language*. Unpublished doctoral dissertation, University of California, Berkley.

Gesell, A. (1940). *The first five years of life*. New York: Harper & Row.

Guess, D., Benson, H., & Siegel-Causey, E. (1985). Concepts and issues related to choice making among persons with severe handicaps. *Journal of The Association for Persons with Severe Handicaps, 10*(2), 79–86.

Halverson, H.M. (1973). An experimental study of prehension in infants by means of systematic cinema records. *Genetic Psychology Monographs, 10*, 212–215.

Harris, D. (1978). *Descriptive analysis of communication interaction processes involving nonvocal severely handicapped children*. Unpublished doctoral dissertation, University of Wisconsin, Madison.

Hooper, C., & Helmick, R. (1977). Nonverbal communication for the severely handicapped: Some considerations. *AAESPH Review, 2*, 47–52.

Hurlbut, B.I., Iwata, B.A., & Green, J.D. (1982). Non-vocal language acquisition in adolescents with severe physical disabilities: Blissymbol versus iconic stimulus formats. *Journal of Applied Behavior Analysis, 15*, 241–258.

Illingsworth, R. (1970). *The development of the infant and young child: Normal and abnormal* (4th ed.). Baltimore: Williams & Wilkins.

Illmer, S., Rynders, J., Sinclair, S., & Helfrich, D. (1981). Assessment of object permanence in severely handicapped students as a function of motor and prompting variables. *Journal of The Association for the Severely Handicapped, 6*, 30–40.

Ingram, D. (1974). The relationship between comprehension and production. In R. Schiefelbusch & L. Lloyd (Eds.), *Language perspectives: Acquisition retardation and intervention*. Baltimore: University Park Press.

Kegl, J., & Wilbur, R. (1976). When does structure stop and style begin? Syntax morphology and phonology vs. stylistic variation in ASL. In S. Mufwene, C. Walker, & S. Steever (Eds.), *Papers from the 12th regional meeting, Chicago Linguistic Society* (pp. 376–396). Chicago: University of Chicago Press.

Kent, L. (1974). *Language acquisition program for the retarded or multiply impaired*. Champaign, IL: Research Press.

Light, J., Collier, B., & Parnes, P. (1985). Communicative interaction between young nonspeaking physically disabled children and their primary care givers: Part 1, Discourse patterns. *Augmentation and Alternative Communication, 1*, 74–83.

McIntire, M. (1974). *A modified model for the description of language acquisition in a deaf child*. Unpublished master's thesis, California State University, Northridge, CA.

Miller, J., Chapman, R., Branston, M., & Reichle, J. (1980). Communicative assessment in twelve (12) to twenty-four (24) months: A reliable method. *Journal of Speech and Hearing Research, 32*, 284–311.

Moore, M., Clark, D., Mail, M., Rajotte, P., & Stoel-Gammon, C. (1977, March). *The relationship between language and object permanence development: A study of Down's infants and children.* Paper presented at the meeting of the Society for Research in Child Development, New Orleans.

Moores, D. (1974). Nonvocal system of verbal behavior. In R.L. Schiefelbusch & L. Lloyd (Eds.), *Language perspectives: Acquisition, retardation, and intervention* (pp. 377–417). Austin, TX: PRO-ED.

Owens, R., & House, L. (1984). Decision-making processes in augmentative communication. *Journal of Speech and Hearing Disorders, 49*, 18–25.

Reichle, J., & Brown, L. (1986). Teaching the use of a multipage direct selection communication board to an adult with autism. *Journal of The Associate for the Severely Handicapped, 11*, 68–73.

Reichle, J., & Karlan, G. (1988). Selecting augmentative communication interventions: A critique of candidacy criteria and a proposed alternative. In R.L. Schiefelbusch & L.L. Lloyd (Eds.), *Language perspectives: Acquisition, retardation, and intervention* (2nd ed., pp. 321–339). Austin, TX: PRO-ED.

Reichle, J., & Ward, M. (1985). Teaching discriminative use of an encoding electronic communication device and signing exact English to a moderately handicapped child. *Language, Speech, and Hearing Services in Schools, 16*(1), 58–63.

Reichle, J., & Yoder, D.E. (1985). Communication board use in severely handicapped learners. *Language, Speech, and Hearing Services in Schools, 16*, 146–157.

Reichle, J., York, J., & Eynon, D. (1989). Influence of indicating preferences for initiating, maintaining, and terminating interactions. In F. Brown &

D. H. Lehr (Eds.), *Persons with profound disabilities: Issues and practices* (pp. 191–211). Baltimore: Paul H. Brookes Publishing Co.

Remington, B., & Clarke, S. (1983). Acquisition of expressive signing by autistic children: An evaluation of the relative effects of simultaneous communication and sign-alone training. *Journal of Applied Behavior Analysis, 16*, 315–328.

Rice, M. (1983). Contemporary accounts of the cognition/language relationship: Implications for speech-language clinicians. *Journal of Speech and Hearing Disorders, 48*, 347–359.

Shane, H. (1980). Approaches to assessing the communication of nonoral persons. In R.L. Schiefelbusch (Ed.), *Nonspeech language and communication: Analysis and intervention* (pp. 197–224). Baltimore: University Park Press.

Shane, H., & Baskir, A. (1980). Election criteria for the adoption of an augmentative communication system: Preliminary considerations. *Journal of Speech and Hearing Disorders, 45*, 408–414.

Sheridan, M.D. (1975). *Children's developmental progress from birth to five years: The Stycar sequences.* Windsor, Berkshire, England: NFER Publishing.

Stillman, R., Alymer, J., & Vandivort, J. (1983, June). *The functions of signalling behaviors in profoundly impaired, deaf-blind children and adolescents.* Paper presented at the 107th Annual Meeting of the American Association on Mental Deficiency, Dallas, TX.

Welch, S.J., & Pear, J.J. (1980). Generalization of naming responses to objects in the natural environment as a function of training stimulus modality with retarded children. *Journal of Applied Behavior Analysis, 13*, 629–643.

Wilbur, R. (1979). *American sign language and sign systems.* Baltimore: University Park Press.

3

Using Ecological Inventories to Promote Functional Communication

Jeff Sigafoos and Jennifer York

TRADITIONALLY, THE CONTENT of many language intervention programs was based on the literature on normal language development (e.g., Miller & Yoder, 1974; Stremel & Waryas, 1974). While this developmental approach to intervention seemed appropriate when applied to very young children (Sailor & Guess, 1983), older learners with disabilities exposed to such an approach were often taught communication skills that had little relevance to their daily lives (Guess, Sailor, & Baer, 1974). Communication demands and opportunities vary with age, and also depend to a great extent upon the nature and diversity of the daily environments in which learners function.

In order to establish communication skills that enable learners to participate more effectively in their daily lives, a functional approach to communication must be adopted. With this approach, intervention priorities for learners with severe disabilities are based upon the unique characteristics of the individual learner, as well as upon the demands and opportunities

of the various environments in which the learner is expected to function. Careful analysis of the demands and opportunities presented in the typical domestic, school, vocational, community, and recreation environments experienced by the learner yields critical information for ensuring that the content of intervention is relevant to the learner's current and future life. Such analyses have been referred to as ecological analyses or ecological inventories (Brown, Branston, et al., 1979; Brown et al., 1988; Falvey, 1986; Ford et al., 1989; Snell & Grigg, 1987).

Various types of information needed in designing communication intervention can be derived from natural environments using ecological inventory strategies (Figure 1).

First, an inventory of the demands and opportunities that exist in an environment is the basis for determining priority targets for instruction. This includes both communication and other instructional targets. Second, after priority instructional targets have been identified, addi-

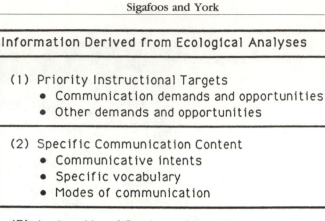

Figure 1.   Information derived from ecological analyses.

tional information, such as delineation of natural cues and consequences, is derived from the environment and used in designing an instructional program. For example, for each priority communication target, interventionists analyze actual environments to determine: 1) the specific communicative intents to be taught so that the learner can effectively respond to environmental demands and opportunities, 2) the mode of communication (e.g., vocal, graphic, gestural) to be used, 3) specific vocabulary, 4) the natural cues and consequences that need to be highlighted for the learner, 5) the time or times during the day at which instruction should take place, and 6) the way in which teaching opportunities can be sequenced or scheduled.

This chapter describes the types of information that can be derived from an analysis of the environment and how this information can be used to design communication programs. An example of a strategy for conducting an ecological inventory to gather relevant information about the learners' typical environments and activities is also provided.

COMMUNICATION INFORMATION DERIVED FROM ECOLOGICAL ANALYSES

Communicative Demands

A properly conducted ecological analysis provides a detailed picture of the communicative demands found in relevant environments. Some of these demands will be obvious (e.g., ordering a meal is a communicative demand in most restaurants). Other demands may be more subtle because they may be contingent demands. Requesting additional materials from a supervisor is a communicative demand that may be necessary in the work place, but only when needed items have been used up. Many communicative demands will have relevance in a variety of environments. When the communicative demands of the learner's daily environments have been listed, instructional priorities can be selected.

Communicative Opportunities

In addition to determining the communicative demands of various activities, it is also important to identify opportunities for teaching communication skills. At a fast food restaurant, for example, there is typically one opportunity to make a request. Additional opportunities for requests can be created, however, by teaching requests for condiments or utensils when these are not provided. In many activities, a large number of communicative opportunities go unrecognized because learners with severe disabilities are given assistance before they have had a chance to request help. Another often unrecognized opportunity is that of social discourse. Learners with disabilities may be excluded from a conversation because others fail to recognize that they might be able to contribute. The opportunity to interact with other people is part of many environments and activities. An ecological inventory of various activities helps the interventionist identify opportunities for communication in such activities.

Communicative Intents to Meet Demands and Opportunities

The communication demands and opportunities that arise in the learner's daily environments will determine to a great extent the type of communicative intents that need to be established. At restaurants, for example, learners will need to be taught how to make requests. Other environments or activities may require the learner to describe aspects of the setting. When interacting with a peer during a leisure activity, initiating and maintaining a conversation will prove important. Different activities will often call for different types of communicative functions (e.g., requesting, rejecting, commenting). A single activity will often require the use of multiple communicative functions. When dining with a peer, for example, a learner may have opportunities to *request*, to *reject*, and to *converse*.

Vocabulary

An ecological inventory can also provide information on specific vocabulary that will prove useful to the learner. At the baseball stadium, for example, vocabulary such as "run," "fly ball," "strike out," and "hot dog" are used frequently. In contrast, the grocery store requires a different vocabulary. Some interventionists have relied upon predetermined lists of initial vocabulary for determining what vocabulary to teach learners with severe disabilities. Such lists are often based upon the words that are used most frequently by young children without disabilities. Selecting vocabulary from such lists may not, however, ensure that the learner will acquire vocabulary that is most relevant to the communication demands and opportunities of current and future environments. Vocabulary targeted for instruction must be determined for each learner by considering the demands of the environments in which he or she is expected to function.

Communication Modes

Learners with severe disabilities will often communicate by speaking, by signing or gesturing, or by selecting symbols, drawings, or photographs. Often the characteristics of the environment will determine which mode is most likely to be effective. A speaker who is unintelligible to strangers may be able to use speech when surrounded by familiar listeners. Signs may be effective when communicating with others who sign. Other environments may include listeners who are not able to comprehend poorly articulated speech or are not familiar with signs. In these settings, graphic communication systems may prove to be the best option (Rotholz, Berkowitz, & Burberry, 1989). (See Chapter 2 for a discussion of the selection of communication modes.)

Learners who communicate primarily through the use of signs or gestures will face situations in which their listeners are not able to interpret their communication attempts. It may be necessary to teach such learners to use another means of communication when these situations arise. An interventionist faced with the task of providing a learner with a back-up system has two options. The first is to teach the learner to use an alternative method, such as a graphic system, whenever communication difficulties arise. Teaching the learner to use an alternative method when the primary method does not result in a response from a communication partner is one strategy for dealing with problems that may arise with unfamiliar listeners. With this method, the learner is taught to engage in a behavioral chain whenever his or her regular communication method fails. For example, a learner going through the lunch line at school may encounter an unfamiliar substitute dining room worker who looks baffled when the learner signs a request for orange juice. Seeing that his efforts to communicate are not succeeding, the learner would then open a communication wallet and point to a symbol for orange juice.

A second strategy is to teach the learner to use a graphic mode of communication in one environment and a gestural mode in another environment. Often differential use strategies are setting specific. For example, a learner might use the gestural mode at home and the graphic mode in the community (see Chapter 2).

Natural Cues and Consequences

Another type of useful information derived from the ecological inventory is the identification of the natural cues and consequences that should control a particular communicative behavior. When one performs the necessary actions required for making coffee, for example, the natural consequence is that one is able to drink the finished brew. Inability to find an item at the grocery store is a natural cue for requesting assistance. An ecological inventory can help identify these natural cues and consequences. Once identified, instructional strategies can be implemented to bring required communicative behaviors under the control of these natural cues and consequences (see Chapter 8).

Skill Cluster Instruction

Teaching communicative skills in the context of functional activities is consistent with a model of instruction that has come to be called *skill cluster instruction* (Sailor & Guess, 1983) or the Individualized Curriculum Sequencing Model (Guess & Helmstetter, 1986). A skill cluster refers to the range of specific behaviors that make up a particular activity. For example, dressing involves a range of specific skills. Selecting appropriate clothing requires choice-making behaviors. Putting on the clothes requires various gross motor and fine motor behaviors. Certain steps (e.g., zipping the back of a dress) may require the learner to request assistance, thus involving a specific communicative behavior. Other activities involve an even wider range of activities. Going out to dinner, for example, may involve making choices (e.g., selecting a restaurant), motor skills (e.g., hailing a taxi cab), communicative skills (e.g., ordering and conversing), and money management skills (e.g., paying the bill, leaving a tip). Each of these skills in turn consists of many component behaviors.

Rather than teaching component behaviors (e.g., gross and fine motor skills) as isolated skills, a skill cluster approach teaches specific behaviors as parts of functional activities. Action sequences, rather than isolated responses, are taught. Rather than teaching fine motor skills in an isolated manipulation task, for example, improved use of the hands would be incorporated during a dressing activity. Rather than teaching learners to name objects in an isolated therapy session, this skill could be incorporated into some larger functional activity, such as commenting on some aspect of the environment, maintaining a conversation at dinner, or reporting to a supervisor at work. Using a skill cluster approach, initial communicative objectives are incorporated into other functional activities. During a snack routine, for example, a learner may be involved not only in intervention designed to teach requesting skills, but also in an intervention designed to teach the learner to pass a tray of snacks to peers, pour juice, manipulate utensils, and use a napkin appropriately. A single routine thus forms the basis for teaching several specific behaviors.

When a skill cluster is selected, the parameters of intervention are determined somewhat by the constraints imposed by the nature of the task. Some activities may lend themselves to multiple intervention sessions per day (e.g., toileting, meal preparation). Other activities may occur only once a day (e.g., dressing) or less frequently (e.g., going to a movie). Opportunities to teach communicative objectives will, therefore, depend upon the types of activities into which these objectives have been incorporated. (Several options for scheduling intervention [e.g., massed, distributed, spaced] are described in Chapter 10.)

CONDUCTING AN ECOLOGICAL ANALYSIS

Numerous formats can be used to conduct ecological inventories depending on the specific purpose of the inventory. An ecological inventory strategy that can be used as the basis for conducting assessments of learner performance in typical environments is presented here (Brown, Branston, et al., 1979; Brown, Branston-McClean, et al., 1979; Falvey, 1986; Snell & Smith, 1983). Included as part of the inventory are descriptions of opportunities for the learner to produce communicative behavior. The first step in the process is to develop the natural environment assessment tool. The second step is to use the assessment tool to assess learner performance in the environment. The third step is to determine priority instructional targets or objectives. The final step is to design the instructional program.

Developing the Assessment Tool

After the team identifies a natural environment in which the learner will receive instruction, an assessment tool is developed that delineates the competencies required for participation in the identified environment (Snell & Smith, 1983; York & Vandercook, in press). The assessment tool can be organized into sections by the subenvironment of each environment. For example, subenvironments of the home would include the kitchen, bathroom, bedroom, dining room, and basement. The next step is to record the activities and related skills that occur in each subenvironment. For example, activities that might take place in a kitchen include making a sandwich, getting drinks, setting the table, clearing the table, and washing the dishes. One way to identify activities and related skills is to observe the activities people perform in each environment and list the component skills required for participation. A task analysis that lists each step of the activity in its proper sequential order should be developed for each activity (Cuvo, Leaf, & Borokove, 1978; Horner & Kelitz, 1975; Popovich, 1981; Wacker & Berg, 1983).

For the purpose of communication intervention, the task analysis must be expanded to include steps involving communicative behavior. For example, a task analysis of collating papers in the office might be expanded to include a step to request additional staples when the stapler is empty. A task analysis of grocery shopping might include a step to ask for assistance if an item cannot be located. Thus, task analyses of activities can easily be expanded to include steps for communicative behavior. Many of these steps might represent contingency steps: *if* (items run out, cannot be located, or are not forthcoming), *then* (ask for more, ask where, or make a request for the desired item). When task analyses are expanded in such a fashion to include steps for communicative behavior, many objectives will have to be taught with negative exemplars (Horner, Bellamy, & Colvin, 1984) or conditional use of communicative behavior (see Chapter 10).

Figure 2 presents part of an assessment tool

Domain: Domestic   Environment: Home   Subenvironment: Kitchen

Activity	Skills	Step performed independently	Step performed with verbal prompt	Step performed with gesture/model	Step completed after physical prompt	Step completed by staff (learner unable to perform step)	Other (describe)
Choosing an item for lunch	1. Approach listener.				+		
	2. Request preferred item.				+		
Making a peanut butter sandwich	1. Gather materials.					+	
	2. Remove two slices of bread from bag, place on flat surface.				+		
	3. Open jar of peanut butter.				+		
	4. Use knife to collect approximately 2 tbsps. of peanut butter.				+		
	5. Spread peanut butter on one slice of bread.			+			
	6. Repeat steps 4 and 5 until entire surface is covered.			+			

Task	Col 1	Col 2	Col 3	Col 4	Col 5
7. Place other slice of bread on top of surface covered with peanut butter.		+			
8. Close jar.		+			
9. Close bread bag.	+				
10. Return jar and bread.		+			
11. Wash knife and return.		+			
Eating lunch					
1. Put sandwich on plate.			+		
2. Bring plate to table.			+		
3. Sit at table.					+
4. Eat sandwich.					+
5. Return plate to sink.				+	
6. Wash plate.				+	

Figure 2.   Sample assessment tool for determining priority instructional targets.

developed to assess learner performance in three different activities: choosing an item for lunch, preparing the chosen item, and eating lunch. Assessments such as these—conducted in actual task situations—will yield information on whether the learner has the skills to complete a particular step independently, or if some type of assistance is needed for the learner to complete the step.

Assessing Learner Performance

After the skills required to complete the designated activities have been identified through a task analysis, the learner's performance on each step is assessed. It is essential that the learner's performance be assessed in the environment in which the behavior will be required. The skills that a learner cannot perform or has difficulty performing during the assessment then become instructional priorities. While team members can make best guesses about intervention targets prior to assessment in natural environments, learners must engage in the designated activities in the actual environment before instructional targets can be finalized.

The assessment process itself is similar to implementing a baseline opportunity to determine the learner's current skill level. Specifically, the interventionist may instruct the learner to perform a task and record the level of assistance required for the learner to complete each step (Figure 2). Often, several such assessments will be needed to obtain a valid assessment of the learner's skills. Assistance is provided by the interventionist as needed, so that each step is completed in its proper sequence. Before completing any step for the learner, however, the interventionist should give the learner an opportunity to complete the step independently. Similarly, after each step has been performed, the learner must have an opportunity to initiate performance of the next step.

Establishing Instructional Priorities

Skills found lacking or deficient during the assessment are identified as potential instructional priorities. Skills with the highest priorities are those that are: 1) most relevant to activities in which the learner engages, 2) of greatest interest to the learner, 3) most easily accomplished, 4) applicable in various environments and activities, 5) required for health and safety reasons, and 6) fostering of positive interactions with peers.

Designing Instructional Intervention Programs

Once priorities have been targeted for instruction, specific intervention programs must be designed. Independent performance need not be the goal of all intervention programs. The fact that a learner may never achieve independent performance of all steps required to complete an activity should not exclude him or her from participating in an activity (Brown, Branston-McClean, et al., 1979). Rather, adaptations can be made to promote partial participation (Baumgart et al., 1982). (The array of prompting strategies available and ways in which to design instruction are examined in Chapter 9.)

Information collected during an assessment may indicate the need to teach specific communication behaviors, either because they are indicated as a regular part of an activity or because they are an appropriate adaptation for allowing a learner to participate to a greater degree in a specific activity. For example, the assessment data recorded in Figure 2 indicate that even with physical assistance the learner was unable to untie the bag of bread and open the jar of peanut butter. For these steps, it may be possible to establish an appropriate communicative alternative (i.e., requesting help) instead of aiming for independence.

Table 1 provides a format that may help organize the design of instructional programs related to communication objectives. For each communication target, specific communicative intents, modes, vocabulary, cues, and consequences are determined through analysis of both the learner and the environment.

Table 1. A format for organizing instructional content derived from ecological analyses

Communication target	Intent	Mode	Vocabulary	Natural cue	Consequence
Recruit listener attention	Request attention as part of chain to request object	Vocal	Vocalization	Proximity of listener	Listener approaches.
Request preferred item	Request for object	Graphic	Explicit "sandwich" symbol	Listener present in kitchen at lunchtime. Listener may ask, "What do you want for lunch?"	Permission to make sandwich granted.
Gather materials	Request assistance	Graphic	Generic "help" symbol	Needed materials placed out of reach.	Listener retrieves needed items.
Open jar of peanut butter	Request assistance	Graphic	Generic "help" symbol	Jar lid is too tight for learner to open independently.	Listener opens jar for learner.

SUMMARY

Selection of appropriate instructional objectives is critical to the ultimate success of any intervention program. It is important to select for instruction those skills that will enable the learner to participate more fully in his or her domestic, vocational, community, recreation, and school environments. Use of an ecological inventory ensures a proper match between the demands and opportunities of these environments and the communication objectives targeted for intervention. Relevance to the real world is an important principle of learning for all individuals, but is particularly important for learners with disabilities. Communication skills targeted for instruction must, therefore, be of direct relevance to a learner's daily life. An ecological approach to designing communication interventions also can be used to determine *what* to teach, *where* to teach, and *when* to teach. (Specific instructional sequences and procedures are described in Chapters 5, 6, 8, 9, and 10.)

REFERENCES

Baumgart, D., Brown, L., Pumpian, I., Nisbet, J., Ford, A., Sweet, M., Messina, R., & Schroeder, J. (1982). The principle of partial participation and individualized adaptations in educational programs for students with severe handicaps. *Journal of The Association for the Severely Handicapped*, 7(2), 17–27.

Brown, L., Branston, M.B., Hamre-Nietupski, S., Pumpian, I., Certo, N., & Gruenewald, L.A. (1979). A strategy for developing chronological age appropriate and functional curricular content for severely handicapped adolescents and young adults. *Journal of Special Education, 13*, 81–90.

Brown, L., Branston-McClean, M.R., Baumgart, D., Vincent, L., Falvey, M., & Schroeder, J. (1979). Utilizing the characteristics of current and subsequent least restrictive environments in the development of curricular content for severely handicapped students. *AAESPH Review, 4*, 407–424.

Brown, L., Shiraga, B., Rogan, P., York, J., Albright, K.Z., McCarthy, E., Loomis, R., & Van

Deventer, P. (1988). The "why" question in programs for people who are severely intellectually disabled. In S.N. Calculator & J.L. Bedrosian (Eds.), *Communication assessment and intervention for adults with mental retardation* (pp. 139–153). Boston: Little, Brown.

Cuvo, A.J., Leaf, R.B., & Borakove, L.S. (1978). Teaching janitorial skills to the mentally retarded: Acquisition, generalization and maintenance. *Journal of Applied Behavioral Analysis, 11*, 345–355.

Falvey, M.A. (1986). *Community-based curriculum: Instructional strategies for students with severe handicaps*. Baltimore: Paul H. Brookes Publishing Co.

Ford, A., Schnorr, R., Meyer, L., Davern, L., Black, J., & Dempsey P. (1989). *The Syracuse community-referenced curriculum guide for students with moderate and severe disabilities*. Baltimore: Paul H. Brookes Publishing Co.

Guess, D., & Helmstetter, E. (1986). Skill cluster instruction and the individualized curriculum sequence model. In R.H. Horner, L.H. Meyer, & H.D. Bud Fredericks (Eds.), *Education of learners with severe handicaps: Exemplary service strategies* (pp. 221–248). Baltimore: Paul H. Brookes Publishing Co.

Guess, D., Sailor, W., & Baer, D.M. (1974). To teach language to retarded children. In R.L. Schiefelbusch & L.L. Lloyd (Eds.), *Language perspectives: Acquisition, retardation, and intervention* (pp. 529–563). Baltimore: University Park Press.

Horner, R.D., & Kelitz, I. (1975). Training mentally retarded adults to brush their teeth. *Journal of Applied Behavior Analysis, 8*, 301–319.

Horner, R.H., Bellamy, G.T., & Colvin, G.T. (1984). Responding in the presence of nontrained stimuli: Implications of generalization error patterns. *Journal of The Association for Persons with Severe Handicaps, 9*, 287–296.

Miller, J.F., & Yoder, D.E. (1974). An ontogenetic language teaching strategy for retarded children. In R.L. Schiefelbusch & L.L. Lloyd (Eds.), *Language perspectives: Acquisition, retardation, and intervention* (pp. 505–528). Baltimore: University Park Press.

Popovich, D. (1981). *Effective educational and behavioral programming for severely and profoundly handicapped students: A manual for teachers and aides*. Baltimore: Paul H. Brookes Publishing Co.

Rotholz, D.A., Berkowitz, S.F., & Burberry, J. (1989). Functionality of two modes of communication in the community by students with developmental disabilities: A comparison of signing and communication books. *Journal of The Association for Persons with Severe Handicaps, 14*, 227–233.

Sailor, W., & Guess, D. (1983). *Severely handicapped students: An instructional design*. Boston: Houghton Mifflin.

Snell, M.E., & Grigg, N.C. (1987). Instructional assessment and curriculum development. In M.E. Snell (Ed.), *Systematic instruction of persons with severe handicaps* (3rd ed., pp. 64–109). Columbus, OH: Charles E. Merrill.

Snell, M.E., & Smith, D.D. (1983). Developing the IEP: Selecting and assessing skills. In M.E. Snell (Ed.), *Systematic instruction of the moderately and severely handicapped* (2nd ed., pp. 76–112). Columbus, OH: Charles E. Merrill.

Stremel, K., & Waryas, C. (1974). A behavioral-psycholinguistic approach to language training. In L. McReynolds (Ed.), *Developing systematic procedures for training children's language*. Rockville, MD: American Speech and Hearing Monographs, No. 18.

Wacker, D.P., & Berg, W.K. (1983). Effects of picture prompts on the acquisition of complex vocational skills by mentally retarded adolescents. *Journal of Applied Behavior Analysis, 16*, 417–433.

York, J., & Vandercook, T. (in press). Designing an integrated education through the IEP process. *Teaching Exceptional Children*.

4

Describing Initial Communicative Intents

Joe Reichle

THIS CHAPTER ATTEMPTS to define the range of actions and gestures that may be used to convey communicative intent, and examines ways of describing emerging communicative intents.

EARLY COMMUNICATIVE SIGNALS

McLean and Snyder-McLean (1988) identified a hierarchy of communicative forms that reflects growing sophistication in a learner's ability to produce speech acts. This hierarchy is comprised of primitive acts, conventional acts, and referential acts. Primitive acts encompass learner actions that occur with sufficient frequency that they have become conditioned (e.g., pulling away when an undesired item is offered or offering a cup to obtain more of a beverage). Conventional acts are actions that have been altered (streamlined) from their earlier primitive act forms (e.g., requesting by offering an open palm without an object in one's hand, or pointing at an object of interest rather than taking an adult's hand and placing it directly on an item of interest). Referential acts include speaking, sign-

ing, or using conventional graphic symbols. Examples of primitive, conventional, and referential communicative acts are shown in Figure 1.

The progression from primitive act to referential act reflects growing sophistication. However, in many instances, primitive acts may communicate more clearly to a listener, and conventional speech acts do not necessarily ease the listener's role in a communicative interaction. For example, proffering a cup to request a drink (a primitive act) is more explicit than requesting a drink by extending an open empty palm (a conventional act). Of course, mastery of only the primitive act means that the learner will always require a cup in order to request a drink.

Although children without disabilities progress from primitive to conventional to referential speech, it has not been established that learners with severe disabilities need do so. In fact, forcing learners with primitive speech to master conventional acts before referential speech is taught may merely strengthen a behavior that will subsequently be replaced. In many cases,

Primitive	Conventional	Referential
Learner pushes a bowl of lima beans away from his place at the table (to reject a nonpreferred item).	Learner shakes head "no" in response to the question "Do you want to take your bath now?"	Learner points to the "milk" symbol on his communication board to indicate he would like milk with his lunch.
Learner takes adult's hand and pulls toward refrigerator (to request pop stored in the refrigerator).	Learner waves good-bye to his mother as she is leaving for work in the morning.	Learner produces the sign for "cat" and points to the window of the pet shop to call attention to the cats in the window.
Learner tries to remove a twist tie from a bread wrapper while alternating gaze from bread wrapper to nearby adult (to request assistance).	Learner points to the cookie jar on the counter to indicate he would like a cookie.	At Burger King, learner points to the symbols "want hamburger, french fries, chocolate shake" in his communication wallet while placing his order.

Figure 1.   Examples of primitive, conventional, and referential communicative acts.

replacing an existing gesture with a new one may be more difficult than establishing a new behavior from scratch.

Sometimes what appear to be relatively minor features of an instructional opportunity may influence significantly the probability of a response or the intrusiveness of the prompt required to obtain a response approximation. Many learners have a history of idiosyncratic communicative behavior. These idiosyncratic forms may have been shaped over a very long period of time and may have been very efficient. Interventionists often throw away the baby with the bath water by refusing to honor existing communicative behaviors and attempting to replace them with more sophisticated communicative behaviors. For example, formats to establish the use of communication boards have focused on teaching a learner to touch a symbol or symbols affixed to a portable surface, such as a communication board or wallet. At first glance this instructional format does not seem very different from the format the learner has been using. It is easy to reason that because a learner was using objects representationally, switching the format of a response from offering an object to touching the object affixed to an array would not be a problem. In working with learners who are accustomed to offering objects to communicate, the author has found it useful to change one characteristic of the communication at a time when transforming an actual object into a two-dimensional representation.

Unfortunately, no guidelines govern which aspect of the learner's communication system to implement first. With Sam, a 25-year-old man with severe retardation, a set of keys used to request a car ride and an empty soda can used to request a Diet Pepsi™ were transformed into two-dimensional stimuli before Sam was taught to point to the symbols rather than pick up the objects and hand them to his communication partner, as he had been doing. The intervention procedures described in Chapter 5 were used to make this transition. Once Sam was picking up two-dimensional laminated representations of a key and a Diet Pepsi™ logo, the intervention focused on teaching Sam simply to touch these symbols rather than pick them up. During the phase of intervention in which the three-dimensional symbols were replaced with two-dimensional symbols, the symbols were located on the dresser in Sam's room. After two-dimensional symbols were established, a fabric wallet was introduced. Velcro™ strips were affixed to a page of the wallet and to the laminated two-dimensional symbols. A history was established that the learner could pull the symbols off the page of his wallet and bring them to significant others. Once a history of selecting symbols from the wallet and taking them to the interventionist was established, the symbols were affixed permanently to the wallet. Using symbols with Velcro™ backing permitted the interventionists to randomize the positions in which the symbols were attached to the learner's wallet. (See Chapter 10 on teaching symbol discriminations.) Upon retrieving his wallet and failing to remove the symbols, Sam picked up the entire wallet and presented it to a staff member, who then asked, "What do you want, Sam?" As Sam began tugging at the symbol, the staff member immediately delivered the desired item. Over successive opportunities, Sam was taught that the slightest contact with the symbol resulted in a successful request.

With Derek, another learner with severe disabilities, small objects were used to represent desired items on a communication board that was attached to the lap tray of Derek's wheelchair. As soon as Derek started to pull the object from his communication board he was reinforced. Over successive opportunities, Derek began to touch the items. Procedures were implemented to transfer instructional control from the real miniature objects being used as symbols to the two-dimensional representations of the product logo for each item. Thus, although Sam's program and Derek's program started very differently, both resulted in the same outcome.

Occasionally, the interventionist encounters a learner who has an extensive history of idiosyncratic but socially acceptable communicative behavior. For example, Paul, a learner with severe retardation, had a history of getting a quart of milk from the refrigerator and handing it to one of his parents to request a beverage at home. This requesting routine was so well established that attempts to modify it met with aggressive behavior. Rather than deploying significant resources to alter the form of this existing response, the author allowed it to remain in Paul's repertoire. A symbol representing milk and lemonade (two beverages stored in cartons) was successfully introduced at school. Eventually, Paul became proficient in using symbols in school and community settings, although he continued to use his idiosyncratic requesting behavior at home. Thus, idiosyncratic communicative forms need not always be replaced with more conventional forms. On some occasions the form of the learner's communicative response is changed from one type of stimulus (real object) to a more representational one (line drawing), but the format of the learner's response (picking up something and giving it to the listener) is maintained. Some examples of unacceptable communicative repertoires are described in Chapter 11. Unfortunately, overzealous interventionists sometimes shoot themselves in the feet attempting to alter radically what may already be a functional communicative behavior. For example, a teacher asked an augmentative system user if he wanted some ice cream. The learner enthusiastically nodded his head, but the teacher instructed him to use his communication board. The learner did not, and the ice cream melted.

In most of the instances described here, the learners were already producing social behavior directed toward others in their environments. However, learners who do not appear to engage in any such intentional (i.e., for the benefit of a listener) behavior are also frequently encountered. Such learners provide a tremendous challenge for the communication interventionist. Many speech and language pathologists believe that certain cognitive prerequisites must be in place before efforts can be made to teach learners an initial repertoire of communicative intents. The author believes that intervention should not be ruled out because of the absence of certain cognitive skills, but rather that intervention can proceed as soon as positive or negative reinforcers have been identified. (The issue of cognitive prerequisites to the establishment of a repertoire of beginning communication skills is addressed in Chapter 2.) However, it is clear that to use intentional communication, the learner must come to understand how his or her actions come to control the actions of others. In the next section, the issue of how to ensure that the learner understands the contingent relationships between his or her behavior and environmental events is addressed.

ESTABLISHING CONTINGENT RELATIONSHIPS BETWEEN BEHAVIOR AND SIGNIFICANT ENVIRONMENTAL EVENTS

The developmental literature presents a strong case that children without disabilities are unable to engage in goal-directed actions or intentional communicative behavior before 8 months of age. As Keogh and Reichle (1985) have pointed out, however, infants exert a significant amount of control over their environment prior to this time. Skinner (1957) provided an eloquent description of how over time a discrete voluntary behavior, such as a cry, can come to serve the function of a social signal. Cries tend to be consequated immediately by a variety of desirable outcomes. When a cry is emitted at meal time, a bottle is delivered; when cries are emitted upon getting a hand caught in a drawer, someone rushes to provide assistance. Over time, therefore, a child may come to cry when hungry, or in order to get help. Often parents report subtle differences between cries of, say, hunger and cries of pain. The exact point at which the child's vocal behavior becomes intentional is unclear. What is clear is that pairing particular vocal behaviors with particular desired outcomes serves to increase the probability that the vocal behavior will be performed in the future when the child finds him- or herself in a similar situation. For children without disabilities, the literature is replete with examples of the influence of predictable positive outcomes on the performance of vocal behavior (Rheingold, Gewirtz, & Ross, 1959; Weisberg, 1963).

This phenomenon is not unique to vocal behavior. Watson (1978) reported a game in which 8-week-old infants could control a crib mobile by establishing contact between their heads and a pressure transducer. The infants quickly acquired the contingent relationship involved in the game. Contingent head turning responses have been taught to infants less than 2 weeks old (Papousek, 1978).

An important facet of learning to understand that there are relationships between one's action, the environment, and people in that environment involves the performance of anticipatory behavior. For example, around 7–8 months of age, many children become interested in the game of "pat-a-cake." Typically, the caregiver sings as he or she guides the child's hands through the motions of the game. Over time, the need to assist the child diminishes. At some point, the child begins to produce the movements of the game when he or she hears the song. Other examples occur even earlier. By 5–6 months infants smile and begin laughing when they see an adult's hand moving toward them as an overture to a tickle. Experience has taught the child that the approach of a large hand is generally followed by a tickle. Not all contingent relationships involve pleasant situations. Infants soon learn to move their heads away to avoid undesired foods. Thus, contingent relationships between events and corresponding behavior that may be used to display communicative intent are naturally established and maintained in the context of daily routines.

DOES CONTINGENCY BETWEEN A PARTICULAR BEHAVIOR AND A PREDICTABLE SUBSEQUENT EVENT CONSTITUTE COMMUNICATION?

Stillman, Alymer, and Vandivort (1983) found learners' behavior to be contingent upon the presence of a desired object or event (request), or upon the presentation of an undesired event (reject or terminate) regardless of whether a listener was present to receive the message. Traditionally, children have been said to engage in communicative behavior when they engage a listener with the purpose of conveying intent. This position assumes that the learner would communicate a message given the presence of a listener, and that in the absence of a listener, the learner would first seek out a listener before communicating.

An alternative point of view is that the establishment of a contingent relationship between the learner's use of a gesture or selection of a symbol and a predictable environmental result will be useful to both the learner and others in the environment, even if social agency is not established. For example, Stillman et al. (1983) established that voluntary behaviors taught to their subjects were useful in the presence of a listener (and not useful in the absence of a listener).

MOVING FROM PERLOCUTION (UNINTENTIONAL) TO ILLOCUTIONARY (INTENTIONAL) COMMUNICATIVE INTENTS

As discussed in previous chapters, Bates, Camioni, and Volterra (1975) identified three stages in which intentional communicative behavior emerges in children without disabilities. During the *perlocutionary* stage an adult assigns intent to actions of a learner that may not have been directed to a listener. For example, when an infant smiles, an adult may conclude that the infant is trying to express to a listener that he or she is happy. When an infant fusses, an adult may conclude that the infant is attempting to communicate to a listener that he or she is hungry. As infants mature, they begin to produce these same behaviors, but may begin to alternate their attention between the referent and a prospective listener. Bates et al. (1975) referred to these instances in which the learner intended to convey a message to the listener as *illocutionary*. Eventually, specific linguistic forms emerge that are clearly intentional (*locutionary* acts).

The distinction between perlocutionary and illocutionary behavior may be easier to observe among users of augmentative or alternative communication systems. Vocal behavior has the unique characteristic of eliciting a listener's attention at the same time that the message is conveyed. Nonelectronic graphic and gestural modes require that some additional behavior be produced in order to elicit a listener's attention if such attention is not already present. Consequently, if a learner displays a history of using a gesture in the absence of an attending listener, it is fairly safe to conclude that the gesture is not intentional. In graphic and gestural modes, the interventionist can address intentionality at the level of establishing an attention-getting response. This, in turn, offers perhaps a clearer point of discrimination for the learner regarding what functionally must occur to ensure an intentional communicative emission. Most learners find it difficult to determine when they need to obtain a listener versus when they can take the listener's presence for granted. Examples of perlocutionary, illocutionary, and locutionary communicative acts are shown in Figure 2.

Hart (1985) has noted that interaction is one-to-one in the initial phases of most naturalistic intervention procedures aimed at establishing communicative behavior. That is, the interventionist makes him- or herself readily accessible to the learner in the context of regularly occur-

Perlocutionary Communicative Acts

Behavior	Context
An infant's crying or fussing	The behavior occurs whether or not a listener is present or available to attend to crying
An infant's smiling	The behavior occurs whether or not a listener is present
A learner touches a "drink" symbol on his communication board	Random symbol selection occurs whether or not a learner is thirsty

Illocutionary Communicative Acts

Behavior	Context
Learner hands empty glass to parent.	Learner has just finished drinking his milk and is requesting more.
Learner shakes her head "yes" and smiles.	Her father has just asked if she wants to go to the zoo.
Learner tugs on mother's sleeve and then points to the front yard.	She looks in the direction of his point and sees a dog running through the yard.

Locutionary Communicative Acts

Behavior	Context
Learner says, "Juice please."	At the breakfast table, as a result of the learner's request, the parent pours her a glass of juice.
Learner signs "Dad ball where?"	Her father responds by saying "Your ball is in your room."
At lunch time, a learner uses his communication wallet and points to the symbols "want eat McDonald's."	His mother responds by saying, "What would you like to eat at McDonald's?"

Figure 2.   Examples of perlocutionary, illocutionary, and locutionary communicative acts.

ring routines. Over time, the learner recognizes that a listener is usually in close proximity when there is something significant to communicate. As a result, the learner may fail to learn that the presence of a listener constitutes part of the dis- criminative stimulus for a communicative be- havior. For example, consider the learner who sees other children at lunch eating cookies and proceeds repeatedly to touch a symbol to re- quest a cookie even though no prospective listener is present. The learner needs to recognize the need first to obtain a listener's attention (by waving an arm, raising a hand, vocalizing, etc.) and only then to indicate the appropriate symbol. Teaching the learner to discriminate between the use of a single symbol when he or she already has the listener's attention, and the use of a chain of attention getting behavior plus a symbol when he or she does not have the listener's attention represents a challenge to the interventionist. Bobby, a 6-year-old with multiple disabilities including severe intellectual deficits, was taught to make explicit requests for each of four items that represented powerful reinforcers for him. He quickly learned to touch the corresponding graphic symbol in the presence of a desired object or objects. Given an array of items, Bobby almost always selected the item that corresponded to the symbol that he had just selected. Most of Bobby's instruction had occurred in the presence of an interventionist. Consequently, he never had to obtain his listener's attention prior to producing a communicative behavior. As a result, it was not clear whether Bobby would seek out an adult when one was not within his vicinity. On several occasions, items that Bobby was interested in were placed on a shelf beyond his reach. Eventually, Bobby brought himself to the room containing the items. He immediately focused on the items and touched his symbol requesting them, repeating this action approximately 15 times. Meeting with no success, he switched his selection to a different symbol and repeated that selection five or six times before giving up.

Bobby's behavior led the author to conclude that using an adult as a mediator to obtain items and using a symbol as a mediator to obtain items represent two very separable classes of behavior. Because all of Bobby's prior intervention had taken place in the presence of an adult, Bobby made no attempt to seek out a listener when none was present. To communicate efficiently, the learner must be able to chain together an attention-getting behavior and the se-

lection of the appropriate symbol. However, the ability to seek out a listener should not serve as a prerequisite for learning intentional use of symbols. A learner need not be engaging in intentional behavior before he or she begins to communicate. Eventually, given a contingent reinforcer, the learner may learn to perform the targeted behavior in the presence of the cues associated with receipt of the reinforcer.

The learner need not consider the perspective of the listener in order to perform a communicative act. Perlocutionary behavior has been described as the production of discrete voluntary behavior that is interpreted by a listener as conveying intent. In both normally developing and intellectually delayed populations, perlocutionary communicative behavior tends to precede the intentional communicative behavior (Bates, Benigni, Bretheton, Camioni, & Volterra, 1979a; McLean & Snyder-McLean, 1988). From a practical standpoint, perlocutionary behaviors are less efficient than intentional behaviors. However, there is a significant body of literature suggesting that for learners with very severe disabilities perlocutionary communication may be far more efficient than no functional communicative behavior.

SELECTING INITIAL COMMUNICATIVE FUNCTIONS TO TEACH

Most interventionists who work with people with severe developmental disabilities have concluded that initial intervention targets should focus on establishing communication skills that allow learners to exert the greatest degree of control over their environments. Traditionally, this overriding principle has resulted in programs designed to teach learners to request desired objects, access to activities, or attention. More recently, interventionists have begun to recognize the importance of establishing communicative skills that enable the learner to refuse offered items or events. Initial intervention pri-

orities should include teaching an initial repertoire of both requesting positive reinforcers and
rejecting negative reinforcers. The types of requests (i.e., requests for object, requests for
action, requests for attention) and rejecting responses (i.e., reject undesired objects, taking
leave) to be taught initially will vary. The authors
have found that the initial success of the intervention program depends on the power of the
reinforcers. For some learners, attention represents the most powerful reinforcer, while other
learners care little about attention. The specific
subclass of rejecting and requesting taught
should be based on the learner's strongest likes
and dislikes. As Chapters 5 and 6 show, learners
with severe disabilities tend to fail to generalize
across subclasses of communicative intents
without careful intervention.

There is a plethora of procedures designed to
describe the range of expressed communicative
intents. From an instructional perspective, the
author has found the protocols developed by
Cirrin and Rowland (1985) and Coggins and
Carpenter (1981) to be the most acceptable. In
many respects, the systems describe the same
range of communicative intents. Coggins and
Carpenter (1981) examined the communicative
acquisitions of children with Down syndrome,
while Cirrin and Rowland (1985) and McLean,
Snyder-McLean, and Cirrin (1981) studied adolescents with severe and profound mental retardation. The taxonomy of Cirrin and Rowland
(1985) is examined in the next several sections,
since it is one of the few that has been used
with learners with severe and multiple disabilities. Definitions for each communicative function identified by these authors are included in
Table 1.

Generalized Requesting

Cirrin and Rowland (1985) defined requesting
objects as ". . . the receipt of a specific object
from the listener when the child makes a response. The object may be out of reach due to
some physical barrier . . ." (p. 55). Young
children without disabilities acquire generalized

Table 1.   Definitions of communicative function categories

Request action	Seeks the performance of an action by the listener where the child awaits a response. The child may specify the action (e.g., "sit") or the child's immediately preceding behavior gives evidence that he realizes that some action is a necessary step to obtaining some object (e.g., signaling "help" to open a jar).
Request object	Seeks the receipt of a specific object from the listener where the child awaits a response. The object may be out of reach due to some physical barrier.
Request information	Seeks information, approval, or permission from the listener where the child awaits a response. This includes directing the listener to provide specific information about an object, action, or location.
Direct attention to self	Direction of listener's attention to the child as a general attention-getter for some unspecified social purpose.
Direct attention for communi-cation	Direction of listener's attention to self as a preface to another communicative behavior that follows immediately.
Direct attention to object	Direction of listener's attention to an external, observable referent, or some object identified by the child. This includes the speaker taking notice of an object, or labeling an object in absence of a request.
Direct attention to action	Direction of listener's attention to an ongoing action or event in the environment. The focus may be the movement or action of an object rather than the object itself. A "comment" on some ongoing activity.
Answer	A communicative response from a child to a request for information from the adult listener. This typically takes the form of indicating a choice or answering a question.

From Cirrin, F.M., & Rowland, C. (1985). Communicative
assessment of nonverbal youths with severe/profound retardation. *Mental Retardation, 23*(2), 52–62; reprinted with permission.

strategies that can be used to request a variety of objects at very early ages. Between 10 and 12 months of age, infants eye desired items that are out of reach, and then focus on someone in a position to grant a request. Subsequently, the child vocalizes when reaching toward the desired item with an outstretched arm, with the hand opening and closing in rapid succession. Often, this behavior is reinforced by access to a wide variety of objects and activities. This type of requesting strategy is known as a *generalized request* because the form of the child's behavior remains the same across all objects and activities.

From a child's perspective, generalized requesting of objects and activities is very efficient. Those people who spend time with the child have become efficient in deciphering the combined pointing and vocalizing, particularly if there are a variety of additional contextual cues. Thus from the child's perspective, the use of a generalized request is economical in that specific vocabulary need not be matched to specific objects or activities in the environment. The open-hand reach accompanied by vocalizing approximates the noncommunicative behavior that would be performed if the child became frustrated by his or her inability to procure a desired item. The initial use of a generalized requesting strategy is thus efficient in that it enables the child to communicate about a large array of objects and activities with very little effort or discriminative skills. Some data suggest that children without disabilities more readily acquire more generic (e.g., doll) as opposed to more explicit (e.g., Barbie™) or even

more generalized (e.g., toy) vocabulary when learning to name a class of objects (Anglin, 1977). To date, however, no study has addressed this issue with respect to people with severe disabilities.

The primary drawback to the establishment of a generalized requesting strategy is the burden it places on the listener to determine exactly what it is the learner wants. Both the learner and the listener can become frustrated by the listener's failure to understand a generalized request.

Explicit Requesting

Explicit requests are often required for clear communication in the community at large. Explicit requests thus place less burden of interpretation on the part of the listener, thereby reducing the frequency of requests for clarification. Explicit requesting may represent the most practical option for learners with a few specific and relatively stable preferences, or for those who tend to acquire vocabulary relatively quickly. (This topic is taken up in greater detail in Chapter 5.) A final possibility is that explicit requests may be acquired more readily by some learners because they are associated with specific response–reinforce relationships that, as shown in Chapter 5, may have an impact on intervention. Examples of the relationship between the communicative intent and the specificity of the consequence are shown in Table 2.

Requesting Attention

Cirrin and Rowland (1985) distinguish among several types of requesting attention. A child

Table 2. Relationship between a communicative event and the specificity of consequence

Referent	Antecedent	Communication	Consequence	Communicative intent
Cookie	Child sees peer eating cookie.	"Want cookie."	Provision of cookie	Request
Cookie	Interventionist asks, "What's he eating?" and points to child sitting beside learner.	"Cookie."	"Right, you had one, too. How about some milk?"	Provision of information

may solicit attention for some unspecified social purpose (e.g., yelling, "Hey, Mom!" after
placing a Halloween mask on his face). This
sort of request serves to *direct attention to self.*
Here the goal is a brief episodic interaction.
Alternatively, attention may be solicited as a
preface to another communicative behavior. For
example, a child might initiate an interaction by
yelling, "Hey, Mom." This sort of communication serves to *direct attention for communication.* Once the mother's attention has been obtained, the child requests a cookie. In a third
type of request for attention the listener's attention is directed to an external, observable referent or some object identified by the child. This
sort of communication serves to *direct attention
to an object.* Finally, the learner may *direct attention to action,* that is, direct the listener's
attention to an ongoing action or event in the
environment.

The available evidence suggests that solicit-
ing the attention of adults prior to requesting an
object or activity or prior to directing the listener's attention to an object or activity develops somewhat concurrently in children without
disabilities. Bates et al. (1979a) have reported
that the emergence of protoimperatives (requesting goods or services) and protodeclara-
tives (requesting attention) begins to emerge
near the end of the child's first year in children
without disabilities. Reichle and Keogh (1985)
speculated that learner preferences may have a
significant effect on the order of emergence,
that is, some learners may find the attention of
an adult to be more reinforcing than any available object or activity. Other learners may find
particular objects more reinforcing than attention from others in the environment. It seems
plausible that a learner's prior history of reinforcement may significantly influence the specific nature of requests that he or she finds most
salient.

***Requesting Attention to Communi-
cate*** Some of the types of attention described
by Cirrin and Rowland (1985) and McLean et

al. (1981) appear to involve chains of behavior.
For example, a learner might vocalize (e.g.,
"Hey") to direct attention to him- or herself. As
soon as the listener gazes in the learner's direction, the learner asks "Can I have ice cream?"
Interestingly, most intervention programs designed to teach requesting focus on directing
attention to communicate. Neither directing attention to self nor directing attention to communicate occurs frequently in the beginning phases
of communication, with each accounting for
less than 10% and 5%, respectively, of the communicative behaviors produced by learners who
rely primarily on actions, on adults, or on objects to communicate. As learners become more
sophisticated in using communicative behaviors
(using intelligible words or signs), it becomes
even less necessary to direct the attention of
another as a precursor to a communicative exchange (Cirrin & Rowland, 1985; McLean et
al., 1981).

Direct attention to an object follows a somewhat different course of development, according to Cirrin and Rowland (1985) and McLean
et al. (1981), among people with severe mental
retardation. Directing attention to objects accounts for less than 5% of the communicative
behaviors produced by learners using adults or
objects to communicate. Among learners using
intelligible words or signs, directing attention to
objects accounts for approximately 40% of communicative behaviors (McLean et al., 1981).
These data suggest that too little emphasis may
be being placed on teaching learners to produce
behaviors that direct the listener's attention to
objects.

***Requesting Attention to Self or to Ob-
jects*** Within the earliest repertoires of people
with severe disabilities, requests for objects account for a very high proportion of communicative behaviors, while requests for attention
to self and requests for attention to objects account for a very small proportion (McLean et
al., 1981). McLean et al. reported that among
learners who engaged in primitive or conven-

tional communicative acts, approximately 40% of their utterances were requests for objects while fewer than 10% consisted of requests for attention to objects or to self.

Interestingly, learners who engaged in somewhat more sophisticated communicative behavior tended to direct attention to objects more often and to request objects relatively less often than primitive communicators. For example, among learners with severe disabilities who were producing single-word utterances (five or more accurate words), approximately 25% of their communicative acts consisted of requests for objects, while 40% were requests for attention to objects.

The implication of these preliminary data is that learners with severe disabilities who have limited forms of communicating appear to be more likely to produce requests for objects. The reason for this phenomenon is not clear. It may be that interventionists tend to teach such learners requests for object as an initial communicative skill. If this is the case, the Cirrin and Rowland (1985) and McLean et al. (1981) observations may merely reflect the history of intervention. A second explanation may be that adult listeners presume that communicative overtures produced by people with severe disabilities are requests. As a result, the learner is shaped into using communicative behavior only to request.

Whether or not learners readily acquire the ability to direct attention to objects may depend to a large degree on whether they enjoy social contact with others. Learners who do not enjoy interacting with others may actively avoid producing communicative behaviors intended to solicit a listener's attention. Learners who do not enjoy the company of others may also produce fewer behaviors to direct attention to self, and most of their behaviors to direct attention to communicate are likely to be followed by requests for objects.

A final possibility is that a learner enjoys social attention but has little to communicate once the listener's attention has been obtained. For example, a learner may say "hi" in an effort to solicit attention. However, once the attention of a listener has been obtained, the learner may continue to say "hi" repeatedly, because of the paucity of his or her repertoire. In this case the listener is likely to retreat from the interaction at the earliest opportunity.

Regardless of the cause, many learners with the most severe disabilities may display a propensity to request objects as one of the earliest communicative functions. The author's experience suggests that learners with severe disabilities can be taught to request attention if the requests are taught as part of a chain of behavior that is necessary to procure an object, or if attention serves as a powerful reinforcer.

In the vocal mode, procuring attention does not require the production of a chain of behaviors, since whenever the learner speaks he or she is likely to obtain the attention of anyone within earshot. In nonelectronic graphic and gestural modes, however, any behavior designed to procure access to an object or activity must be preceded by a separate discrete behavior to solicit a listener's attention (unless the listener is already attending). The attention-getting response may consist of pushing a call button, raising a hand, or walking over to the prospective partner and tapping him or her on the shoulder.

Directing Attention as a Preface to Providing Information Investigators have suggested a variety of strategies for teaching attentional requests. McLean and Snyder-McLean (1988) have described interactional sequences in which something novel or unusual is introduced into the setting. For example, while a learner is interacting with an instructor, a large black spider may walk across the table within obvious view of the learner. McLean and Snyder-McLean (1988) have reported success in teaching some learners to direct their listener's attention to this novelty. The most common application of this type of stimulus novelty may occur around domestic examples, such as spills on floors, rain entering via an open window, and so forth. All of these examples presume that there is some level of stimulus novelty to which a learner will respond.

Requesting Action

Among children without disabilities, requests for actions emerge as early as 15 months of age, although they appear to occur somewhat less frequently than requests for objects. Among the less advanced communicators observed by McLean et al. (1981), requests for action accounted for just over 25% of all communicative behaviors and represented the second most frequent type of behavior, after requests for objects or protests. As learners with severe disabilities began using formal signs or spoken words, requests for actions fell in importance, becoming the third most frequent type of behavior (after requests for objects and directing attention to objects), accounting for just over 15% of all communicative behaviors.

In a request for action, the appearance or presence of a familiar activity or person motivates the learner to request the participation of another person in a routine game or activity. The literature is replete with descriptions of the emergence of early social games in which the learner requests the continuation of an activity that does not involve materials. For example, as an adult enters the room, the learner raises his hand to engage in "high five." This act serves to request the corresponding reciprocating action of the listener.

In a second situation, the learner has procured an object but cannot use it without the help of another person. For example, a learner may have a baseball glove and a ball, but lack someone with whom to play catch. In still a third variation, the learner may have procured a desired object but cannot use it effectively. For example, the learner may have found a wrapped piece of candy but be unable to unwrap it. Young learners have been observed to take a

listener's hand and move it to the toy or object as a prompt to activate it. A preschool child interested in a wind-up ferris wheel would attempt to activate it himself after it had wound down. After failing to do so, he would seek out an adult, bring him or her to the toy, and place the adult's hand on the wind-up knob. Clearly, the learner intended to communicate to the listener that he wanted the crank turned. The learner's behavior was easily recognizable as a request for assistance or a request for action from the listener.

Requesting Assistance While Engaging in Nonpreferred Activities

Requests for assistance may appear in conjunction with other communicative intents. The requests for assistance addressed so far have been requests for assistance in gaining access to a preferred activity. Assistance may also be required to help a learner perform a task that he or she does not desire. For example, say a learner is unable to mop the floor because the bucket is empty. Although the learner does not particularly enjoy mopping the floor, the task must be completed. It is thus important that a learner be able to request assistance related to undesired activities.

One interesting aspect of the development of requests for assistance involves the learner's propensity to use requests for assistance both to procure direct access to a reinforcer and to terminate more quickly an undesired event. For example, a learner who plugs in a vacuum and discovers that it does not work requests assistance so that he can get on with the (relatively undesired) task in order to complete it more quickly. Completion of the task, in turn, results in receipt of a reinforcer. The author has found that for some people with severe disabilities, teaching a requesting assistance response to obtain a desired item does not generalize to situations in which the learner has encountered a problem that keeps him or her from engaging in a task that may not be desired.

An interesting area for future exploration involves the relationship between a learner's ability to offer assistance and his or her ability to request assistance. Virtually no work has been done on the ability of people with severe disabilities to offer assistance. In order for a learner to offer assistance, he or she must be able to recognize that there is a problem. It is unclear whether teaching a learner to request assistance generalizes to offering assistance or vice versa. It seems reasonable, however, to speculate that a learner might be more likely to generalize from offering assistance to requesting assistance than vice versa. This seems more plausible in that the potential natural reinforcing contingencies may be more powerful in an episode of requesting assistance. That is, offering assistance is apt to result in the receipt of generalized social reinforcement, while requesting assistance is apt to be reinforced by receiving access to a reinforcer or by removal of a potentially aversive stimulus that is important to the learner.

Providing Information

Cirrin and Rowland (1985) divide the pragmatic intent of providing information about the environment into several separate categories. *Directing attention to object* includes "directing the listener's attention to an external, observable referent . . . [including] the speaker taking notice of an object or labeling an object in the absence of a request . . ." (p. 55). *Directing attention to action* involves "direction of the listener's attention to an ongoing action or event . . . . The focus may be the movement or action of an object rather than the object itself . . ." (p. 55). Finally, a learner's provision of information may take the form of an *answer,* defined by Cirrin and Rowland (1985) as "a communicative response from a child to a request for information from the adult listener . . . "(p. 55). Among primitive communicators, these categories accounted for less than 15% of communicative behaviors. Among

learners with severe disabilities who had acquired some conventional vocabulary these categories accounted for just under 50% of their communicative behaviors, with direct attention to object alone accounting for 40% of all communicative acts (McLean et al., 1981).

Providing information is a communicative intent that, for the most part, has not been addressed in a functional manner for learners with severe disabilities. Although "providing information" has been one of the initial foci of many language intervention programs designed for people with severe disabilities (Guess, Sailor, & Baer, 1974; Kent, 1974; Lovaas, 1977), in most of these programs this has been synonymous with labeling objects.

Like most communicative intents, providing information can be spontaneous or it can occur as a response to a communicative act by another. Early initiated provisions of information are described in terms of *showing* routines. Around 9–10 months of age, most infants begin to pick up objects of interest, approach adults, and extend the hand or arm that contains the object. After receiving an approving comment from the adult, the infant will pull the object back in toward his or her body and depart. If the communicative partner incorrectly presumes that the infant is attempting to give him or her the item and offers a hand to receive it, the infant is apt to depart, becoming at least mildly distressed. By 1–2 years of age, these showing routines are accompanied by the vocal attention getting behavior described earlier.

Providing information also occurs in formats in which the child's communicative partner solicits information, a category that Cirrin and Rowland (1985) call "answers." For example, when a 2-year-old plays with the car keys, a parent might ask, "Where are the car keys?", to which the child might respond by pointing to the keys on the floor. In this example, the child both showed that he understood his communicative partner's message and provided his partner with information.

Answers to questions account for a very small proportion of the communicative acts provided by people with severe disabilities. McLean et al. (1981) reported that even with the learners in their study who used spoken words, produced signs, or used representational graphic symbols, fewer than 15% of their communicative acts involved answering questions. The reasons for this paucity are many. First, learners' ability to answer questions is affected by their ability to understand the communicative behavior (including contextual cues) addressed to them. Second, it is possible that reinforcers are not associated directly with provisions of information. Learners may thus have seen little benefit in responding. (This topic is discussed in greater detail in Chapter 7 in the discussion of developing conversational skills in people with severe disabilities.)

Rejecting

Rejecting emerges very early in an infant's development. Many early rejection responses are highly situation specific. For example, a 5-month-old infant who does not want to eat the food being offered rejects it by turning his head away from the spoon. If the mother approaches the infant from another angle, he turns his head away again. A learner with disabilities may reject going on an outing by going to her room, as far away from the front door as possible. Both of these strategies are effective. The job of the interventionist, as described in Chapter 6, is to select a topography that can be used across a wide variety of rejecting opportunities.

Cirrin and Rowland (1985) described a protest as ". . . an indication that the speaker opposes or disapproves of the listener's behavior or action . . ." (p. 55). Among people with severe disabilities, protests account for a relatively large proportion (25%) of the communicative behaviors produced by learners using primitive forms of communication. Interestingly, as learners become more sophisticated in their use of communicative behavior, the pro-

portion of protests decreases: among learners using conventional speech, signs, or graphic communication protests account for only approximately 5% of their total utterances (Cirrin & Rowland, 1985). The apparent decrease in the use of protests may relate to increases in the use of other communicative intents. For example, if offered an undesirable object, a more sophisticated learner may request an alternative rather than merely protest. Alternatively, a learner may request action (e.g., "go away"). Both of these behaviors function to allow the learner to avoid receiving the object proffered.

A rejecting behavior (e.g., "no") can be used to reject objects or activities under a variety of circumstances. A rejection can be used in an effort to avoid the offer of something that is undesired. It can also be used in an effort to avoid an object that although usually a reinforcer is not desired. For example, although television may represent a very powerful reinforcer at 10 o'clock in the morning, it may be rejected at 3 o'clock in the morning, or after 15 hours of viewing. Offers of desired objects or activities may also be rejected because a prior commitment had been made (e.g., "I'd like to go to the party, but I have to mow the yard.").

To complicate things further, the form of the communicative behavior typically used to reject may be used for other purposes as well. For example, a learner might respond "no" to the question, "Did Mom go to the store?" In this instance, "no" does not signify rejection, but rather is used to deny the truth of the proposition stated.

One additional distinction of interest regarding rejecting behaviors should be made. Rejection is usually thought of in the context of avoiding an undesired stimulus. However, in the case of leavetaking it is actually used as an attempt to escape some ongoing activity. As described in Chapter 6, the discriminative stimuli for an avoidance response may differ from those for an escape response. The offer of the item serves as the provoking stimulus in avoiding an undesired object or activity. In escape the discriminative stimulus may be more conditional as a function of length of participation and the availability other potentially more interesting activities. For example, in order to engage in a neutral but slightly boring activity it may help to arrange to have powerful reinforcers available.

Using the Same Vocabulary to Indicate Different Communicative Intents

Even though learners may articulate a vocabulary item clearly, the intent of the communicative act may be unclear. Say, for example, a learner is consuming cookies and milk at snacktime. Just as the last sip of milk is consumed, a peer spills his milk all over the floor. After obtaining the teacher's attention, the learner touches a symbol signifying milk. In the absence of any additional communicative behavior, it may be difficult to determine whether the learner's utterance was intended as a request for more milk or a comment describing the accident that had just occurred. In describing her own child's emerging repertoire, Bloom (1970) observed that vocabulary initially tended to be used to express a singular communicative intent quickly began to be expanded to other communicative intents. Lamarre and Holland (1985) investigated the functional independence of requests and provisions of information in preschool children. Some participants initially learned to direct the experimenter's placement of objects with the prepositional phrases "on the left" and "on the right." At regular intervals during acquisition, probes were implemented to determine collateral acquisition of a corresponding repertoire using the same vocabulary to describe the position of objects that had been placed. The remaining children learned to describe the location of objects with the same phrases in which they were asked to direct others to place objects. Results demonstrated that acquisition of the phrases as directives did not lead to collateral acquisition of a corresponding describing repertoire and vice versa, even though

the same vocabulary was involved in both repertoires. For six of the nine children, requests and provisions of information remained functionally independent after acquisition. A similar lack of generalization across these response classes has been observed in chimpanzees (Savage-Rumbaugh, 1984), disadvantaged preschool children (Hart & Risley, 1968), and learners with developmental disabilities (Glennen & Calculator, 1985; Hall & Sundberg, 1987; McCook, Cipani, Madigan, & LaCampagne, 1988; Reichle & Yoder, 1985; Romski, Sevcik, & Pate, 1988), although among learners with developmental disabilities there appear to be certain training parameters that may facilitate transfer from describing to requesting relationships (Sigafoos, Doss, & Reichle, 1989; Sigafoos, Reichle, Doss, Hall, & Pettitt, in press).

Using Different Vocabulary to Refer to the Same Object

The selection of different vocabulary (and sometimes different communicative intents) depending on the conditions under which the object is presented represents a critical aspect of communicative intents.

The main difficulty in learning to generalize a particular vocabulary item from one communicative function (i.e., requesting) to another (i.e., describing) seems to rest with failure to receive opportunities to express different communicative intents using the same referent. First, some vocabulary items are predisposed to be matched with particular communicative intents. For example, Snickers™ bars may be so strongly preferred by a particular learner that the word or symbol for Snickers™ tends to be used largely for requests. The interventionist must carefully engineer opportunities for this vocabulary item to be used in expressing other communicative intents. For example, after the learner has consumed the Snickers™ bar, another person in the learner's environment might ask, "What did you have for a snack?", thus creating an opportunity in the same setting to use a word or symbol usually associated with requesting to provide information.

Early in the learner's intervention history, some vocabulary may be somewhat overused to express a single communicative intent, thereby creating a communicative intent bias for some vocabulary. The solution to this problem appears to lie in creating instructional opportunities in which the same vocabulary item must be used to express several different communicative intents. This topic has received little attention in the literature.

The main objection to the concurrent implementation of several different intents using the same vocabulary is that it represents a more sophisticated discrimination task for the learner. Keogh and Reichle (1985) suggested a strategy that involved the use of stimulating response generalization as a method of clarifying communicative intent. Initially, the learner was taught a generalized communicative symbol to signify an entire class of communicative intent (i.e., "want" for requesting). Concurrently, object labels were introduced as provisions of information. Once these two pragmatic classes had been introduced, opportunities were created in which producing more explicit requests would be advantageous. To handle these opportunities, the learner was taught to chain his or her generalized requesting symbol to one of the previously learned object labels. Over time the rule established was to request an explicit item by marking the object label with "want." If the learner were simply commenting or providing information, he or she was taught to use the object label in isolation. (This strategy is described in greater detail in Chapter 5.)

Whether the interventionist pursues the generalization strategy suggested by Keogh and Reichle (1985) or chooses to introduce two different intents that may be expressed using the same vocabulary item, he or she must carefully consider whether the intent to be addressed is relevant for the learner. Too often learners are taught to comment or provide information when

they have virtually no interest in sharing information. Intervention procedures must therefore ensure an appropriate match between the expressed intent and the related context.

Applying Two Different Communicative Intents to the Same Referent Object

The selection of different vocabulary (and in this case different communicative intents) as a function of the conditions under which the referent object is presented represents a critical aspect of producing communicative intents. Often, interventionists teach communicative intents under such rigid and nonvarying stimulus conditions that acquisition of a particular communicative intent has very limited applicability. For example, if rejecting responses are always taught in the presence of disliked items, the learner may never learn to reject an item that is normally a strong reinforcer, but is not desired on a particular occasion. A learner who has been taught to reject only in the presence of undesired items is not likely, for example, to reject an offer of a sixth cup of coffee but is apt either to produce no response or to request the coffee but then refrain from drinking it.

Often the conditions selected for instruction too rigidly define the class of behavior being taught. The interventionist must carefully perform an ecological inventory (see Chapter 3) to determine those conditions that are likely to be most useful to each learner. The conditional use of different communicative intents as a function of conditional relationships between the learner and aspects of his or her environment represents a critical aspect of the social validity of any communicative behavior that a learner acquires. (Chapter 8 deals more directly with this important issue at a procedural level.)

SUMMARY

Since virtually all learners are assumed to engage in some form of communicative behavior, a primary responsibility for the interventionist is to upgrade the form of the learner's behavior to a level that meets the community's standards of social acceptability. The interventionist must also establish strategies to lessen the learner's dependence upon a listener to interpret his or her perlocutionary behavior as communicative. The author's experience and other data suggest that learners with severe disabilities tend to be highly motivated to obtain access to desired objects or activities and to avoid contact with objects and activities that are not desired. Of course, this may not be true of all learners. An

ecological analysis, described in Chapter 3, should thus be applied to determine which initial intents to teach.

The selection of initial communicative intents to teach is closely related to the selection of specific vocabulary to teach. The examples cited in this chapter focus on the selection of generalized rather than more explicit communicative symbols. The use of communicative intents requires that the learner acquire relatively sophisticated conditional uses of communicative intents. Often these conditional uses focus on the same referent object or event.

REFERENCES

Anglin, J.M. (1977). *Word, object, and conceptual development*. New York: Norton.

Bates, E., Benigni, L., Bretheton, I., Camioni, L., & Volterra, V. (1979a). Cognition and communication from 9–13 months: Correlational findings. In E. Bates, L. Benigni, I. Bretheton, L. Camioni, & V. Volterra (Eds.), *The emergence of symbols: Cognition and communication in infancy* (pp. 69–140). New York: Academic Press.

Bates, E., Benigni, L., Bretheton, I., Camioni, L., & Volterra, V. (1979b). *The emergence of symbols: Cognition and communication in infancy*. New York: Academic Press.

Bates, E., Camioni, L., & Volterra, V. (1975). The acquisition of performatives prior to speech. *Merrill-Palmer Quarterly, 21*(3), 205–226.

Bloom, L. (1970). *Language development: Form and function in emerging grammars*. Cambridge: MIT Press.

Cirrin, F., & Rowland, C. (1985). Communicative assessment of nonverbal youths with severe/profound mental retardation. *Mental Retardation, 23*(2), 52–62.

Coggins, T., & Carpenter, R. (1981). The communication intention inventory: A system for observing and coding children's early, intentional communication. *Applied Psycholinguistics, 2,* 235–252.

Glennen, S.L., & Calculator, S.N. (1985). Training functional communication board use: A pragmatic approach. *Augmentative and Alternative Communication, 1,* 134–142.

Guess, D., Sailor, W., & Baer, D. (1974). To teach language to retarded children. In R.L. Schiefel-

busch & L. Lloyd (Eds.), *Language perspectives: Acquisition, retardation, and intervention* (pp. 529–563). Baltimore: University Park Press.

Hall, G., & Sundberg, M.L. (1987). Teaching mands by manipulating conditional establishing operations. *Analysis of Verbal Behavior, 5,* 41–53.

Hart, B. (1985). Naturalistic language training techniques. In S. Warren & A. Rogers-Warren (Eds.), *Teaching functional language* (pp. 63–88). Baltimore: University Park Press.

Hart, B.M., & Risley, T.R. (1968). Establishing use of descriptive adjective in the spontaneous speech of disadvantaged preschool children. *Journal of Applied Behavior Analysis, 1,* 109–120.

Kent, L. (1974). *Language acquisition program for the retarded or multiply impaired*. Champaign, IL: Research Press.

Keogh, W., & Reichle, J. (1985). *Communication instruction for learners with severe handicaps: Some unresolved issues*. Unpublished manuscript, University of Minnesota, Minneapolis.

Lamarre, J., & Holland, J.G. (1985). The functional independence of mands and tacts. *Journal of the Experimental Analysis of Behavior, 43,* 5–19.

Lovaas, O.I. (1977). *The autistic child: Language development through behavior modification*. New York: Irvington.

McCook, B., Cipani, E., Madigan, K., & LaCampagne, J. (1988). Developing requesting behavior: Acquisition, fluency and generality. *Mental Retardation, 26*(3), 137–143.

McLean, J., & Snyder-McLean, L. (1988). Application of pragmatics to severely mentally retarded children and youth. In R. Schiefelbusch & L.L.

Lloyd (Eds.), *Language perspectives: Acquisition, retardation and intervention* (pp. 255–288). Austin, TX: PRO-ED.

McLean, J., Snyder-McLean, L., & Cirrin, F. (1981). *Communication performatives and representational behaviors in severely mentally retarded adolescents.* Miniseminar conducted at the annual meeting of the Speech-Language-Hearing Association, Los Angeles.

Papousek, H. (1978). The infant's fundamental adaptive response system in social interaction. In S. Trotter & E.B. Thoman (Eds.), *Social responsiveness of infants* (pp. 27–37). New York: Johnson & Johnson.

Reichle, J., & Keogh, W. (1985). A selected review of what, when, and how to teach. In S. Warren & A. Rogers-Warren (Eds.), *Teaching functional language* (pp. 25–59). Baltimore: University Park Press.

Reichle, J., & Yoder, D.E. (1985). Communication board use in severely handicapped learners. *Language, Speech and Hearing Services in Schools, 16,* 146–157.

Rheingold, H., Gewirtz, J., & Ross, H. (1959). Social conditioning of vocalization in the infant. *Journal of Comparative Psychology, 52,* 68–73.

Romski, M.A., Sevcik, R.A., & Pate, J.L. (1988). Establishment of symbolic communication in persons with severe mental retardation. *Journal of Speech and Hearing Disorders, 53,* 94–107.

Savage-Rumbaugh, E. (1984). Verbal behavior at a procedural level in a chimpanzee. *Journal of the Experimental Analysis of Behavior, 41,* 223–250.

Sigafoos, J., Doss, S., & Reichle, J. (1989). Developing mand and tact repertoiries in persons with severe developmental disabilities using graphic symbols. *Research in Developmental Disabilities, 10,* 183–200.

Sigafoos, J., Reichle, J., Doss, S., Hall, K., & Pettitt, L. (in press). "Spontaneous" transfer of stimulus control from tact to mand contingencies. *Research in Developmental Disabilities.*

Skinner, B.F. (1957). *Verbal behavior.* New York: Appleton-Century-Crofts.

Stillman, R. Alymer, J., & Vandivort, J. (1983, June). *The functions of signaling behaviors in profoundly impaired deaf-blind children and adolescents.* Paper presented at the 107th annual meeting of The American Association on Mental Deficiency, Dallas, TX.

Watson, J. (1978). Perception of contingency as a determinant of social responsiveness. In S. Trotter & E. Thoman (Eds.), *Social responsiveness of infants.* New York: Johnson & Johnson.

Weisberg, P. (1963). Social and nonsocial conditioning of infant vocalizations. *Child Development, 39,* 377–388.

5

Establishing an Initial Repertoire of Requesting

Joe Reichle and Jeff Sigafoos

OBJECTS AND ACTIVITIES in the environment that learners make some effort to pursue can be described as "liked" or "preferred." Obtaining such preferred items often requires the mediation of a listener. At a restaurant, for example, patrons generally do not enter the kitchen and rummage through the pantry looking for something to eat, but instead order, or request, their meals from a server. In this example, the server can be viewed as a listener who mediates the customer's request. Many preferred objects and activities are best obtained through the mediation of another person, and such situations call for some type of requesting behavior on the part of the learner. In the request, preferred items are presented as reinforcement of the response. This chapter highlights factors to consider in establishing an initial repertoire of requests, describes the types of requests that can be taught, and outlines procedures for teaching learners to request preferred objects and activities appropriately in vocal, gestural, and graphic modes. Assuming there are at least some objects and activities that the learner will make some effort to pursue, developing an effective repertoire of

communicative behavior can begin by teaching requests. Reasons for teaching requesting are summarized in Table 1.

REASONS FOR TEACHING REQUESTING

One expected outcome of communication intervention involving people with severe disabilities is the ability to express wants and needs. Teaching learners to request preferred or needed items is one way to achieve this outcome. Teaching learners to name an internal state,

Table 1.   Reasons for teaching requesting

—Provides the learner with a means of obtaining access to preferred objects and activities

—Provides the learner with a means of obtaining needed objects or actions

—Allows the learner to exert some measure of control over the environment

—Allows initial intervention demands to be associated with receipt of preferred items, perhaps facilitating future intervention efforts

—May replace existing repertoires of attention or object-motivated excess behaviors

such as a toothache or chest pains, is also important (Sundberg, 1983). Occasionally, both skills—requesting a preferred item and naming an internal state—are used simultaneously, as, for example, when a learner requests an aspirin to counteract a headache. The ability to label the internal pain as a "headache," however, will not necessarily lead to the corresponding action of requesting an aspirin, although the prior label may serve as a rationale for the subsequent request.

Learners who can request are able to express their wants and needs (Guess, Sailor, & Baer, 1974). Requesting is thus functional in the sense that it often produces changes that are of benefit to the speaker (Skinner, 1957). Once learners can express their wants they can, for example, receive food when hungry or a drink when thirsty. Most other classes of communicative behavior function primarily for the benefit of the listener (Skinner, 1957). It is the listener who benefits from being told "It's raining," for example, because he or she can then take steps to keep dry, such as staying indoors or using an umbrella. The role of the speaker in commenting upon an event such as an imminent rain shower is maintained by the social reinforcement supplied by the listener (e.g., "Thank you."). Many learners with severe disabilities are not reinforced by such social attention and, hence, efforts to teach communicative behaviors with purely social consequences may prove difficult as an initial intervention target. In contrast, when requesting is taught as an initial communicative behavior, learners are exposed to interventions that benefit them directly. By beginning with requesting, these once "asocial" learners may eventually become more receptive to the types of interventions designed to teach the more social forms of communication (Michael, 1988). Teaching requests provides learners with a useful skill, and may also facilitate the teaching of other communicative intents.

Related to these benefits is the possibility that interventionists implementing requesting strategies may become reinforcers through their roles as providers of preferred objects and activities. As a result of requesting intervention, the initially asocial learner may show an increased tendency to approach and interact with others, particularly with the interventionists. This increased tendency for interaction provides the opportunities for implementing procedures to teach more social or conversationally related communicative skills in an incidental format (see Chapter 8).

Another reason for teaching requesting is that doing so may help to replace existing repertoires of excess behavior maintained by positive reinforcement contingencies (see Chapter 11). Even learners who have not learned conventional or formal systems of requesting are likely to desire access to certain objects or activities. These learners may have learned unconventional or unacceptable means of requesting. Some learners, for example, may have learned that grabbing is an effective means of obtaining items (Horner & Budd, 1985). Other learners may engage in aggressive or self-injurious acts because such actions have been followed by access to effective reinforcers, such as attention from staff. Appropriate requests for preferred objects (Horner & Budd, 1985) or attention (Carr & Durand, 1985) may serve as functional equivalents to such excess behaviors (Carr, 1988).

There are, thus, several reasons for teaching requesting. The potential number of requests that can be taught is infinite. It may be best to begin by teaching a few relatively simple requests, such as teaching learners to request preferred objects or activities when offered (Sundberg, 1983). A prerequisite to beginning intervention to teach such requests is, therefore, the identification of those objects or activities that are preferred by the learner. Strategies for identifying preferred items are described in the following sections.

IDENTIFYING REINFORCERS

Interviews

Objects or activities that can be used in a requesting program can be identified in several ways (Table 2). The easiest way would be simply to ask the learner which things he or she likes. Of course, if the learner could respond, he or she would probably not require communication intervention in the first place. This dilemma is commonly solved by querying people familiar with the learner. Parents, teachers, or caregivers are asked which objects or activities the learner likes or dislikes. The items generated by such interviews are then used as consequences for correct responses when teaching requesting or rejecting. Items that are liked are assumed to be positive reinforcers and become the focus of requesting intervention. Items that are disliked are assumed to be negative reinforcers and become the focus of rejecting intervention, described in Chapter 6.

Identifying reinforcers by interviewing people familiar with the learner rests upon two assumptions. First, the information obtained is assumed to be reliable. The reliability of this information may depend on several factors, such as how well the person knows the learner or how clearly the learner indicates preferences. Some learners may show little or no change in behavior when presented with potential reinforcers, making it difficult to determine if they

Table 2. Strategies for identifying reinforcers

—Ask the learner.

—Ask parents, instructors, peers, and significant others which objects and activities the learner likes.

—Observe the learner to determine activities frequently engaged in, or the effort expended to obtain access to objects or activities.

—Measure approach to presented items.

—Record selections among presented objects, both when one item is offered at a time and when several items are offered simultaneously.

prefer a particular object. In addition, the presence of motor disabilities may limit the extent of interaction with materials, thus making it difficult for caregivers to judge a learner's preferences. Second, objects or activities identified as likes or dislikes are assumed to function as effective positive or negative reinforcement. In fact, reinforcement involves a relationship. Before it is meaningful to call an object a reinforcer that object must be shown to strengthen the behavior upon which it is contingent. Often objects or activities identified by caregivers as preferred are simply assumed to be reinforcers. These objects or activities may show little correlation with the actual reinforcing capacity of these objects, however (Green et al., 1988).

Because of the problems associated with identifying reinforcers by asking, this technique should be used as a preliminary method of screening with which to identify a set of potential reinforcers. Objects or activities identified can then be subjected to more rigorous and systematic assessment to determine if they are indeed functional reinforcers.

Systematic Preference Testing

More systematic assessments have been used to identify potential reinforcers. Most of these efforts involve gauging a learner's preference for presented stimuli (Dattilo & Mirenda, 1987; Green et al., 1988; Pace, Ivancic, Edwards, Iwata, & Page, 1985; Wacker, Berg, Wiggins, Muldoon, & Cavanaugh, 1985).

Watching a Learner Approach an Item Pace et al. (1985) presented 16 objects 10 times to 6 children and adolescents with profound mental retardation. During each presentation learners were observed to determine their preferences. An item was said to be "preferred" when it was approached within 5 seconds on at least 80% of the trials. The items that were preferred varied, indicating the individualized nature of preferences. Most learners did approach some items, suggesting the usefulness of the approach/nonapproach dichotomy.

Preferred and nonpreferred items were then tested to determine if they did, in fact, function as reinforcers. For each learner a specific response (e.g., reach, look, say "eat") was selected. These responses were followed by either a preferred or a nonpreferred stimulus. Generally, the use of preferred objects as consequences increased the rate of correct responses. Thus, preference, as defined by high levels of approach to presented stimuli, appears to be positively correlated with reinforcing effectiveness. Gauging preferences in terms of approach/nonapproach to presented objects thus appears to be one reliable method of identifying reinforcers—a method that is perhaps more reliable than staff opinions regarding a learner's likes and dislikes (Green et al., 1988).

Measuring the Degree of Effort Exerted to Gain Access to an Item Preference for objects has also been gauged by determining how much effort a learner will put forth to gain access to an object. For example, Wacker et al. (1985) arranged so that some motor movements (e.g., raise arm, raise head) exhibited by five learners with multiple disabilities would activate a microswitch that in turn operated various devices (e.g., taped music, colored lights, a toy robot). The length of time learners activated each device served as the measure of preference. Microswitches were also used by Dattilo and Mirenda (1987) to determine preferences among learners with severe disabilities. Both studies found that learners responded at different rates depending on the device that was activated by the microswitch. These differential response rates indicate a sensitivity to the programmed consequences. The two studies also showed that objects identified as "preferred" were indeed functional reinforcers. That is, some objects effectively reinforced the movements that activated the devices. Learners thus requested an object by activating a particular device. The microswitch thus became the mediator through which access to the operation of devices was achieved. In a similar man-

ner, pointing to a "want" symbol may be the method by which a learner requests preferred objects, access to which is mediated by a listener.

Watching A Learner Select An Item Another technique for identifying reinforcers involves offering objects to learners and noting those items most frequently accepted (Keogh & Reichle, 1985). The procedure is similar to the microswitch technique. In this task, however, the learner indicates preference in a more direct manner by actually reaching for and grasping an item, as opposed to touching a switch to activate various devices. Initially, these items might be those reported by caregivers as highly preferred. Each time the items are offered the learner is allowed to select one item. This sequence is repeated until clear trends emerge in the learner's choice of items.

This assessment can be performed in two ways. Objects can be offered one at a time, or several objects can be offered simultaneously. In the first approach, a preferred item would be one that was selected relatively often. As a general rule, items selected 80% or more of the time they are offered tend to be functional reinforcers (Pace et al., 1985). In the second approach, preference is gauged by comparing the number of times a particular item is selected relative to other items (Sigafoos, 1989). Unfortunately, in comparing rates of selection across a number of items, there are no rules or guidelines for determining when a difference becomes important.

In both approaches preference is gauged by the frequency with which a particular item is selected relative to the number of times the item is made available. Items selected more frequently are assumed to be preferred over items selected less frequently. If all items are selected with equal frequency, they are assumed to be preferred equally. Such a result, however, may indicate that the learner fails to discriminate among the offered items. Lack of discrimination may arise because all of the items offered represent reinforcers. Since any selection the learner makes is reinforced, there is no need for the learner to note which item is being selected. One way to force the learner to pay attention to which item he or she selects is to include some neutral or undesirable objects. A piece of scrap paper or an empty cup is not likely to be a preferred item relative to, say, a favorite snack food. To avoid obtaining a nonpreferred item, the learner must attend more carefully to the objects he or she selects.

Another potential problem occurs when none of the offered items is a reinforcer. In this case the problem is a lack of selection. Assuming motoric impairments can be ruled out as the reason for the lack of selection, new items should be added to those being offered. Ideas for new items to add might come from interviews with caregivers, or from observations of the learner, noting in particular those objects and activities to which the learner willingly subjects him- or herself.

A final potential problem is that the learner may select all available items. This type of selection pattern may create difficulties when attempting to implement more than one or two instructional opportunities without the learner becoming satiated, or the supply of reinforcers being exhausted. It may, therefore, prove useful to teach a learner who selects all items in an array to make a single choice. Several methods can be used. The offered items can be spaced far enough apart so that any attempt by the learner to reach for a second item can be easily interrupted. One simple way to interrupt a reach for a second item is to remove the available items after a single choice has been made. If removal of the items is not feasible, the interventionist may instead unobtrusively block any attempt of the learner to select more than one item. A third potential solution, which could be used in combination with the other two, is to reinforce selection of a single item. Should the learner select only one item, for example, he or she could then be given a second preferred item. Although giving the learner an additional preferred item for selecting just one may seem counterintuitive, such a procedure should eventually teach the learner that the magnitude of reinforcement is greater for initially selecting only one item, provided the learner is willing to tolerate a slight delay in receiving the second reinforcer.

A learner may also show a very strong preference for one particular item, selecting it to the exclusion of all others. For example, a learner may always select the potato chip, regardless of what else is offered. In order to get a broader view of the learner's preferences it may help to remove the highly preferred item from the array after it has been selected, say, three consecutive times (Keogh & Reichle, 1985). Once the highly preferred item is removed, the learner may no longer reach for any of the other available objects. If this happens it may be that for this learner there is only one preferred item. Before reaching this conclusion, however, several attempts should be made to replace the highly preferred item. It may be that the learner is simply waiting for the preferred item to reappear and may ultimately select other items once he or she realizes that the original item will not reappear.

Some learners will lack the motor skills necessary to select offered objects. For those learners an alternative method of selection may be necessary. Some other reliable response, such as looking at an item for several seconds, may serve as a replacement for reaching. Green et al. (1988), for example, accepted as "approach" behavior such diverse actions as: 1) "an apparent voluntary . . . movement . . . ," 2) ". . . maintaining contact with the stimulus . . . ," or 3) ". . . positive facial expression[s] . . . positive vocalizations" (p. 32). Systematic assessment protocols to identify reinforcers can be adapted to accommodate learners with physical impairments (Wacker et al., 1985).

Other Measures Other measures that may

reliably indicate a learner's likes and dislikes are also available. For example, the rate at which a particular food or beverage item is consumed may be a good indicator of how much the item is preferred. Consider a young child who eats her vegetables in a very slow and methodical fashion and tends to spill them frequently, with little or no inclination to pick them up. Should a morsel of a candy bar find its way to the floor, however, it would be retrieved and consumed enthusiastically. Rate of consumption, amount spilled or left untouched, and anticipatory behaviors may thus be used as estimates of preference, in addition to or as supplements for more direct measures of approach or selection. Table 2 summarizes the strategies described for identifying preferences. These strategies will typically yield a list of preferred objects or activities. Some of these items may be used as reinforcers when teaching requests.

Testing the Validity of the Preferences as Reinforcers   Whether these potential reinforcers are indeed functional in the sense of strengthening a request must be determined empirically. A behavior could be selected and access provided to the potential reinforcers each time that behavior occurs. If the number of times the selected behavior was performed increases as a result, then the item selected is validated as functional reinforcers. It is useful to test the reinforcing effect of various items by having the learner point to a symbol that serves to communicate "I want something." In this way the reinforcer is tested and the learner may acquire a useful skill. Of course, the skill is useful only if the learner is considered to be a good candidate for a graphic-mode requesting program. It makes sense, therefore, to implement a requesting program after a list of potential reinforcers has been generated by interviews and systematic assessment techniques. Testing these potential reinforcers for their actual reinforcing effects can then occur in the context of teaching the request. If the requesting behavior is acquired during intervention, the results establish that the objects and/or activities used did indeed function as reinforcers. If the skill is not acquired during intervention, the problem may or may not result from the lack of effective reinforcers.

MODES OF REQUESTING OFFERED OBJECTS

In the prototypic request, a preferred item is offered, the learner makes the appropriate request, and the preferred item is received. This sequence is illustrated in Figure 1. The actual requesting response in this prototypic example could have consisted of a speech act (vocal mode), a manual sign (gestural mode), or the selection of a given line drawing or photograph (graphic mode). Specific intervention issues related to establishing an initial repertoire of requesting in each of those three modes are examined in the following sections.

Vocal Mode

Requesting in the vocal mode is straightforward: a preferred item is offered and delivered after the learner utters or vocalizes the appropriate response. Intervention is often needed to establish this sequence, because many learners will not vocalize a request.

To learn to request preferred objects or activities vocally, the learner must be capable of producing vocal behavior, and the interventionist must have some effective means of prompting the learner's vocalization at the appropriate time. These two requirements mean that either the learner will independently produce some consistent vocalization—in which case intervention will focus on bringing that vocalization under the control of appropriate motivational or contextual variables—or the learner will correctly imitate the interventionist's modeled speech—in which case intervention will focus on fading the imitative prompt and bringing the vocalization under appropriate stimulus control. For learners who do not vocalize or

Prototypic Requesting Sequence (Objects)

Stimulus

Response

Consequence

Interventionist offers a preferred item or an array of preferred items. May also ask, "What do you want?" → Learner produces requesting response (e.g., "want" or "want" plus "apple"). → Interventionist delivers preferred item or provides access to array.

Prototypic Requesting Sequence (Actions)

Stimulus

Response

Consequence

Difficult task → Learner requests assistance (e.g., "help"). → Listener supplies needed assistance.

Figure 1. Prototypic requesting sequence showing stimulus, response, and consequences.

who do so infrequently, efforts will first be directed at increasing the frequency of vocal behavior. For learners who vocalize but do not imitate speech, efforts should be directed at teaching vocal imitation.

Once the frequency of vocal behavior has been increased or a repertoire of imitative speech has been acquired, transfer of stimulus control procedures can be implemented to establish vocal-mode requests. Suppose, for example, that the current controlling variables for a learner's speech are the imitative models supplied by others. The learner shows no tendency to ask for a preferred object when presented with one, but will readily utter the correct response when prompted to do so. A functional request is sought, however, in which the learner asks for the preferred item when it is offered without having to be prompted. Functional requests can

be established in this case by initially prompting the learner to say "want" when offered preferred items and gradually fading the imitative prompt over successive opportunities. Imitative prompts might be faded by delaying the model or by providing less and less of a model over trials (e.g., "say 'want,' " "say 'wan,' " "say 'wa,' " "say"), eventually providing no model at all, but simply waiting for the learner to request. It is important to realize that as control by the imitative prompt is being faded, stimulus control over the response is being acquired by other aspects of the environment, such as the general context in which the offer is made.

Gestural Mode

A request in the gestural mode serves the same function as a request in the vocal mode. Rather than vocalize the request, however, the learner makes an appropriate gesture, and the gesture is reinforced by access to the preferred object or activity. Gestures might consist of formal signs (i.e., American Sign Language [ASL], Signed Exact English [SEE] signs), natural gestures (e.g., nodding one's head up and down to indicate "yes"), or idiosyncratic movements (e.g., raising an arm to a certain height).

Sign languages and sign systems are understood by a relatively small number of people, and the signs themselves are for the most part not highly guessable. Repertoires of requests consisting of manual signs may not be reinforced by listeners unfamiliar with the sign, and hence such repertoires may become extinguished. Similar problems may be faced by learners whose idiosyncratic gestures are understood by only a few close friends, family members, educators, or caregivers. Thus, although their breadth and specificity is limited, natural gestures appear to have the largest potential audience.

Candidates for gestural mode requesting might engage in some acceptable motor behavior, or might need to be taught a completely new gesture. In the former case, intervention efforts focus on the transfer of stimulus control from the current controlling variable to the offer and subsequent receipt of preferred items. In the latter case, intervention could follow a more standard prompt and fade procedure. It is not clear whether it is easier to change the stimulus control of existing gestures or to establish new gestures. In either case, a wider range of prompts is available in teaching requests in the gestural mode than in the vocal mode.

To prompt a correct request in either the gestural or the vocal mode, an interventionist might display an object, speak or sign a specific instruction, or model appropriate behavior (by demonstrating the correct sign or telling the learner what to say). Should these prompts prove ineffective in recruiting a correct response, the interventionist teaching in the vocal mode is left with no recourse, whereas the interventionist teaching in the gestural mode can physically prompt the desired response by taking hold of the learner's hands and arms and guiding them through the correct movement. Because gestures can be physically prompted, procedures to teach requesting can be implemented with learners who do not vocalize or imitate speech. Generalized imitation of motor movements might facilitate gestural mode instruction, but intervention can proceed even in the absence of such a response class.

The basic requesting sequence in the gestural mode can initially be arranged as shown in Figure 1. In this sequence a single or perhaps an array of preferred items is offered. Access to offered items occurs immediately after the learner's requests. During the early phases of intervention, learners may show little tendency to form the desired gesture when offered preferred items, but may instead attempt to reach for the offered item or items. The early phase of intervention may thus require substantial response prompting. At first, as soon as the preferred item is offered the learner is prompted to make the request gesture. Any prompt (e.g., verbal, model, physical) that will reliably recruit the request is given. Prompts can also be arranged from least to most intrusive.

Eventually, of course, the learner should request without the assistance of an instructional prompt. Instead, the natural cue or natural discriminative stimulus of an offered item should be sufficient to evoke a request, provided the item offered is an effective reinforcer at that moment. Instructional prompts must therefore be faded or eliminated. Such fading can begin shortly after a few initial responses have been successfully prompted. Once a learner has been prompted to make a gestural mode request, that prompt can then be delayed a few seconds and delivered at a slightly lower intensity on the next opportunity. If successful the delay interval is increased and the magnitude of the prompt decreased. If at some point the now delayed and reduced prompt fails to recruit the request, the interventionist can return to a previously effective level of prompting and continue to fade, this time more gradually. Fading continues in this manner until eventually the learner requests offered objects by producing the correct gesture without having to be prompted. Fading has proved to be effective in eliminating the need for response prompts.

Gestures themselves can be broken down into a series of discrete steps. By doing so, interventionists can then direct prompts to individual steps of the gesture, or to only those steps that require assistance. Figure 2 shows a task analysis for the ASL sign "want." Four steps have been delineated. Initially, learners may require prompting at every step to produce the gesture, as was the case on June 21. The next day (June 22) only the first three steps required prompting, with the final step completed independently. Subsequent days (June 23 and June 24) showed continued improvement, with the learner independently completing the final two steps but continuing to need prompting for steps one and two. This trend suggests that continued intervention and efforts to fade prompts would eventually establish independent productions of the entire "want" sign. Figure 2 shows how a

task analysis can be adapted for use as a data collection form.

Graphic Mode

The requesting relationship in the graphic mode follows essentially the same sequence as in the vocal and gestural modes. In the prototypic sequence, the offer of preferred objects or events provides optimal conditions for a request to be reinforced. The only difference is that instead of the requesting response consisting of some distinct vocalization or gesture, the requesting response typically consists of the learner selecting a particular symbol, line drawing, or photograph. In the generalized request, for example, access to an array of preferred objects is made contingent upon selection of a "want" symbol.

Typically, learners are taught to select a symbol by pointing to it with an isolated index finger. Some learners will not be able to do this, and may instead point with a group of fingers or an assisting device, such as a head- or mouthstick, or brush the symbol with their hands. Other learners may have to look at the symbol (eye gaze) for a predetermined length of time. As long as at least one reliable method can be identi-

Step	Motor Movement	Performance			
1	Learner brings both hands to waist level.	-	-	-	-
2	Learner turns hands so that palms are directed upwards.	-	-	-	-
3	Learner flexes all fingers and thumbs inward as if gripping a softball.	-	-	+	+
4	Learner pulls both arms toward chest, without actual bodily contact.	-	+	+	+
Date		6/21	6/22	6/23	6/24

Key
+ = Correct (performed without prompts)
 - = Incorrect (required physical prompts)

Figure 2. Task analysis of the ASL sign "want."

fied for selecting symbols the graphic mode can be considered.

In teaching a repertoire of requests, the interventionist can use a variety of response prompts, including physical prompts. As in the gestural mode, learners can, if necessary, be prompted to point to a symbol by actually guiding their fingers to touch the line drawing, photograph, or other type of symbol. Other prompts that may be effective include the modeling of a symbol selection (e.g., the interventionist points to the correct symbol), or verbal prompts (e.g., telling the learner to point to "want"). In addition, several types of stimulus prompts are available to recruit the desired behavior. As in other modes, prompts are delivered initially to recruit a correct symbol selection, and then gradually faded to obtain independent performance.

TYPES OF REQUESTS

Requesting can be viewed as part of a larger class of communicative or verbal behavior termed *mands* (Skinner, 1957). A mand is a type of verbal behavior whose form is often said to specify its reinforcement. For example, "stop" is reinforced as a mand by someone stopping. The mand "help" is reinforced when a listener supplies assistance. Some mands (e.g., "Tell me your name," "What time is it?") are reinforced by other verbal behavior (information). The response class of manding includes such diverse relationships as commanding, demanding, requesting, and rejecting. Requesting consists of at least two broad classes. So far this chapter has focused on only one of these types, the requests for objects and activities. In this type of request the effective reinforcer is the receipt of or granting of access to the requested object or activity. This is the type of request diagramed in Figure 1. Within this class of request, several levels are possible. The request for an object can occur in the presence or absence of the object. A request for a donut can be made after an unopened package of donuts is seen. Alternatively, a bowl of soup unaccompanied by a spoon can motivate the request "spoon, please." Requests for objects can also be explicit or generalized, as discussed later in this chapter.

A second broad class of requests involves forms that specify a particular listener action. In this type of request, known as requests for listener action, the effective type of reinforcer is a corresponding action on the part of another. "Sit here" is reinforced as a mand when the listener locates him- or herself in a particular place and position. Requesting assistance is a good example of a mand reinforced by a particular action. Assistance from another is often an effective type of reinforcement when confronted with a difficult task, and thus requests for assistance are likely to occur under such conditions. Such a sequence is outlined in the bottom half of Figure 1. Like requests for objects and activities, requests for listener action can consist of generalized (e.g., "Help") or more explicit (e.g., "Open this") forms. The next section considers the advantages and disadvantages of explicit versus generalized requests. Procedures for teaching both generalized and explicit requests are then detailed. Finally, special considerations for teaching both requests for listener action and requests for assistance are described.

Levels of Explicitness

Communicative forms refer to the sounds, words, phrases, signs, or gestures that a learner uses to request, or to the symbols, photographs, or line drawings a learner is taught to select. All of these forms can be considered the *vocabulary* of the communication system. Vocabulary taught as requests can be represented at various levels of generality. The level of generality, in turn, affects the nature of the request taught. Vocabulary items such as "want," for example, are more general than "food" or "drink," which are in turn more general than "cookie," "fruit," or "juice." The nature of the request corresponding to these different levels of vocabulary might best be conceptualized along a continuum from generalized requests ("want") to more explicit requests ("apple"). Figure 3 illustrates this continuum, with intermediate levels of vocabulary arbitrarily designated as generic requests. For a learner who prefers cookies, fruit, music, and perhaps several other such classes of items, the interventionist must decide whether to teach explicit, generic, or more generalized requests.

Operationally, when a learner makes a request, he or she is provided as a consequence with the item specified. Different types of requests imply different types of consequences. For example, when a learner points to a "cookie" symbol on a communication board, any one of several types of cookies could be provided.

In contrast, a more explicit request, such as a request for an Oreo™, is likely to be met with a particular type of cookie. The differences in reinforcement strategies associated with these different types of requests are likely to influence various aspects of intervention, such as the rate of vocabulary acquisition.

Data generated from studies of language development among children without disabilities provide conflicting guidelines for the selection of an initial requesting strategy. Some data show that children without disabilities more readily acquire generic (e.g., "collie") or more generalized (e.g., "animal") vocabulary when learning to name a class of objects (Anglin, 1977). However, naming an object represents a different class of behavior from requesting an object (Hall & Sundberg, 1987; Lamarre & Holland, 1985; Skinner, 1957). In addition, Bloom and Lahey (1978) have noted that a child's use of vocabulary may not always correspond to the adult usage of those same terms. A common observation is that children often overgeneralize and/or undergeneralize when using a particular term. For example, one child may use the term "dog" only in the presence of the family pet (undergeneralization), whereas another child may call all four-legged animals "dogs."

Generalized Requests

There may be several advantages to teaching more generalized or generic forms of requests. For example, learners with several varied reinforcers may benefit from learning a more generalized request. The generalized request "want" or the generic request "cookie," for example, could be used to gain access to the entire range of preferred items or cookies. These skills provide the learner with an immediately useful requesting strategy without having to establish a large vocabulary. More generalized requests may also be effective with learners whose preferences shift. Even if some preferences change

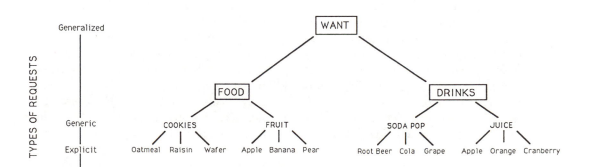

Figure 3.   Levels of vocabulary generality and the type of request corresponding to each level.

there may still be a large enough pool of reinforcers available to maintain generalized requesting. Third, the varied reinforcement associated with more generalized requesting may enable the interventionist to implement a higher density of instructional opportunities without the learner becoming satiated (Egel, 1980, 1981). This may be especially important for learners who acquire new skills only after repeated instruction. Finally, generalized requests may be more resistant to extinction, because they are more likely to be intermittently reinforced (Ferster & Skinner, 1957). Consider, for example, a learner who, given the choice, would select chocolate chip over oatmeal cookies. Should this learner point to a "cookie" symbol and be offered either an oatmeal or chocolate chip cookie on a random basis, approximately half the time the request might go unreinforced because it is followed by the less preferred cookie. At other times, however, the request is reinforced by the preferred cookie. In this example, selecting the "cookie" symbol is reinforced on a *variable-ratio schedule* (Catania, 1979). Had the learner been taught the explicit request "chocolate chip cookie," every request would have been followed by the preferred item and hence reinforcement would occur on a *continuous schedule*. However, the learner's communication partners may not be consistent in their reinforcement practices. A listener may be unable ("Sorry we are out of cookies.") or unwilling ("No! It will spoil your appetite.") to mediate a speaker's request. Whereas continuous reinforcement tends to speed acquisition (White & Haring, 1980), such "extinction trials" may be disruptive. In addition, resistance to extinction may represent an important dependent variable, particularly when one considers that many of the attempts to communicate made by augmentative users are likely to be ignored by listeners (Calculator, 1988).

Explicit Requests

Explicit requests are often required for clear communication in the community at large. For example, a learner could not order dinner at a restaurant by asking for "food." Explicit requests reduce the need for the listener to interpret, thus reducing the frequency of requests for clarification. For learners with a few specific and relatively stable preferences, or for learners who tend to acquire vocabulary relatively quickly, explicit requesting may represent the most practical option. For learners with few preferences, only a small vocabulary is needed, and a complete repertoire can thus be established relatively quickly. Learners who acquire vocabulary quickly are also able to develop a complete repertoire readily.

The nature of the explicit requesting relationship may itself facilitate the acquisition of the targeted vocabulary. Explicit requests are associated with specific response–reinforcer relationships. When a speaker requests "apple," "coffee," or "pencil," the form of the reinforcer in each case is restricted to a fairly narrow class of objects. The more explicit the request, the more circumscribed is the class of objects that will effectively serve as reinforcement. Only a particular type of apple will suffice when one requests a MacIntosh apple or a Granny Smith apple. The specific reinforcement associated with an explicit request may facilitate acquisition because of this one-to-one correspondence between the form of the response and the form of the consequence (Ferster, 1967, 1972), a relationship that has been called "reinforcer specificity" (Goetz, Schuler, & Sailor, 1979).

Several studies have investigated the effects of reinforcer specificity on teaching receptive (Litt & Schreibman, 1981; Saunders & Sailor, 1979) and expressive (Rogers & Siegel, 1984) language skills to learners with severe disabilities. The receptive language tasks have involved teaching learners to select the one object named by the interventionist from a two-item array. In contrast, expressive tasks involve teaching the learner to name an object displayed by the interventionist. With both types of tasks, reinforcer specificity consists of reinforcing correct responses by delivering the object selected or named. When the learner correctly selects the cookie when told "find cookie," or correctly names a cookie when asked, "What is that?", the reinforcer is the cookie selected or named. This stands in contrast to more arbitrary or nonspecific conditions, in which correct responses are reinforced with some other equally preferred but unrelated item (e.g., an apple, a sip of juice), or perhaps with one of several reinforcers presented on a random basis. With receptive tasks, acquisition is generally improved by use of reinforcer-specific strategies, although this advantage does not hold for all learners. The one case study that investigated the effects of reinforcer specificity on an expressive task failed to find any advantage over an arbitrary reinforcement strategy (Rogers & Siegel, 1984). Many of the studies investigating reinforcer specificity are plagued by methodological problems. Such difficulties lead Reichle, Lindamood, and Sigafoos (1986) to conclude that "specificity as an intervention strategy may not be a best practice for all learners with severe handicaps . . . ." (pp. 134–135).

Since that review, however, more recent investigations have found some evidence to support the use of specific over nonspecific reinforcement when teaching communicative behavior (Carroll & Hesse, 1987; Stafford, Sundberg, & Braam, 1988). In these studies, specific reinforcement was used when teaching requests, whereas nonspecific reinforcement was used when teaching object names. Carroll and Hesse (1987) compared two conditions in teaching six preschool children to name various toy parts. In the "name only" condition, a toy part was placed in front of the learner. The experimenter then said, "This is a _____. What is this?" Correct responses were followed by generalized conditioned reinforcement (e.g., "Good job."). When the learner responded incorrectly or failed to respond, the interventionist modeled the correct response. Trials to criterion in this condition for a set of toy part names were compared to the number of trials required for a comparable set of toy parts in a "requesting to naming" condition. Between each naming trial in this latter condition the learner was asked to assemble one of the toys, a skill previously developed. Part of this assembly task required the learner to request the missing part. Acquisition of toy part names required fewer trials to criterion in the "requesting-naming" condition. Requests in this study were reinforced by receipt of a specific toy part, which then enabled the learner to assemble the toy. Correctly naming a toy part, in contrast, resulted in purely social reinforcement. Specific reinforcement associated with requests may, therefore, speed the acquisition of object names. However, the learners in this study were also allowed to play briefly with the toys assembled during requesting trials. If toy play was an effective reinforcer, the superiority of the condition that included requesting may not have been due necessarily to specific reinforcement. Still, Stafford et al. (1988) found in a case study that specific reinforcement tended to be preferred over nonspecific (arbitrary) reinforcement. While this preference did not translate to improved acquisitions—the learner acquired responses rapidly under both reinforcement conditions—such preferences may no doubt prove important for other learners.

Comparing Explicit and Generalized Requests

Although relatively sparse and replete with potential problems, the literature on reinforcer specificity does suggest that the differences in reinforcement practices associated with explicit (i.e., specific reinforcement) and generalized (i.e., varied reinforcement) requests may significantly affect the acquisition, generalization, and maintenance of requesting skills among learners with severe disabilities. To date, however, there have been no direct comparisons of explicit and more generalized requesting strategies (see Sigafoos, 1989). Table 3 summarizes the differences between explicit and generalized requests.

Table 3.   Generalized versus explicit requests

Aspect	Generalized requests	Explicit requests
Vocabulary	Broad (e.g., "want," "food")	Narrow (e.g., "apple," "cookies")
Interpretation	Requires greater interpretation by listener	Requires less interpretation by listener
Reinforcement	Varied, intermittent	Specific, continuous
Teaching opportunities	Relatively more	Relatively fewer

Several studies have demonstrated that these different types of requests can be taught to learners with severe disabilities. Reichle, Rogers, and Barrett (1984) taught an adolescent girl with severe mental retardation to request a variety of preferred objects by producing the ASL sign "want." Initially, the learner was physically prompted to sign "want" when offered a tray of preferred items, and then allowed to select one item from the tray. Over successive opportunities, prompts were faded until the generalized request occurred independently each time the tray was offered. The learner consistently performed at 80% or better after 25 days of training.

Keogh and Reichle (1985) suggest that once a generalized (e.g., "want") request has been established, more explicit requests can be added by teaching learners to combine the generalized request with an object label (e.g., "want" and "cookie"). This intervention sequence has been implemented successfully. For example, Reichle and Brown (1986) taught an adult with autism to select a single symbol ("want") as a generalized request. The learner was then taught to identify some of the objects previously requested by selecting matching line drawings. Finally, explicit requests were established by teaching the learner to select two symbols (e.g., "want" and "cookie") when offered a specific preferred item.

While explicit requests have generally been taught after generalized requests they have also been maintained concurrently with a more generalized requesting strategy. In the vocal mode,

a learner who was blind and severely retarded was taught to discriminate between generalized and explicit requesting based upon object availability (Reichle, Sigafoos, & Piché, 1989). If the name of an item had not yet been taught, requesting it required the generalized form ("want"). Known items required the appropriate explicit form (e.g., "want and cracker"). Sigafoos, Reichle, Doss, Hall, and Pettitt (in press) taught two adults with severe retardation to request needed utensils (e.g., spoon, opener, straw) by selecting explicit symbols. Once the learners had requested a preferred food or beverage item (e.g., applesauce, a soft drink, juice) by selecting a generalized request symbol ("want"), an explicit request was required to obtain the utensil needed for gaining access to that item. The complete requesting episode thus included an explicit request subsequent to a more generalized request. Both types of requests were maintained in the learners' repertoires and both types were acquired rapidly. Yet, in this study, the generalized request ("want") was taught prior to more explicit requests.

It is unclear from these studies whether acquisition of explicit requests is facilitated by the prior development of a more generalized requesting strategy. Although these studies demonstrated that explicit requests can be taught subsequent to more generalized forms, it has also been shown that a repertoire of explicit requests can be acquired by learners with severe disabilities in the absence of any more generalized requests. Sigafoos, Doss, and

Reichle (1989), for example, taught three adults with severe disabilities explicit requests for each of three preferred objects and the utensils required to gain access to those items. When offered a bottle of water, for example, the learner requested it by opening a communication wallet and pointing to the line drawing of a bottle of water. Once the bottle had been delivered, a bottle opener was needed to open the bottle, hence the learner was taught to select the line drawing of a bottle opener. In this study, repertoires of up to six explicit requests were eventually established and subsequently maintained. Hall and Sundberg (1987) and Sundberg (1980) have also taught explicit signed requests as the initial and only requesting strategy.

Other investigators have successfully taught vocabulary corresponding to generic requests from the beginning of intervention. McCook, Cipani, Madigan, and LaCampagne (1988) taught two learners to ask for juice during morning break at a day program. Although the vocabulary item taught implied a generic request, it was unclear from the methodology if requests were reinforced with a single type of juice (e.g., orange juice), thus reflecting an explicit request, or if several types of juice (e.g., orange, grape, and apple juice) were dispensed as reinforcement, thus conforming to a generic request. Romski, Sevcik, and Pate (1988) also failed to specify the nature of reinforcement in their study on teaching requests to people with severe mental retardation using generic graphic symbols (e.g., "cereal").

Thus, through relatively standard instructional procedures (e.g., reinforcement, prompt fading), both explicit and generalized requests can be taught to learners with severe disabilities. Explicit requests can be taught subsequent to more generic requests, with both strategies then maintained concurrently. It is not clear, however, whether the differences between explicit and generic requests affect aspects of interventions, such as speed of acquisition.

TEACHING GENERALIZED REQUESTING

A generalized requesting episode consists of the discriminative stimulus, the response, and the consequence, as shown in Figure 1. Such a division is somewhat oversimplified, since ordinarily, requesting episodes occur in rapid and fluid interchanges between a speaker and a listener. Slowing down and segmenting such episodes is useful for teaching communication skills initially, however.

Discriminative stimuli are arranged by the interventionist to set the occasion for a requesting episode. To establish a generalized request initially it is helpful to arrange specific discriminative stimuli. There are two basic types of discriminative stimuli. The first is the offer or availability of potential reinforcers. The second is the query posed by the interventionist as he or she presents the reinforcers (i.e., "What do you want?" or perhaps "Want something?"). In initiating instructional opportunities with such questions there is a danger that requests may fail to occur spontaneously. That is, the learner may learn to make requests only when instructed or otherwise prompted to do so. Indeed, it has often been noted that communicative repertoires taught to learners with severe disabilities lack spontaneity (Carr, 1982; Carr & Kologinsky, 1983; Charlop, Schreibman, & Thibodeau, 1985; Gobbi, Cipani, Hudson, & Lapenta-Neudeck, 1986; Halle, 1987; Lovaas, Koegel, Simmons, & Long, 1973; Oliver & Halle, 1982; Schaeffer, 1978; Sosne, Handleman, & Harris, 1979).

One reason for this lack of spontaneity may be that learners are often given the opportunity to make requests only when others present discrete instructional stimuli. Thus, to avoid establishing such questions as the only condition under which requests occur, it may be prudent to omit these questions as consistently presented discriminative stimuli, thereby ensuring that, on some occasions, learners have the opportunity to make requests without having first been prompted by an interventionist's questions. However, if such questions are reliable response prompts, they may prove useful in establishing the requesting response. Once established, transfer of stimulus control procedures could be implemented to bring requests under the control of more natural discriminative stimuli (Halle, 1987).

Following the offer of preferred items, many learners will attempt to reach for an item from the array without producing an approximation of a communicative request. This tendency to reach for and select items should result from a prior history of choosing preferred objects. For example, during reinforcer preference testing, learners might be offered a tray containing five or six objects, from which they could reach for and select one item. The primary difference between preference assessment and teaching a generalized request is that in the latter the learner is required to vocalize a request, produce the appropriate gesture, or make contact with the appropriate symbol before reaching for and selecting an item. In the graphic mode, contacting the appropriate symbol may flow directly from the reaching and selecting component of the reinforcer preference test. Procedures for teaching generalized requesting in the graphic mode are described in detail in the following sections. Through standard prompting and fading procedures, generalized requesting is also applicable to vocal and gestural modes.

Teaching Generalized Requesting Using Backward Chaining

Establishing the generalized request provides the learner with an immediately useful skill, since it facilitates access to a variety of preferred objects and activities without the learner having to learn the name of each potentially reinforcing item. While the learner should eventually be taught to name some objects or request some items explicitly, as an initial skill a generalized request serves a useful function and

demonstrates to the learner the benefits of communication.

Generalized requests can be analyzed as a chain of two behaviors. The second step of this chain involves reaching for and selecting an item from among those offered. Reaching for and selecting an item is directly related to obtaining the item, which can then be consumed, in the case of edibles, or otherwise manipulated (e.g., playing with a selected toy). Pointing to an appropriate symbol (e.g., "want") is the first part of the chain. The second part of this chain—reaching for and selecting items—is generally already a part of most learners' repertoires. This link may also be strengthened as a result of the prior history with the reinforcer preference tests described earlier. Establishing the generalized request (i.e., pointing to "want") can therefore be added onto this chain.

Once a history of reaching for desired items has been established, the interventionist may begin physically placing the "want" symbol into the learner's path as he or she reaches for a preferred item. As an array is presented and the learner reaches for an item on it, the "want" symbol is put up as a barrier. In order to gain access to the item the learner must touch the symbol. As soon as the symbol is touched, it is removed and the learner can then successfully reach the item. This technique builds a history of contacting the symbol en route to the item. Initially, learners may attempt to reach around or over the symbol to gain access to the preferred objects. It may, therefore, be necessary to use an oversized symbol to ensure that all reaches can be blocked. Eventually, most learners will stop trying to reach around the symbol and will come to touch the symbol quickly. When this is observed, the next step is to alter the size and location of the symbol. If an oversized symbol was used, its size is gradually reduced. The interventionist observes the learner to make sure that he or she continues to touch the symbol while reaching for the array of items offered.

Simultaneously, the location of the symbol with respect to the array is altered. Initially, the symbol is placed directly in front of the array, blocking access to the items offered. Once contact occurs reliably in this location the symbol is moved slightly to the side, so that it is only partially blocking access to the items. It is important to ensure at this and all subsequent fading steps that the learner touches the symbol before selecting an item. In a series of gradual and discrete steps the location of the symbol is moved farther and farther from the array of offered items. Eventually, it will appear on a suitable work surface in front of the learner, perhaps flat on a table, or in a communication board or wallet.

An alternative to such a prompting strategy involves applying a response prompt directed at the learner's hand. For example, the "want" symbol is placed in front of the learner and an array containing several preferred items is offered. The learner may also be asked, "What do you want?" or "Want something?" The learner may then reach for one of the items offered. However, instead of bringing the symbol up to meet the learner's hand as in the inserting technique, the interventionist brings the learner's hand down to contact the symbol. Once the symbol has been touched, access to the preferred items is permitted. Any kind of prompt that can reliably recruit the desired performance can be used. Because prompts are delivered immediately prior to or during a learner's reach for an offered item, physical guidance or modeling a correct response are usually used. These prompts are then faded until the learner points to the "want" symbol in the absence of prompts before reaching for offered objects. Thus, with both prompting strategies, the terminal performance is for learners to select a "want" symbol placed in front of them before reaching for offered items.

During the initial opportunities of a generalized request intervention procedure there is little reason to expect the learner will point to the "want" symbol independently. Nonetheless, this lack of correct responding should be verified during an initial baseline phase in which the "want" symbol is placed in front of the learner, either to the right or to the left of center on a random basis. The interventionist displays the array of potential reinforcers, asking "Want something?" An appropriate period of time—perhaps 4 seconds—is then allowed for the learner to respond. Instead of pointing to the "want" symbol during baseline, learners will most often try to reach for the offered items. Should the initial baseline phase reveal that the learner does not independently point to the "want" symbol within 4 seconds of being asked, "Want something?" intervention procedures should be implemented to teach the skill.

During intervention it is helpful to distinguish between several types of possible responses. A request is defined as any time the learner independently points to the "want" symbol, vocalizes correctly, or signs "want" after having been offered a preferred item. Requests that occur within some predetermined amount of time are defined as independent or correct. An incorrect response would be scored if the learner pointed to, said, or signed something other than "want." Incorrect responses will be minimized during the early phases of intervention, when "want" is the only available request. At a later point in intervention, discrimination between two or more vocalizations, signs, or symbols will be introduced. The initial "errorless" intervention involving a single request form will often ease the transition to discriminations involving other words, signs, or symbols (Terrace, 1963). Another likely pattern of responding is for the learner to fail to produce the correct request within the allotted time frame.

Establishing Contingent Consequences

Each of the three types of responses—independent, incorrect, and no response—should be subject to differential consequences during intervention. Contingent consequences refer to the changes that occur as a result of an act. During intervention to teach a generalized request, the act of pointing to the "want" symbol, for example, has several contingent consequences. Some of these consequences follow directly from the act. For example, the learner's finger lands on the symbol, a result that can be felt by the learner and seen by the learner as well as by others who happen to be looking. Other consequences, however, follow only indirectly. For example, upon seeing the learner's finger touch the symbol the interventionist moves an array of potential reinforcers within reach, allowing the learner to select one of the available items.

Correct requests are typically reinforced by presenting the learner with access to preferred items. These procedures specify a *contingency*. A contingency is essentially an if/then statement (Lee, 1988). In this case, if the learner points to "want," then a preferred item can be selected. Should the frequency of pointing to the want symbol increase as a result of this contingency, the contingency does indeed involve reinforcement and the objects selected by the learner are indeed effective reinforcers.

Establishing Symbol Discriminations

Once the learner has been taught that a single action (e.g., producing a gesture, touching a symbol, vocalizing) exerts control over his or her environment, additional symbols may be added to the learner's array, and he or she can be taught to discriminate among them. In progressing toward teaching the learner to discriminate among symbols, it is important to introduce *distractors* early in the intervention process. A distractor is a stimulus that is presented simultaneously with the target stimulus. The distractor should differ from the target stimulus just enough to allow the learner to avoid responding to the distractor, instead selecting the target stimulus. The advantage of

introducing distractors early is that a discrimination between responses can be established as the generalized requesting skill is being taught. However, this strategy may also increase the probability of errors during the early stages of intervention. Such errors can be minimized by using more intensive prompting procedures, or by introducing the second response only after the generalized request has been acquired (e.g., after 10–20 independent generalized requests have been made). In the graphic mode, for example, the learner is taught to continue pointing to the "want" symbol even when confronted with it and some other symbol. Here the possibility exists for incorrect responses. Several options are available in the event of an incorrect response. Incorrect responses can be interrupted before they actually occur. As the learner starts to reach for the second symbol, or as the learner starts to form an incorrect sign, the interventionist can immediately deliver a response prompt to ensure correct performance. Delivering prompts to interrupt incorrect responses has the desirable feature of preserving the integrity of an errorless teaching strategy. Of course, in order to be effective it must be possible to catch and prevent errors before they actually occur. This may prove difficult, particularly when instruction occurs in the vocal mode. One simple way to increase the odds of preventing errors in the graphic mode is to space symbols far enough apart so that reaches for the incorrect symbol can be detected in time to allow the interventionist to redirect the learner.

Errorless learning techniques may not always ensure the complete absence of errors. When errors do occur, therefore, the interventionist must decide how to deal with them. One option is simply to ignore errors, pausing briefly before the next intervention opportunity. Incorrect responses could also be followed by an error correction procedure. Using this technique, the correct response is prompted after an error occurs. Practicing the correct response two to three times is often part of the error correction procedure (Braam & Poling, 1983; Hall & Sundberg, 1987). Error correction procedures are generally effective (Ault, Wolery, Doyle, & Gast, 1989), particularly when combined with procedures designed to minimize errors (e.g., stimulus shaping, stimulus fading, most-to-least prompting).

Data Collection and Analysis

The data collected during implementation of a generalized requesting intervention are classified in terms of their accuracy (correct or incorrect) and their subtype (independent or prompted). Collecting these data enables the effects of intervention to be evaluated. To be useful, the data must be collected in a systematic and reliable fashion. Early phases of programs to teach requesting are typically implemented in a massed trial format, as described in Chapter 10. A record should be kept of the type of response that occurred during each learning opportunity. This record contains the raw data of the program. Because each opportunity is introduced initially by a discrete discriminative stimulus, and a clear separation between successive opportunities is maintained, it is relatively easy to secure a record of the responses made on a trial-by-trial basis. After each session—which may have consisted of 10 instructional opportunities—these data can be converted into a per-

cent score and graphed in the manner shown in Figure 4. During the two baseline sessions, no independent responses were noted. Intervention procedures were associated with a steady increase in the percent of independent responses, reaching 100% by the ninth intervention session. Intervention will not always yield such clear gains. When graphed trends reveal no acquisition of the desired skill, a change in teaching methodology may be warranted. (For a discussion of graphing options see Haring & Kennedy [1988]. For a discussion of the evaluation of graphed data, see Parsonson & Baer [1986]).

Close inspection of the data collected during intervention will often provide clues as to what type of revisions may be warranted. Suppose, for example, that the primary problem was a large percentage of trials during which the learner made no response. This pattern may indicate a failure to find objects or activities that functioned as reinforcers. Another learner may require physical assistance to produce the response. Although it is often said that such a learner is "prompt dependent," such a classification offers little instructional guidance. What is needed is a more effective method of transferring stimulus control from physical assistance to the discriminative stimuli that are arranged by the interventionist (e.g., offering preferred

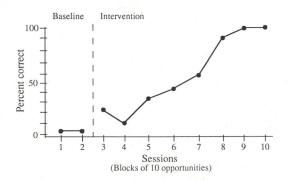

Figure 4. Percentage of correct, unprompted requesting responses across blocks of 10 opportunities during the baseline period and during intervention.

objects, asking "Want something?"). Several techniques, reviewed in Chapter 8, can be used to achieve such a transfer of stimulus control (Striefel & Owens, 1980).

Other types of problems often emerge when a second response is introduced. Sometimes the established response breaks down when a second response is taught. The learner may, for example, point to each of the two symbols on a random basis. Such a pattern often requires the implementation of stimulus fading or stimulus shaping techniques (Etzel & LeBlanc, 1979; Etzel, LeBlanc, Schilmoeller, & Stella, 1981; Sidman & Stoddard, 1967; Terrace, 1963). Another common problem when two or more responses are available is an indiscriminant chaining of the two. The learner may, for example, point to every available symbol or produce all the signs in his or her repertoire on every opportunity. This pattern may develop because the learner eventually hits upon the correct response and is dutifully reinforced. Breaking this pattern can often be achieved through a combination of interruption, stimulus control, and response prompting techniques. (More details on such strategies are provided in Chapter 10.)

The range of potential problems, their nature, and origin is too great to cover exhaustively here. Common types of problems may also be affected by idiosyncratic histories of individual learners. In addition, solutions to particular problems may depend on individual learner characteristics (Farlow & Snell, 1989; Grigg, Snell, & Loyd, 1989). By collecting, graphing, and evaluating data in a systematic fashion, interventionists will at least be able to determine when a revision in teaching methods is needed.

TEACHING EXPLICIT REQUESTS

An explicit requesting episode is comprised of the discriminative stimulus, the symbol selection, and the consequence. Access to an item (e.g., an apple) is the consequence of selecting a particular symbol (e.g., a line drawing of an apple) in the presence of a relevant discriminative stimulus, such as the interventionist offering an apple and asking, "What do you want?" Such requests are explicit in that the symbols depict more precisely the consequences.

At least two types of explicit requesting strategies can be taught. The first involves teaching learners to point to a single symbol to request a specific item. The second involves teaching learners a choice of behavior (e.g., "want" and "cookie") to request a specific item. Within this latter strategy, there are two options for establishing such as chain.

In the first type of explicit request, pointing to the generic symbol for "cookie," "cracker," or "book," for example, is reinforced by access to cookies, crackers, and books, respectively. To teach a single explicit request, the interventionist can implement opportunities by offering a specific item (e.g., a cookie) while at the same time during some teaching opportunities asking, "Want this?" When the learner says, signs, or points to the symbol for "cookie" the requested item is given. Initially, "cookie" may be the only response taught. Alternatively, the learner may be taught two or more explicit requests and taught discriminative use of each explicit request. If one of the requests previously taught to the learner is a generalized "want," then the learner may need to be taught to produce "want" when there is no more specific symbol for the offered item, but produce the more explicit form when there is (Reichle et al., 1989). In this case, the learner requests with either a generalized (i.e., "want") or explicit (i.e., object label) strategy, depending on the item offered.

The second type of explicit requesting involves teaching learners to produce a chain of behaviors consisting of "want" and an object label (e.g., "want" and "cookie"). When the second strategy is pursued, a chain of at least two responses is required to make an explicit request. One strategy for teaching a chained request involves a three-step process. First, a generalized request ("want") is taught. Next, a few explicit symbols (e.g., "cookie," "cracker," "milk") are taught as object labels. That is, the interventionist holds up an object, asks, "What is this?", reinforcing correct responses with some unrelated item. Finally, when one of the explicit items is offered with the question "Want this?" the learner is taught to produce "want" and then the corresponding explicit form (e.g., "want" and "cookie").

In order successfully to maintain generalized requests, explicit labels, and explicit requests, the learner needs to distinguish among the various questions being asked (e.g., "Want this?" versus "What is this?") and the object being offered (e.g., a reinforcer with versus a reinforcer without a corresponding explicit name). Basic discrimination training procedures are used to establish such skills (Keogh & Reichle, 1985; Lovaas, 1977; Reichle et al., 1984). Explicit object labels are first taught as object names rather than requests. Such a strategy is appropriate when it would later be important for the learner to maintain such object names in isolation. For example, on some occasions, a learner may produce "cookie" as a comment, for example, when pointing out that someone is making a batch of cookies. Other learners may have little need or inclination to make such comments, reserving such responses instead for requesting. In these cases, it may be possible to teach explicit requests by teaching the learner to select two symbols (e.g., "want" and "cookie") without first teaching "cookie" as an object name. Using this second strategy, a cookie, for example, may be offered. Since the learner is familiar with generalized requesting, offering him or her a cookie would probably evoke the communication "want." When this occurs, the learner can then be prompted to add "cookie," at which point he or she is supplied with a cookie. Other preferred objects would continue to be appropriately requested using only "want."

Additional explicit requests can also be estab-

lished in the same manner. The only difference between this strategy and the first strategy is that the explicit vocabulary items are not first taught as object names. It is unclear which strategy for teaching or sequencing requests is more efficient. A recent study (Sigafoos, 1989) notes that concurrent instruction to teach both explicit and generic requesting may prove problematic, leading to a high rate of errors, suggesting that it may be better to teach explicit and generalized requests separately. Reichle et al. (1989) suggest that once established, both requesting repertoires can be maintained, with a generalized request used for unfamiliar items and explicit requests used for particular items the learner is taught to request explicitly.

Explicit requests can be taught initially without teaching either generalized requests or explicit labels when the single symbol strategy is adopted. To use the more sophisticated strategy, generalized requesting and explicit labels are necessary. While explicit symbols may often be difficult to interpret as requests or labels, the use of "want" preceding an explicit symbol renders meaning unambiguous. When an explicit form is produced alone (e.g., "cookie") it is interpreted as a comment.

The basic procedures for both strategies are straightforward: a preferred item is offered, and the interventionist asks, "Want this?" or "What do you want?" If the learner says, signs, or selects the appropriate word, sign, or symbol he or she is then reinforced by being given the requested item. Incorrect responses or a failure to respond call for the use of stimulus or response prompts. Any prompts used will then have to be faded.

These basic procedures do not represent a set of fixed steps, nor must discrete-trial intervention sessions, consisting of a block of massed opportunities, represent the structure of instruction. While such a massed trial format may prove effective in the initial acquisition of the skill (Mulligan, Guess, Holvoet, & Brown, 1980; Mulligan, Lacy, & Guess, 1982), opportunities for generalized and/or explicit requests are often available in the natural environment. For example, incidental teaching paradigms can be adopted to teach requests under more natural conditions (Hart, 1985; Hart & Risley, 1968, 1974, 1975), as discussed in Chapter 8. Because generalized requests are less tied than explicit requests to any single source of reinforcement, more opportunities may arise in the natural environment for teaching them. Of course, once a large number of explicit requests is available, opportunities in the natural environment will also arise regularly. If they do not, the need to have taught that vocabulary should be reevaluated.

TEACHING REQUESTS FOR ACTIONS

Requests for objects and activities are appropriate under a variety of conditions. In general, requests for objects and activities should occur when a particular item is wanted or needed, but not readily accessible. That is, if a spoon is readily available to the learner, a request is not needed. Instead, the learner should simply reach for the item directly.

Just as requests for objects are appropriate under a variety of conditions, so, too, are requests for listener actions. A request to have one's coat buttoned, for example, must be made when a cold breeze is blowing, in which case the action of the listener will help terminate an aversive event. Requests for listener actions might also be made when some type of assistance is needed to obtain an item. For example, a learner who likes pickles may occasionally need assistance in opening the jar. Once the jar has been opened by another the learner may then be capable of selecting a pickle without further assistance.

Requesting Attention

Another condition that might require listener action is when a learner requests attention. Learners should be taught to request attention

for two reasons. First, some learners may enjoy the attention of others. In this case, requesting attention is similar to requesting a preferred object or activity, and comes close to commenting behavior. Second, in many situations, a learner may first need to recruit a listener in order to engage in other communicative exchanges, such as requesting. In this case, requesting attention is part of a chain of behavior leading to the receipt of some desired item.

Intervention procedures to teach communicative behavior are typically implemented when the learner already has the attention of a listener and vice versa. This does not ensure, however, that learners will come to recruit a listener before engaging in a communicative exchange. It will thus often be necessary to teach learners to recruit attention. One strategy is first to establish a communicative behavior (e.g., requesting, rejecting, commenting) when the learner already has the interventionist's attention. Opportunities can then be implemented when the interventionist is not overtly attending to the learner. Over successive opportunities the interventionist can further withdraw his or her attention. For example, a learner might first be taught to request help in opening a jar when the interventionist is near. Once this skill is established, the interventionist could position him- or herself some distance from the learner. The learner would then be prompted first to obtain the interventionist's attention (by perhaps walking over to the interventionist, or producing some auditory or visual signal) and then to request help.

An alternative strategy would be first to establish the request for attention, and then to introduce steps to teach more explicit requesting or some other communicative behavior. Once the learner had been taught to request attention, he or she would then be taught to make a request. This option may be problematic because it requires that a condition of no attention serve as the discriminative stimulus for beginning the intervention opportunity.

To prompt a learner to recruit attention, however, the interventionist will often need to approach the learner. This may make it difficult to establish no attention as the condition for recruiting attention. During the early phases of intervention, therefore, it may sometimes be necessary to use two interventionists—one to prompt a request for attention if needed, and the other to provide attention and continue teaching more explicit requests.

Introducing Negative Teaching Exemplars

Just as there are appropriate (positive) conditions and inappropriate (negative) conditions for requesting objects, so too are there positive and negative exemplars for requesting listener action. Learners with severe disabilities may need instruction both to make requests in the presence of positive exemplars, and to refrain from requesting under conditions in which objects or activities can be independently accessed, or when assistance is not needed to proceed with or complete a task. An important instructional issue, therefore, concerns when to introduce negative teaching exemplars. (The use of negative teaching exemplars is discussed in detail in Chapter 10.)

Requesting Assistance

Teaching a request for listener action can be illustrated by considering a request for assistance. In the presence of a difficult task, the request "help" is reinforced by the resulting assistance supplied by another person. In order to teach this skill, the interventionist might select several tasks that are important to the learner. Tasks that include one or two difficult steps with which the learner will require assistance should be selected. As the learner participates in the task he or she will eventually reach the step or steps that require assistance. Some learners might first try to complete the step independently, but be unable to do so. This failure could precipitate excess behaviors, such as yell-

ing, hitting, or attempting to damage the task materials. It may be wise, therefore, to select steps that generate only mild emotional behavior (Alwell, Hunt, Goetz, & Sailor, 1989; Goetz, Gee, & Sailor, 1985). Alternatively, a prompt to request assistance might be given as soon as the difficult step is encountered, before any excess behaviors occur. Over consecutive opportunities, requests for assistance would be prompted after longer and longer intervals, thus fading the prompts with time delay.

Request for assistance can occur as generalized or explicit forms. The advantage of generalized forms is the potential relevance to a greater variety of conditions. "Help" is appropriate in a wide range of circumstances, whereas "open" is more restricted. Thus, in establishing a generalized request for assistance ("help"), general case instruction can be adopted. Several difficult steps for which assistance is needed are selected from the full range of tasks that the learner encounters. A single response is established as appropriate across the entire range of these tasks. Some situations may require the learner to specify more precisely the nature of the assistance required. A listener who asked for "help" may be confused as to what kind of help is needed. "Open," in contrast, narrows the options to a particular type of assistance.

SUMMARY

Teaching learners to request objects and activities ensures that the benefits of communication are realized early in intervention. Interventions to establish a repertoire of requests can begin as soon as a set of potential reinforcers has been identified. Requesting can be taught in the vocal, gestural, and graphic modes. Both requests for objects and activities and requests for listener action can be taught. Both classes of requests can be taught as generalized, generic, or explicit requests.

REFERENCES

Alwell, M., Hunt, P., Goetz, L., & Sailor, W. (1989). Teaching generalized communicative behaviors within interrupted behavior chain contexts. *Journal of The Association for Persons with Severe Handicaps, 14,* 91–100.

Anglin, J.W. (1977). *Word, object, and conceptual development.* New York: Norton.

Ault, M.J., Wolery, M., Doyle, P.M., & Gast, D.L. (1989). Review of comparative studies on the instruction of students with moderate and severe handicaps. *Exceptional Children, 55,* 346–356.

Bloom, L., & Lahey, M. (1978). *Language development and language disorders.* New York: John Wiley & Sons.

Braam, S.J., & Poling, A. (1983). Development of intraverbal behavior in mentally retarded individuals through transfer of stimulus control procedures: Classification of verbal responses. *Applied Research in Mental Retardation, 4,* 279–302.

Calculator, S.N. (1988). Promoting the acquisition and generalization of conversational skills by individuals with severe disabilities. *Augmentative and Alternative Communication, 4,* 94–103.

Carr, E.G. (1982). Sign language. In R. Koegel, A. Rincover, & A. Egel (Eds.), *Educating and understanding autistic children* (pp. 142–157). San Diego: College-Hill Press.

Carr, E.G. (1988). Functional equivalence as a mechanism of response generalization. In R. Horner, G. Dunlap, & R. Koegel (Eds.), *Generalization and maintenance* (pp. 221–241). Baltimore: Paul H. Brookes Publishing Co.

Carr, E.G., & Durand, V.M. (1985). Reducing behavior problems through functional communication training. *Journal of Applied Behavior Analysis, 18,* 111–126.

Carr, E.G., & Kologinsky, E. (1983). Acquisition of sign language by autistic children II: Spontaneity and generalization effects. *Journal of Applied Behavior Analysis, 16,* 297–314.

Carroll, R.J., & Hesse, B.E. (1987). The effects of alternating mand and tact training on the acquisition of tacts. *Analysis of Verbal Behavior, 5,* 55–65.

Catania, A.C. (1979). *Learning.* Englewood Cliffs, NJ: Prentice-Hall.

Charlop, M.H., Schreibman, L., & Thibodeau, M.G. (1985). Increasing spontaneous verbal responding in autistic children using a time delay procedure. *Journal of Applied Behavior Analysis, 18,* 155–166.

Dattilo, J., & Mirenda, P. (1987). An application of a leisure preference assessment protocol for persons with severe handicaps. *Journal of The Association for Persons with Severe Handicaps, 12,* 306–311.

Egel, A.L. (1980). The effects of constant versus varied reinforcer presentation on responding by autistic children. *Journal of Experimental Child Psychology, 30,* 455–463.

Egel, A.L. (1981). Reinforcer variation: Implications for motivating developmentally disabled children. *Journal of Applied Behavior Analysis, 14,* 345–350.

Etzel, B.C., & LeBlanc, J.M. (1979). The simplest treatment alternative: The law of parsimony applied to choosing appropriate instructional control and errorless-learning procedures for the difficult-to-teach child. *Journal of Autism and Developmental Disorders, 9,* 361–382.

Etzel, B.C., LeBlanc, J.M., Schilmoeller, K., & Stella, M. (1981). Stimulus control procedures in the education of young children. In S.W. Bijou & R. Ruiz (Eds.), *Contributions of behavior modification to education* (pp. 3–37). Hillsdale, NJ: Lawrence Erlbaum Associates.

Farlow, L.J., & Snell, M.E. (1989). Teacher use of student performance data to make instructional decisions: Practices in programs for students with moderate to profound disabilities. *Journal of The Association for Persons with Severe Handicaps, 14,* 13–22.

Ferster, C.B. (1967). Arbitrary and natural reinforcement. *Psychological Record, 17,* 341–347.

Ferster, C.B. (1972). Clinical reinforcement. *Seminars in Psychiatry, 4,* 101–111.

Ferster, C.B., & Skinner, B.F. (1957) Schedules of reinforcement. New York: Appleton-Century-Crofts.

Gobbi, L., Cipani, E., Hudson, C., & Lapenta-Neudeck, R. (1986). Developing spontaneous requesting among children with severe mental retardation. *Mental Retardation, 24,* 357–363.

Goetz, L., Gee, K., & Sailor, W. (1985). Using a behavior chain interruption strategy to teach communication skills to students with severe disabilities. *Journal of The Association for Persons with Severe Handicaps, 10,* 21–30.

Goetz, L., Schuler, A., & Sailor, W. (1979). Teaching functional speech to the severely handicapped: Current issues. *Journal of Autism and Developmental Disorders, 9,* 325–343.

Green, C.W., Reid, D.H., White, L.K., Halford, R.C., Brittain, D.P., & Gardner, S.M. (1988).

Identifying reinforcers for persons with profound handicaps: Staff opinion versus systematic assessment of preferences. *Journal of Applied Behavior Analysis, 21,* 31–43.

Grigg, N.C., Snell, M.E., & Loyd, B. (1989). Visual analysis of student evaluation data: A qualitative analysis of teacher decision making. *Journal of The Association for Persons with Severe Handicaps, 14,* 23–32.

Guess, D., Sailor, W., & Baer, D.M. (1974). To teach language to retarded children. In R.L. Schiefelbusch & L.L. Lloyd (Eds.), *Language perspectives: Acquisition, retardation, and intervention* (pp. 529–563). Baltimore: University Park Press.

Hall, G., & Sundberg, M.L. (1987). Teaching mands by manipulating conditioned establishing operations. *Analysis of Verbal Behavior, 5,* 41–53.

Halle, J.W. (1987). Teaching language in the natural environment: An analysis of spontaneity. *Journal of The Association for Persons with Severe Handicaps, 12,* 28–37.

Haring, T.G., & Kennedy, G.H. (1988). Units of analysis in task-analytic research. *Journal of Applied Behavior Analysis, 21,* 207–215.

Hart, B. (1985). Naturalistic language training techniques. In S.F. Warren & A.K. Rogers-Warren (Eds.), *Teaching functional language* (pp. 63–88). Austin, TX: PRO-ED.

Hart, B., & Risley, T.R. (1968). Establishing use of descriptive adjectives in the spontaneous speech of disadvantaged preschool children. *Journal of Applied Behavior Analysis, 1,* 109–120.

Hart, B., & Risley, T.R. (1974). Using preschool materials to modify the language of disadvantaged children. *Journal of Applied Behavior Analysis, 7,* 243–256.

Hart, B., & Risley, T.R. (1975). Incidental teaching of language in the preschool. *Journal of Applied Behavior Analysis, 8,* 411–420.

Horner, R.H., & Budd, C.M. (1985). Acquisition of manual sign use: Collateral reduction of maladaptive behavior and factors limiting generalization. *Education and Training of the Mentally Retarded, 20,* 39–47.

Keogh, W., & Reichle, J. (1985). Communication intervention for the "difficult-to-teach" severely handicapped. In S. Warren & A. Rogers-Warren (Eds.), *Teaching functional language* (pp. 157–194). Austin, TX: PRO-ED.

Lamarre, J., & Holland, J.G. (1985). The functional independence of mands and tacts. *Journal of the Experimental Analysis of Behavior, 43,* 5–19.

Lee, V.L. (1988). *Beyond behaviorism.* Hillsdale, NJ: Lawrence Erlbaum Associates.

Litt, M., & Schreibman, L. (1981). Stimulus-specific reinforcement in the acquisition of receptive labels by autistic children. *Analysis and Intervention in Developmental Disabilities, 1,* 171–186.

Lovaas, O.I. (1977). *The autistic child: Language development through behavior modification.* New York: Irvington.

Lovass, O.I., Koegel, R., Simmons, J.Q., & Long, J.S. (1973). Some generalization and follow-up measures on autistic children in behavior therapy. *Journal of Applied Behavior Analysis, 6,* 131–166.

Martin, G., & Pear, J. (1983). *Behavior modification: What it is and how to do it* (2nd ed.). Englewood Cliffs, NJ: Prentice-Hall.

McCook, B., Cipani, E., Madigan, K., & LaCampagne, J. (1988). Developing requesting behavior: Acquisition, fluency, and generality. *Mental Retardation, 26,* 137–143.

Michael, J. (1988). Establishing operations and the mand. *Analysis of Verbal Behavior, 6,* 3–9.

Mulligan, M., Guess, D., Holvoet, J., & Brown, F. (1980). The individualized curriculum sequencing model (1): Implications from research on massed, distributed, or spaced trial training. *Journal of The Association for the Severely Handicapped, 5,* 325–336.

Mulligan, M., Lacy, L., & Guess, D. (1982). Effects of massed, distributed, and spaced trial sequencing on several handicapped students' performance. *Journal of The Association for the Severely Handicapped, 7,* 48–61.

Oliver, C.B., & Halle, J.W. (1982). Language training in the everyday environment: Teaching functional sign use to a retarded child. *Journal of The Association for Persons with Severe Handicaps, 8,* 50–62.

Pace, G.M., Ivancic, M.T., Edwards, G.L., Iwata, B.A., & Page, T.J. (1985). Assessment of stimulus preference and reinforcer value with profoundly retarded individuals. *Journal of Applied Behavior Analysis, 18,* 249–255.

Parsonson, B.S., & Baer, D.M. (1986). The graphic analysis of data. In A. Poling & R.W. Fuqua (Eds.), *Research methods in applied behavior analysis: Issues and advances* (pp. 157–186). New York: Plenum.

Popovich, D. (1981). *Effective educational and behavioral programming for severely and profoundly handicapped students: A manual for teachers and aides.* Baltimore: Paul H. Brookes Publishing Co.

Reichle, J., & Brown, L. (1986). Teaching the use of a multi-page direct selection communication board to an adult with autism. *Journal of The Association for Persons with Severe Handicaps, 11*, 68–73.

Reichle, J., Lindamood, L., & Sigafoos, J. (1986). The match between reinforcer class and response class: Its influence on communication intervention strategies. *Journal of The Association for Persons with Severe Handicaps, 11*, 131–135.

Reichle, J., Rogers, N., & Barrett, C. (1984). Establishing pragmatic discriminations among the communicative functions of requesting, rejecting, and describing. *Journal of The Association for Persons with Severe Handicaps, 9*, 43–50.

Reichle, J., Sigafoos, J., & Piché, L. (1989). Teaching an adolescent with blindness: A correspondence between requesting and selecting preferred objects. *Journal of The Association for Persons with Severe Handicaps, 14*, 75–80.

Rogers, N., & Siegel, G. (1984). *Reinforcement strategies with a language disordered child*. Unpublished master's thesis, University of Minnesota, Minneapolis.

Romski, M.A., Sevcik, R.A., & Pate, J.L. (1988). Establishment of symbolic communication in persons with severe mental retardation. *Journal of Speech and Hearing Disorders, 53*, 94–107.

Saunders, R., & Sailor, W. (1979). A comparison of three strategies of reinforcement on two choice learning problems with severely retarded children. *AAESPH Review, 4*, 323–333.

Schaeffer, B. (1978). Teaching spontaneous sign language to nonverbal children: Theory & method. *Sign Language Studies, 21*, 317–352.

Sidman, M., & Stoddard, L.T. (1967). The effectiveness of fading in programming a simultaneous form discrimination for retarded children. *Journal of the Experimental Analysis of Behavior, 10*, 3–15.

Sigafoos, J. (1989). *Comparing explicit to generic vocabulary in teaching requests*. Unpublished doctoral dissertation, University of Minnesota, Minneapolis.

Sigafoos, J., Doss, S., & Reichle, J. (1989). Developing mand and tact repertoires in persons with severe developmental disabilities using graphic symbols. *Research in Developmental Disabilities, 10*, 183–200.

Sigafoos, J., Reichle, J., Doss, S., Hall, K., & Pettitt, L. (in press). "Spontaneous" transfer of stimulus control from tract to mand contingencies. *Research in Developmental Disabilities*.

Skinner, B.F. (1957). *Verbal behavior*. Englewood Cliffs, NJ: Prentice-Hall.

Sosne, J.B., Handleman, J.S., & Harris, S.L. (1979). Teaching spontaneous-functional speech to autistic type children. *Mental Retardation, 17*, 241–245.

Stafford, M.W., Sundberg, M.L., & Braam, S.J. (1988). A preliminary investigation of the consequences that define the mand and the tact. *Analysis of Verbal Behavior, 6*, 61–71.

Striefel, S., & Owens, C. (1980). Transfer of stimulus control procedures: Applications to language acquisition training with the developmentally handicapped. *Behavior Research of Severe Disabilities, 1*, 307–331.

Sundberg, M.L. (1980). *Developing a verbal repertoire using sign language and Skinner's analysis of verbal behavior*. Unpublished doctoral dissertation, Western Michigan University, Kalamazoo.

Sundberg, M.L. (1983). Language. In J.L. Matson & S.E. Breuning (Eds.), *Assessing the mentally retarded* (pp. 285–310). New York: Grune & Stratton.

Terrace, H.S. (1963). Discrimination learning with and without "errors." *Journal of the Experimental Analysis of Behavior, 6*, 1–27.

Wacker, D.P., Berg, W.K., Wiggins, B., Muldoon, M., & Cavanaugh, J. (1985). Evaluation of reinforcer preferences for profoundly handicapped students. *Journal of Applied Behavior Analysis, 18*, 173–178.

White, O.R., & Haring, N.G. (1980). *Exceptional teaching* (2nd ed.). Columbus, OH: Charles E. Merrill.

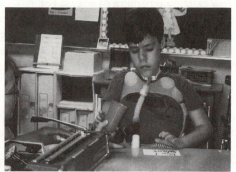

6

Establishing an Initial Repertoire of Rejecting

Jeff Sigafoos and Joe Reichle

OBJECTS OR ACTIVITIES learners attempt to obtain are referred to as liked or preferred. Such objects or activities can often be used effectively as reinforcement when teaching learners to request. Objects or activities learners attempt to escape or avoid are said to be "disliked" or "nonpreferred." Such objects or activities can be used to teach learners to reject. In teaching requesting, the interventionist presents the learner with a preferred object or activity after the learner has made the desired response. In contrast, in teaching rejecting, nonpreferred objects or events are removed or terminated when the learner makes the desired response. This chapter examines strategies for establishing an initial repertoire of rejecting, describes the types of rejections that can be taught, and outlines intervention procedures for teaching learners to reject nonpreferred objects or activities appropriately in the vocal, gestural, and graphic modes.

REASONS FOR TEACHING REJECTING

One rationale frequently given for teaching requesting is that doing so provides learners with

a means of expressing their wants and needs. A similar rationale can be offered for teaching rejecting as an initial communicative behavior. Rejecting allows learners to indicate to listeners which objects or activities are disliked or undesired at the time they are offered. Listeners can then remove or terminate these objects or events, thus reinforcing the rejection. Rejecting thus enables the learner to direct the actions of others.

For people without disabilities, the repertoire of rejecting includes such phrases as "no," "stop that," and "no, not that one, this one." All of these types of rejections can be effective in directing the actions of others, thus providing the speaker with a means of changing the environment in order to reduce contact with nonpreferred objects or activities.

Many learners with severe disabilities have not been exposed to enough contingencies to establish appropriate rejecting behavior. Many such learners have instead learned other, often socially inappropriate (e.g., aggressive acts, self-injurious behaviors, tantrums) methods of rejecting. Teaching rejecting may thus involve replacing an existing repertoire of excess behavior. A learner who throws nonpreferred items might be taught to shake his head "no" when offered such items. A learner who hits others to escape from work might initially be taught to select a "break" symbol to take a break after working a short period of time. Where choices are available, a learner might be taught to reject one item and request an alternative. (Replacing excess behaviors with more socially acceptable communicative behavior is discussed in detail in Chapter 11.) The important point here is that rejecting may often be implemented not only to provide an effective means for learners to indicate dislikes, but also to replace an existing repertoire of excess behaviors that are maintained by negative reinforcement contingencies (Carr, 1977; Iwata, 1987). In this case, negative reinforcement refers to the fact that the excess behavior functions to remove some aversive aspect of the environment. For example, a learner is at least temporarily released from work if he or she has a tantrum. A learner need not finish dinner if he or she throws the dinner plate from the table. Teaching a more socially appropriate rejecting response, such as saying "no," shaking one's head "no," or selecting a "no" symbol allows the same negative reinforcement contingency to operate, but in a way that is less likely to harm or damage people or property, and is perhaps more likely to be reinforced consistently by listeners.

Teaching rejecting also provides learners with self-protection. Learners with severe disabilities are often vulnerable to abuse. Part of this vulnerability may stem from the fact that, like young children, learners with disabilities are taught to be compliant, to follow the instructions of others. Compliance training is not considered complete until it generalizes across persons and directives, so that any stranger can give the learner any type of instruction and get compliance. This type of training could leave a learner vulnerable to exploitation or abuse. Teaching

a rejecting response may, therefore, comprise one part of a self-protection strategy. Rejecting certain objects or activities could also be considered as a self-regulation skill under some conditions. For example, a weight-conscious learner could be taught politely to reject an offer of more chocolate cake. In this case, the learner is taught to reject an item that might ordinarily be the object of a request.

Developing an initial repertoire of rejecting thus provides the learner with a socially acceptable means of removing or terminating nonpreferred objects or activities, with a means of protecting him- or herself in the face of inappropriate requests, and with a means of self-regulating his or her behavior. Reasons for teaching rejecting are summarized in Table 1.

Learners who engage in excess behaviors to escape or avoid certain objects or activities are good candidates for intervention designed to establish a more socially acceptable method of rejecting. Rejecting may also be selected as an initial communicative behavior for learners who have few preferences, but at least some stable nonpreferred objects or activities. Rejecting may also be targeted for learners who need self-protection or self-regulation skills.

One important consideration should be noted, however, before teaching rejecting as the initial communicative behavior. By introducing rejecting first, the interventionist may become established in the learner's mind as someone who presents undesired events. To teach a learner to

Table 1.   Reasons for teaching rejecting

—May provide a means of removing or terminating nonpreferred objects or activities

—May provide a means of avoiding nonpreferred objects or activities

—May serve as a self-protection skill

—May serve as a self-regulation skill

—May replace existing repertoires of escape-motivated or demand-related excess behaviors reject a nonpreferred food item, for example, the interventionist will have to offer the disliked food to the learner repeatedly. If this is the interventionist's only interaction with the learner, he or she will be associated only with the presentation of an aversive event. Over time the learner may exhibit some tendency to escape from or avoid the interventionist. An interventionist who implements rejecting opportunities should thus also interact with that learner at other times in the context of different types of tasks (e.g., implementing requesting opportunities).

Not all candidates for rejecting intervention will be taught in the same mode. While the principles underlying teaching rejecting are similar across modes, the instructional techniques will vary depending upon the mode.

PROCEDURES FOR TEACHING REJECTING IN VARIOUS MODES

Traditionally, a rejecting response was taught by offering a nonpreferred item, having the learner perform the rejecting response, and removing the item. This sequence is illustrated in Figure 1. The rejecting response may be taught in the vocal mode (e.g., the learner says "no" or some approximation of "no"), in the gestural mode (e.g., the learner signs "no," shake his or her head from left to right, or perhaps moves his or her hand as if pushing the object away), or in the graphic mode (e.g., the learner selects a "no" symbol). There are several subtle differences in establishing rejecting responses in different modes.

Vocal Mode

To establish a rejecting response in the vocal mode, the learner must be able to speak or at least produce some discrete vocalization. If the learner does not already imitate speech it will be helpful first to teach him or her to do so. In the vocal mode, the only effective way for the interventionist to prompt a correct response is to provide a model (i.e., say "no") for the learner to imitate. Because prompting will often be necessary, at least initially, imitative models must be established as effective prompts. Occasionally, a learner may independently produce some discrete vocalization, such as an undifferentiated sound, that could be accepted as an initial approximation of the rejecting response. The interventionist could then attempt to shape a more conventional topography, such as "no," or train listeners to react appropriately to the unformed sound.

Teaching the prototypic rejecting response is relatively straightforward in the vocal mode. Objects or activities are first identified as nonpreferred using procedures similar to those described in Chapter 5 for selecting reinforcers. First, a variety of items is offered. Those items never selected or actively avoided are assumed to be disliked. A disliked item is then offered. The interventionist may also ask, "Want this?" If an initial baseline assessment phase is implemented to ascertain the learner's initial skills, no other types of cues or prompts are provided. After some predetermined period of time (e.g., 4, 5, or 10 seconds) the interventionist can ei-

<u>Stimulus</u>		<u>Response</u>		<u>Consequence</u>
Interventionist offers nonpreferred item (may also ask "want it?").	→	Learner produces rejecting response (e.g., "No").	→	Interventionist removes nonpreferred item.

Figure 1. The prototypic rejecting sequence includes stimulus, response, and consequence.

ther withdraw the object or give it to the learner. The interventionist initially prompts the correct rejecting response immediately after presenting the nonpreferred item. After several pairings of the nonpreferred item with the prompt, the interventionist can begin to fade the prompt by first increasing the delay interval between the presentation of the nonpreferred item and the delivery of the prompt. The prompt may also be faded in loudness. Correct unprompted responses are recorded whenever the learner says "no" after a nonpreferred item is offered, but before the interventionist prompts a correct response. Withdrawing the object constitutes reinforcement and should never follow a socially unacceptable behavior. Giving the learner the item may enable the interventionist to determine which strategies the learner uses to escape from a nonpreferred item. For example, the learner might produce some discrete vocalization that could be shaped into a rejecting response. However, if these strategies include severe excess behavior (e.g., yelling, self-injury), it is probably better to end each baseline opportunity by removing the nonpreferred item rather than giving it to the learner.

The learner's behavior should be recorded after each baseline opportunity. Learner behavior may be recorded in several ways. If the learner produced the appropriate rejecting response, the behavior should be recorded as a correct response. If the learner produced some other (inappropriate) response (e.g., said "yes" or "want"), the behavior should be recorded as an incorrect response. Of course, if the learner responds with "want" to what the interventionist believed to be a nonpreferred item, the item may in fact be preferred. This could be checked by giving the learner the item and seeing if it was accepted willingly or avoided actively. If accepted, "want" would constitute a correct response, and it may be necessary to reevaluate preferences. If avoided, "want" would constitute an "incorrect" response, since the learner did not want that item. If the learner makes no response, it should be scored as such.

Finally, it will often be useful to record in some detail what the learner did rather than simply scoring his or her behavior as correct, incorrect, or absent. For example, if the learner looked away or attempted to leave when presented with the undesired objects, these actions indicate existing rejecting strategies, and may also indicate the degree to which a particular item is disliked.

Baseline data can also be used to determine what form of behavior to accept as the rejecting response. For example, if the learner frequently produces a particular sound when the nonpreferred item is offered, this sound may initially be accepted as the rejecting response, and intervention efforts might focus on shaping a more conventional response (i.e., "no"). Should the dominant baseline pattern consist of nonresponding, intervention would focus on prompting the desired response (i.e., "say 'no' "), and then fading the prompts, perhaps by a combined time delay and stimulus fading procedure (i.e., "say 'no'," "Say 'N'," "say," "s___")(Risley & Wolf, 1967), provided, of course, that the learner can imitate vocalizations. Finally, baseline data can be used to evaluate the effectiveness of intervention. If the trend during intervention does not show acceptable progress, the teaching procedures may need to be modified.

Figure 2 shows hypothetical data from a rejecting program. During the baseline period, no correct responses occurred. During intervention there was a steady increase in the percentage of correct, unprompted rejecting responses, and the rejecting response was well established after the eighth block of 10 learning opportunities. Such a trend suggests that the intervention procedures were effective in teaching the learner to reject nonpreferred objects.

For learners who fail to acquire a functional repertoire of speech even after months of instruction, gestural or graphic modes of communication may be more appropriate. Even among learners who may acquire a vocal mode repertoire, it may make sense to teach rejecting in the gestural mode first, since the gestural mode

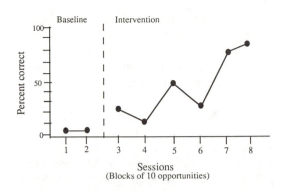

Figure 2. Percentage of correct, unprompted rejecting responses across blocks of 10 opportunities during the baseline period and during intervention.

does not require imitation. Later, if the learner masters imitation, the gesture can be chained to the spoken approximation "no."

Gestural Mode

To establish a rejecting response in the gestural mode, the learner must be physically capable of consistently producing some discrete motor behavior that will serve as the rejecting response. Such a behavior may consist of a natural gesture, such as shaking one's head back and forth; a conventional gesture, such as the ASL sign for "no" or an idiosyncratic gesture, such as pursing the lips and drawing away. A gesture that is directly related to the reinforcing effect (e.g., a sweep of the hand) could also be used. Many learners have a natural tendency to push away or throw nonpreferred objects. In such cases, the interventionist must decide whether to accept as the rejecting response a motor behavior that is already part of the learner's repertoire or to try to establish a new gesture.

One drawback of accepting existing idiosyncratic gestures as the rejecting response is that those gestures may not be readily understood by others. Idiosyncratic gestures are typically not very guessable. Suppose, for example, that a learner waves his right arm when confronted with nonpreferred items. Over the years, primary caregivers may have learned that arm waving means "no." While understood by caregivers, it is unlikely that this gesture would be

correctly interpreted by the community at large. Moreover, the existing rejecting response might consist of an excess behavior, such as throwing objects or pounding on a table. As a general rule, any action to be included in the learner's communicative repertoire should not be part of an existing unacceptable excess repertoire and should be guessable in the community. In both of these cases, then, the interventionist may elect to establish a new rejecting response, even though the learner already exhibits a gesture for rejecting. The old rejecting response could be replaced by either a natural gesture (e.g., shaking one's head back and forth) or a formal sign.

Unlike vocal mode intervention, where prompting is somewhat limited to providing an imitative model (e.g., "Say 'no'."), in the gestural mode, physical prompts can be delivered to recruit the correct response. Many learners will imitate motor movements or can be taught to do so (Baer & Deguchi, 1985). To recruit a correct headshake, for example, the interventionist may be able simply to model the movement. However, if the learner does not engage in generalized motor imitation, the interventionist can use a physical prompt, placing his or her hands gently on the learner's head and guiding it back and forth. A correct rejecting response may be effectively prompted by delivering a stimulus prompt. For example, many learners will reliably turn their hands away from an oncoming spoon containing a nonpreferred food item. Bringing a spoon to one side of the learner's face may, therefore, prompt the first part of a headshake. The spoon is then quickly moved to the other side, thus compelling the learner to shake his or her head back and forth in a "no" gesture. The spoon is then removed to reinforce the desired response. The prompt will need to be faded before a functional rejecting response is obtained. Fading can occur by gradually presenting the stimulus farther and farther from the learner.

Consider a typical intervention sequence for teaching a "no" headshake as a rejecting response. First, a nonpreferred item is offered and the learner is immediately prompted to shake his or her head "no." As soon as the response occurs, the nonpreferred item is removed. Suppose the interventionist was using a physical prompt. After several pairings of the prompt with the presentation of the nonpreferred item, the interventionist may attempt to fade the prompt by delaying it by 4, 5, 10, or 15 seconds (Handen & Zane, 1987). If during this delay interval the learner independently shakes his or her head "no," the item is immediately removed. If the rejection response does not occur within the delay interval, the physical prompt is delivered and the item is removed. In addition to delaying the prompt, physical guidance may be faded by giving less and less assistance across successive opportunities (i.e., magnitude fading). For example, initially the interventionist may place one of his or her hands on each side of the learner's head and move it gently from side to side. On the next opportunity only one hand may be placed on one side of the learner's head and a gentle nudge given to start a shake to one side. Eventually, a light touch to the head may be all that is required to recruit a headshake, and after several opportunities even this prompt may be completely faded. Physical prompts can thus be faded by delaying the prompt and by systematically reducing the level of assistance given.

In a similar manner, for learners who will imitate a headshake, this modeling prompt can be eliminated using both time delay and magnitude fading. For example, the interventionist may both delay modeling the headshake and model less and less of the response. Initially, the modeled response may consist of an exaggerated and slow-motion sweep of the head from the right to the left and back again. Eventually, the interventionist quickly moves his or her head a few inches to one side to model the "no" headshake.

A gestural mode rejecting sequence can also accommodate a formal sign. However, before deciding to teach a gestural sign as a rejecting strategy it is important to remember that such signs may not be readily understood in the community at large. It may also be unwise to teach natural gestures and formal signs to serve the same function.

If the intervention procedure calls for the use of response prompts, gestures often lend themselves to a more traditional task-analytic approach to instruction (Haring & Kennedy, 1988; Popovich, 1981; Schleien & Ray, 1988; Snell, 1983). With this approach, prompts can be delivered as needed at each step of the gesture. A task analysis is a step-by-step listing of the component skills of a task. Figure 3 shows a task analysis of the ASL sign "no." When teaching this sign, physical prompts can be given for each step, as needed. After one step has been completed, the learner is provided with an opportunity to complete the next step independently. If he or she does not respond independently, that step is then prompted. This strategy is then repeated for the remaining steps. Step-by-step prompting may reveal that the learner is having difficulty with a particular step. For example, in Figure 3 the learner performed correctly on steps 1 and 3, but required prompting to complete step 2. More practice may, therefore, be required on this step of the task. Thus, gestural mode responses can be more readily prompted than vocal mode responses, because both physical response prompts and stimulus prompts can be delivered to elicit correct performances, even among learners who are not imitative (vocally or motorically.) Learners entering gestural mode programs need not be generalized imitators of motor movements, although this skill may facilitate acquisition.

Graphic Mode

To acquire a rejecting response in the graphic mode, the learner must be able to select a symbol, in any of the manners described in Chapter 2. Requesting in the graphic mode follows the

Step	Motor Movement	Performance		
1	Learner raises right arm in front of body so that hand is approximately chin level.	+	+	+
2a	Learner isolates thumb.	-	-	-
2b	Learner isolates index finger.	-	-	-
2c	Learner isolates middle finger.	-	-	-
3	Learner brings thumb, index, and middle finger together in a quick motion so that pads of all three touch.	+	+	+
	Date	6/21	6/22	6/23

Key
+ = Correct (performed without prompts)
- = Incorrect (required physical prompts)

Figure 3.   Task analysis of the ASL sign "no."

prototypic sequence: a nonpreferred item is offered, the learner selects a "no" symbol, and the nonpreferred item is removed. During the initial phases of intervention, it will often be necessary to prompt the learner to point to the "no" symbol. Two types of response prompts could be used to obtain a correct pointing response. Some learners, for example, may have some imitative control and a modeling or gestural prompt (i.e., the interventionist points to the correct symbol) may prove effective. Other learners may require a physical prompt (i.e., the interventionist physical guides the learner's finger to the correct symbol).

Response prompts can be eliminated using a time-delay and magnitude fading procedure. If correct responses can be prompted by modeling pointing, the prompt can be faded by having the interventionist point at the symbol from farther and farther away. Stimulus prompts may also be used effectively. A learner might be induced to point to a "no" symbol, for example, by somehow emphasizing or drawing the learner's attention to its presence. A symbol could for example, be moved around or initially made very large.

When teaching the learner to select a single symbol (in this case, "no") a *response shaping* procedure may also be useful. In shaping the desired form (e.g., pointing to a "no" symbol) is gradually established by reinforcing closer and closer approximations to the desired topography (Martin & Pear, 1983; Popovich, 1981; Skinner, 1953). For example, suppose in teaching a rejecting response the interventionist begins by placing the "no" symbol in front of the learner. Any movement of the learner's hand in the direction of the symbol is then reinforced by immediately removing the nonpreferred object. Because of this reinforcement, the learner will acquire some tendency to reach toward the symbol. The interventionist can then withhold reinforcement until the learner's hand moves a little closer to the symbol, and still later wait for the learner's hand actually to make contact with the symbol. At that point a successful selection of the "no" symbol will have been shaped.

Shaping procedures have often been criticized for being slow and laborious. The process is difficult to quantify and remains somewhat of an art. Shaping a rejecting response may prove particularly difficult. Recall that in learning to request preferred objects learners often exhibit a tendency to reach for the offered item. The selection of a "want" symbol can often be shaped by inserting that symbol into the oncoming reach. No such opportunity exists in teaching learners to reject nonpreferred items. In fact, if removal of the nonpreferred object is indeed an effective form of negative reinforcement, then learners may try to escape from those objects by attempting to leave the area, turn away, or otherwise withdraw. These types of escape behaviors will then compete with the desired response of staying in the area and pointing to the "no" symbol. To prevent this problem, the interventionist could prime the learner to respond appropriately prior to offering the nonpreferred item (Carr, 1988). For example, the learner could be prompted to point to the "no" symbol several times. Once this routine was established, the learner could then be taught to select in the presence of nonpreferred objects.

Selecting a "no" symbol can be established in an errorless manner by making only a single symbol available (Terrace, 1963). While the use of a single symbol will likely produce rapid acquisition of the desired skill, it will not ensure that the skill will be maintained when additional symbols are added to the learner's repertoire. The learner may believe that simply pointing to a piece of paper, rather than to a particular symbol, causes the withdrawal of the nonpreferred item. In order to discriminate between two or more symbols, a learner need not be able to read, as long as he or she can somehow tell the difference between various symbols. The basis of this discrimination may simply be the fact that the marks "no" look different from the marks "want." Once the learner can reliably point to the "no" symbol, for example, to reject nonpreferred objects, a second symbol can be introduced and discrimination training implemented. The second symbol can be introduced gradually or faded into the array to minimize errors. Differential reinforcement is given so that pointing to the "no" symbol is reinforced in the presence of nonpreferred objects, while pointing to the "want" symbol is reinforced in the presence of preferred objects (Reichle, Rogers, & Barrett, 1984). (Discrimination training is described in more detail in Chapter 10.)

One disadvantage of learning rejecting in the graphic mode is that listeners have to approach the learner to see which symbol he or she selected. The approach of the interventionist to see the symbol is inconsistent with removal of the nonpreferred object, which is the reinforcement for a rejection.

TYPES OF REJECTIONS

Like requests, rejections can be generalized or explicit, and can serve various functions. A learner can be taught to reject an offer of a nonpreferred object or to terminate an activity in which there is no provoking stimulus that serves as the discriminative stimulus for its termination. Both the level of generality and the function of the rejection are examined in the following sections.

Generalized Rejections

A generalized rejection (e.g., saying "no," pointing to a "no" symbol) can be established as a method of rejecting the entire range of nonpreferred objects or activities. The advantages of generalized requesting hold as well for generalized rejecting. Specifically, a generalized rejection:

1. Provides a means for the learner to reject any nonpreferred object without having to be able to discriminate among symbols
2. Enables a greater number of intervention opportunities to be implemented because a variety of items is available as discriminative stimuli or reinforcers. (This advantage may be less important in teaching rejecting than in teaching requesting, since a learner is unlikely to be satiated by the removal of an object as he or she might by the presentation of an object.)

3. Applies to a wide range of circumstances, promoting the generalization and maintenance of the behavior in natural environments

One drawback to generalized communicative behavior is that it places more of a burden on the listener, who must attempt to determine what it is the learner is rejecting. This is probably more critical in teaching requesting, in which an incorrect interpretation results in the learner not receiving the item that he or she wanted. Rejections, however, generally occur when the nonpreferred object or activity is actually present, thus diminishing the need for the listener to interpret. A generalized rejection may be the most practical type of rejecting behavior to establish initially.

Explicit Rejections

In generalized rejecting a single response is taught as a means of rejecting a particular object. For example, a learner might be taught to reject a nonpreferred food item with "no." In contrast, with explicit rejecting, intervention is conducted initially with a single specific nonpreferred item, making this approach most applicable for learners who have one or two objects or activities they dislike. If these nonpreferred items are likely to remain disliked, it may make sense to teach more explicit rejecting behavior.

Many learners have a fairly large list of nonpreferred items, which can be handled with generalized rejection, as well as a smaller number of intensely disliked items, which can be handled with a more explicit rejection. In this case both types of rejecting strategies may be implemented, with explicit rejection probably established after more generalized rejection. First, a learner could be taught the generalized rejection "no." Next, specific object labels could be taught. For example, a learner could be taught to say, sign, or point to the appropriate symbol when shown a particular item. The

learner would then be taught to combine the generalized "no" with the spoken word, gesture, or symbol corresponding to the object in question. Nonpreferred objects that the learner has not learned to name would continue to be rejected by the generalized "no."

These two types of rejections may be appropriate under slightly different conditions. For example, when offered a five-course meal containing one nonpreferred item, a learner would like to be able to reject the one nonpreferred item, while accepting the rest of the meal. This situation calls for an explicit rejection ("no spinach"). When offered a meal consisting entirely of nonpreferred items, however, the learner can use the generalized rejection ("no"). One way to deal with these different situations is to establish both explicit and more generalized forms of rejecting behavior. Explicit rejections are appropriate when many objects are offered, any one of which might be nonpreferred. Generalized rejections are appropriate when a single nonpreferred object or a group of equally nonpreferred items is offered.

Although generalized and explicit rejections have been described as if they represent distinct skills, in fact the two strategies are part of a continuum of behaviors. At one end of this continuum are generalized forms ("no") that are used to reject a wide range of nonpreferred objects or activities. Toward the middle of the continuum are forms such as "no vegetables" or "no noise" that are useful for particular classes of objects or activities. Further down this continuum are more explicit forms (e.g., "no spinach"), which occur in the presence of specific nonpreferred items.

Learners with severe disabilities have been taught to reject nonpreferred items with generalized rejections (Hung, 1980; Reichle et al., 1984). No study has documented the successful use of explicit rejection strategies by learners with severe disabilities, however, and no research has been done to determine which type of rejection (generalized or explicit) is more readily established, generalized, or maintained. In the absence of data, the logical strategy is to teach generalized rejecting before more explicit rejecting.

Rejections to Escape or Avoid

The underlying principle for rejecting behavior is negative reinforcement (Carr, 1977; Iwata, 1987). This principle is most readily seen in the contingency called "escape." A contingency is simply an if/then statement describing the relationship between some action and the resulting consequence (Lee, 1988). For example, if you drop an egg, then it will break. If you say "no," then the listener will remove the nonpreferred object. Each of these if/then statements describes a contingency. The first example (i.e., dropping an egg) holds because this is how the physical world works. In such a contingency the action is directly responsible for the consequences. In the second example, however, the action of saying "no" achieves its effect (i.e., the removal of the nonpreferred item) only indirectly, through the mediation of a listener. That is, saying "no" does not result in the removal of an object in the same way that, say, hurling the object through the air would. It is this indirect nature that separates simple mechanical actions from that class of behavior that variously been called language, verbal behavior (Skinner, 1957), or communicative behavior.

Unlike contingencies in which the consequence follows directly from the action, communicative behaviors are not inevitably effective. For communicative behavior to be effective, at the very least there must be a listener present who understands the speaker and is willing and able to reinforce his or her behavior. In both the direct and indirect contingencies, the conditions under which the actions occur determine to a large extent the consequences that follow. For example, if an egg is dropped gently on a soft pillow, it will not break. If a listener is not present rejecting an object will not cause it to be removed. Even if a listener is present, a rejection may not be honored. Statements of contingencies are often expanded to include the conditions under which the if/then statement holds true. For example, an egg is dropped, then it will break, given that it is dropped from a height of, say, 6 feet onto a concrete surface. Similarly, if a learner says "no," then the nonpreferred object will be removed, given that an obliging listener is present. Several conditions may need to prevail for an if/then contingency to hold. For example, not only a listener but a nonpreferred object must be present, and the speaker must have the listener's attention in order for the response "no" to be effective in having the object removed.

A learner can be taught to escape from an offered object or activity under at least two basic conditions. In one condition, the learner is taught to reject an offered item before actually coming into contact with the stimulus (e.g., a learner rejects an undesired food before tasting it). This condition comes close to an avoidance contingency. In an avoidance contingency, if the rejecting response is produced, then the nonpreferred stimulus is postponed or not presented at all. Most reported efforts to teach learners to reject nonpreferred items have established a type of pseudoavoidance contingency ("pseudo" because the nonpreferred event is offered or shown to the learner. True avoidance contingencies allow the learner to postpone or prevent any presentation of the aversive stimulus). Reichle et al. (1984) taught an adolescent girl with severe mental retardation to reject nonpreferred objects in the gestural mode. The learner was offered a variety of nonpreferred objects and asked, "Want one?" When she produced an approximation of the sign "no," the nonpreferred items were removed. Initially, the learner had to be prompted to make the correct sign, but physical guidance was successfully faded and the girl eventually used the rejection sign spontaneously when offered nonpreferred items. One aspect of this study involved giving the learner one of the nonpreferred items if the "no" sign did not occur independently. If the learner showed resistance when given the nonpreferred item, this was taken as evidence that the item was indeed disliked. The learner was then prompted to produce the "no" sign and then the item was removed. In this study, then, the learner could avoid receiving a nonpreferred object by signing "no" when such an object was offered.

A similar avoidance contingency was established for two children with autism in a study reported by Hung (1980). In this study, several food items were identified that were either consistently accepted and consumed ("yes" items) or consistently rejected ("no" items). The learners were then taught to say "yes" when offered "yes" foods and asked if they wanted a particular "yes" food. Correct response were reinforced by provision of the preferred food. The learners were then taught to say "no" when offered a "no" food item. Correct responses were reinforced by removal of the item. If the learner said "yes" to a "no" item, he or she was given a small taste of that item. Both learners eventually became very proficient at responding "yes" to offers of preferred foods and responding "no" to offers of nonpreferred foods. These learners avoided receiving nonpreferred objects by responding "no." Although the nonpreferred items were offered, the learners in these studies did not actually have to receive the item before it could be rejected. This type of rejecting behavior might be desirable if the actual receipt of the nonpreferred item is likely to generate behaviors that are unacceptable (e.g., aggressive, self-injurious) or may interfere with teaching the skill. For example, if giving the learner a nonpreferred item makes it more difficult to prompt the rejection response, then this first condition may represent the initial context within which to establish a reject response.

Under the second basic condition, the rejecting contingency is similar to the classic escape paradigm. Nonpreferred items are presented in an escape contingency, and the rejecting response functions to remove or terminate the object or activity. The learner can reject an object only after first trying it. This type of contingency is often used by parents in trying to get their children to eat a new type of food.

Escape contingencies arise in many situations. For example, in teaching blind learners to reject nonpreferred foods, it may be necessary to offer a taste of the object (if it cannot be smelled or touched) and prompt the reject response. Trying an offered item before rejecting it may also open the door to new experiences, since some learners may have a tendency to reject anything that is new without first trying it. Sometimes, however, after trying a new object or activity, learners discover that they like it.

An application of teaching rejecting was described in a study by Yamamoto and Mochizuki (1988). In this study, three children with autism were first taught to request an object from a "supplier" when instructed to do so by another. The children were instructed to bring a pencil from the teacher. They were then taught to approach the teacher (supplier), say, "Give me a pencil.", and return with the pencil. Sometimes, however, the children were supplied with an item that did not correspond to the request. When this occurred the children were taught to reject the mismatched offer (e.g., "That's not it. Give me a pencil."). Each of the children learned to reject items that did not correspond to the prior request. Such a rejecting strategy is useful in a variety of situations. For example, restaurant customers occasionally receive items they did not order. In such cases, a rejecting strategy (e.g., "That's not what I ordered. I had the _____.") may be appropriate.

As these examples suggest, rejecting does not always involve escaping from or avoiding an aversive or highly disliked object or event. A relatively neutral item might be rejected because it is not appropriate. Or a usually preferred item might be rejected after the learner has become saturated with that particular item.

A fourth piece of cake, for example, might be rejected, although cake is a preferred food.

Rejections to Take Leave

Leavetaking is a type of escape behavior in which a person removes him- or herself from an ongoing activity. For example, a person may want to terminate a conversation if it is boring or if he or she has something else to do. This desire to terminate is often signalled by conspicuously glancing at the clock, by averting the other person's attention, or by ceasing to respond. Eventually, one of several fairly standard forms appears to end the conversation (e.g., "Nice talking to you.", "See you later.", "Well, I must go."). These forms can be viewed as a type of escape behavior, or more specifically as a means of leavetaking.

It is important to distinguish between rejecting an activity and taking leave of an activity. A rejection occurs before the learner begins to participate in the activity. Leavetaking occurs at some point during participation or at the completion of an activity when the learner may become fatigued, the task may become too boring, a more attractive alternative may become available, or the time for the activity may be up. A single leavetaking form—"done" or "stop," for instance—could be established as a generalized form appropriate for a variety of activities. In contrast, the same response could be taught as an explicit response appropriate only to a particular task. There are few data to guide the interventionist in these matters. As with rejecting, it may, therefore, be most logical to teach generalized leavetaking.

Complicating matters even further is the fact that the same vocabulary may be included in more than one pragmatic class. "Done," for example, may represent both a comment on a certain state of affairs (i.e., the learner has actually finished a task) and a leavetaking. As discussed in Chapter 4, there is little reason to expect that vocabulary taught as a comment will occur automatically as a mand. Rejecting and leavetaking-exiting are types of mands that are reinforced by a characteristic consequence (i.e., the removal of a nonpreferred object or termination of a nonpreferred activity).

The distinction between rejecting and leavetaking may best be viewed in terms of a continuum. At one end of the continuum are pure requests, such as asking for a particular item. At the other end of the continuum are pure rejections, such as refusing an offered item. Between these two points are mands that contain elements of both requesting and rejecting (e.g., "Please stop doing that.") Leavetaking often contains elements of both requesting and rejecting. For example, a leavetaking response may terminate participation in some activity so that the learner can enter some other more preferred setting.

Determining Activities That Support Leavetaking Intervention   Not all nonpreferred activities should be the focus of leavetaking intervention. Some learners with severe disabilities may dislike a particular activity partially because of their lack of proficiency. Rather than teach such learners how to take leave of such activities, intervention should seek to increase their proficiency through skill training, thus perhaps changing the status of the activity from nonpreferred to preferred, and eliminating the learner's desire to take leave of the activity.

Learners who refuse to participate to any degree in a work task might first need to have some level of participation shaped. For example, if every time a learner is brought near a table containing work materials, he or she throws a violent temper tantrum, some work skills might first be established and the tantrums must be extinguished. The interventionist could, for example, determine how close a learner can be brought to the work materials without throwing a tantrum. Some powerful reinforcers could also be identified. Suppose, for example, the learner likes grapes and there are no contraindications to the learner receiving a few extra grapes each day. The interventionist then might stand as close to the work materials as the learner will go without throwing a tantrum, and call the learner over. When the learner approaches, he or she is given a grape. After the learner consumes the reinforcer, the interventionist asks, "Want to work?" and then immediately prompts the learner to produce the selected rejecting response, which might be a headshake "no" in this case. Over successive opportunities the interventionist stands closer and closer to the work materials, as long as no tantrum behavior is observed. Gradually, additional demands are introduced. For example, the learner may be offered a reinforcer only after approaching the interventionist and complying with a second request (e.g., "Sit down."). Later the learner may be required to sit at the work table for increasingly long periods of time (e.g., 10, 20, 30 seconds; 1, 2, 5, 10 minutes). Next, a minimal amount of work may be required before the reinforcer is provided and before an opportunity to take leave is offered. Through such a shaping procedure, the learner should eventually come to work readily and participate for increasingly longer periods of time before engaging in the leavetaking response (e.g., a headshake "no").

If leavetaking behavior is not consistently reinforced during the early stages of intervention, the behavior may be extinguished and the tantrums may resume. Once the behavior is well established, however, conditions can be placed on when and where leavetaking will and will not be accepted. For example, the contingency might be established that leavetaking will be honored only after the learner has worked, on average, a certain amount of time (i.e., a variable-interval schedule) or after completing a certain amount of work (e.g., ratio schedules).

Use of a Safety Signal   Some learners may participate in a work task for a certain period of time before attempting to take leave. If the amount of time the learner spends on the task is unacceptable or if the method used to take leave (e.g., throwing materials) is unacceptable,

steps can be taken to increase the amount of time spent working and to establish a more appropriate leavetaking behavior. One method of achieving both of these goals is *safety signal conditioning*.

A safety signal is any external stimulus that correlates with the end of an activity. The function of a safety signal may be to sustain performance on a task until the end. For example, one might consider taking a break from mowing the lawn, but continue if only a small amount of additional effort is required to finish the job. In this case, the fact that the task is almost over is a type of safety signal that will often generate sustained performance. Similarly, being informed that another 2 minutes of work are required before a break may be sufficient to keep one working until the end.

For learners who perform excess behavior to escape from a task, simply adding a safety signal may help reduce the frequency of excess behavior (Carr & Newsom, 1985). The effectiveness of a safety signal may first need to be established. This is done by introducing the safety signal just prior to the point in the task when excess behavior is likely to occur. At first, the task is terminated as soon as the signal is given. For example, if a learner typically works at a task for 3 minutes, the safety signal (e.g., "O.K., almost break time.") would be delivered by the interventionist after, say, 2½ minutes. Initially, the learner is prompted to request leavetaking as soon as the safety signal is given. The task demands are then removed. As several work periods elapse without a display of excess behavior, the interval between the introduction of the safety signal and the opportunity to request leavetaking can gradually be lengthened. In addition, the safety signal can gradually be given at a later and later point in the task.

Figure 4 shows a sequence for teaching a leavetaking behavior in conjunction with safety signal conditioning. First, the learner's behavior is assessed to determine at what point in a task excess behavior occurs. In this example, the

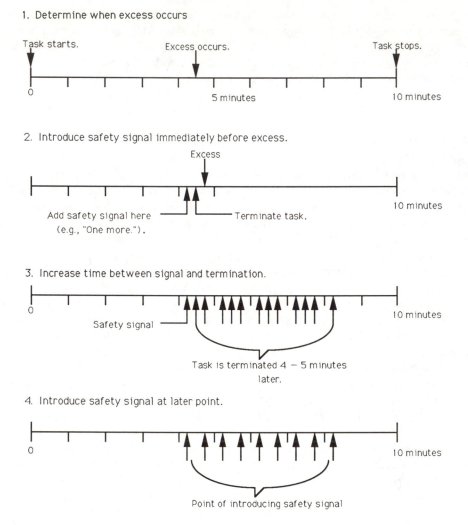

1. Determine when excess occurs

Task starts.   Excess occurs.   Task stops.

0   5 minutes   10 minutes

2. Introduce safety signal immediately before excess.

Excess

Add safety signal here
(e.g., "One more.").   Terminate task.   10 minutes

3. Increase time between signal and termination.

0   10 minutes

Safety signal

Task is terminated 4 — 5 minutes
later.

4. Introduce safety signal at later point.

0   10 minutes

Point of introducing safety signal

Figure 4.   Conditioning a safety signal.

learner typically completes 4½ minutes of a 10-minute task before attempting to take leave by engaging in excess behavior. Next, the safety signal (e.g., "Almost done.") is introduced after the learner has worked for about 4 minutes, that is, just before he or she generally attempts to take leave. Initially, the learner is immediately prompted to select a leavetaking symbol after the safety signal is given, and the task then ends. In step 3, the interval between the safety signal and the opportunity to take leave is increased. Eventually, the safety signal is given and the opportunity to request leavetaking is delayed by 4–5 minutes. The last step is to introduce the safety signal at a later and later point in the task, thus shaping 10 minutes (or more) of work behavior.

When teaching a leavetaking response or any type of rejecting behavior, it is wise to start with situations that do not represent the worst problems. It may be easier to establish the desired leavetaking or rejecting response with relatively neutral objects or activities rather than with objects or activities the learner dislikes intensely. Such objects or activities may generate emotional or excess behavior that may interfere with the interventionist's ability to prompt a correct response. If, however, the response form can be established in the presence of mildly disliked items, then the use of this response can perhaps be generalized to situations involving more aversive characteristics.

Discriminative Use of Leavetaking Behavior At some point it will be important to teach the learner to discriminate between situations in which leavetaking is allowed and situations in which it is not. During activities in which leavetaking is allowed, the learner will be prompted after the safety signal to request leavetaking, with the prompts eventually faded. During activities in which leavetaking is not acceptable (e.g., dressing, bathing, toothbrushing) requests to take leave will not be honored. Instead, participation in the activity could be reinforced.

One situation in which leavetaking behavior may be appropriate is when others are engaging in similar behavior. The actions of others provide important discriminative stimuli for behavior. Learners with severe disabilities may have learned to "follow the lead of others" because doing so is often reinforced. In some leavetaking situations the action of others leaving is an important controlling variable and should come to control the learner's own leavetaking.

Other situations in which leavetaking behavior may be appropriate are when the novelty of an activity or task wears off, when a once preferred task has become tedious, or when fatigue has set in. The new toys a child receives at Christmas may be played out by spring. New toys are abandoned, temporarily, in favor of old and vice versa. After playing tennis for 45 minutes a learner may become overheated or fatigued, and therefore wish to quit. After stuffing 50 envelopes, a learner may be worn out by the drudgery of the task and need a break. In order to provide a sufficient number of teaching opportunities, activities that turn over in 5–10 minutes are probably best for teaching a leavetaking response.

For any given activity, then, it will be necessary to determine the amount of time a learner will typically participate before indicating a desire to take leave. For example, a learner may typically spend 3 minutes on a new activity and then throw the materials across the room before moving on to the next activity. When such a pattern is consistently observed, opportunities to reject the materials more appropriately can be implemented after the learner has participated for 2½ minutes. After 2½ minutes the interventionist asks, "Want to quit?" and then prompts the learner to point to a "done" or "break" symbol. When this response occurs, the materials are removed and the learner is allowed to move on to some other activity. Over successive opportunities the prompts are faded. Eventually, the learner should master appropriate leavetaking skills. Finally, learners can be taught appropriate leavetaking behaviors in the face of preferred activities. In this case, leavetaking behavior is very similar to requesting an alternative activity.

TEACHING REQUESTS FOR ALTERNATIVES

The basic principles of teaching requests for alternatives are similar to those for teaching requesting in general. As a type of rejecting behavior, a request for an alternative provides learners with a means of making choices. It is a good option to consider when options do exist and when members of a particular class of objects (fruits, drinks, cookies, work tasks) can be ranked in terms of preference. For example, sometimes a learner may prefer to bathe, at other times to shower. Choices can be incorporated into learners' lives by providing them with the means to request a bath as an alternative to a shower.

Learners with severe disabilities can be taught to request an alternative when offered some less preferred item. Suppose, for example, that a learner likes fruit, but prefers some fruits (e.g., grapes, apples, cherries) to others (e.g., bananas). When the learner is offered a banana, he typically throws it across the room. It may be possible to teach the learner to reject the offer by communicating "no." Alternatively, the learner could be taught to request some other type of fruit. When a banana is offered, the learner is taught to select the "apple" symbol, the banana is removed, and the apple is presented. To execute such a task, the learner would need symbols corresponding to each available alternative.

A similar technique could be established at the single symbol level with an intermediate level vocabulary. For example, a learner may have been taught to request a number of fruits by pointing to a single "fruit" symbol. At snacktime the learner selects the "fruit" symbol. Not knowing which type of fruit to deliver, the interventionist offers the learner a banana. If the learner does not really want the banana, he or she could be taught to request an alternative by pointing again to the "fruit" symbol. A new item would then be offered and this process would continue until the learner accepts an offer. Thus, an alternative is requested by simply repeating the previous generic request, thus obviating the need to acquire a large repertoire of symbols. The drawback to this technique is that many offers and counteroffers may be required before the interventionist determines which item the learner is requesting.

A third technique would be to teach the learner first to reject the offered item ("no"), and then to request the alternative ("want" and "apple"). There is evidence to suggest, however, that requests for alternatives may not readily occur on occasions when a nonpreferred item is offered in the absence of organized instruction. Reichle (1988) reported on an adult with severe disabilities who had been taught to request preferred items and reject nonpreferred items. Each of these skills had been established sepa-

rately by presenting the learner with either a preferred or a nonpreferred object. The learner showed no tendency to reject a usually preferred item after having become satiated with it. Specifically, the learner liked coffee and would typically request four to five cups. He would not reject an offer for a sixth cup even though he would not drink it if given. Thus, he failed to generalize his rejecting skills, which had been learned exclusively in the context of nonpreferred items, to a situation in which a usually preferred item needed to be rejected. Learners taught to request preferred items and reject nonpreferred items may similarly fail to request an alternative when offered a usually preferred item they do not currently want. Requesting an alternative may thus need to be taught directly, as it is unlikely to emerge even if the appropriate request form is available. For example, although the learner may know how to request an apple, he or she may not think to do so when offered a banana. To learn to use "apple" as a request for an alternative, the learner is taught first to reject the banana ("no") and then to request the alternative ("want" plus "apple"). Initially, this sequence may require substantial prompting, but such prompts eventually can be faded until the chain occurs independently under the appropriate conditions.

TEACHING REJECTIONS IN THE CONTEXT OF INTEROCEPTIVE STATES

Often learners who have been taught to reject nonpreferred objects when they are offered will fail to do so under more natural situations. That is, although learners may know to reject a nonpreferred food when it is offered, they may be unable to reject a food they normally like but do not want (because, say, of illness or lack of appetite) (Sosne, Handleman, & Harris, 1979).

Reichle (1988) investigated this issue of generalization of rejecting behavior from situations involving the offer of nonpreferred items to situations involving continued offers of preferred items. Learners with severe retardation were taught a generalized rejecting gesture to use in the presence of highly nonpreferred objects or activities. Two probe conditions were then implemented. In one condition, other nonpreferred objects or activities were offered to test for stimulus generalization to untrained exemplars. In the other condition, the learners were satiated with preferred items and continued offers were made to test for generalizations from nonpreferred to preferred objects or activities under a state of satiation. Generalization extended to other nonpreferred objects or activities, but the rejection response did not occur when preferred objects or activities were repeatedly offered. These results suggest that rejecting usually preferred items in the face of satiation is not likely to emerge simply by teaching a learner to reject nonpreferred items, and may require instruction.

TEACHING
CONDITIONAL USE OF REJECTION

Just as conditions can be placed on when it is and when it is not appropriate to request (as discussed in Chapter 5), similar conditional control of rejecting may need to be taught. Some objects (e.g., medications) or activities (e.g., work, self-care routines) cannot be avoided and are thus inappropriate to reject. Such mandatory objects and activities should thus be excluded when teaching rejecting behavior, thus imposing conditions on the circumstances under which rejecting behavior will be effective. In some circumstances rejecting will never be effective. Other situations, however, will accommodate leavetaking or rejecting to some degree. For example, a learner may have some leeway in deciding what clothing to wear, what foods to

eat, or what work tasks to perform. These situations may thus permit some rejecting.

In some instances, rather than trying to place conditions on the use of an appropriate rejecting response while attempting to establish the behavior itself, it may be wiser first to teach the skill and increase its frequency, and only then to place conditions on its use. For example, each time a learner produces a rejection response, he or she is allowed to avoid participation in a nonpreferred housekeeping task. Once this rejecting response is firmly established, the rejecting response may then be honored only after the learner has participated in the task for a brief period of time. Alternatively, only every other rejection might be honored, so that sometimes the learner rejects a task but is not allowed to avoid it. "Yes" trials (i.e., rejections that are honored) should be distinguished from "no" trials (i.e., rejections that are not honored) in some predictable way. This can be achieved by verbally cueing the learner (e.g., "Today you will have to dust your room." versus "Today you can dust your room if you like.").

SUMMARY

Rejecting has been largely neglected by language intervention programs for learners with severe disabilities. Teaching learners to reject nonpreferred objects or activities is important for ensuring them a degree of autonomy and control. Learners can use generalized or explicit vocabulary to reject nonpreferred objects, to take leave, and to request an alternative. These skills can be taught in the vocal, gestural, and graphic modes. Two challenges facing the interventionist are teaching the learner to reject spontaneously and teaching him or her to use rejecting responses conditionally.

REFERENCES

Baer, D.M., & Deguchi, H. (1985). Generalized imitation from a radical-behavioral viewpoint. In S. Reiss & R.R. Bootzin (Eds.), *Theoretical issues in* *behavior therapy* (pp. 179–217). New York: Academic Press.
Carr, E.G. (1977). The motivation of self-injurious

behavior: A review of some hypotheses. *Psychological Bulletin, 84,* 800–816.

Carr, E.G. (1988). Functional equivalence as a mechanism of response generalization. In R.H. Horner, G. Dunlap, & R.L. Koegel (Eds.), *Generalization and maintenance: Life-style changes in applied settings* (pp. 221–241). Baltimore: Paul H. Brookes Publishing Co.

Carr, E.G., & Newsom, C.D. (1985). Demand-related tantrums: Conceptualization and treatment. *Behavior Modification, 9,* 403–426.

Handen, B.L., & Zane, T. (1987). Delayed prompting: A review of procedural variations and results. *Research in Developmental Disabilities, 8,* 307–330.

Haring, T.G., & Kennedy, G.H. (1988). Units of analysis in task-analytic research. *Journal of Applied Behavior Analysis, 21,* 207–215.

Hung, D.W. (1980). Training and generalization of yes and no as mands in two autistic children. *Journal of Autism and Developmental Disorders, 10,* 139–152.

Iwata, B.A. (1987). Negative reinforcement in applied behavior analysis: An emerging technology. *Journal of Applied Behavior Analysis, 20,* 361–378.

Lee, V.L. (1988). *Beyond behaviorism.* Hillsdale, NJ: Lawrence Erlbaum Associates.

Martin, G., & Pear, J. (1983). *Behavior modification: What it is and how to do it* (2nd ed.). Englewood Cliffs, NJ: Prentice-Hall.

Popovich, D. (1981). *Effective educational and behavioral programming for severely and profoundly handicapped students: A manual for teachers and aids.* Baltimore: Paul H. Brookes Publishing Co.

Reichle, J. (1988). *Stimulus control applications in the establishment of an initial communicative repertoire.* Unpublished manuscript, University of Minnesota, Minneapolis.

Reichle, J., Rogers, N., & Barrett, C. (1984). Establishing pragmatic discrimination among the communicative functions of requesting, rejecting, and commenting in an adolescent. *Journal of The Association for Persons with Severe Handicaps, 9,* 31–36.

Risley, T.R., & Wolf, M. (1967). Establishing functional speech in echolalic children. *Behaviour Research and Therapy, 5,* 73–88.

Schleien, S.J., & Ray, M.T. (1988). *Community recreation and persons with disabilities: Strategies for integration.* Baltimore: Paul H. Brookes Publishing Co.

Skinner, B.F. (1953). *Science and human behavior.* New York: Macmillan.

Skinner, B.F. (1957). *Verbal behavior.* Englewood Cliffs, NJ: Prentice-Hall.

Snell, M.E. (1983). *Systematic instruction of the moderately and severely handicapped.* Columbus, OH: Charles E. Merrill.

Sosne, J.B., Handleman, J.S., & Harris, S.L. (1979). Teaching spontaneous-functional speech to autistic type children. *Mental Retardation, 17,* 241–245.

Terrace, H.S. (1963). Discrimination learning with and without "errors." *Journal of the Experimental Analysis of Behavior, 6,* 1–27.

Yamamoto, J., & Mochizuki, A. (1988). Acquisition and functional analysis of manding with autistic students. *Journal of Applied Behavior Analysis, 21,* 57–64.

7

Developing Communicative Exchanges

Joe Reichle

Initial communicative exchanges are often comprised of a single exchange in which an initiation is followed by a single response. As interactions become more sophisticated, an initiation is followed by some period of maintenance, followed by a termination response by one of the participants. When teaching learners with severe disabilities to use communicative intents during interactions, attention must be paid to the learner's ability to initiate, maintain, and terminate interactions. Without these competencies, the value of acquiring communicative intents is limited.

Several topics related to teaching functional interaction skills are addressed in this chapter. First, interactions are defined as either social or nonsocial, and the implications of this distinction are examined. Second, the three components of an interaction (i.e., maintenance, initiation, and termination) are discussed, and suggestions for teaching each are provided. Third, critical elements of communicative interaction are examined. Fourth, procedural issues are addressed. Finally, conversational difficulties experienced by learners with severe

disabilities and suggestions for practical ways to facilitate greater participation in communicative exchanges are examined. The sections on learners with severe disabilities reflect relatively new information and perspectives. Because these perspectives are new, a data base is lacking. Programmatic suggestions are derived primarily from seemingly logical applications of research on children without disabilities to people with severe disabilities, as well as from considerable experience in the field.

We all interact with different aspects of our environments. For example, in purchasing a beverage from a vending machine, we interact with the machine. In sitting down to eat, we interact with eating utensils and food items. The terms *initiate, maintain,* and *terminate* can be applied to activities regardless of the presence of other people in the environment. For example, a learner can initiate participation in a meal by retrieving his lunch box, going outside, sitting under a tree, and opening the lunch box. The mealtime routine can be maintained as the learner moves from food item to food item over the course of the meal. Mealtime may be terminated with the learner closing his lunch box, returning inside, and placing the lunch box in a locker. In this example, no other people were involved in the series of interactions with aspects of the environment.

In other situations, the terms *initiate, maintain,* and *terminate* may apply to participation in activities that involve other people. For example, during lunchtime a learner might initiate a communicative interaction by saying, "Boy, it's cold outside." The learner's partner, in turn, could maintain this interaction by nodding "yes" and saying, "It was cold yesterday, too." At the conclusion of the exchange, one of the participants may say goodbye in order to terminate the interaction.

Little empirical work has been done to determine the relationship between ability to initiate, maintain, and terminate interactions in nonsocial activities (i.e., those engaged in individually) and the ability to initiate, maintain, and terminate interactions in social routines (i.e., those engaged in with other people). It seems reasonable to speculate that learners who have a difficult time initiating, maintaining, and terminating participation in activities that do not involve other people are prone to the same difficulties in activities involving people. Some learners appear unable to generalize between social and nonsocial activities. Interactions in both types of activities are very important if learners are to function independently in home and community environments.

QUALITATIVE ASPECTS
OF SUCCESSFUL INTERACTIONS

The goal of most communication intervention programs appears to be to establish skills that permit a back and forth exchange that has a logical beginning and end. Grice (1975) suggests that the qualitative criteria of truthfulness, informativeness, and relevance be applied to any desirable communicative interaction.

Truthfulness

An operational definition of truthfulness suggests that the learner recognizes the correspondence between his or her actions and his or her communicative behavior. For example, if a learner requests a cookie, the listener must assume that he actually wants one. In asking a peer, "What did you do at work today?", the learner assumes that the response will correspond to what the listener actually did. Failure to link communicative behavior correctly with actions appears to be common among young children and learners with severe disabilities.

Risley and Hart (1968) reported discrepancies between the actions of school-age children described as disadvantaged and their subsequent verbal reports describing their actions. Israel and Brown (1977) reported a similar lack of correspondence among preschool children. The reasons for the lack of correspondence were unclear. It is possible that during the interval between engaging in an activity and reporting about it learners were unable to remember exactly what had happened. It is also possible that the learners did not want to engage in a social interaction and thus provided the least costly response that would be acceptable to the listener. For example, if a 4-year-old is asked what he did at school while he is engrossed in a cartoon on TV, he may respond, "We played" to "get rid" of the inquisitor.

Several investigators have described intervention procedures designed to improve the correspondence between communicative behavior and the corresponding actions (Baer, Williams, Osnes, & Stokes, 1984; Guevremont, Osnes, & Stokes, 1986a, 1986b). In all instances, successful correspondence between actions and communicative behavior improved when reinforcement was contingent on a match between actions and verbal reports. These findings suggest that, among many learners, inability to remember may not be the major cause of the lack of correspondence between actions and utterances. The importance of confused recall was tested using a strategy originally referred to by Constantine and Sidman (1975) as delayed matching. The interventionist shows the learner an item (e.g., an apple). The item is then removed. After a predetermined number of seconds, the choice array is placed near the learner. In order for the learner to produce a correct response, he or she must remember the item during the interval between the time the item is removed and the time the choice array is presented. There is some evidence to suggest that learners who do not do well in a delayed matching task can be taught to do so through the systematic application of a delay procedure. The delay procedure is designed systematically to increase the length of the interval between the delivery of the item and the presentation of the choice array.

Correspondence between a learner's communicative behavior and his or her actions is critical if the learner's communication is to have social validity. The listener must be able to assume that, for the most part, a speaker's communicative behaviors are representative of actual events.

Frequently, the explanation for a lack of correspondence may be found in the learner's history with his or her initial repertoire of symbols. Often a learner's initial communicative repertoire may consist almost exclusively of symbols representing preferred items. Consequently, touching any symbol will result in good things happening. In many instances, learners may not attend to the symbols they select since any symbol touched results in the receipt of a desirable object or activity.

Informativeness and Relevance

Children between 1 and 1½ years old and some learners with severe developmental disabilities often demand high levels of attention but lack a sufficiently extensive communicative repertoire to participate in a conversation. They may spend a significant amount of time pointing out the obvious. For example, a cat may walk into a room while both the child and the caregiver observe. In spite of the fact that the adult has been attending to the event, the child will call attention to the event. Subsequently, the child may label the items several times during a short period of time. Of course, adults interacting with their children contribute directly to this phenomenon by asking children to provide information that is already known to both the child and the adult.

Some people with severe disabilities appear to have tremendous difficulties being informative. For example, some learners seek to continue an interaction by engaging in echolalic behavior. Other learners will seek to maintain an interaction by engaging in perseverative behavior. For example, after saying "How are you doing?" to enter an interaction, the learner continues to repeat the phrase "How are you doing?"

Sometimes the learner's communicative behavior is not understandable to the listener. In these instances, the learner must be able to revise the original message to meet the needs of the listener. Sensitivity in listener feedback coupled with the ability to repair conversational breakdowns represent skills critical to the maintenance of conversational interaction. There is a growing body of data examining these skills among both children with and children without developmental disabilities. These studies indicate that children understand the obligation to clarify an unsuccessful communicative attempt at a very early age, provided that their partner clearly marks the utterance as being problematic (e.g., " I don't get it."). Children without developmental disabilities understand this responsibility by about 18 months of age (Gallagher & Darnton, 1978). Calculator and Delaney (1986) have suggested that users of augmentative communication systems perform similarly to children without disabilities in recognizing the need to clarify an incomprehensible communicative act.

The strategies that are used to repair unsuccessful communicative attempts appear to change as the child gets older or becomes more sophisticated linguistically. Gallagher (1977) reported that among children without developmental disabilities with a mean length of utterance of less than 2.0 units, phonetic elaboration (altering the articulation of the original utterance) was a prevailing clarification strategy. As children became more sophisticated linguistically, they began to rely more heavily on strategies that involve reduction, elaboration, and utterance substitution (Figure 1). All of these strategies involve changing substantially the organization of the original utterance (reduction/elaboration), or adding vocabulary items that were not part of the original utterance (elaboration/substitution). Gallagher and Darnton (1978) found that as language-impaired children became more proficient in language (in terms of mean length of utterance), their strategies for revising unclear utterances differed from those used by people without disabilities, as reported by Gallagher (1977).

Prekker (1988) compared conversational repair strategies used by 24- to 30-month-old children without developmental disabilities with strategies used by 5- to 12-year-old children with intellectual delays. She found that among children with a mean length of utterance under 2.0, the younger group used significantly more elaboration repairs. Among the more linguistically sophisticated learners, no significant qualitative differences in repair strategies were observed between the two groups.

Calculator and Delaney (1986) investigated the clarification strategies used by five speaking and five nonspeaking learners with mental retardation. The learners' mental ages ranged from 3 years, 8 months to 5 years, 6 months. Mean length of utterance ranged from 2.05 to 4.50 and their age equivalent scores on the Peabody Picture Vocabulary Test ranged from 2:11 to 7:7. Each subject received 40 neutral requests for clarification (e.g., "Huh?", "What?") during the course of a 90-minute interaction (one request about every 2 minutes). The two groups of learners performed similarly. Repetition was the most prevalent repair strategy for 9 of the 10 subjects. There were no significant differences between the two groups with respect to the types of revision strategies adopted. Elabora-

Strategy	Definition	Example
Reduction	Deletion of one or more words from the original utterance	Child: "My tire." Adult: "What?" Child: "Tire."
Elaboration	Addition of one or more words to the original utterance	Child: "That?" Adult: "What?" Child: "What that?"
Substitution	Replacement of one or more words in the original utterance	Child: "Get it out." Adult: "What?" Child: "Get that out."

Figure 1.   Strategies used to repair unsuccessful communicative attempts. (Adapted from Gallagher, 1977.)

tions accounted for the greatest proportion of revisions, and substitutions were used sparingly. Both groups failed to respond to approximately 18% of the requests for clarification. Calculator and Delaney concluded that conversational breakdown often linked to use of communication boards may not be due to the use of the augmentative system per se, but instead may be a function of repair skill deficits in this population.

Most of the rather sparse literature suggests that augmentative system users perform more acceptably in obligatory communicative situations. This appears to be the case in providing answers to questions as well as in revising original communicative attempts after the listener indicates that a clarification is required.

DEVELOPING COMMUNICATIVE EXCHANGES IN THE VOCAL MODE

Maintaining an Interaction

Most of us have observed learners fuss or cry at the termination of an activity that they wish to experience again. A somewhat more sophisticated method of maintaining an interaction in a play situation with another person may involve taking turns in a game of catch. In the presence of a terminated event or an event with an uncharacteristic pause, a learner may produce a behavior to maintain participation. It may be difficult to tell whether the learner is requesting reentry into the activity or whether he or she is protesting the original termination of the activity. Initial repertoires of protesting (or rejecting) and requesting may be more similar than the interventionist realizes. Additionally, there may be difficulty differentiating between initiating and maintaining. If a learner approaches an adult who has not been attending to obtain assistance in activating a toy, the adult is apt to perceive the learner's behavior as an initiation. However, from the learner's perspective, the approach made to the adult may be simply part of a chain

of behavior to maintain an interaction with the toy. At first glance this may be a seemingly unimportant point. However, the relative time between stopping an activity and restarting it may serve as a critical feature distinguishing early aspects of initiation and maintenance. It also underscores the importance of defining exactly what we mean by interactional maintenance.

In the toy example, the learner's interaction was motivated by the desire to get something; it was not purely social. Among children without disabilities, purely social interactions appear to emerge somewhat concurrently with nonsocial interactions. Children interact with their caregivers in games such as "peek-a-boo," "so-big," "waving hi," and "give me five." These interactions are social in that the purpose of the game appears to be to have fun with another person by taking turns over a sustained period of time. Interactional maintenance thus begins with the learner's awareness that someone or something in his or her environment has initiated an action, and includes the learner's reaction to changing aspects of his or her environment. This reaction, in turn, may result in the learner's communicative partner producing another communicative act further to maintain the interaction.

Reacting to Events   Reacting to environmental events represents a critical skill required in maintaining an interaction with one's environment. For many people who have been described as passive participants, documenting their awareness of environmental events is a significant initial step in the establishment of interaction maintenance skills. Changes in a learner's visual orientation subsequent to the presentation of an environmental event have often been used as evidence of environmental awareness. For example, a mother enters the room carrying a bottle of milk. The child immediately takes notice as he or she visually glances at the mother, the milk, or both. Home environments, as well as educational and community environments, provide a wealth of visual and auditory events to which a learner may react. The newspaper boy throws the paper on the front porch creating a loud noise, pots and pans bang, siblings yell, toilets flush, door bells ring. Cats walk into the room, a peer holding an ice-cream cone walks by.

Interactions that occur between very young children and others in their environment may be very limited by the motor and vocal competencies of the infant. The earliest emergence of interactional maintenance among infants is difficult to pinpoint. In summarizing the available literature, Owens (1984) concluded that the first 6 months of life are characterized by the mastery of "joint attention," that is, the child quickly develops a propensity to spend much of his waking time "looking at objects and events in tandem with his mother" (p. 147). Brazelton, Koslowski, and Main (1974) reported rhythmic cycles of attention and nonattention during face to face interaction between mothers and children. Mothers appear to use two slightly different variations of the same strategy to promote joint attention. In an initial technique, the mother initiates face to face gazing with her child (typically making smiling faces with accompanying soft sounds). When the infant is between 1 and 2 months of age, mothers begin to incorporate bringing objects into the child's field of vision, or they follow the infants "line of regard." In this latter strategy, when the mother observes an object on which the child appears to have focused, she transfers her gaze to that item and in some instances retrieves it and brings it close to the child for inspection. During these episodes, mothers often attempt to enhance the saliency of the item by shaking and waving it to ensure maintenance of the child's attention.

By about 8 weeks of age, the infant has gained increasing competence in the ability visually to track the movement of both the mother and the objects she may be handling. By around 4 months of age, the child's proficiency in attend-

ing to maternally initiated cues has improved to the extent that the young child can follow his or her mother's line of regard (Scaife & Bruner, 1975). Shortly after line of regard emerges, the infant begins to attend to and act upon slightly more peripheral cues associated with the mother's action. For example, if a history develops in which the mother says "look" just before she initiates movement to items of interest, over time the child will come to engage in "line of regard" in the presence of only a verbal cue produced by the mother. Near the end of the first 6 months, the child has learned to attend to very subtle maternal cues.

Several instructional strategies are available for learners who fail to attend to or to respond to events that occur in their surroundings. The first strategy involves enhancing the saliency of stimuli to which the interventionist wishes the learner to respond. The second strategy involves establishing a reliable response given the assumption that the learner is aware of an environmental event but does not yet have an interpretable response to provide to demonstrate awareness. For some learners with severe or multiple disabilities, subtle gazing cues offered by the interventionist may not be sufficient to attract the learner's attention or cause the learner's line of regard to shift. If joint attention is a critical aspect of interactional development, at the earliest level, the interventionist must consider procedures that might facilitate behaviors such as those described. A reasonable starting point has been to determine whether a learner will engage in line of regard.

Attending to Line of Regard   Superficially, line of regard resembles imitation. After establishing eye contact with the learner, the interventionist looks at an item located some distance from both the interventionist and the learner. The learner then shifts his or her eye gaze to the new area of interventionist focus. In this sequence, the learner has replicated the behavior performed by the interventionist. However, an alternative explanation for this behavior may exist. Suppose, for example, that a child's mother arrives home from work at approximately 5 P.M. each day bearing a treat for her child. Everyday the child's father sees the child's mother as he gazes out the front window. Just prior to the mother opening the door and saying "I'm home," the father shifts his gaze to the door. Initially, it may be the sound of the door opening or the mother saying "I'm home" that prompts the learner to turn his or her head in the direction of the door. Over time, however, the child may begin to observe that the father usually shifts his gaze to the door just before it opens. Consequently, the father's glance at the door can come to be associated with the mother's arriving home from work. Careful scrutiny of this episode suggests that the child's ability to localize represents a critical skill that facilitates the acquisition of line of regard.

A conditioning procedure is depicted in Figure 2 in which a controlling stimulus (opening of the door) paired with a noncontrolling stimulus (eye gaze of caregiver) resulted in the target behavior (the learner looking at the door). Over time because the caregiver's eye gaze was paired systematically with the opening of the door, the caregiver's eye gaze came to take on the stimulus properties of the door opening, resulting in a learner response. Table 1 presents components of a procedure for teaching line of regard.

Typically, learners are not content simply to look at items of interest. Among learners with functional use of their arms, approximations of reaching readily begin to occur. Learners with severe physical disabilities often have to exert significant effort to reach toward an object or person of interest. Learners may inadvertently have been taught to wait for objects and people of interest to come to them. That is, their history of interactions with the environment may have taught them to be helpless. Sometimes,

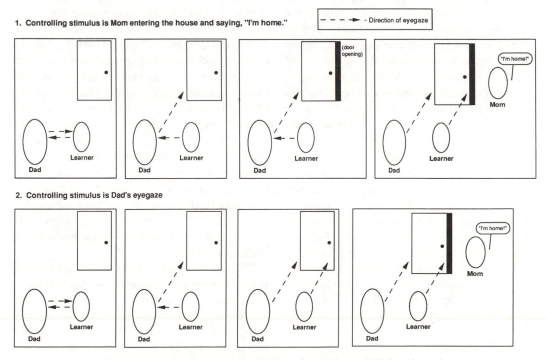

Figure 2.   An example of a conditioning procedure used to establish line of regard.

Table 1. Components of a procedure to teach "line of regard"

—An auditory or visual event that results in the learner localizing to it is identified.

—After establishing eye contact with the learner, the interventionist diverts his gaze to the location where the auditory or visual event is about to occur.

—Over successive intervention opportunities the amount of time between the interventionist's eye gaze and the auditory or visual spectacle increases.

this helplessness culminates in a learner looking at an object or person of interest but failing to reach forward, even though he or she is physically capable of doing so. For these learners, intervention strategies that involve teaching reaching as an interactional maintenance strategy can be appropriate.

Acting on Objects or Activities Introduced by Others

Reaching   Around 5 months of age infants begin to engage in visually directed reaching. That is, in reaching for a target that moves, the infant will adjust his or her reach. Bruner (1978) has reported that two distinct classes of reaching behavior emerge by about 8 months of age. In one, learners reach without attending to their communicative partners. These reaches are used primarily to procure desired items or examine unfamiliar items. In the second, reach is accompanied by gaze directed to the communicative partner. Bruner refers to this type of reach as "reach for signal." Reach-for-signal behavior paves the way for a variety of interpersonal games that begin to enter the learner's repertoire. Bruner (1975) refers to these emerging social routines as "joint action." Joint actions consist of routine actions that occur in familiar well learned contexts. Examples of joint action games engaged in by mothers and their young children include peek-a-boo, tickling, "I'm gonna get you," eensy weensy spider, and pat-a-cake.

The emergence of some of these games was described in Chapter 1. Initially, the child's turn

in the game may consist only of a laugh, smile, or wiggle at the appropriate moment. Over time, as the child becomes more familiar with the game and becomes more sophisticated in terms of motor abilities, he or she may begin to imitate the behavior produced by his or her partner. For example, in a game of peek-a-boo, a learner may smile or chuckle as his partner removes her hands from his face. Over time he may begin to raise his own hands to his face at about the same point as his partner. Eventually, the learner may come to take turns in the game. That is, during one turn, he may be the passive partner in the game and in the next turn he may be the active partner. The learner's growing propensity for use of his hands and arms allows the reach-for-signal behavior to be expanded into several routines. Around 8–10 months of age, infants begin to coordinate their motor movement to engage in what have come to be referred to as *take, show,* and *give* routines.

Taking   In taking routines, desired objects or activities are offered to the learner. For example, the author offered soup crackers to his 12-month-old daughter. The child took the first 15 crackers and consumed them. From that point on, however, the child took the cracker offered, moved several feet away, and placed it on the table. She remained at the table until offered another cracker. This game continued for 23 more repetitions. Interestingly, crackers on the floor were not touched during the game. It thus appeared that taking was the main purpose of the game. It is not clear what it is that is so intrinsically enjoyable about taking, although it seems likely that some of the enjoyment was derived from the social interaction between the child and father.

This taking routine can be observed in people with developmental disabilities. Such learners often engage in a task and then take offered reinforcers only to discard them. In at least some of these instances it is possible that the social interaction engaged in by the learners sustained their performance.

"Reaching for" routines are of instructional value with people with severe disabilities who do not engage in interactions. Reaching for an offered object represents a fairly simple method of maintaining an interaction with another person. Being able to move toward a communicative partner contingent on the offer of a reinforcer establishes the important condition of close proximity that is important if an interaction is to proceed. There may be several separate and distinct reasons why people extend their hands to accept an offered object. If an offered object represents a desired object, taking it is a probable event. Of course, if the item offered is preferred, it is likely that the learner would reach for it if the item were set on a nearby table. A second motivation for taking an offered item is to satisfy one's curiosity. The interventionist may be offering a brand new item with which the learner has no experience. The learner's curiosity serves to motivate a reach. A third motivation for taking is social. A learner may have very little interest or curiosity in the item being offered. However, he or she may be interested in interacting with the person who is extending the item. A summary of the possible motivations for engaging in taking is shown in Table 2.

Some learners with severe disabilities are motivated to participate in taking routines solely as a function of their interest in the reinforcers being offered. However, it is possible that, over time, such learners may acquire an interest in social interactions if such interests are cultivated by the interventionist during taking routines. The next several sections describe the establishment of a taking routine in learners who may not be interested in social interactions at the outset.

Teaching the Learner to Self-Select Items of Interest   With learners who seem to show little interest in interacting with people, it may be helpful to separate interactions that take place with objects from interactions that take place with people. This is particularly important if there is reason to believe that access to particular objects may be more reinforcing than access to particular people. The first step is to identify items in the environment that the learner will be taught to select. In doing so, interventionists must keep in mind that some learners may exhibit learned helplessness and may be uninterested in items in their environment.

Learned helplessness occurs when it is unclear to the learner that he or she is able to exert control over the environment. Guess, Benson, and Siegel-Causey (1985) suggest that learners who exhibit helplessness see no relationship between their actions and environmental outcomes. For many learners, their social history has offered few opportunities to self-select desired objects, people, or activities. At mealtime, plates are prepared and distributed. Additional servings are provided automatically. Coats are handed out and doors opened when it is time to go outside. Thus, throughout the day, the caregivers do virtually everything for the learners. Initially, some learners may have attempted to self-select items or activities of interest, but were actively encouraged not to do so. For example, while at a restaurant, the learner may reach for a pitcher of milk. Fearing a spill, the caregiver may quickly intervene by prompting the learner's hand away from the pitcher. Over time, the learner's self-selecting behavior may be extinguished.

The primary intervention strategy used to remedy learned helplessness involves the establishment of the learner's contingent control over some aspect or aspects of the environment. Several intervention studies have demonstrated that

Table 2.   Motivations for "taking"

—Obtaining desired reinforcer

—Satisfying curiosity

—Establishing social contact with another person

—Perpetuating a habit of reaching for an offered object (since in the past it often resulted in obtaining something desirable)

very young children can be taught to control their access to desirable activities as a result of their actions (Watson & Ramey, 1969). Perhaps the greatest challenge facing the interventionist who works with an apparently passive learner is selecting an environmental event that he or she values sufficiently to motivate him or her to learn an accessing response. These strategies, called reinforcer sampling, are discussed in detail in Chapter 5.

Teaching the Learner to Obtain Access to Desired Items Using People as Mediators Often learners who have developed preferences for certain objects or activities have not yet cultivated an interest in people who may be associated with those objects and activities. Consider the case of a shy child who visits someone's home. She may admire a bowl of candy on the coffee table at a distance. However, she will not approach because of the strong need to maintain distance between herself and a novel adult. The child's apprehensiveness may result from a variety of reasons.

In the case of people with severe disabilities, the reasons may be even more complex. There may be a history in which other people are associated with task demands. In some cases, other people may be associated with the interruption of repertoires of stereotypic behavior. Some learners may have grown up in a living environment in which approaching another person who had a desired object resulted in the delivery of warnings intended to preempt possible stealing. Regardless of the reason for the learner's reticence, such a situation affords the interventionist an excellent opportunity to establish people as "things that one should want to approach." If the adult picks up a piece of candy and offers it to the child, the child may still refrain from initiated movement. If so, the adult may place the candy farther away from him- or herself in an attempt to coax movement from the child. Over time the people who are offering the reinforcers may become conditioned reinforcers as a result of the history of pairing themselves and the desired

object. When this occurs the offer may begin to take on some of the qualities of the original reinforcer in the eyes of the recipient.

Of course, it is always possible that the item or activity being offered is not desired. Perhaps the safest method of ensuring that the learner is interested in the object being offered is to make the offer after the learner has produced a self-selecting response. For example, suppose that a learner self-selects apples from a bowl. On some occasions, as the learner begins to reach for the apple, another person in the environment may pick up the apple and place it in the learner's hand. During other opportunities, the learner may continue to self-select the apple. Across successive opportunities, the interventionist might make the offer earlier and earlier in the context of this situation. Assuming that such actions continue to meet with success, the interventionist would initiate the apple selecting routine. That is, when the learner was not in the process of procuring an apple, the interventionist would approach. Initially, the interventionist would all but place the item in the learner's hand. Across successive opportunities, the interventionist would move the item toward the learner, waiting just a bit to see if the learner could be coaxed into moving slightly toward the item of interest. At some point, the learner will spot the interventionist with a desired item, move to the interventionist, and accept the offered item.

Once these routines have been established, it may be helpful to alter them slightly so that on some occasions the delivery of the reinforcer occurs only after the learner experiences elaborated social contact. For example, the interventionist could offer two closed fists to the learner. The learner picks a fist and the fist is opened. If it is empty, the learner tries the other. On some occasions, the desired item may be in the interventionist's pocket rather than in his or her hand. These variations on a common routine afford valuable opportunities to increase the social component of a routine that was motivated initially by the immediate receipt of a reinforcer. In some instances, such scenarios have led to the successful establishment of a purely social interaction.

Setting the Stage for the Learner to Interact with Others Many learners with severe disabilities may have limited experience interacting with others. They may not have discovered that interacting with others can be enjoyable. The activities described involve chaining a social experience to the procurement of a desired item that already has a well-established history as a reinforcer. For example, as the learner approaches, the interventionist may smile and move to tickle a preschool child, or prompt a "give-me-five" response with an older person. Initially, receipt of a primary reinforcer may have been the motivating factor behind the routine. Over time, however, the social component of the interaction may begin to become a motivating factor in its own right. Thus by following the program logic put forth here, the interventionist has an opportunity to establish other people as positive reinforcers.

Often the prior behavior of staff toward the learner may establish a history in which the learner is prone to avoid interactions with others. For example, upon scrutinizing their own behavior, staff members are sometimes surprised to learn that much of their interaction with a learner centers on task demands and/or intrusive correction procedures. If this is the case, interventionists should try to increase the proportion of nondirective communication initiatives.

Importance of Vocalizations in Maintaining Interactions Teaching a learner to produce spoken communicative behavior is in many respects more challenging than establishing a graphic or gestural repertoire. Perhaps the biggest challenge in establishing speech is identifying a strategy for prompting verbal approximations. In both gestural and graphic modes a plethora of prompting strategies may be used. With even the most passive learner, physical response prompts are available to establish re-

sponse approximations from the outset of an intervention program. In the verbal mode, however, the range of available prompting strategies is limited.

The most efficient response prompt in teaching an initial verbal repertoire involves the provision of imitative models. The interventionist produces a spoken word or word approximation that the learner replicates. Unfortunately, many learners with severe disabilities cannot use imitative models, since they have never learned to imitate. The importance of establishing an imitative model as an instructional prompt is evidenced by the importance given to imitation in empirically validated intervention programs that emerged during the 1970s (Bricker & Bricker, 1974; Bricker, Dennison, & Bricker, 1976; Guess, Sailor, & Baer, 1974; Kent, 1974; Lovaas, 1981; McDonald, 1985). All of these programs emphasized establishing imitation as the earliest repertoire of communication production.

Piaget (1929) provided an exacting description of the emergence of vocal and verbal imitation. He and his colleagues noted that the probability that a child would vocalize was influenced by early environmental factors. That is, if others in the child's environment were vocalizing, the child was more apt to do so. This phenomenon has been referred to as *vocal contagion*. Within the next several months, the infant comes to engage in child-initiated turn-taking. During these episodes, the child produces a vocal behavior and waits for the adult to vocalize before producing the next vocalization. As the child nears the end of the first year of life, he or she begins to participate in vocal chains in which the adult initiates a vocal utterance and the child produces a contingent vocalization.

Establishing More Frequent Vocalizations The majority of vocal turn-taking intervention strategies have focused initially on attempting to increase the frequency with which a learner vocalizes. Generally, the teacher and/or caregiver is encouraged to select the time, place, and activity during which the learner's vocalizations will be reinforced. One of the earliest empirical demonstrations that social contingencies could serve to increase the frequency of vocalizations produced by an infant was reported by Rheingold, Gewirtz, and Ross (1959). These investigators used a "triple treat contingency." That is, every time an infant vocalized, the experimenter leaned over the crib and smiled, vocalized "tsk-tsk," and tickled the infant gently. This contingency resulted in a systematic increase in vocal behavior observed. This initial investigation prompted an extensive line of research attempting to differentiate types of reinforcers that could be used and whether, in fact, the vocal behavior produced by the interventionist served as a reinforcer or as a discriminative stimuli for the next vocalization.

The basis for teaching a learner to vocalize more often is that in child-initiated imitation, the child actually initiates an instructional opportunity. Unless the learner is vocalizing often, few instructional opportunities will be generated to teach the learner to produce contingent vocal behavior. Once the learner is vocalizing fairly often (e.g., 15 vocalizations within a 10-minute period) he or she will begin to be reinforced for participating in interactional chains that consist of child vocalization—adult vocalization—child vocalization. Finally, once the learner participates consistently in vocal turn-taking routines, more traditional vocal imitation intervention is implemented in which the learner is taught to replicate the vocal behavior modeled by the interventionist.

Participating in Vocal Turn Taking (Learner-Initiated Imitation) By several months of age, infants begin to exhibit a propensity to vocalize more in the presence of a familiar person than they do in the presence of an unfamiliar person. At about this time, children have been reported to begin to participate in interpersonal vocal chains in which the child initiates a vocalization. The adult then contingently replicates the child's sound. This, in turn, results in the child contingently reproducing a vocalization that may or may not replicate his or her original vocalization. This phenomenon has been referred to as child-initiated imitation.

It appears that in child-initiated imitation, the child focuses more on vocalizing at the correct time, and less on replicating the exact form of the vocalization that has been modeled. Children thus seem to segment the competence of vocal imitation into vocalizing at the right time and vocalizing the right thing at the right time. Slightly later they master replication of the qualitative features of the sounds that have been modeled by others in their environment. Many interventionists have elected to ignore the establishment of vocalizing at the right time in favor of teaching vocalizing the right thing at the right time. Generally, these procedures involve the interventionist arbitrarily selecting several sounds that he or she wishes to teach the child to imitate. The interventionist then approaches the child, produces the target sound, and allows an interval of time for the learner to reproduce the sound modeled. Each successful approximation is then reinforced immediately.

There is an extensive body of literature suggesting that young children are more apt to produce vocal turn taking when the adult utterance was produced as part of a vocal sequence initiated by the child. For example, a child produces a vocal behavior. Upon hearing this vocalization, the adult imitates it. The child then reproduces his or her original behavior. This phenomenon of child-initiated imitation has been reported to be a significant aspect of caregiver–child interactional sequences.

If the interventionist chooses to address child-initiated imitation as an intervention objective, he or she is committing to teaching the learner to vocalize at the right time regardless of the form of the learner's vocal behavior. Initially, the interventionist is available to observe for vocal behavior. As soon as the learner vocalizes, the interventionist jumps in with a vocalization. If the learner vocalizes again the interventionist repeats the learner's vocalization. Once this routine has been established, the interventionist begins conducting probe opportunities. During a probe opportunity, the routine proceeds as usual, with one notable exception. After the learner produces the initial vocalization, the interventionist pauses slightly longer than usual before taking his or her turn. If the learner remains silent during the slightly longer pause, the next opportunity conducted maintains the same time constraints. Gradually, across successive opportunities, the length of the pause between the learner's vocalization and the contingent adult-produced replication increases.

A skeptic might suggest that a learner who appears to be engaging in learner-initiated imitation is simply vocalizing, and that a clever caregiver is simply fitting his or her verbal productions into the blank space available. A simple probe can be implemented to ensure that this is not the case. Across successive vocal initiations produced by a learner, the interventionist can vary the length of time prior to taking his or her turn. If the learner usually waits for the interventionist's vocalization prior to producing the second vocalization, learner-initiated imitation is occurring. If the learner is not waiting for his or her turn, it may be possible to implement procedures to assist in the establishment of learner-initiated imitation.

It seems reasonable to propose that child-initiated imitation serves at least two functions. First, it may be used as an instructional technique to begin to establish vocal imitation skills that can later be used as a response prompt to teach more sophisticated communicative productions. Second, initial chains of child-initiated imitation may result in an efficient technique to begin to teach the learner the rudiments of verbal skills required to maintain a verbal interaction.

Participating in Partner-Initiated Imitation Partner-initiated imitation marks a distinct shift in the pattern of discriminative stimuli that precede the learner's vocalization. One technique for establishing partner-initiated imitation involves subtly introducing a shift in the discriminative stimulus presented to the learner, while maintaining the topographical features of the learner's response. For example, after the initial learner vocalization, the interventionist can systematically delay reproducing the child's initiation. Over repeated successful opportunities this delay is systematically lengthened. As the interval of time between the learner-produced and partner-produced imitation grows longer, the three-component vocal chain begins to resemble partner-initiated imitation. This sequence of intervention is summarized in Figure 3.

Other strategies for teaching imitation have employed an array of response-shaping and, in some instances, response-prompting strategies. For example, Lovaas, Berberich, Perloff, and Schaeffer (1966) suggested selecting an initial repertoire of sounds to teach that involved producing lip closure (e.g., /m/, /b/). Initially, the learner was reinforced for vocalizing frequently. Once this occurred, reinforcement was provided for producing a single sound uttered after the interventionist's vocal model. Finally, after the interventionist's model was given and the learner was contingently producing sound, the interventionist would physically prompt lip closure. If the learner vocalized in accordance with the prompt, he or she was reinforced. If he or she did not, a brief period of time was allowed to elapse and another instructional opportunity was implemented. Over time, the physical prompt for lip closure was systematically faded. Next, a second sound was introduced to contrast with the first. This sequence of intervention is in contrast to the more developmentally based intervention sequence depicted in Figure 3.

Other interventionists (Bricker et al., 1976) have suggested selecting sounds to teach based on those that already constitute the more frequently produced sounds in the learner's repertoire. Although helpful, this strategy can back-

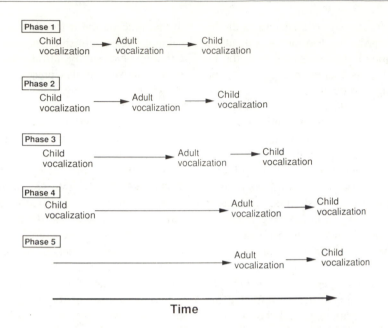

Figure 3. Moving from child-initiated imitation to adult-initiated imitation. The latency between child initiation and adult initiation increases over time.

fire if the interventionist selects a sound that occurs so frequently that the learner is apt to engage in verbal perseveration, thereby making the introduction of new sounds more difficult. The most successful intervention procedures appear to have used a mixed sequence of introducing new vocal stimuli. That is, first one particular sound is established contingent on the production of an interventionist-initiated model. Next, opportunities for the learner to imitate a second sound are interspersed with maintenance opportunities on the original sound. One of the less desirable features of some original vocal imitation programs was their reliance on training that took place out of natural context (Guess et al., 1974; Kent, 1974; Lovaas et al., 1966). Consequently, the number of teaching opportunities required to establish target skills may not have benefitted from other natural cues available in the learner's environment.

Imitating Sounds Produced by Objects Many children play with toys that produce dis-

tinctive sounds. Cars go "vroom-vroom," dogs bark, cows moo. When one considers the typical array of toys with which children play, it is safe to assume that they encounter thousands of opportunities in which the sound that a toy produces is paired either with procurement of the toy or with some action on it by the child. When a toy is selected by the child, it usually represents a strong preference, and the child's attention is thus highly focused. In many respects these situations can be thought of as incidental teaching opportunities in which a vocal representation for an object is paired systematically with the object. Thus, it is not unusual to see learners initially refer to dogs as "arf-arf," cows as "moo," ducks as "quack," and so forth.

When a learner's emerging vocal repertoire consists of a variety of sounds produced by objects, the prognosis for vocal mode communication development is good for two reasons. First, the learner can match a specific sound or sound combination to a particular referent. Second, the learner has shown that he or she may be able to engage in imitative behavior to acquire new vocabulary.

Initiating an Interaction

Many occasions arise in which a learner wishes to interact with others. For example, a learner who knows that he is not allowed to cross the street alone may initiate taking a peer's hand as he says "here" or "give your hand" because he knows that he will not be allowed to cross the street without doing so. On other occasions, a learner may see a group of children laughing on the playground. The expectation that there must be something interesting going on may motivate the learner to ask to join the group. In still other situations, the learner may initiate from habit. For example, while passing out milk at snack-time the learner may say, "Here you go," as he or she distributes the milk. Finally, among sophisticated communicators, social motivations may arise as a thoughtful consideration of a perspective partner. For example, upon seeing someone dropping a package as he struggles to open a door, a learner may approach, pick up the package, and say, "You dropped this—here you go." Certain learner and environmental characteristics appear to increase the probability of an initiation occurring. These conditions are summarized in Figure 4 and described in the following sections.

Joining an Ongoing Activity   Often we are more likely to engage in an activity if we see others doing so—we all know the story of how Tom Sawyer interested his peers in painting a fence. Observing an ongoing activity reminds the learner of the options available. People with

Circumstance	Example
Joining activities that are already in progress	Tom Sawyer instilling an interest among his peers in painting a fence
Beginning well-established routines	A learner (taught that you can't eat your snack unless all the children in the group have some), upon receiving several cookies turns to a peer who doesn't have any, offers her a cookie, and says "here."
Calling attention to novel events	At snacktime when a child spills his milk, a learner obtains the teacher's attention to point out what has happened.
Protesting the undesirable actions of another	A waitress, assuming that a customer has finished his meal, attempts to remove a plate that still contains a small amount of food. When this happens, the customer says, "I'm not done."

Figure 4.   Circumstances that may promote initiation of interactions.

severe disabilities appear to be more likely to join a new activity in which others in their environment are engaging.

Beginning with Well-Established Routines Some social initiations occur as part of well-rehearsed routines. For example, upon approaching a familiar individual, a learner may say "hello," thus initiating an interaction. Other initiations may have an extensive idiosyncratic history. For example, a mother may have instilled a measure of social etiquette in her 8-year-old by teaching him to share. The rule may have been consistently taught that when given a snack, the child should not eat it unless all of the children in the group are also given some. If this rule has been well established, one would expect a learner who receives several cookies to turn to a peer and say "here" as he offers the peer a cookie. In still other routines, leaving the cafeteria may serve as a cue to approach the snack bar. Seeing the clerk may then serve as a cue to initiate a request. The establishment of initiations may be most easily established in situations that have common natural cues for which there are numerous intervention opportunities during the course of a typical day.

Calling Attention to Novel Events McLean and Snyder-McLean (1978) described a communication assessment activity in which very novel events were introduced so that they could be observed clearly by the learner but could not be observed by the communicative partner. They report that many learners with severe disabilities called the interventionist's attention to the item, apparently because of its novelty.

Many novelties exist in the natural environment. For example, when a child spills a carton of milk at snacktime, learners who rarely communicate obtain a teacher's attention to point out the mishap. Although using novelty is a potentially effective strategy for setting the occasion for an initiation, it usually cannot provide a sufficient number of instances in which to teach initiation. The instances it does provide

represent an important source of at least some instructional opportunities, however.

Protesting the Actions of Another A learner may be motivated to initiate a social interaction as a protest of an action performed by a third person. For example, a waitress may attempt to remove a plate before a diner has finished eating. Upon observing the waitress, the customer may explain, "I'm not done." The desire to interrupt the ongoing activity of another may thus prompt the learner to communicate. In this example, the learner may have had no prior interaction with the person who removed the plate. Consequently, the learner's protest represents a communication initiation. Goetz, Gee, and Sailor (1985) described an instructional procedure they call *interrupted chain training* that capitalizes on these opportunities.

A Continuum from Maintaining to Initiating an Interaction Initiating, maintaining, and terminating interactions do not represent distinct and separate skills. Consider a mother playing a vocal turn-taking game with her child. The mother jumps from behind a chair and says "boo." Initially, the child reciprocates by engaging in the same behavior. The mother then repeats her behavior and the game continues in this fashion. At some point the interval of time between turns may increase as the child begins to become interested in a cartoon show on the television in an adjoining room. At some point in this game, a full minute may occur between turns. Eventually, the interval of time becomes great enough so that the child's behavior no longer serves to maintain an interaction, but rather represents an initiation for interaction. This progression represents a viable strategy with a learner who responds efficiently in a social interaction but fails to initiate at the outset of intervention.

Relationship between Social Initiations and Spontaneity In many cases, spontaneity overlaps with initiation of communicative behavior. In the examples provided in the previous section, the learner initiated interactions spontaneously. A learner may also initiate a social interaction nonspontaneously. For example, a learner may wish to join a game of tag, but refrain from doing so, instead lingering near the edge of the activity. The caregiver may observe this and provide verbal coaxing (e.g., "Go ahead, ask if you can play too. Go say 'Can I play too?' ") If this prompt is successful, the learner's utterance represents a nonspontaneous initiation.

Terminating an Interaction

Terminating an interaction is not usually taught as part of establishing an initial repertoire of interactive communication skills. However, as discussed in detail in Chapter 11, many repertoires of socially unacceptable behavior begin as attempts to terminate interactions. Thus, for learners with severe disabilities, being able successfully to conclude an interaction represents a critical achievement.

Because socially motivated excess behavior is often the catalyst for teaching terminating responses, the communicative intents of protesting and rejecting are often equated with terminating interactions. In fact, protesting and rejecting to escape or avoid undesired objects or activities represent only some of the kinds of situations in which terminating can be used. For example, a learner who is eating lunch in the school cafeteria with his friends hears the bell signaling the end of lunch. Immediately, he says, "Oops, I've gotta go. Goodbye." Alternatively, a learner may be having a pleasant conversation with another person when she begins to notice that her partner is beginning to look at his watch. Noticing this, the learner may say, "Oh, I see that you have to get going, so long." At other times, a learner may be enjoying playtime outside with a friend. Upon seeing his mother, he remembers that he had been told not to go outside. He thus says to his friend, "I have to go." Finally, a learner may be pleasant-

ly interacting with a peer. Upon hearing his baby sister crying, he may say, "I gotta go."

All of these examples provide instances in which responses can be made to terminate an interaction. These terminations may occur for a variety of reasons and may thus involve several different communicative intents. Figure 5 summarizes these instances. Classes of cues that may be important for learners to attend to in order to be able to end interactions are described in the following sections.

Terminating an Undesired Interaction   Chapter 6 examined instances in which a learner may be highly motivated to terminate an interaction in order to escape or avoid an undesired event. In some instances a learner may want to avoid a provoking event (e.g., being offered a food he or she hates). In other instances a learner may realize that his or her interest level is not adequate to sustain performance in a particular activity. For example, a learner may become bored playing cards and say, "Let's stop." In both of these situations the activities are undesired. One activity is always undesired, the other activity becomes undesired depending on the conditions. Learners with severe disabilities appear to view the two situations as involving different response classes. Reichle (1989) reported that learners who had been taught to terminate interactions concerning offers of undesired items often failed to generalize to situations in which the learner became bored or satiated and wished to depart. There thus appears to be merit in adopting a "general case" approach in selecting teaching examples that sample the entire field of situations in which the interventionist wishes the target behavior to be performed. It is particularly important to sample the range of situations in which terminating responses are apt to occur. Earlier chapters have examined escaping or avoiding offers of undesired objects or activities and leave-taking events that have become undesirable even though there is no preferable activity in sight. In

Circumstance	Example
Ending undesired interactions	A learner becomes bored participating in a game of cards and says, "Let's stop."
Concluding desirable interactions in order to accommodate a schedule	When the bell rings in the school cafeteria, a learner may have to terminate his lunchtime interaction with a peer in order to avoid being late to his next class.
Finishing pleasant interactions to take advantage of a more attractive alternative.	A 7-year-old child may be content to play with a 3-year-old child provided no other playmates are available. However, the appearance of another 7-year-old may result in the interaction with the 3-year-old being abruptly terminated.
Discontinuing pleasant interactions due to environmental disruptions.	A learner who sees his little brother fall off his bike may need to terminate a play activity in order to render assistance.

Figure 5.   Circumstances that may promote termination of interactions.

the next section several other situations in which a learner may be called upon to perform a socially acceptable behavior to terminate an interaction are examined.

Terminating a Desired Interaction to Accommodate a Schedule   Learners with severe disabilities are required to follow some kind of daily routine. They must, therefore, be able to terminate activities in order to accommodate their schedules. For example, when the bell rings in the school cafeteria, a learner may have to terminate his lunchtime interaction with a peer in order to avoid being late in getting to his next class. Learning to terminate an interaction in this instance may be particularly challenging because there may be no clear reinforcer for appropriate behavior, since the school or work activity that follows lunch may not be a preferred activity. It may thus be necessary to establish a reinforcer that the learner can receive

as a result of appropriately terminating his activity. For example, a learner who successfully terminates a lunchtime activity to go to work may receive a break shortly after arriving at work.

Terminating a Pleasant Interaction Because of a More Attractive Alternative   Some interactions seem adequate to sustain a learner's participation without additional inducements. For example, a 7-year-old child may be happy to play with a 3-year-old provided that no older playmates are available. However, the appearance of another 7-year-old may result in the 3-year-old being abandoned. It is particularly important that learners with disabilities be taught socially acceptable strategies for extricating themselves from such situations. Such situations demand a careful ecological analysis of solutions that are most likely to occur given the demands of the learner's environment and his or her current repertoire. Interestingly, learning to terminate interactions in a situation similar to the one described here may be particularly important in fostering friendships. Learners with disabilities may become distracted by other events in the environment and simply wander away from interactions. This behavior may offend the peer or peers with whom the learner was interacting and influence future interactions.

Terminating a Pleasant Interaction Because of an Environmental Disruption Often a learner may need to terminate an interaction briefly. For example, if a learner sees a younger sibling fall off of a bike, it may be desirable to terminate a play activity in order to render assistance.

The bulk of the literature on generalized use of communicative behavior suggests that unless the range of contexts in which one expects the target skill to be performed is addressed during intervention, the learner should not be expected to generalize the new skill. Teaching a learner to terminate interactions politely yet efficiently represents relatively uncharted territory for the communication interventionist. This is a very important area to address if the learner is to be able to establish pleasant interactions with others in the environment.

CHALLENGES FOR USERS OF GRAPHIC MODE AUGMENTATIVE SYSTEMS

Learners who use electronic and nonelectronic communication aids have been reported to be limited in their ability to engage in communicative exchange (Light, Collier, & Parnes, 1985). Some of these limitations are examined here in terms of maintaining, initiating, and terminating an interaction.

Maintaining an Interaction

Light et al. (1985) observed that, for the most part, graphic mode users produce utterances that respond to communicative demands made by speakers without disabilities in their environment. Users of graphic mode augmentative systems are most likely to generate an utterance when there is an obligation to do so (e.g., "What time is it?"). Graphic mode users are less likely to respond when a response is not obligatory (e.g., "It's really cold outside.").

There may be many reasons why users of augmentative systems fail to maintain interactions in a conversational manner. These include learned helplessness, lack of efficiency in terms of speed, and lack of efficiency in terms of physical effort required.

Overreliance on the Conversational Partner Many users of augmentative communicative systems have learned to refrain from independently engaging in regular daily activities because they have received assistance in virtually every aspect of their life (Guess et al., 1985; Seligman, 1975). Among users of graphic mode systems, it has been well documented that when a learner's partner produces an utterance to which the learner fails to respond, the partner will frequently alter his or her interactional style and ask a series of questions that can be answered "yes" or "no." For example, suppose that the learner's partner asks, "What did you do in school today?" and receives no response. The partner is likely to follow up with questions such as "Did you go to the zoo? To the store? To McDonald's?" These questions constitute an opportunity for the learner to participate in auditory scanning (described in Chapter 13). That is, when the learner's communicative partner arrives at a topic the learner wishes to affirm or deny, he or she signals accordingly.

This strategy has several advantages for the learner using a graphic mode system. First, it demands less physical effort. There is evidence to suggest that many users of augmentative systems tend to match specific classes of communicative opportunities with the response that is physically least demanding to perform. Second, the learner may lack sufficient vocabulary to provide the flexibility required to generate an answer. When the conversational load begins to fall too heavily on the verbal mode participant, he or she may begin to shorten periods of interaction with the augmentative system user, or even avoid interactions (Reichle, 1989). The burden of carrying the interaction cannot be borne inordinately by one member of the dyad. If this happens, the quality, if not the quantity, of interactions may be jeopardized.

Lack of Truthfulness   Sometimes the fear of losing one's speaking partner is so great that the user of an augmentative system may knowingly provide misinformation to keep the interaction flowing. For example, an adult user of an electronic communication aid is asked if he is going home. He nods "yes." An hour later he is seen going to a friend's house. When asked why he has not been truthful, the learner indicates that the time required to generate a correct answer would have slowed up the interaction, possibly jeopardizing his opportunity to introduce the topic that he really wanted to discuss.

The preceding example suggests that at least some sophisticated users of augmentative systems may consider where they can cut corners in an interaction in order to enhance conversational efficiency. Obviously, this strategy may alienate listeners if they discover the learner's white lies. It is also risky for the augmentative system user to place him- or herself in the position of attempting to predict the significance of a topic to current and future interactions once misinformation has been given.

Users of augmentative systems may choose their entrance into communicative exchanges more carefully than verbal mode learners. It may be that some graphic mode learners are reluctant to engage in communicative exchanges because of a lack of opportunities. Among other learners, constraints may be the result of excessive planning on how to behave during an interaction. For yet other learners, poor communicative skills may be the result of a history of learned helplessness ("If I wait, the listener will simplify my role in the interaction."), or fear of being ignored ("If I take the time to produce an accurate message, I will lose the attention of my listener.").

Accommodating the Interactional Style of Vocal Mode Users   Most vocal mode users have difficulty tolerating slowness in communicative exchanges. Even in interacting with young children, most people rarely pause longer than 2 seconds during an interactional exchange. In contrast, in interacting with users of graphic mode systems rarely is there a pause of less than 5 seconds. To reduce the length of the silent pauses, conversational partners adopt several strategies, described in the following sections.

Asking Yes/No Questions   Several investigators (Harris, 1978; Light et al., 1985) have demonstrated that speaking partners tend to engage in communicative exchanges that require the learner simply to confirm or deny the vocal mode user's statements. This strategy speeds up an interaction, but provides the learner with very limited experience in learning to direct an exchange by steering the topic in a new direction. It also limits opportunities to teach symbol combinations that may be part of the graphic mode system. Furthermore, it limits the amount of time the graphic mode user can practice using his or her augmentative system.

Producing Utterances That Require No Response   Vocal mode users often engage learners in polite, superfluous, communicative exchanges (e.g., "That's a nice dress."). Such utterances allow interaction to proceed without creating critical communicative opportunities or obligations for the learner. In terms of beginning to learn to participate discriminatively in an interaction, it is important that the learner be shown clearly what constitutes an opportunity for a turn. This can best be accomplished when there is an obligation to respond. For example, when a peer approaches with an outstretched hand and says, "Give me five," the communicative obligation is clear. When a ball is rolled back and forth, obligatory turns are marked clearly. Learners using augmentative communication systems have an extremely limited number of these opportunities.

Failing to Be Informative Learners often produce utterances that do not obligate the listener to respond by stating the obvious or failing to be informative. This phenomenon is common when speakers talk to young children. There is a propensity to talk about what the learner is doing. Although this is consistent with an instructional strategy in which modeled language behavior is paired with the learner's action, it also means that the speaker states the obvious. Once a learner has a beginning communicative repertoire, stating the obvious violates the rule of informativeness put forth earlier. Stating the obvious tends to result in nonparticipation on the part of the graphic mode user, and fails to model the competency of adding critical and relevant information to a communicative exchange.

Initiating an Interaction

Investigators who have examined the propensity for graphic mode communicators to initiate a communicative exchange agree that communicative initiations are rare. Clearly, such learners have fewer opportunities to initiate an interaction than vocal mode communicators. Numerous investigators (Buzolich, 1982; Harris, 1978; Light et al., 1985) have reported that vocal mode communicators with disabilities tend to control communicative interactions and are reluctant to relinquish their turn when communicating with users of graphic systems. This inequity in opportunity for initiation may represent some defect inherent within populations with multiple or severe disabilities. However, Beukelman and Yorkston (1982) report that much the same phenomenon occurs when speakers without disabilities are placed in the role of an augmentative system user and required to interact with speaking partners.

It is also possible that some learners are afraid to initiate a conversation because doing so increases later communicative demands. For example, if the learner says, "My dad got a new car," the listener is apt to respond, "Oh yeah, what kind?" This then obligates the augmentative user to respond. Most users of augmentative system view initiating a communicative exchange much as one would view planning strategy in a chess game. That is, they attempt to anticipate what vocabulary (or phrases) will be needed over the next several speaking turns. Because significant concentration may be required to plan participation, users of augmentative systems may tend to be very discriminating in selecting those situations in which they can pull off a successful communicative initiation.

Users of augmentative systems are more likely to initiate a communicative exchange that focuses on requesting (Light et al., 1985). In a request, the learner can exert some control over the number of exchanges that occur in an interaction provided he or she can be sufficiently explicit. For example, a learner may approach a clerk at a fast food restaurant and order a medium Diet Coke™. In many instances, no further turn taking will be necessary. If there is further exchange, it can efficiently be handled with a "yes" or "no" response (i.e., "Do you want fries with that?"). Requesting opportunities also tend to occur during events in which a successful consequence of the request will be strongly reinforcing.

Terminating an Interaction

Users of augmentative communication systems with severe disabilities are often unable to terminate communicative exchanges efficiently (Reichle, 1989). Often, augmentative system users simply fail to terminate an interaction. For example, a learner may miss a ride home because he fails to terminate an interaction. Later, the learner may indicate that he knew he would miss his ride but did not know how to end the conversation without interrupting his partner. Because the graphic mode is slow, some graphic mode users report difficulty being able to break into the interaction and obtain the speaking floor in order to terminate an interaction politely. That is, most of the verbal mode partner's utterances may obligate the learner to provide an answer. In essence, the learner is so busy producing answers that he has little time to terminate the interaction. In other cases, the learner appears to fail to consider the learner's subtle cues that represent indirect requests for the termination of an intervention. For example, a learner may fail to recognize that a communicative partner's edging his way to the door suggests his desire to terminate the interaction. The learner may be so involved in formulating an utterance that he or she fails to attend to cues being provided by the listener.

Sometimes failure to terminate an interaction efficiently occurs because the learner has no symbol that can be used to terminate an interaction politely. One learner the author knew used a representation for "I have to go to the bathroom" to terminate interactions. This symbol worked successfully for a while. However, eventually the utterance became the focus of jokes among the learner's speaking peers.

Some learners may be reluctant to terminate an interaction because they are afraid that it will be difficult to regain the attention of their communicative partner. In these instances, the learner can be provided with a mechanism for scheduling a future meeting (e.g., a message that communicates, "Gee, I'm sorry, I've got to go. When can we get together again?").

SUMMARY

This chapter has focused on establishing the interactional use of initial communicative reper-toires. Teaching individual communicative intents such as requesting and rejecting will not guarantee that a learner will be able to use them to initiate, maintain, or terminate interactions with others. This chapter has summarized the emergence of some types of interactional exchanges among learners without disabilities. Those aspects of interaction chosen for discussion seem to be applicable to learners with severe disabilities.

It is apparent that establishing interactive use of communicative repertoires involves the behavior of both the learner and his or her communicative partners. In this respect, the ecology supporting people with severe disabilities may represent a particular challenge. Kennedy, Horner, and Newton (1989) reported that there is tremendous turnover among people interacting with learners with severe disabilities. That is, few companions remain part of the learner's social sphere for more than a few months. This means that learners must constantly be adjusting to different interactive partners who may bring a variety of interactional styles to the interaction.

This chapter has focused on the challenges encountered by the graphic mode user. In terms of interacting with a communication partner, graphic mode users face the greatest challenges. Establishing interactional flow is very dependent on the timing of utterances produced by both partners in an interactive exchange. Graphic mode users can produce only 20%–25% as many utterances as speakers during the same period of time. Consequently, the graphic mode user has a significant communicative burden in attempting to "keep up" during an interactional exchange.

REFERENCES

Baer, R.A., Williams, J.A., Osnes, P.G., & Stokes, T.F. (1984). Delayed reinforcement as an indiscriminable contingency in verbal/nonverbal correspondence training. *Journal of Applied Behavior Analysis, 17,* 429–440.

Beukelman, D., & Yorkston, K. (1982). Communication interaction of adult communication augmentative system use. *Topics in Language Disorders, 2,* 39–53.

Brazelton, T., Koslowski, B., & Main, M. (1974). The origins of reciprocity: The early mother–infant interaction. In M. Lewis & L. Rosenblum (Eds.), *The effects of the infant on its caregiver* (pp. 49–77). New York: John Wiley & Sons.

Bricker, D., & Bricker, W. (1974). An early language training strategy. In R.L. Schiefelbusch & L.L. Lloyd (Eds.), *Language perspectives: Acquisition, retardation, and intervention.* Baltimore: University Park Press.

Bricker, D., Dennison, L., & Bricker, W. (1976). *A language intervention program for developmentally young children* (MCCD Monograph Series I). Miami: Mailman Center for Child Development, University of Miami.

Bruner, J. (1975). The ontogenesis of speech act. *Journal of Child Language, 2,* 1–19.

Bruner, J. (1978). On prelinguistic prerequisites of speech. In R.N. Campbell & P.T. Smith (Eds.), *Recent advances in the psychology of language* (Vol. 4a, pp. 194–214). New York: Plenum.

Buzolich, M.J. (1982). *Intervention analysis of adult augmented communicators: A pilot study.* Unpublished manuscript, University of California, San Francisco.

Calculator, S., & Delaney, E. (1986). Comparison of nonspeaking and speaking mentally retarded adults' clarification strategies. *Journal of Speech and Hearing Research, 51,* 252–259.

Chapman, R. (1981). Exploring children's communicative intents. In J. Miller (Ed.), *Assessing language production in children* (pp. 111–136). Baltimore: University Park Press.

Constantine, B., & Sidman, M. (1975). Role of naming in delayed matching to sample. *American Journal of Mental Deficiency, 79,* 680–689.

Gallagher, T.M. (1977). Revision of behaviors in the speech of normal children developing language. *Journal of Speech and Hearing Research, 20,* 303–318.

Gallagher, T.M., & Darnton, B.A. (1978). Conversational aspects of the speech of language-disordered children: Revision behaviors. *Journal of Speech and Hearing Research, 21,* 118–135.

Goetz, L., Gee, K., & Sailor, W. (1985). Using a behavior chain interruption strategy to teach communication skills to students with severe disabilities. *Journal of The Association for Persons with Severe Handicaps, 10,* 21–30.

Grice, H.P. (1975). Logic and conversation. In P. Cole & J.L. Morgan. (Eds.), *Syntax and seman-*

tics: *Vol. 3: Speech acts* (pp. 41–58). New York: Academic Press.

Guess, D., Benson, H., & Siegel-Causey, E. (1985). Concepts and issues related to choicemaking and autonomy among persons with severe disabilities. *Journal of The Association for Persons with Severe Handicaps, 10*(2), 79–86.

Guess, D., Sailor, W., & Baer, D. (1974). To teach language to retarded children. In R.L. Schiefelbusch & L. Lloyd (Eds.), *Language perspectives: Acquisition, retardation, and intervention* (pp. 529–563). Baltimore: University Park Press.

Guevremont, D., Osnes, P., & Stokes, T. (1986a). Preparation for effective self-regulation: The development of generalized verbal control. *Journal of Applied Behavior Analysis, 19,* 99–104.

Guevremont, D., Osnes, P., & Stokes, T. (1986b). Programming maintenance after corresponding training interventions with children. *Journal of Applied Behavior Analysis, 19,* 215–219.

Harris, D. (1978). *Descriptive analysis of communication interaction processes involving nonvocal severely physically handicapped.* Unpublished doctoral dissertation, University of Wisconsin, Madison.

Israel, A., & Brown, M. (1977). Correspondence training prior to verbal training and control of nonverbal behavior via control of verbal behavior. *Journal of Applied Behavior Analysis, 10,* 333–338.

Kennedy, G.H., Horner, R.H., & Newton, J.S. (1989). Social contacts of adults with severe disabilities living in the community: A descriptive analysis of relationship patterns. *Journal of The Association for Persons with Severe Handicaps, 14*(3), 190–196.

Kent, L. (1974). *Language acquisition program for the retarded or multiply impaired.* Champaign, IL: Research Press.

Light, J., Collier, B., & Parnes, P. (1985). Communicative interaction between young nonspeaking physically disabled children and their primary caregivers: Part 1—Discourse patterns. *Augmentative and Alternative Communication, 1,* 74–83.

Lovaas, O. (1981). *Teaching developmentally disabled children.* Austin, TX: PRO-ED.

Lovaas, O.I., Berberich, J.P., Perloff, B.F., & Schaeffer, B. (1966). Acquisition of initiative speech by schizophrenic children. *Science, 151,* 705–707.

McDonald, J.D. (1985). Language through conversation: A model for intervention with language-delayed persons. In S.F. Warren & A.K. Rogers-

Warren (Eds.), *Teaching functional language* (pp. 89–122). Austin, TX: PRO-ED.

McLean, J., & Snyder-McLean, L. (1978). *A transactional approach to early language training.* Columbus, OH: Charles E. Merrill.

Owens, R. (1984). *Language development.* Columbus, OH: Charles E. Merrill.

Piaget, J. (1929). *The child's conception of the world.* New York: Harcourt, Brace and World.

Prekker, J. (1988). *Conversational repair strategies among intellectually delayed children.* Unpublished master's thesis, University of Minnesota, Minneapolis.

Reichle, J. (1989). *Generalized use of a generalized rejecting response: Practical replications for a beginning communication system.* Unpublished manuscript, University of Minnesota, Minneapolis.

Rheingold, H., Gewirtz, J., & Ross, H. (1959). Social conditioning of vocalizations in the infant.

Journal of Comparative Psychology, 52, 68–73.

Risley, T., & Hart, B. (1968). Developing a correspondence between the nonverbal and verbal behavior of preschool children. *Journal of Applied Behavior Analysis, 1,* 267–281.

Scaife, M., & Bruner, J. (1975). The capacity for joint visual attention in the infant. *Nature, 253,* 265–266.

Seligman, M. (1975). *Helplessness: On depression, development and death.* San Francisco: W.H. Freeman.

Watson, J. (1978). Perception of contingency as a determinant of social responsiveness. In S. Trotter & E. Thoman (Eds.), *Social responsiveness of infants* (pp. 6–10). New York: Johnson & Johnson.

Watson, J., & Ramey, C. (1969, March). *Reactions to response contingency stimulation in early infancy.* Paper presented at biennial meeting of the Society for Research in Child Deelopment, Santa Monica, CA.

8

Establishing
Spontaneity and Generalization

Joe Reichle and Jeff Sigafoos

Many learners with developmental disabilities are described as passive or prompt dependent (Reichle, York, & Eynon, 1989). This description is often based on the observation that the learner rarely initiates behavior spontaneously. Communicative repertoires taught to learners with developmental disabilities have often been characterized by a lack of spontaneity (Carr, 1982; Carr & Kologinsky, 1983; Charlop, Schreibman, & Thibodeau, 1985; Gobbi, Cipani, Hudson, & Lapenta-Neudeck, 1986; Halle, 1987; Lovaas, Koegel, Simmons, & Long, 1973; Oliver & Halle, 1982; Schaeffer, 1978; Sosne, Handleman, & Harris, 1979).

LACK OF SPONTANEITY

Lack of spontaneity in the use of newly established communicative repertoires poses many problems. Requesting repertoires, for example, are often established to provide a means for learners to express their wants or needs. However, if learners express wants or needs only when prompted to do so, then they are not fully able to affect their environments. In this case, the requesting repertoire is not very useful in meeting the learners' needs. In general, communicative repertoires are most useful when the behaviors established occur spontaneously (e.g., the learner requests a drink when thirsty).

Learners with developmental disabilities also often fail to generalize acquired behaviors to new people, settings, tasks, or materials (Stokes & Baer, 1977). A learner taught to request a drink by one interventionist may not do so with another. Failure to generalize limits the usefulness of newly established communicative behaviors.

Fortunately, there is a growing body of literature on establishing spontaneous and generalized use of newly established communicative behavior. Spontaneity and generalization represent important aspects of the various communicative intents (i.e., requesting, rejecting, offering information), as well as important aspects of communicative exchanges (i.e., initiating, maintaining, terminating). This chapter thus serves to extend the discussions presented in Chapters 4 and 7.

Definitions of Spontaneity

Several definitions of spontaneous communication have been put forth. Perhaps the most widely accepted is that which defines communicative behaviors as spontaneous when they occur without having to be prompted by instructional cues (i.e., vocal, gestural, modeling, or physical prompts) that are not part of the natural conditions under which the behavior is expected to occur. Spontaneous speech, for example, occurs when the learner does not have to be provided with an imitative model (Bricker & Bricker, 1974; Charlop et al., 1985; MacDonald, 1976; MacDonald & Blott, 1974).

Explicit verbal instructions are often relied upon to prompt communicative behavior. Some procedures, such as the mand-model procedure described later (Rogers-Warren & Warren, 1980; Warren, McQuarter, & Rogers-Warren, 1984), rely on instructor-initiated questions (e.g., "What is this?") or commands (e.g., "Tell me what you want?") to create instructional opportunities in the natural environment. One potential problem with such procedures is that learners may then communicate only when instructed to do so.

Explanations for the Lack of Spontaneity

Several investigators (Carr & Kologinsky, 1983; Gobbi et al., 1986; McCook, Cipani, Madigan, & LaCampagne, 1988; Oliver & Halle, 1982) have attributed the lack of spontaneity to certain characteristics of structured interventions for teaching communicative behaviors. Procedures for teaching communicative behavior have often been implemented by a single instructor, in a single setting, with each intervention opportunity initiated in an identical manner. Distinct cues and intrusive response prompts may be delivered at the beginning of an intervention opportunity to evoke a "correct" response that could then be quickly reinforced. Responses

that occurred at other times (i.e., spontaneously) were not likely to have been reinforced, as these were considered "incorrect."

Not surprisingly, this structure resulted in communicative repertoires that were under rather narrow stimulus control. Repertoires established in such a fashion were not typically used when these controlling stimuli were absent, as was usually the case outside the intervention setting. Logical solutions involved implementing procedures to teach communicative behaviors in more natural settings and bringing the learner's repertoire under the control of a broader range of stimuli.

Facilitating Spontaneity

Carr and Kologinsky (1983) attempted to establish the use of spontaneous requests in three learners with autism. These learners had repertoires that ranged between 25 and 50 expressive signs (used as requests). Carr and Kologinsky (1983) believed that the learners' requests were prompted by the sight of preferred objects. Therefore, to set the occasion for spontaneous requests, no objects were made visible to the learners and no verbal prompts were given by the interventionist. When a request did not occur within a certain period of time, the interventionist provided an imitative prompt. At the conclusion of the investigation, the rate and variety of spontaneous signs had increased for all three learners. Carr and Kologinsky (1983) concluded that spontaneous signing was facilitated as a result of a shift in stimulus control from imitative prompting to the presence of an attending adult.

Halle, Baer, and Spradlin (1981) taught six learners with mental retardation to request preferred materials. A constant time delay was used to fade the use of a verbal instructional prompt, thus bringing requests under the control of more natural contextual cues. Charlop et al. (1985) also used a time-delay procedure in teaching seven learners with autism to use spoken words to request desired objects spontaneously. They reported that spontaneous requests generalized across settings, people, and objects that had not served as stimuli during acquisition. Gobbi et al. (1986) implemented a procedure they described as "quick transfer" to establish spontaneous requesting responses in two learners with severe disabilities. The instructional procedure consisted of a 30-second time-delay procedure that was incorporated with the use of graduated levels of stimulus prompts. Gobbi et al. (1986) reported high rates of spontaneous requesting as a result of the intervention procedure. Furthermore, they reported that spontaneous requesting generalized to other settings and other people.

Facilitating Spontaneous Requesting Requests are often controlled by certain motivational variables. Michael (1982, 1988) distinguished between two types of motivational variables, *establishing operations* and *conditioned establishing operations*. An establishing operation is defined as ". . . any change in the environment which alters the effectiveness of some object or event as reinforcement and simultaneously alters the momentary frequency of the behavior that has been followed by that reinforcement" (1982, pp. 150–151). For example, not eating for a lengthy period of time can be viewed as a change in the environment. This change is likely to result in food becoming an effective and powerful type of reinforcement. Because of this change, behaviors that lead to access to food (e.g., preparing a meal, requesting a meal) are more likely to occur.

Some establishing operations do not depend on a learning history. No one has to learn to be hungry after being deprived of food, for example. Changes that do not depend on past experience (e.g., physical deprivation or satiation) are called *unconditioned establishing operations*.

When the goal of intervention is to bring communicative behavior under the control of interoceptive states, the number of opportunities may be difficult for the interventionist

to control. The interventionist must take advantage of natural opportunities as they arise. Some of these opportunities may be easy to predict. Requests for food, for example, can be taught at mealtimes. Requests for beverages can be taught after the learner has exerted energy or eaten salty foods. Requests for warm clothing can be taught after the learner has been exposed to cold. The interventionist must be able to identify such natural opportunities and be in a position to implement instructional opportunities as they occur.

Conditioned establishing operations are often easier to create (Michael, 1988). For example, one has to learn the value of a spoon when confronted with applesauce. The receipt of a bowl of applesauce can be viewed as a change in the environment that makes a spoon an effective type of reinforcement. It thus increases the frequency of any behavior that has previously resulted in receipt of a spoon (e.g., searching the kitchen, asking for a spoon). Creating natural opportunities for teaching learners spontaneously to request spoons is straightforward—applesauce is provided without a spoon. Assuming the learner has already learned that spoons are used to eat applesauce, the interventionist may employ incidental teaching, mand-model procedures, and/or time-delay procedures to bring requests under the control of the relevant conditioned establishing operation (i.e., the receipt of applesauce). Similar conditional establishing operations can be created to provide opportunities for learners to request needed utensils, tools, toy parts, and so forth (Sosne et al., 1979).

Empirical Results Several studies have reported procedures for bringing communicative behavior under the control of conditioned establishing operations. Hall and Sundberg (1987) taught two learners with profound hearing and severe intellectual impairments to sign the names of several common household utensils (e.g., cup, can opener). Using a transfer of stimulus control procedure, these signs were

then established as requests for those same
utensils when they were needed to complete
tasks (e.g., making soup, opening a can of
fruit). Specifically, at the point in the task when
the utensil was needed, the interventionist initially displayed the item and signed, "What's
that?" or provided a model of the correct sign.
As these prompts were eliminated using time
delay and graduated levels of stimulus fading,
spontaneous requests occurred at the appropriate point in the task.

Using similar intervention procedures, Sigafoos, Doss, and Reichle (1989) taught three
learners with severe mental retardation to point
to a line drawing to request the utensils required
for consuming each of three preferred food or
beverage items. In a follow-up study (Sigafoos,
Reichle, Doss, Hall, & Pettitt, in press), two
additional learners came to request a spoon, a
bottle opener, and a straw spontaneously when
these items were needed to open and consume a
coup of applesauce, a bottle of carbonated beverage, and carton of juice, respectively. In both
the Hall and Sundberg and the Sigafoos et al.
studies, opportunities for requesting the needed
utensil were created by offering the desired food
or beverage item, but delaying the presentation
of the corresponding utensil until an appropriate
request was made.

A slightly different procedure was developed
by Goetz, Gee, and Sailor (1985). In their
study, two adolescents from a classroom serving students with severe retardation were taught
to point to graphic symbols to request either
initiation or continuation of various activities
(e.g., making toast). Conditioned establishing
operations were manipulated by requiring an
appropriate request (e.g., pointing to a toast
symbol to engage in making toast) either prior
to beginning or at some pre-determined point
during the task. For both learners, unprompted
requests occurred more frequently during opportunities that took place during, rather than
before, the activity.

Hunt, Goetz, Alwell, and Sailor (1986) later
replicated this "behavior-chain interruption strategy" in a study involving three children with
severe retardation. One explanation for the
viability of this intervention strategy is that continuation of a task is a more powerful motivator
than is beginning a task. Both Goetz et al. (1985)
and Hunt et al. (1986) provided evidence that
interruption of the desired tasks was moderately
upsetting to the learners. That is, when interrupted, the learners showed visible signs of distress and attempted to continue the task. By
being allowed to continue with the task, the
learner not only escaped from a mildly aversive
situation (negative reinforcement), but also got
back on track toward receipt of the reinforcer.

Creating opportunities for teaching requests in
the natural environment can be arranged not only
by withholding needed items or interrupting an
ongoing task, but also by withholding needed
assistance. Reichle, Anderson, and Schermer
(1986) manipulated the twist tie on a bread package to teach an adult with autism to request help.
After the learner had requested bread in order to
make a sandwich, he was confronted with either
a loosely wrapped or a tightly wrapped bread
package. Given the loosely wrapped bread bag,
the learner proceeded to make a sandwich. However, given the tightly wrapped bag, the learner
could not get at the bread and was thus unable to
make a sandwich. Under these latter conditions
the learner was taught to open a communication
wallet, search the pages, and select a "help"
symbol, at which point the interventionist un-
wrapped the package.

Identifying Interoceptive States   The environment can be arranged in ways that opti-
mize the probability that the learner will make
requests spontaneously. The learner's propensity to make requests spontaneously may depend on the interaction between conditions imposed by the environment and the learner's state
at any particular point in time. For example,
regardless of how overt the cues to request a
drink of water are, if the learner is not thirsty,
he or she is not likely to request a drink. Thus,

when learners fail to generalize newly established communication, it may be that relevant controlling variables are not in effect.

Some of the relevant controlling influences may be difficult to identify. Indirect evidence must often be used to determine how a particular object or activity will coincide with a learner's interoceptive state at a particular point in time. Skinner (1945) identified several types of indirect evidence that provide a connection with such interoceptive states, or "private events." Two of these connections may prove useful to interventionists when attempting to establish communicative repertoires controlled by interoceptive states. First, private events are frequently accompanied by public events. For example, we can infer that a learner is hot or cold based upon the temperature of the environment to which he or she has been exposed. Hunger may be inferred from a growling stomach. The interventionist can use these public accompaniments to teach the learner to label the internal state (e.g., "I'm hot," "I'm cold," "I'm hungry"). These opportunities could also be used to teach the learner to request objects or events to alter the existing state (e.g., "water," "heat," "food").

Second, the appearance of collateral behavior may provide evidence for an existing interoceptive state. For example, a person who shivers can be assumed to be cold. Sundberg (1983) described how public accompaniments and collateral behaviors could be used as the basis for assessing the extent of a learner's communicative repertoire with respect to private events. The appearance of these behaviors provides natural opportunities for implementing intervention procedures that may be designed to alert others to the learner's bodily state so that appropriate actions can then be taken or, alternatively, to teach learners a more direct means of achieving a satisfying state of affairs (e.g., "water," "heat"). For example, the interventionist may approach a shivering learner and ask, "What do you need?" and then prompt a request for a warm sweater. Over successive opportunities, the prompts are faded until the learner independently requests warm clothes when cold. Thus, by implementing intervention opportunities in the presence of public accompaniments or collateral behaviors, interoceptive states may eventually come to control appropriate communicative behaviors.

In addition to public accompaniments and collateral behaviors, knowledge of a person's history can be used to infer certain bodily states. For example, a person who has not eaten for a while can usually be assumed to be hungry. A natural opportunity to teach requests for food, therefore, arises each time a learner has been without food for 3–4 hours. Clearly, it is unethical deliberately to withhold food in order to create a relevant motivational state. However, interventionists can make use of naturally occurring states of deprivation. For example, requests for food can be taught at mealtimes. Through transfer of stimulus control procedures, requests for food may eventually occur spontaneously whenever the learner is hungry.

Because requesting desired objects or activities represents an extremely motivating situation for most learners, interventionists often choose this communicative intent for developing procedures to increase spontaneity. However, spontaneity represents an important attribute of other communicative intents, such as rejecting and offering information, as well.

Facilitating Spontaneous Rejecting Since rejecting implies that an offer of a nonpreferred object or activity was made, it might appear that rejecting can never be truly spontaneous. If spontaneity is viewed along a continuum, it is clear that qualitative aspects of the conditions under which the rejecting behavior is performed may influence significantly the flow of the interaction. Sometimes, for example, an offered item may need to be experienced before a rejection occurs. At other times, the mere anticipation of the offer may be sufficient to precipitate rejecting behaviors. Consider a learner who has had limited experience with a particular food, and may not recognize it as being undesired until he or she tastes it. In this case, a rejecting response might consist of spitting. In contrast, a learner who was familiar with the item and did not like it, or a learner who had become satiated with the item, might begin to perform a rejecting behavior far in advance of the actual delivery of the food.

Facilitating Spontaneous Offers of Information Contextual cues for offering information often involve a combination of very subtle contextual and interoceptive variables. Consider, for example, 10- to 14-month-old children who are beginning to show objects to others in their environment. Initially, young children learn to accept an offer from another person. Over time they may begin to find it entertaining to pass the object back. At some point, the child may find an item used frequently in a "passing routine," but be some distance from a prospective interactive partner. If the child picks up the object, his or her interactive partner may take notice and make positive social comments (reinforcement). Over time, the learner's behavior of "showing" may thus be shaped.

An alternative scenario for the emergence of showing behavior is grounded in the contextual variables of stimulus novelty. It is commonly accepted that novel events in the environment tend to recruit our attention. Upon seeing an expensive automobile, one might say "Wow," whether or not a listener is present. Similarly, when young children see a novel spectacle, they are apt to engage in motor and vocal accompaniments (e.g., laughing, squealing, pointing). In some instances, a learner may produce an utterance in an effort to share novel information (e.g., "That's neat."). On other occasions there may be an implicit call for help in the message (e.g., "Look at this spider!"). Some learners may call attention to a novel event, and then produce a more explicit request regarding the observations. For example, a child may point to a tricycle that has tipped over. An interactive

partner may comment, "Oh, it fell over." The learner may then begin to fuss as he or she pulls at the tricycle, thus prompting the partner to respond, "Oh, you want me to pick it up?" The distinction raised in the last example is very important. It suggests that to be efficient communicators, learners must acquire the ability to chain a variety of different communicative intents into a single interactive chain to meet both their own and their listeners' needs.

Facilitating Spontaneous Communicative Exchanges It is important to establish spontaneity across all types of communicative intents (requesting, rejecting, offering information) as well as across all aspects of communicative exchanges (initiating, maintaining, terminating). Figure 1 illustrates the interaction of these two dimensions.

Initiating Interactions Spontaneity is most important with respect to the initiation of communicative exchanges. Spontaneous initiations may occur to request, to reject, or to offer information. A hungry learner initiates a spontaneous request, for example, when he or she asks for food without being prompted. Communicative exchanges can also be initiated when a learner spontaneously rejects an object or activity. Finally, many communicative initiations involve a learner commenting on some novel or interesting aspect of the environment to initiate a conversation.

Maintaining Interactions Certain conditions represent natural cues for maintaining a communicative exchange. For example, a learner may spontaneously ask to continue rough housing with a parent. Elaborating on a prior comment or rejecting something that had previously been accepted in order to obtain a more preferred item also represent spontaneous communicative acts that function to maintain an interaction. Maintaining a communicative exchange presupposes that an initiation has been made. Some learners may need to be prompted to initiate an exchange, but be able to maintain that exchange spontaneously. At snacktime, for

		Initiate	Maintain	Terminate
Request	Context	A 6-year-old sees a peer on the playground.	A preschool child is watching his mother blow bubbles.	A learner has lost interest in playing with his younger sibling.
	Utterance	He approaches the peer and says, "Wanna play?"	He says, "Do it again."	He says, "Wouldn't you like to watch cartoons now?"
Reject	Context	Two children are standing together. Adult asks one child if he wants to go to a movie.	A preschool child is playing games with his dad.	A learner and his friend are working on a jigsaw puzzle.
	Utterance	The other child says, "I don't want to go to a movie today."	He says, "I don't want to take a bath."	He says, "I'm tired of doing this."

Figure 1.   Interaction between communicative intents and stages of communicative exchanges.

example, the interventionist may have to prompt the initial request, but once this request is reinforced the learner may be able to request more of the snack spontaneously.

Terminating Interactions   One way to terminate participation in an activity is to request to take leave. Such a request is considered spontaneous when it occurs without prompting after the learner has participated in the activity for some time. A rejection often terminates a communicative exchange. When a learner is offered an item, rejects it, and no further offers are made, the exchange has been terminated. Another way to terminate an exchange spontaneously is to complete an offer of information. This might happen when a learner describes a novel item so completely that there is nothing left to add.

Determining Which Discriminative Stimuli Should Control the Learner's Responses   A potentially wide range of stimuli may come to control a particular class of communicative behavior. Some of these may reflect irrelevant or inappropriate sources of control

(Koegel & Rincover, 1976; Lovaas, Koegel, & Schriebman, 1979). Other controlling variables may be the instructional prompts delivered by interventionist to recruit learner responses. Several investigators have proposed that instructional prompts be arranged in a continuum (Charlop et al., 1985; Halle, 1987), in which responses that need to be prompted physically are considered less spontaneous than those prompted by imitative models, gestures, or questions. Responses controlled by contextual cues or other more natural discriminative stimuli are in turn considered even more spontaneous.

One goal of intervention may be to ensure that communicative behaviors occur in environments that are more natural than those used for teaching. It is thus important for interventionists to determine which discriminative stimuli in the learner's environment should control the learner's responses. Combined with knowledge of the variables, prompts, or stimuli that currently control the learner's behavior, such a determination represents a type of discrepancy analysis between the variables that currently control behavior and the natural stimuli that should control the behavior, thus indicating the transfer of stimulus control that is needed.

FAILURE TO GENERALIZE ACQUIRED BEHAVIORS

Stokes and Baer (1977) defined generalization as the occurrence of a class of behavior under conditions different from those prevailing during acquisition, either without direct instruction or without the same degree of intervention. Stokes and Baer (1977) went on to delineate strategies that promote generalization. Four of these strategies are described in the following sections, and summarized in Figure 2.

1. Train Sufficient Exemplars

Generalization across a range of settings, materials, people, and tasks can be improved by including multiple exemplars during intervention (Stokes, Baer, & Jackson, 1974). For example, ordering a meal in a restaurant is more likely to generalize to unfamiliar restaurants if the initial intervention includes training in several restaurants, rather than just one. The exemplars selected for intervention should represent the range of variation within that class of objects (Horner, McDonnell, & Bellamy, 1986).

2. Use Contingencies That Are Maintained Naturally

Another strategy for promoting generalization is to teach behaviors that are likely to be rein-

Strategy	Description
Train sufficient exemplars	Teach the same behaviors under a variety of conditions (e.g., vary the materials, settings, people).
Use contingencies that are naturally maintained	Teach in conditions that include naturally available cues and consequences so that the behavior comes under control of natural conditions (e.g., teach during naturally occuring daily routines).
Train loosely	Systematically vary the conditions of instruction--specifically the stimuli (e.g., questions, cues, prompts) to prevent the development of narrow stimulus control.
Choose common stimuli	Use stimuli (e.g., materials, people) that are naturally available or present in the array of conditions in which performance is desired.

Figure 2.   Strategies for promoting generalization.

forced in natural settings. Requesting preferred objects and activities, for example, is a skill that is likely to be reinforced in the home, in school, and in some community settings. Behaviors that are reinforced are more likely to be maintained. When selecting initial communicative objectives it is, therefore, important to ensure that the learner's current and future environments will continue to provide natural reinforcements when the behaviors occur.

3. Train Loosely

A third strategy for promoting generalization involves the introduction of variation into the intervention procedures. In the past, most intervention programs were rigid in the delivery of antecedent cues. Using a loose training strategy, however, an effort is made to vary the procedures across opportunities. For example, in teaching requesting the interventionist may vary his or her questions (e.g., "What do you want?", "Want something?", "Can I get you something?") and on some occasions refrain from asking anything at all. Using this strategy, generalization occurs because precise control over the instructional stimuli is "loosened," resembling the natural variation found in most environments (Campbell & Stremel-Campbell, 1982).

4. Choose Common Stimuli

Bringing stimuli found in the natural environment into instructional settings (i.e., programming common stimuli) may also promote generalization (Rincover & Koegel, 1975). In this strategy, the training setting is made to resemble more natural settings. This can be done by ensuring that the same people, materials, procedures, and perhaps even furniture present during instruction are also part of natural environments. One means of incorporating more natural discriminative stimuli into the instructional process would be to implement intervention procedures in the natural environment. Several such procedures have been developed for

teaching communicative behaviors in more natural contexts.

NATURAL ENVIRONMENT INTERVENTION PROCEDURES

Incidental teaching (Hart, 1985) and the mand-model procedure (Rogers-Warren & Warren, 1980; Warren et al., 1984) represent two empirically validated options for teaching functional communication skills in more natural environments. Figure 3 highlights the characteristics of these procedures and suggests considerations for the use of each. Both procedures are described in the following sections.

Incidental Teaching

In the incidental teaching paradigm, the interventionist waits for the learner to initiate an interaction to start an instructional opportunity. Once a learner has indicated some interest in a particular object or activity—for example, by reaching for a ball—the interventionist approaches and makes the learner ask for it using the appropriate response (e.g., "red ball"). If the learner fails to ask for the item appropriately, a prompt is provided.

A teaching episode is always initiated by the learner. The learner may do so by looking at an object, by approaching a particular place or person, or by reaching for a desired object that is just out of reach. The interventionist can increase the frequency of such initiations by arranging the environment so that potentially desired objects or activities are present. When initiations by the learner are observed, the interventionist approaches the learner and pauses briefly before providing access to the desired object or activity. This pause provides a natural opportunity for the learner to request or comment upon the object of interest. If the learner does not independently produce the required communicative behavior at this point, the interventionist prompts the required communicative act. Finally, the learner's communicative behav-

Option	Characteristics	Considerations for use
Incidental teaching	Uses learner-initiated teaching opportunities	Learners must currently initiate approximations of target behavior. Effective reinforcers must be available in the natural environment.
Mand-model	Uses interventionist initiated teaching opportunities	Learners need not initiate. Most effective when learners have shown propensity to act on verbal prompts Mands for communicative behavior may reduce spontaneity.
Time delay	Interventionist delays the delivery of the controlling mand-mode prompt. Interventionist makes use of naturally arising opportunities.	Learner must be consistently responding to an instructional prompt (e.g., to a mand or model). Learner has shown little or no propensity to initiate approximations of target behavior.

Figure 3.   Characteristics and considerations for use of natural environment interventions.

ior is reinforced by the interventionist delivering the appropriate consequence.

Incidental teaching has been used successfully with preschool children (Hart & Risley, 1968, 1974, 1975) and with learners with severe disabilities (Haring, Neetz, Lovinger, Peck, & Semmel, 1987; McGee, Krantz, Mason, & McClannahan, 1983; McGee, Krantz, & McClannahan, 1985). A major advantage of the incidental teaching paradigm is that since the learner initiates the learning opportunity, a high degree of motivation can be assumed. A major disadvantage is that the number of instructional opportunities depends solely upon the learner. Some learners may show interest only rarely because of their limited initiation repertoires.

To obtain a sufficient number of teaching opportunities with such learners, interventionists may need to consider other options.

Mand-Model Procedures

The mand-model teaching procedure uses teacher-initiated instructions to generate instructional opportunities in the natural environment. For example, a teacher may approach a child at snacktime and say, "Tell me what you want.", or approach a child who is playing with a toy car and ask, "What are you doing?" The major difference between mand-model procedures and incidental teaching is in the arrangement of the verbal cues or instructions provided by the interventionist. In the incidental teaching paradigm, teachers ask questions to prompt responses after a child has initiated an exchange but has not made the required communicative response. In contrast, in a mand-model paradigm the teacher mands a response by either asking a question or providing a direct instruction to initiate an instructional opportunity. If the learner fails to respond to the mand correctly or in a timely fashion, additional prompts (e.g., imitative models) are used to prompt the desired communicative behavior.

Mand-model procedures thus solve the problem of limited initiation by using teacher-initiated opportunities. The teacher must identify naturally occurring situations in which mand-model opportunities are to be initiated.

Rogers-Warren and Warren (1980) used mand-model procedures to teach children to make a request or provide information concerning certain play materials. Appropriate replies from the child resulted in teacher-mediated access to the materials and praise. Additional instructions (e.g., "Give me a whole sentence.") or imitative models (e.g., "Say 'red ball.' ") were used if needed to obtain an appropriate response. Teachers for three children with language delays quickly learned to implement the mand-model procedure in their classrooms and did so during daily 30-minute free-play periods. All three children in the study showed increased frequency of vocal responses, including a substantial number of untrained words and phrases. Warren et al. (1984) systematically replicated the mand-model procedure and confirmed its effectiveness in generating increased talking in three preschool children with language delay.

Part of the success of the mand-model procedure is likely to be attributable to the increase in the number of opportunities to communicate. This increase is a direct result of teacher-initiated mands using instructions to verbalize (e.g., "Tell me _____"), questions (e.g., "What is this?"), and models (e.g., "Say 'car.' ").

Time Delay

Time delay has received increased attention in recent years (Halle, 1982; Halle et al., 1981; Handen & Zane, 1987). The procedure refers to the practice of introducing a designated pause between presentation of the natural cue and delivery of the instructional prompt. This brief interval allows the learner an opportunity to respond in the presence of the natural cue prior to delivery of an instructional prompt.

Time delay can be used to provide opportunities for learners to communicate in the natural environment. In a time-delay procedure controlling cues are withheld briefly to give the learner time to respond. Time-delay procedures have been used to teach a variety of communicative behaviors, including requests for displayed objects (Charlop et al., 1985; Gobbi et al., 1986; McCook et al., 1988) and statements of affection (Charlop & Walsh, 1986). Halle, Marshall, and Spradlin (1979) withheld the delivery of food trays to six children with mental retardation for 15 seconds. If the learner uttered an appropriate request (e.g., "Tray please.") within that 15 seconds, the interventionist provided the meal. If the learner did not utter an appropriate request, he or she was prompted to imitate a request, and was then given the tray. For two of the six children, the 15-second delay was sufficient to evoke requests. Increased requesting occurred for three children when prompting and delay were combined. One child required more intensive training to establish appropriate requesting behavior. A follow-up study (Halle et al., 1981) demonstrated that teachers can quickly learn to implement the delay technique in a variety of activities with a resulting increase in child initiations.

While time delay alone may provide learners the opportunity to display already established communicative behaviors, it cannot be used to teach new communicative responses. Because of this limitation, time-delay procedures are generally implemented after a given communicative behavior has been established through the use of mands, models, or other types of response prompts. Time delay can also be used as a means of fading these type of response prompts. This approach is known as *delayed prompting* (Handen & Zane, 1987). With delayed prompting, the interventionist waits a predetermined amount of time for a response to occur. If the response is not forthcoming, the interventionist delivers a prompt at the end of the delay interval to recruit the desired action. Delayed prompting procedures can be implemented subsequent to or during acquisition of the communicative behavior. Time delay is appropriate for increasing existing communicative behavior. Time delay can also be combined with other procedures both to create opportunities and to establish new communicative behaviors.

Synthesizing Natural Environment Intervention Procedures

Incidental teaching, mand-model procedures, and time-delay procedures can be integrated, so that the limitations of each procedure can be partially offset by the others (Halle, 1982). Incidental teaching, for example, may not be appropriate for learners with low rates of communicative initiation. The mand-model procedure could thus be used to increase the number of instructional opportunities. Extensive use of mand-model procedures may bring communicative behavior under the narrow control of the interventionist's instructions (e.g., "Tell me _____") or models (e.g., "Say 'ball.'") (Carr, 1982). This can create a situation in which learners actually initiate less, because they learn to produce a response only after a teacher provides a prompt. To be functional, initiations must ultimately come under the control of natural cues present in the learner's environment.

To overcome the narrow stimulus control that may result from extensive use of mands and

models, time-delay procedures can be implemented to separate the learner's communicative behavior from its dependence upon prompts. One purpose of time-delay procedures is to transfer stimulus control from the interventionist's prompts to more natural controlling variables. Suppose a learner's requests occur only when a verbal cue is provided by the interventionist. The interventionist gives the learner some applesauce and then asks, "What do you need?", to which the learner responds, "Spoon." On successive trials the question, "What do you need?" is progressively delayed. When the learner is reliably requesting a spoon without being prompted, a transfer of stimulus control has been achieved. Requests for spoons have effectively been transferred from the interventionist's questions to the more natural circumstance of having applesauce but no spoon.

Time-delay procedures may, at times, need to be combined with other prompt-fading techniques. For example, the verbal prompt (e.g., "Say, 'I want a spoon.'") can be reduced in complexity, loudness, or length (i.e., "Say, 'I want a _____'," "Say, 'I want _____'," "Say '_____,'" and finally no verbal prompt at all) (Risley & Reynolds, 1970; Risley & Wolf, 1967). Similar combinations of time delay and prompt fading can be used to eliminate the need for physical prompts often required to establish gestural or graphic mode communicative responses. For example, initially, molding a learner's hands to execute the sign "cookie" may require full physical assistance (i.e., taking the learner's hands and putting them through each step of the sign). Physical assistance can be faded by systematically reducing the amount or magnitude of the assistance provided. In getting a learner to point to a graphic symbol it may first be necessary physically to guide the learner's finger to the symbol. Time-delay and prompt-fading procedures can also be used to eliminate the need for this level of physical guidance.

SUMMARY

Learners often fail to use newly acquired communicative behaviors spontaneously or to generalize them to people, objects, or settings other than those used in teaching. This chapter described procedures to facilitate spontaneity and promote generalization. Several nonintrusive intervention procedures—incidental teaching, mand-model procedures, and time delay—that promote the establishment of spontaneous communicative behavior were reviewed.

REFERENCES

Bricker, W.A., & Bricker, D.D. (1974). An early language training strategy. In R.L. Schiefelbusch & L.L. Lloyd (Eds.), *Language perspectives: Acquisition, retardation, and intervention* (pp. 431–468). Baltimore: University Park Press.

Campbell, R.C., & Stremel-Campbell, K. (1982). Programming "loose training" as a strategy to facilitate language generalization. *Journal of Applied Behavior Analysis, 15,* 295–301.

Carr, E.G. (1982). Sign language. In R. Koegel, A. Rincover, & A. Egel (Eds.), *Educating and understanding autistic children* (pp. 142–157). San Diego: College-Hill Press.

Carr, E.G., & Kologinsky, E. (1983). Acquisition of sign language by autistic children II: Spontaneity and generalization effects. *Journal of Applied Behavior Analysis, 16,* 297–314.

Charlop, M.H., Schreibman, L., & Thibodeau, M.G. (1985). Increasing spontaneous verbal responding in autistic children using a time delay procedure. *Journal of Applied Behavior Analysis, 18,* 155–166.

Charlop, M.H., & Walsh, M.E. (1986). Increasing autistic children's spontaneous verbalizations of affection: An assessment of time delay and peer modeling procedures. *Journal of Applied Behavior Analysis, 19,* 307–314.

Gobbi, L., Cipani, E., Hudson, C., & Lapenta-Neudeck, R. (1986). Developing spontaneous requesting among children with severe mental retardation. *Mental Retardation, 24,* 357–363.

Goetz, L., Gee, K., & Sailor, W. (1985). Using a behavior chain interruption strategy to teach communication skills to students with severe disabilities. *Journal of The Association for Persons with Severe Handicaps, 10,* 21–30.

Hall, G., & Sundberg, M.L. (1987). Teaching mands by manipulating conditioned establishing operations. *Analysis of Verbal Behavior, 5,* 41–53.

Halle, J.W. (1982). Teaching functional language to the handicapped: An integrative model of natural environment teaching techniques. *Journal of The Association for the Severely Handicapped, 7,* 29–37.

Halle, J.W. (1987). Teaching language in the natural environment: An analysis of spontaneity. *Journal of The Association for Persons with Severe Handicaps, 12,* 28–37.

Halle, J.W., Baer, D.M., & Spradlin, J.E. (1981). Teachers' generalized use of delay as a stimulus control procedure to increase language use in handicapped children. *Journal of Applied Behavior Analysis, 14,* 389–409.

Halle, J.W., Marshall, A.M., & Spradlin, J.E. (1979). Time delay: A technique to increase language use and facilitate generalization in retarded children. *Journal of Applied Behavior Analysis, 12,* 431–439.

Handen, B.L., & Zane, T. (1987). Delayed prompting: A review of procedural variations and results. *Research in Developmental Disabilities, 8,* 307–330.

Haring, T.G., Neetz, J.A., Lovinger, L., Peck, C., & Semmel, M.I. (1987). Effects of four modified incidental teaching procedures to create opportunities for communication. *Journal of The Association for Persons with Severe Handicaps, 12,* 218–226.

Hart, B. (1985). Naturalistic language training techniques. In S.F. Warren & A.K. Rogers-Warren (Eds.), *Teaching functional language* (pp. 63–88). Austin, TX: PRO-ED.

Hart, B., & Risley, T.R. (1968). Establishing use of descriptive adjectives in the spontaneous speech of disadvantaged preschool children. *Journal of Applied Behavior Analysis, 1,* 109–120.

Hart, B., & Risley, T.R. (1974). Using preschool materials to modify the language of disadvantaged children. *Journal of Applied Behavior Analysis, 7,* 243–256.

Hart, B., & Risley, T.R. (1975). Incidental teaching of language in the preschool. *Journal of Applied Behavior Analysis, 8,* 411–420.

Horner, R.H., McDonnell, J.J., & Bellamy, G.T.

(1986). Teaching generalized skills: General case instruction in simulation and community settings. In R.H. Horner, L.H. Meyer, & H.D.B. Fredricks (Eds.), *Education of learners with severe handicaps: Exemplary service strategies* (pp. 289–314). Baltimore: Paul H. Brookes Publishing Co.

Hunt, P., Goetz, L., Alwell, M., & Sailor, W. (1986). Using an interrupted behavior chain strategy to teach generalized communication responses. *Journal of The Association for Persons with Severe Handicaps, 11,* 196–204.

Koegel, R.L., & Rincover, A. (1976). Some detrimental effects of using extra stimuli to guide learning in normal and autistic children. *Journal of Abnormal Child Psychology, 4,* 59–71.

Lovaas, O.I., Koegel, R., & Schriebman, L. (1979). Stimulus overselectivity in autism: A review of research. *Psychological Bulletin, 86,* 1236–1254.

Lovaas, O.I., Koegel, R., Simmons, J.Q., & Long, J.S. (1973). Some generalization and follow-up measures on autistic children in behavior therapy. *Journal of Applied Behavior Analysis, 6,* 131–166.

MacDonald, J.D. (1976). Environmental language intervention. In F.B. Withrow & C.J. Nygren (Eds.), *Language, materials, and curriculum management for the handicapped learner.* Columbus, OH: Charles E. Merrill.

MacDonald, J.D., & Blott, J.P. (1974). Environmental language intervention: The rationale for a diagnostic and training strategy through rules, context, and generalization. *Journal of Speech and Hearing Disorders, 39,* 244–256.

McCook, B., Cipani, E., Madigan, K., & LaCampagne, J. (1988). Developing requesting behavior: Acquisition, fluency and generality. *Mental Retardation, 26,* 137–143.

McGee, G.G., Krantz, P.J., Mason, D., & McClannahan, L.E. (1983). A modified incidental-teaching procedure for autistic youth: Acquisition and generalization of receptive object labels. *Journal of Applied Behavior Analysis, 18,* 17–31.

McGee, G.G., Krantz, P.J., & McClannahan, L.E. (1985). The facilitative effects of incidental teaching on preposition use by autistic children. *Journal of Applied Behavior Analysis, 18,* 17–31.

Michael, J. (1982). Distinguishing between discriminative and motivational functions of stimuli. *Journal of the Experimental Analysis of Behavior, 37,* 149–155.

Michael, J. (1988). Establishing operations and the mand. *Analysis of Verbal Behavior, 6,* 3–9.

Oliver, C.B., & Halle, J.W. (1982). Language training in the everyday environment: Teaching func-

tional sign language use to a retarded child. *Journal of The Association for the Severely Handicapped, 8,* 50–62.

Reichle, J., Anderson, H., & Schermer, G. (1986). *Establishing the discrimination between requesting objects, requesting assistance and "helping yourself."* Unpublished manuscript, University of Minnesota, Minneapolis.

Reichle, J., York, J., & Eynon, D. (1989). Influence of indicating preferences for initiating, maintaining, and terminating interactions. In F. Brown & D.H. Lehr (Eds.), *Persons with profound disabilities: Issues and practices* (pp. 191–211). Baltimore: Paul H. Brookes Publishing Co.

Rincover, A., & Koegel, R.L. (1975). Setting generality and stimulus control in autistic children. *Journal of Applied Behavior Analysis, 8,* 235–246.

Risley, T.R., & Reynolds, N.J. (1970). Emphasis as a prompt for verbal imitation. *Journal of Applied Behavior Analysis, 3,* 185–190.

Risley, T.R., & Wolf, M. (1967). Establishing functional speech in echolalic children. *Behaviour Research and Therapy, 5,* 73–88.

Rogers-Warren, A., & Warren, S.F. (1980). Mands for verbalization: Facilitating the display of newly trained language in children. *Behavior Modification, 4,* 361–382.

Schaeffer, B. (1978). Teaching spontaneous sign language to nonverbal children: Theory & method. *Sign Language Studies, 21,* 317–352.

Sigafoos, J., Doss, S., & Reichle, J. (1989). Developing mand and tact repertoires in persons with severe developmental disabilities using graphic symbols. *Research in Developmental Disabilities, 10,* 183–200.

Sigafoos, J., Reichle, J., Doss, S., Hall, K., & Pettitt, L. (in press). "Spontaneous" transfer of stimulus control from tact to mand contingencies. *Research in Developmental Disabilities.*

Skinner, B.F. (1945). The operational analysis of psychological terms. *Psychological Review, 52,* 270–277.

Sosne, J.B., Handleman, J.S., & Harris, S.L. (1979). Teaching spontaneous-functional speech to autistic type children. *Mental Retardation, 17,* 241–245.

Stokes, T., & Baer, D. (1977). An implicit technology of generalization. *Journal of Applied Behavior Analysis, 10,* 349–367.

Stokes, J.F., Baer, D.M., & Jackson, R.L. (1974). Programming the generalization of a greeting response in four retarded children. *Journal of Applied Behavior Analysis, 7,* 599–610.

Sundberg, M.L. (1983). Language. In J.L. Matson & S.E. Breuning (Eds.), *Assessing the mentally retarded* (pp. 285–310). New York: Grune & Stratton.

Warren, S.F., McQuarter, R.J., & Rogers-Warren, A.K. (1984). The effects of mands and models on the speech of unresponsive language-delayed preschool children. *Journal of Speech and Hearing Disorders, 49,* 43–52.

9

Defining the Array of Instructional Prompts for Teaching Communication Skills

Jeff Sigafoos, Theresa Mustonen,
Paris DePaepe, Joe Reichle, and Jennifer York

THE ULTIMATE GOAL of communication instruction is for the learner to communicate spontaneously in the presence of naturally occurring cues (e.g., spontaneously waving to a classmate upon arriving at the bus stop in the morning, requesting a drink when thirsty). For some learners, however, naturally available cues are not sufficient to evoke communicative behavior. Additional cues or prompts must thus be provided. The purposes of this chapter are to: 1) introduce a conceptual model for designing instruction, 2) define a variety of options for instructional prompt and examine the advantages and disadvantages of each, 3) examine strategies for sequencing the delivery of instructional prompts and the relative advantages and disadvantages of each, 4) review types of prompts and prompting strategies related to communication intervention, and 5) examine procedures for incorporating newly established communicative behavior into the natural environment.

CONCEPTUAL MODEL FOR DESIGNING INSTRUCTION

Instructional design depends largely upon the stage of learning at which the learner is operating. In the acquisition stage of learning, the goal is to establish the new skill, with emphasis on accuracy. Once skills have been acquired, instructional emphasis may change to improving fluency (timing, efficiency) or other more qualitative aspects of performance. Once accuracy and fluency have been established, maintenance of the skill over time in the absence of instructional assistance is sought. Generalization of the skill to novel and appropriate situations is an additional aspect of instruction that may be incorporated at any of these stages.

General guidelines for instructional design at each stage are shown in Figure 1. Conceptualized in simplest terms, performance of a particular behavior can be influenced by intervening before the behavior is performed (*antecedent instruction*) or after the behavior is performed or is supposed to have been performed (*consequential instruction*). In the acquisition stage of learning, when emphasis is on establishing accuracy, most instruction should be provided before the learner initiates the desired behavior, so that the likelihood of correct responding is increased. Errors should be minimized, since incorrect behaviors are sometimes very difficult to change once established. The purpose of providing instructional prompts is to evoke the behavior so that it may then come under the control of more natural cues. For example, the natural cues associated with greeting a friend include the presence of peers or the initiation of a greeting by a friend. Before prompting the desired greeting response the instructor may point out others engaging in greeting behaviors in the hope that the learner begins to imitate this behavior.

Once skills are fairly well established, greater fluency may have to be sought. The intensity of instructional prompts is faded by employing less intrusive prompts, so that the learner has a greater opportunity to initiate performance. If errors are made, the interventionist must decide whether to intervene to avoid an incorrect response or to allow the learner an opportunity to self-correct. Instructive feedback should be given if self-correction does not occur.

Before moving on to skill maintenance, all

INSTRUCTIONAL COMPONENTS

| | Cue/antecedent | Behavior/response | Consequence | |
			Correction	Reinforcement
Acquisition	Natural cues paired with instructional prompts	Establish accurate behavior	Natural correction paired with instructional correction procedure if error occurs (errors should be infrequent)	Natural reinforcement paired with additional reinforcement and higher rate if necessary
Fluency	Natural cues fading instructional prompts	Maintain accuracy, establish fluency	Natural correction paired with instructional correction procedure, fading to natural corrections	Natural reinforcement fading to natural schedule
Maintenance	Natural cues	Maintain accuracy and fluency (in absence of instruction)	Natural corrections	Natural reinforcement
Generalization	Natural cues in novel and varied conditions	Maintain accuracy and fluency, demonstrate in novel situations (in absence of instruction)	Natural corrections in novel and varied conditions	Natural reinforcement in novel and varied conditions

STAGES OF LEARNING

Figure 1.   Instructional components of various stages of learning.

instructional prompts should be faded and the learner should be able to perform the behavior in the absence of instruction. That is, the behavior must be well established under natural conditions. Several techniques for fading prompts are presented later in this chapter. Reinforcement levels should also be faded to correspond with those operating in the natural environment.

Maintenance of a skill is defined as continued performance of a behavior over time under conditions that were present during acquisition. For example, after the learner has been taught to order a meal at a restaurant, he or she should be able to do so whenever the occasion arises. Generalization is evident when performance occurs in natural situations that are somewhat different from the conditions under which instruction was provided. For example, a learner might demonstrate ordering skills at Hardee's or Burger King with her family even though direct instruction occurred only at McDonald's with her teacher.

One goal of instruction for learners with severe disabilities is to be able to apply useful skills in naturally occurring environments. By keeping in mind stages of learning efficiency and by referencing naturally available cues and consequences, instructional programs can be designed to promote effective communication throughout daily life.

At the start of communication instruction, the interventionist identifies the natural discriminative stimulus for evoking the desired communicative response. Sometimes the natural cue does not evoke the desired response from the learner and some type of response prompt is needed to ensure the response will occur. A prompt refers to any extra cue, stimulus, or assistance that reliably recruits the desired behavior. Gradually, the response or stimulus prompts required to recruit the behavior are faded until the learner consistently produces the desired response in the presence of the natural cue without having to be prompted. Prompts directed at the learner's behavior are called *response*

prompts. Prompts directed at an alteration of the cue or discriminative stimulus for behavior are called *stimulus prompts*.

RESPONSE PROMPTING AND PROMPT HIERARCHIES

Types of Response Prompts

There are several types of response prompts. *Verbal prompts* are simply spoken questions, directions, or instructions that may set the occasion for a response (e.g., "What do you want?"), direct the learner to respond (e.g., "Tell me what you want."), or more explicitly specify the required learner action (e.g., "Sign 'milk.', " "Point to the 'milk' symbol."). A second type of prompt is referred to as *modeling*. The interventionist might, for example, demonstrate the sign "milk," with the learner expected to imitate the modeled sign. In the graphic mode, pointing to the correct symbol for learners using a direct-select system of communication is an example of a modeling prompt. In other modes, however, pointing to the correct item is considered a type of *gestural prompt*. For example, pointing to a glass of milk may prompt a learner to request that item. A fourth type of response prompt is *physical assistance,* which might involve taking hold of a learner's hands and arms and putting him or her through the desired action. The amount of physical assistance provided can vary from a light touch to actual hand-over-hand guidance. Physical guidance is often necessary to prompt desired behavior in learners who do not imitate.

Each type of prompt has advantages and disadvantages, as summarized in Table 1. Verbal prompts are probably the easiest type of prompt to deliver, provided the learner attends to and follows directions. Since the exact wording of the prompt can be specified clearly in written instructional procedures, it can be implemented consistently across interventionists. In addition, verbal prompts are useful with learners with

Table 1. Advantages and disadvantages of various types of prompts

Type of prompt	Advantages and disadvantages
Response prompts	
Verbal	Quick and easy to deliver
	Easy to define
	Requires learner to attend and follow directions
	May be disruptive in some settings
Modeling	Provides nonintrusive visual cue
	Requires visual attending
	Requires imitative repertoire
Gestures	Provides nonintrusive visual cue
	Requires visual attending
Physical	Ensures success
	May prevent errors
	May create dependency, resistance
	May be difficult to fade
Stimulus prompts	
Stimulus fading (size, intensity, color)	Allows discrete fading of steps to be specified
	Non–criterion-related feature is manipulated
	May lead to stimulus overselectivity
	Depends upon finding some stimulus to which the learner will respond that can subsequently be faded
Stimulus shaping	Allows discrete fading of steps to be specified
	Criterion-related feature of stimulus is manipulated
	May be difficult to develop stimulus materials for shaping program
	Depends upon finding some stimulus to which the learner will respond that can subsequently be shaped

visual impairment, or who need only occasional reminders to carry out a task. A disadvantage of verbal prompts is that they may be distracting to others in the environment. Depending on the skill being taught, a verbal prompt may also

require more time to give than a model, gesture, or physical prompt. For instance, if the learner is being taught to take a communication wallet out of his or her pocket as a precursor to making a request, a gesture toward the learner's pocket may prompt the behavior more quickly than the verbal prompt "Take your wallet out of your pocket and open it."

Gestures and models offer several advantages. Gestures provide fairly nonintrusive visual cues that may be sufficient to recruit the behavior. Models demonstrate to the learner exactly what his or her next action should be. In order for these two prompts to be effective, however, the learner must visually attend to the interventionist's model or gesture. The use of models also requires a learner who will imitate the demonstrated action. If the learner does not reliably imitate a model of the desired behavior, physical prompting is likely to be necessary.

Physical prompts can be very valuable for learners who do not imitate or who do not respond to other types of prompts. Learners who are physically unskilled or uncoordinated in the initial stages of an instructional program may benefit from the use of physical guidance that familiarizes them with the motor movements required to accomplish the skill. Physically guiding a learner through a task helps prevent him or her from developing incorrect patterns of responding. However, the use of physical prompts has its drawbacks. Learners who are very passive may become dependent on such assistance, making it difficult to fade the prompts. For some learners, minimizing effort may be more reinforcing than being reinforced for independent performance. Furthermore, use of physical prompts may not be advisable for learners who have a history of engaging in excess behavior when confronted with task demands, or for learners who dislike physical contact. An interventionist should be careful to identify the types of physical prompts that are antecedents to aggression or self-injury, and avoid their use.

Types of Response Prompt Hierarchies

Depending on the learner or task, a single type of response prompt may be effective in recruiting the desired behavior. A learner being taught to request assistance, for example, may always respond appropriately when provided with a verbal prompt (e.g., "What do you need?" or "Ask for help."). Other learners may respond consistently to an interventionist's model (e.g., the interventionist demonstrates the sign for "help"). With many learners, however, a single prompt may not be effective, and physical assistance may be required to prompt the desired behavior. Instructional procedures for such learners may, therefore, need to incorporate and sequence several types of response prompts. Systematic delivery and sequencing of several response prompts follows two basic patterns or hierarchies—*least-to-most intrusive* and *most-to-least intrusive*.

Least-to-Most Prompting Hierarchies In a least-to-most prompting hierarchy, also known as an *increasing assistance method* or the *system of least prompts,* the interventionist applies the least intrusive prompt first, then progresses through the sequence of prompts until the learner performs the desired behavior. As the learner's performance improves, the number and type of prompts are reduced (faded) until the learner responds to natural cues alone. A typical least-to-most prompting hierarchy begins with verbal prompts, followed by gestures, models, and finally physical assistance. For example, in the initial opportunities of teaching a learner to request by pointing to a symbol for "cookie," an interventionist might begin with the verbal prompt, "Point to cookie." If the learner does not respond, the interventionist might repeat the verbal prompt and model the behavior of pointing to the symbol. Should the learner again fail to respond, the interventionist would repeat the verbal prompt and physically assist the learner in pointing to the symbol.

Once the learner began to initiate pointing to the symbol, the interventionist would eliminate the physical prompt, and then the combined verbal and modeling prompt. These prompts would be faded in the same manner, until the learner responded to the more natural cue of an offered cookie in the absence of any instructional prompt. Least-to-most intrusive prompting systems have frequently been used to teach communicative behaviors (Bates & Renzaglia, 1982; O'Brien, 1978).

The least-to-most prompting hierarchy is one of the most frequently used prompting strategies (Schoen, 1986; Snell, 1983). Since the prompting sequence always begins with the least intrusive prompt and progresses to more intrusive prompts, it can be a relatively easy system to implement. The criterion for moving from one prompt to the next is easy to understand — if the learner does not respond the interventionist gives the next level of prompt; if the learner responds correctly the interventionist provides reinforcement and moves on to the next step. However, an interventionist must be familiar with all the prompts in a hierarchy and must remember their order of use, since it may be necessary to apply the entire sequence.

The least-to-most prompting system also gives the learner an opportunity to make errors. The interventionist gives the prompt and then waits a predetermined length of time for the learner to respond before proceeding to the next prompt level. During the wait interval, the learner may either respond correctly, make no response, or begin to respond incorrectly. Although most programs include error correction procedures to interrupt or correct mistakes, the fact that the learner is allowed to respond incorrectly introduces the possibility that errors may persist (Terrace, 1963).

Learner characteristics are a very important consideration in the decision to use an increasing prompt hierarchy. If a learner shows a tendency toward passivity that is unrelated to motor skill ability, using this system may lead to increased dependency. A learner may wait until the highest level of prompt is given because responding then requires the least amount of effort. Fading of physical prompts, which often represent the most intrusive prompts in the hierarchy, may also prove difficult if learners are reinforced by physical contact with the interventionist.

Characteristics of the task also come into play. If the interventionist adopts a skill cluster approach (Sailor & Guess, 1983), embedding communication skills instruction into the teaching of other skills, the resulting task analysis may be very long. Using an increasing prompt hierarchy on multistep tasks may add considerably to the time required to teach all of the skills within a cluster. For example, a task analysis for grocery shopping may include steps performed in a variety of environments, such as the home, city bus, or store entrance, as well as the subenvironments of the grocery store itself. This may be of particular concern when intervention takes place in community environments. For example, when a long line of customers is waiting behind the learner at a fast food restaurant, use of an increasing prompt hierarchy will add to the time it takes the learner to place an order, may call undue attention to the learner, and may be annoying to others.

Most-to-Least Prompting Hierarchies.   In a most-to-least, or decreasing assistance, hierarchy, prompts are arranged from the most intrusive to the least intrusive (Schoen, 1986). The first prompt provided after the natural cue is one that will reliably evoke the desired behavior. Over successive opportunities, this prompt is faded and less intrusive prompts are delivered. A typical most-to-least prompting hierarchy begins with physical assistance, followed by models, gestures, and finally verbal prompts. For example, an interventionist might initially provide physical assistance to a learner as a means of prompting a particular sign. After a few such prompted opportunities, physical assistance

would be faded and a less intrusive model of the correct sign delivered. A similar strategy could be followed to establish first gestures and then verbal cues as instructional prompts. Often prompts representing different levels of intrusiveness can be delivered simultaneously. After several simultaneous pairings, the more intrusive prompt can be systematically faded, while control by the less intrusive prompt is maintained. Decreasing assistance procedures are sometimes referred to as an application of errorless learning procedures because initially learners are not given the opportunity to make errors. The most-to-least intrusive prompt hierarchy has also been used to teach a variety of communication skills, including verbalizations and sign production (Hinerman, Jenson, Walker, & Petersen, 1982; Luiselli, Colozzi, Donnellon, Helfen, & Pemberton, 1978).

Graduated guidance is a variation of a most-to-least prompting hierarchy. In this type of prompt, the amount of physical assistance and the manner in which it is applied are reduced gradually as the learner's performance improves. During initial instructional opportunities an interventionist might place his or her hand over the learner's hand, shaping the learner's finger to point to a symbol. In later opportunities, the interventionist might merely rest his or her fingers on the back of the learner's hand, wrist, and then elbow until finally no contact is necessary. Physical assistance can also be faded by reducing only the magnitude of assistance provided, so that the interventionist continues to touch the learner in the same place but reduces the pressure over time. For example, an interventionist might use full physical guidance to assist the learner to touch a symbol, then over time reduce the amount of contact with the learner until his or her hand moves simultaneously with but does not touch the learner's hand. This is referred to as *shadowing* the learner's movements.

The most-to-least prompting system can be very useful for teaching communication skills.

Since the interventionist begins with the prompt that will result in occurrence of the behavior, the amount of time spent waiting for the learner to respond is minimized. The learner moves through the task faster, and training time is often reduced. Opportunity for errors is also minimized since the first prompt given is the one that typically results in the learner making a correct response. For this reason, using decreasing prompt hierarchies may result in rapid skill acquisition with few errors. However, in this system of prompts it is often more difficult to judge when a prompt should be faded to a lower level. Particularly when physical prompts are used first, the decision to move to a less intrusive prompt may be somewhat arbitrary.

Learner characteristics may also affect the effectiveness of a most-to-least system. More intrusive prompts may prove difficult to fade, for example, if the learner is reinforced by physical contact with an instructor. Other learners may dislike physical contact with an instructor, which can serve as either a training advantage or a disadvantage. If a learner possesses most of the motor skills required for a task but performs it clumsily, using physical prompts may bring about faster independent performance, since the learner may prefer to engage in the behavior independently rather than be assisted. If the learner is unskilled, however, the interventionist may have no choice but to use minimal amounts of physical guidance in the early stages of intervention, and to be alert to the possibility that the learner may become resistant.

Learners who are skilled at some steps of a task but unskilled at others present another type of problem. An interventionist may need to combine approaches for this type of learner, using a decreasing assistance approach for the more difficult steps of the task and an increasing assistance hierarchy, or simply a single type of prompt for steps the learner is capable of completing more independently (Browder & Snell, 1983).

Characteristics of the task should also be con-

sidered. In tasks in which committing an error would be unacceptable (e.g., crossing a busy street), a decreasing prompt hierarchy may be preferred over other strategies. Communication skills, such as signing or gesturing, lend themselves to a decreasing prompt hierarchy, particularly if learners have motor skill difficulties or do not imitate. The environment in which training will occur can also affect the decision to use a decreasing prompting hierarchy. In some environments, it may be less distracting to use this prompting system rather than an increasing prompt hierarchy. For example, teaching a learner to request a "small side salad with French dressing" at a fast food restaurant by pointing to a symbol may be expedited if the interventionist starts by physically guiding the learner to point to the symbol as opposed to verbally prompting, then gesturing, and finally using physical guidance.

In summary, response prompting strategies have wide applicability in teaching communicative behavior to learners with severe disabilities. By the careful sequencing of the various types of response prompts, interventionists can increase their success in establishing the desired behavior. Also built into these sequences are mechanisms for fading the use of such response prompts. Often, there will be instances, however, where the desired form of behavior is already a part of the learner's communicative repertoire. The learner may, for example, already point to or otherwise select graphic symbols. In such cases, the focus of intervention may be to bring existing behavior under appropriate stimulus control so that it occurs at the appropriate times.

Using Time Delay to Fade Response Prompts

Time delay, described in Chapter 8, may be used within the context of naturally occurring activities to teach learners to respond to environmental or other cues, and it can be incorporated into instructional programs as a means of fading response prompts. Halle (1982) described the procedure as a "natural environment intervention designed (1) to provide more opportunities or reasons for handicapped children to talk, and (2) to teach handicapped children to respond to cues other than adult verbalizations" (p. 31). Used in this manner, the procedure allows interventionists to use naturally occurring communication opportunities and capitalize on previously unrecognized opportunities for teaching. Time-delay procedures are also frequently applied as a means of fading instructional prompts that may have been necessary to establish a behavior.

To implement a time-delay procedure, the interventionist waits for a specified period for the learner to produce the target response. If the learner does not respond independently in the presence of the natural cue, an instructional prompt is delivered. Time-delay procedures fall into two categories, those that use a constant prespecified delay, and those that use successively longer delays between the cue and the subsequent prompt. With a *constant time-delay* procedure, the instructional cue and the response prompt are delivered simultaneously during initial teaching opportunities. On subsequent opportunities, the amount of time the interventionist waits after the natural cue before delivering the instructional prompt is increased to a constant specified length of time (e.g., 4 seconds). This delay interval remains at this constant level throughout the remainder of intervention. In *progressive time delay,* the response prompt is initially presented immediately after the natural cue. Over successive opportunities, the length of time between the instructional cue and the additional prompt is gradually increased by prespecified increments until the maximum delay interval is attained.

Time-delay procedures enable the transfer of stimulus control from the instructional prompt to the desired natural controlling stimulus by gradually delaying the delivery of the instructional prompt. Both constant (Browder, Morris, & Snell, 1981; Kleinert & Gast, 1982; Oliver & Halle, 1982) and progressive (Charlop, Schreibman, & Thibodeau, 1985; Wolery, Gast, Kirk, & Schuster, 1988) time-delay strategies have been used to fade response prompts that are required to establish communicative behaviors among learners with developmental disabilities.

Empirical Results on the Effectiveness of Various Prompting and Fading Systems

Response prompts have been used successfully and subsequently faded to teach a variety of communicative behaviors among learners with severe disabilities. Several studies have compared the various response prompting systems. The results of such comparisons provide some empirical basis for the selection of an appropriate response prompting strategy.

Csapo (1981) compared the effects of increasing assistance and decreasing assistance procedures for teaching learners with severe and profound disabilities to make a two-choice discrimination. Learners were presented with two different colored blocks and asked to give one block to the instructor. In the increasing assistance condition, the instructor first made a verbal request. If the learner did not respond correctly, the instructor first pointed, then provided partial physical assistance, then full physical assistance until the correct response occurred. In the decreasing assistance condition, the verbal request was first paired with full physical assistance. After the learner responded correctly three consecutive times, the full physical prompt was faded to partial physical assistance, then to a gestural prompt, then to verbal directions. Learners who were trained initially with the decreasing assistance procedure showed steady increases in correct responding and low error rates. A change to the increasing assistance condition resulted in an initial slight drop in their performance, followed by a rapid increase in correct responses. Correct responses also increased at a faster rate than during the decreasing assistance condition. Learners who first received training using increasing assistance procedures exhibited higher error rates initially. These results suggest that decreasing assistance procedures were more efficient for rapid establishment of correct responses, while increasing assistance procedures were more efficient once the behavior had been established and learners were refining their skills. Day (1987) reported similar results.

Constant time delay and the system of least prompts were compared by Gast, Ault, Wolery, Doyle, and Belanger (1988). Both procedures were used to teach learners with moderate mental retardation to read words found in grocery stores. Three of the learners used spoken language, and the fourth used manual signs. During one of the two daily sessions, learners received instruction using the time-delay procedure. During the other daily session, a system of least prompts was used. Time-delay procedures consisted of a constant 4-second delay between the natural cue and a verbal or signed model. The hierarchy of prompts in the system of least prompts began with a verbal task request, and proceeded to the task request plus verbal description of the item, the task request plus a photograph of the word, and finally, a task request plus a verbal or signed model. A 4-second delay was also used between prompt levels in the least prompts procedure. Both procedures were found to be effective in teaching reading. In terms of efficiency, as measured by the amount of direct instructional time required, the number of sessions required before the learners mastered the tasks, and percentage of errors, the constant time-delay procedure appeared to be the more efficient of the two. McDonnell (1987) also found a time-delay procedure more efficient than a system of least prompts when teaching learners with severe disabilities to make purchases at stores and restaurants. Progressive time-delay procedures have also been found to be more efficient than the system of least prompts (Bennett, Gast, Wolery,

& Schuster, 1986; Godby, Gast, & Wolery, 1987).

Ault, Gast, and Wolery (1988) compared progressive and constant time-delay procedures in a study designed to teach three learners with moderate mental retardation to read words commonly found on signs in community environments. Progressive time-delay procedures were used to teach each learner to read six words out loud. Six different words were taught using the constant time-delay procedure. Progressive time-delay procedures consisted of increasing by 1 second each session the delay between presentation of a card on which a word was written, a verbal prompt ("What word?"), and a verbal model of the correct response until an 8-second delay was reached. Both correct responses (i.e., the learner verbally responded to the prompt by reading the word on the card) and waiting responses (i.e., the learner did not respond during the delay interval, but produced the correct response after the experimenter's model) were reinforced. If the learner produced an incorrect response during the delay, the investigator corrected him or her verbally by instructing the learner to wait for the model if he or she did not know the correct response, removing the card, and looking away from the subject for 10 seconds. Wait errors (incorrect responses after the experimenter's model) and no response errors were consequated by the investigator saying "No," removing the card, and looking away for 10 seconds. Constant time-delay procedures were implemented after the first training session and consisted of a 5-second delay between presentation of the card, the prompt ("What word?"), and the experimenter's model of the correct response. Correct and incorrect responses were consequated in the same manner as under the progressive time-delay procedure. Both procedures led to skill acquisition for all three students. The constant time-delay procedure was found to be more efficient in terms of direct instructional time and number of sessions required. With respect to errors, one learner made more errors during the progressive time-delay training, a second made more errors during the constant time delay, and a third showed no difference in performance.

Sequencing Response Prompts

After selecting a particular prompting hierarchy, the interventionist must determine how to sequence the prompts. A sequence typically used in an increasing prompt hierarchy consists of verbal, gestural, and finally physical prompts. However, this sequence may not represent the least-to-most intrusive hierarchy for every instructional situation or learner. Depending on the skill being taught and the characteristics of the environment, a verbal prompt may represent a more intrusive form of prompt than a gestural prompt or a model. For example, if a learner is being taught to order a meal at a fast food restaurant using a communication wallet, the interventionist's gesture to prompt the learner to remove his wallet from his pocket may be faster and draw less attention to the learner than a verbal prompt.

Analysis of the natural cues that signal the learner to engage in a behavior is important in determining how to arrange cues within a hierarchy. For instance, in a fast food restaurant, "May I take your order?" can be thought of as a verbal prompt to the customer to place an order. In this case, the least intrusive prompt might be a verbal prompt that closely corresponds to the natural cue (e.g., "Order your meal."). The natural cue for picking up one's tray and carrying it to a table is visual (i.e., the counter person sliding the tray forward). A gestural prompt to direct the learner's attention to the tray may be less intrusive than a verbal prompt. Likewise, providing a learner with verbal prompts (e.g., "Take out your wallet and show him what you want.") may hinder the development of spontaneous requesting behavior, and result in the learner attending only to the verbal prompts rather than to the natural cues that should set the occasion for correct responding.

The interventionist must also decide whether to use the same prompting hierarchy on all steps of a skill. Typically, once a hierarchy of prompts is chosen it is applied consistently on every step of the skill being taught. For some steps of a task, however, a verbal cue may represent the least intrusive response prompt, while for other steps, a verbal cue may be a more intrusive prompt. For this reason, it may make sense to use different sequences of prompts for different steps. For example, an interventionist teaching a learner to purchase a soft drink at a movie theatre might first use a verbal prompt ("Do you want to buy a drink?") to teach the learner to approach the counter. If the learner does not respond, the interventionist could then prompt with a gesture (bringing an imaginary glass to his lips). Finally, the interventionist could touch the learner's shoulder to nudge him toward the counter. At the point at which the learner is to remove his wallet from his pocket in order to pay the clerk, the interventionist might decide first to gesture, then to prompt verbally and finally to use physical guidance.

The rigidity of the hierarchy selected must also be considered. For example, instead of always giving a verbal prompt after the learner fails to respond to the natural cue, the interventionist could occasionally vary the prompt by demonstrating the behavior or using a gestural prompt. In doing so, an interventionist might decrease the likelihood that a learner will come under the control of only one type of prompt. For instance, an interventionist teaching a learner to request an apple by pointing to a photograph of an apple after being offered a choice between an apple (a preferred item) and a banana (a nonpreferred item) might on some occasions use the verbal prompt "Point to 'apple.'" On other occasions the interventionist might simply demonstrate touching the photograph, or gesture in its general vicinity.

Another issue is whether prompts, particularly verbal prompts, should always be delivered in the same manner. An interventionist may enhance generalization by providing slightly different forms of the same prompt across teaching opportunities. For instance, instead of always using the verbal prompt "Point to hamburger." on some opportunities, the interventionist might say, "Show him what you want for lunch."or "What do you want to order?" Using this strategy might result in the need for more instructional opportunities before the learner masters the behavior, since the learner needs to come under the control of each variation of the verbal prompt. A potential long-term advantage of this strategy is that it may prepare a learner to respond to a wider variety of natural and environmental cues, thereby promoting generalization and reducing dependency on any particular prompt. Table 2 provides a summary of the characteristics and considerations for use of various prompt sequencing options.

STIMULUS PROMPTING

Discrimination among stimuli occurs when a behavior is performed more frequently or less frequently in the presence of one stimulus relative to another. A good example is picking up a telephone and saying "hello." This behavior occurs more frequently in the presence of a ringing telephone. A person who has learned to answer a telephone only after it has begun to ring demonstrates good discriminative behavior. Such behavior is said to be under the *stimulus control* of a ringing telephone, and the action of picking up the telephone and saying hello is called a *discriminated operant.* Young children learning the mechanics of telephone use for the first time often fail to show such discriminative behavior, often picking up the telephone and talking even when the phone is not ringing. When this happens the child's response goes unreinforced, as there is no listener to talk to. In contrast, when the telephone is ringing, a listener is usually available, providing a source of reinforcement for answering. This differential reinforcement should—and in most cases, will—produce a repertoire of discriminated operants.

Response and stimulus prompts can be viewed along a continuum. At one end are response prompts directed solely at the learner's

Table 2. Characteristics of various prompting strategies

Type of prompt	Characteristics	Advantages and disadvantages
Least-to-most hierarchy	Prompts delivered in sequence from less to more intrusiveness	Clear criteria for moving from one prompt level to the next
	Several distinct prompts included in sequence (e.g., verbal, gestural, model, physical)	May be necessary to apply entire sequence during early stages of intervention
		Allows opportunities for errors
Most-to-least hierarchy	Prompts delivered in sequence from more to less intrusiveness	Time required to recruit response is minimized
	Several distinct prompts included in sequence (e.g., physical, model, gesture, verbal)	Opportunities for errors are minimized
		May preempt opportunity for independence
Time delay	Systematic use of delays before prompting correct response	Provides opportunity for independent performance
	Opportunity for communicative behavior in presence of natural cue	Allows opportunities for errors
		May have greatest applicability in generalization versus acquisition phase

physical actions, such as physically guiding a learner to make a sign. At the other end are stimulus prompts. Stimulus prompts involve alterations to the antecedent stimulus that serve to prompt the desired behavior (Snell, 1983). Between these extremes are prompts that contain elements of both. For example, an interventionist can point to the correct symbol to prompt the learner to do likewise. This prompt is designed to influence stimulus, but it also may be viewed as an imitative model to prompt a pointing response to a graphic symbol. Prompts can also be categorized according to whether they are delivered before or after an opportunity to respond, and according to whether they are delivered to the response side or the stimulus side of the instructional paradigm.

Several types of stimulus prompts have been used successfully to establish communicative behavior. Stimulus prompting involves the manipulation of aspects of a stimulus (e.g., color, size, shape, location) as a means of increasing a learner's propensity to respond appropriately to that stimulus. For example, Figure 2 shows how stimulus prompts might be used to increase a learner's tendency to point to the correct generalized request symbol ("WANT"), as opposed to the incorrect blank symbol. An enlarged "WANT" symbol and a much smaller blank symbol are presented. Correct responses consist of pointing to the "WANT" symbol as a means of requesting preferred items. For learners who already have some tendency to point, the initially much larger size of the "WANT" symbol may effectively prompt correct requests. Over successive opportunities, this stimulus prompt (i.e., size) is gradually faded until it matches the size of the blank symbol. This process is referred to as *stimulus fading*. When the two symbols are the same size, graphics could be gradually added to the blank card until the additional symbol was complete. This process of gradually adding necessary components to the stimulus array, thereby increasing the discriminative demands on the learner, is referred to as

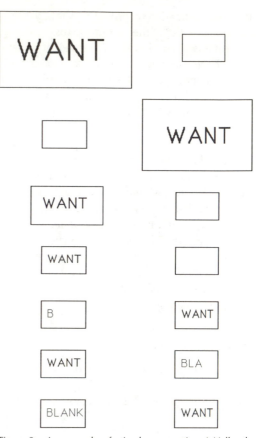

Figure 2. An example of stimulus prompting. Initially, the "WANT" symbol is larger than the other (blank) symbol, thus encouraging requesting responses. Over successive opportunities the size of the symbol is faded and a distractor is added.

stimulus shaping. This second symbol would then serve as a distractor that would be presented concurrently with the "WANT" symbol. Stimulus prompting strategies such as those described here are examples of a technology that can be used to approximate errorless learning (Etzel & LeBlanc, 1979; Terrace, 1963). Errors that could possibly become a part of a chain of responses are minimized through the use of stimulus fading and stimulus shaping.

During communication intervention, the stimulus to which the learner is required to respond may include multiple features. For example, when presented with a card that has a graphic symbol printed on it, the learner could attend to the configuration of the symbol, the color of the card, or the location of the card. This can often lead to difficulties during intervention, since some learners may attend to irrelevant features of the stimulus, such as its position on the table or its color (Rincover, 1978; Schreibman, 1975). As a result of *stimulus overselectivity,* the learner's response can fail to come under the control of the relevant criterion feature of the stimulus. Instead, the behavior of the learner remains under the control of an irrelevant feature of the stimulus. For example, consider a situation in which a learner is being taught to request an apple by pointing to an apple symbol. If the apple symbol is placed in the same position on the table during each instructional opportunity it may be that the position of the symbol, rather than its distinctive shape, will come to control the learner's pointing response. Thus, it is critical that the stimulus prompting procedures used in communication interventions be developed to enhance the likelihood of the transfer of stimulus control to the relevant feature of the stimulus. In the preceding example this could be accomplished by randomly alternating the position of both symbol cards during the intervention opportunities. Prompts can be used that alter some relevant feature of the stimulus. An example would be changing the shape of a picture into the corresponding printed word to establish a sight reading vocabulary. The stimulus prompts will eventually have to be removed so that the discriminative stimulus alone is sufficient to prompt the appropriate behavior.

STIMULUS FADING

Any feature added as a stimulus prompt that is not part of the natural cuing conditions will eventually have to be faded. For example, the goal of an intervention program might be to teach a learner to request potato chips by pointing to a graphic symbol. The learner preferred a brand of potato chips that came in a distinctive package. After determining that the learner would reliably reach out and obtain potato chips from such a bag, a gradual process began to transform the potato chip bag into a symbol for potato chips. First, after the learner reached out and touched the full bag, a few potato chips were delivered to him. Later, some of the contents of the bag were removed and the bag was presented to the learner. The learner was given a few potato chips after he touched the partially empty bag. Over successive opportunities, all of the contents of the bag were removed until only the empty bag was presented to the learner. Potato chips were delivered to the learner after he touched the flattened bag. Gradually, the bag was trimmed away until only the product logo section of the package remained. This product logo then became part of a communication board or wallet symbol system used as a means of requesting potato chips. In this example, stimulus fading procedures were used systematically to transfer stimulus control of the learner's response from the original product package to the product logo. When teaching a learner to make a generalized request, an enlarged "WANT" symbol might be used at the beginning of instruction to maximize the probability of the learner responding correctly. In a stimulus fading procedure, the size of the "WANT" card would be gradually reduced over consecutive instructional opportunities until the "WANT" symbol was the same size as the other symbols. Decreasing the size of the symbol in this way will allow for a greater number of symbols to be included in the communication wallet or board, and also can make the system more portable.

Other stimulus prompts, such as an added picture or enhanced features of a graphic symbol, may be faded by gradually decreasing the visibility of the picture or by reducing or removing features of the symbol. For example, a stimulus fading procedure could be used to transfer stimulus control from a graphic symbol that included both a line drawing and the corresponding printed word to one that consisted only of the printed word, thus teaching a learner to "read." To achieve this goal, a printed word, such as "COFFEE," could be superimposed over a drawing of a coffee cup (Lancioni & Smeets, 1986). In a stimulus fading procedure the drawing of the coffee cup could be faded until only the word "COFFEE" remained, as shown in Figure 3. Goetz, Gee, and Sailor (1983) included such a stimulus fading procedure in a study designed to teach three learners with severe disabilities to respond to auditory cues, thus making assessment of their hearing possible. In this study, a light on either side of the learner was illuminated and reinforcement provided if the learner turned his head toward the direction of the light. The light in this case represented a stimulus prompt. Later, an auditory cue was presented simultaneously with the light cue, and reinforcement again was delivered after a correct response. The transfer of stimulus control from light and sound to only the auditory cue was accomplished through a systematic intensity fading procedure in which the intensity of the light was gradually reduced. The results indicated that the learners maintained correct responding to the auditory cue after the paired visual and sound training and the consequent stimulus intensity fading procedure.

Smeets, Hoogeveen, Striefel, and Lancioni (1985) used stimulus fading to teach eight children and adolescents with moderate retardation to identify printed words receptively. Each of four word pairs was used in the training, with one of the words in each pair selected as the discriminative stimulus. To fade the stimuli, the experimenters first enhanced a distinctive feature of the first letter of the word that was the discriminative stimulus (e.g., thickened the lower area of the letter "V"). This feature was faded over six phases by gradually decreasing the width of the line until it was the same thickness as the rest of the word. A second condition

COFFEE

Figure 3.   A stimulus fading procedure in which stimulus control is transferred from a graphic symbol to the printed word.

that included both the stimulus fading procedure and a letter discrimination procedure was also used to teach the learners to attend to all letters of the discriminative stimulus. The authors reported that both procedures were effective in teaching the learners to acquire the word discriminations, and noted that a low error rate was seen during the stimulus fading and the fading plus letter discrimination training.

Stimulus fading can be used in developing an augmentative communication system for learners with visual impairments. Communication boards or wallets for these learners can be developed to include parts of real objects or other materials of differing shapes or textures. Each partial object used in the augmentative system represents a specific object or activity that could be requested by the learner. The different objects could then be discriminated by the learner touching the communication board or wallet. For example, suppose that a learner with visual impairments preferred a particular type of juice or canned beverage. Initially, a six-pack of the beverage, held together by plastic ring packaging, would be presented to the learner. After touching the plastic ring packaging, the learner would be offered some of the beverage. Gradually, cans of the beverage would be removed from the plastic rings until finally only the plastic rings would be presented to the learner. Some of the beverage would be given to the learner after he or she touched the empty plastic rings. Next, one ring at a time would be cut away from the packaging until only one ring remained. At this time, the complete ring or even a smaller piece of the ring would be mounted on a communication board. Other partial items could be added to the communication board using similar fading procedures, thus increasing the learner's repertoire of symbols.

Stimulus fading procedures could be used in the development of an augmentative communication system that includes a variety of simple graphic symbols. Fading procedures could be used to transfer stimulus control of a learner's pointing response from an enhanced line drawing to a simple graphic symbol. Consider the situation in which a learner consistently responds with a pointing response when presented with an enhanced line drawing of a chair. After the learner touches the line drawing of the chair, the chair would be made accessible. To ensure an appropriate motivation for requesting a chair, a situation could be created in which the learner would for some reason need a chair. In a stimulus fading procedure, the details of the enhanced drawing would be systematically eliminated until a very simple graphic symbol remained. This graphic symbol would then be used as the final stimulus to be incorporated into the learner's symbol repertoire. It is critical that the fading process be done gradually to ensure that the learner maintains his or her pointing response as the drawing is gradually changed into the simpler graphic symbol.

STIMULUS SHAPING

Intervention methods that include stimulus shaping may be used as a part of stimulus prompting strategies. (As used here, the term *shaping* is synonymous with the term *building*.) Procedures of this type involve reinforcing a behavior performed in the presence of a controlling stimulus. As mentioned earlier, necessary stimulus elements are gradually reformed. Gradually, the topography or configuration of this stimulus is altered until a new stimulus is formed that is unlike the original stimulus, but still controls the response (Sidman & Stoddard, 1967).

Stimulus shaping was used by Lancioni (1983) in a study designed to teach the use of pictorial representations as a means of communication. Initially, three children with severe mental retardation were taught a match-to-sample task of touching an object that corresponded to a presented picture card. First, the learners were taught to touch a red block in response to the experimenter pointing to a corresponding picture card of a red block. Later, a second all red card was introduced along with the original card of the red block. A red card with white spots was substituted for the red card after the subjects correctly touched the block after the experimenter pointed again to the red block card. A stimulus shaping procedure was used in which the red area on the card was reduced and the white spots gradually shaped into a drawing of a bottle. A real red bottle was then introduced along with the red block for the object discrimination task. Later a similar process was used to shape the bottle card into a picture depicting a red purse, and to facilitate object discriminations of three green and three yellow objects. A similar stimulus shaping process was also used to teach the subjects to imitate body positions shown on cards.

COMPARING SHAPING AND FADING PROCEDURES

A study by Walsh and Lamberts (1979) compared the effectiveness of a stimulus fading and a stimulus shaping procedure. A repeated measures design was used to assess the effectiveness of each of these procedures in teaching two lists of words to 30 students with moderate mental retardation. The picture-fading procedure involved the individual presentation of 10 words with each of their corresponding pictures. Stimulus fading was used gradually to reduce the visibility of each picture (over six levels) until only the printed word was present.

A second list of 10 words was taught using an errorless discrimination procedure. This consisted of a stimulus shaping procedure in which the word to be taught was initially presented alone with the verbal cue "Point to the word _____." Distractor stimuli (i.e., dashed lines or two letters, such as "FT") were gradually introduced along with the target word until the word was finally presented with two similar printed words. The results indicated that learners recognized more words after the instruction that included the stimulus shaping procedure than they did after the stimulus fading procedure. The shaping procedure also resulted in better performance at a picture–word matching task. It was suggested that the transfer of stimulus control from the pictures to the printed words may have

failed to occur in the stimulus fading condition because of the requirement simultaneously to attend to both the picture and its corresponding printed word.

The effectiveness of a stimulus fading procedure such as the one used by Walsh and Lamberts (1979) might be increased by embedding the picture into the printed word, allowing the learner to attend simultaneously to both the printed word and the picture. The picture could then be faded gradually over trials until eventually only the printed word was visible.

COMBINING STIMULUS SHAPING AND FADING PROCEDURES

Stimulus shaping and stimulus fading strategies have each been used independently to facilitate the acquisition of a variety of skills. In certain situations these techniques can be used effectively in conjunction with each other. A study by Sidman and Stoddard (1967) compared the efficacy of an errorless learning strategy that included both stimulus fading and stimulus shaping procedures, and trial and error learning in teaching children with severe retardation a discrimination between a circle and an ellipse. The errorless learning procedure started out with the presentation of a circle on a bright key while eight other keys were darkened. The learners were then reinforced for pressing the bright key. Gradually, the unmarked dark keys were illuminated until they were identical in illumination to the original bright key and the learners were again reinforced for pressing the original circle key. In this initial phase the intensity of the key lights was faded from dark to light. A stimulus shaping procedure was then employed gradually to add the shape of an ellipse onto each of the unmarked keys. These ellipses were gradually shaped to resemble the shape of a circle, thus making the discrimination more difficult. In the trial and error learning condition the learners were required to discriminate between a circle and an ellipse, with the ellipse introduced at its final criterion level, rather than gradually. Seven of the ten learners who received the training that included the fading and shaping procedures learned to discriminate between the circle and the ellipse. In contrast, only 1 of the 10 learners in the trial and error group was able to do so.

Stimulus fading and shaping procedures can be used concurrently to develop graphic symbol systems. Consider the situation in which a learner is being taught to make an explicit request for a cookie by touching a card with a picture of a cookie drawn on it. In this case, a 4" x 6" card with a drawing of a cookie on it would be presented along with a smaller blank card, in a procedure similar to that shown in Figure 2. Initially, the learner might be more likely to touch the card with the cookie on it, or could be taught readily to do so because the card is larger and has a drawing on it. Gradually, the "cookie" card would be reduced in size (faded) until it matched the size of the blank card. In addition, elements of a second symbol—representing a banana, for example—could be added systematically to the blank card (a shaping procedure) until the banana symbol was complete. At this point, the learner would have been taught a discrimination among two symbols.

ISSUES RELATED TO THE USE OF STIMULUS SHAPING AND FADING PROCEDURES

Many factors must be examined when considering the selection and implementation of stimulus shaping and fading procedures. Both the targeted response and the specific stimuli that will be included as part of the communication instruction will determine, to a great extent, whether a stimulus prompting strategy is appropriate. For example, when providing instruction in the gestural mode, some type of response prompting strategy would be preferable to a stimulus prompting procedure because of the topography of the learner responses. Conversely, communication intervention that includes selecting graphic symbols seems better suited to stimulus shaping and fading procedures, because in each case the response topography (e.g., pointing) is essentially the same, with responses distinguished on the basis of the specific stimulus (e.g., line drawing) that has been selected (Michael, 1985).

Although stimulus prompting is a powerful instructional technique, in some situations a response prompting strategy may need to be added to complement the stimulus prompts used. For example, a response prompt might be needed in situations in which a learner fails to respond to a stimulus prompt. Smeets et al. (1985) used response interruption, repetition of the original verbal instruction, and physical assistance as part of the correction procedure in teaching receptive word identification. Some type of response prompt may need to be included as part of error correction procedures if instructional procedures that include stimulus prompting procedures do not produce completely errorless performance. Thus, when developing an intervention that includes stimulus shaping or fading, a decision must be made regarding the type of response prompts to use in any error correction procedures. In addition, methods for systematically fading any additional response prompts must be selected.

For the most part, the stimulus shaping and fading procedures that have been described in the literature tend to include discrete stimuli that were manipulated easily in a systematic manner (e.g., the intensity of a light, line drawings presented on cards). Stimulus prompting strategies are generally not recommended for situations in which the stimuli would be difficult or impractical to manipulate. The actual development of the stimulus materials to be used in the shaping or fading procedures must be considered. The construction of a graduated series of cards with a graphic symbol systematically faded requires both time and resources. However, once developed, these materials can be saved and duplicated for use in future instruction (Touchette, 1971).

An important consideration related to the development of the stimulus materials to be used in fading procedures concerns the specific feature or dimension of the stimulus that will be manipulated, and whether shaping or fading occurs to the positive or negative stimulus or both. In a previous example, for instance, the size of a "WANT" card was faded. In this case, the "WANT" card was the positive stimulus because it was the symbol correlated with reinforcement. An alternative, however, would be to increase the size of the blank symbol. In this case fading is said to occur on the negative rather than the positive stimulus. There is some evidence to suggest that in teaching line drawing discriminations to children with autism, fading on the positive stimulus is more effective than fading on the negative stimulus (Schreibman & Charlop, 1981).

Other major issues related to the use of stimulus prompts concern the number of levels or steps that will be included in the shaping or fading procedure, as well as the criteria for progressing from one level to the next. Although stimulus shaping and fading procedures generally produce few errors if implemented carefully, error rates may increase dramatically if shaping or fading occurs too abruptly. The number of levels to be used in a shaping or fading procedure depends partly on the complexity of the stimulus prompt used. The shaping or fading steps included must be designed to facilitate the transfer of the stimulus control with few errors, without necessitating an excessive number of instructional sessions.

Another closely related issue is the rate at which the different steps or levels included in the stimulus prompting system should be presented to the learner. Often a specific response criterion (e.g., 10 correct responses at each fading step) is established. This practice may result

in a learner remaining at a specific level longer than is necessary, and in some instances may cause the learner to become lodged at a particular level, possibly resulting in errors when the next fading or shaping step is finally introduced. Monitoring the learner's behavior during the progression through the sequenced fading and shaping levels will be critical to ensure that his or her response rate remains at the desired level at each step of the shaping or fading process. Fading or shaping a stimulus too rapidly can result in the learner failing to engage in the desired response after the next specific fading step is introduced. If errors increase after moving to the next fading level, it is possible that the degree of stimulus change between the levels is too great. A more gradual fading between the two stimulus prompt levels might better facilitate a high rate of correct responding. A procedure requiring the learner to return to the previous stimulus prompt level after making a specified number of errors at any given fading level should be included as part of the instructional protocol.

SUMMARY

In this chapter, instructional methods that can be used to establish communicative behaviors and bring those behaviors under appropriate stimulus control are described. During the initial acquisition of a new communicative behavior, the interventionist has a range of response and stimulus prompts that can be used effectively to evoke the desired behavior. Tables 1 and 2 summarize the characteristics and considerations for use of several instructional prompt options. Once the desired response has been obtained, reinforcement is critical to ensure the maintenance of the behavior. Over time it is desirable to fade the use of any instructional prompts. Several strategies for fading instructional prompts, described in this chapter, can be used.

REFERENCES

Ault, M.J., Gast, D.L., & Wolery, M. (1988). Comparison of progressive and constant time-delay procedures in teaching community-sign word reading. *American Journal on Mental Retardation, 93*, 44–56.

Bates, P., & Renzaglia, A. (1982). Language instruction with a profoundly retarded adolescent: The use of a table game in the acquisition of verbal labeling skills. *Education and Treatment of Children, 5*, 13–22.

Bennett, D.L., Gast, D.L., Wolery, W., & Schuster, J. (1986). Time delay and the system of least prompts: A comparison in teaching manual sign production. *Education and Training of the Mentally Retarded, 21*, 117–129.

Browder, D.M., Morris, W.M., & Snell, M.E. (1981). Using time delay to teach manual signs to a severely retarded student. *Education and Training of the Mentally Retarded, 16*, 252–258.

Browder, D.M., & Snell, M.E. (1983). Daily living skills. In M.E. Snell (Ed.), *Systematic instruction of the moderately and severely handicapped* (2nd ed., pp. 412–444). Columbus, OH: Charles E. Merrill.

Charlop, M.H., Schreibman, L., & Thibodeau, M.G. (1985). Increasing spontaneous verbal responding in autistic children using a time delay procedure. *Journal of Applied Behavior Analysis, 18*, 155–166.

Csapo, M. (1981). Comparison of two prompting procedures to increase response fluency among severely handicapped learners. *Journal of The Association for the Severely Handicapped, 6*(1), 39–47.

Day, H.M. (1987). Comparison of two prompting procedures to facilitate skill acquisition among severely mentally retarded adolescents. *American Journal of Mental Deficiency, 91*(4), 366–372.

Etzel, B.C., & LeBlanc, J.M. (1979). The simplest treatment alternative: The law of parsimony applied to choosing appropriate instructional control and errorless-learning procedures for the difficult-to-teach child. *Journal of Autism and Developmental Disorders, 9*(4), 361–382.

Gast, D.L., Ault, M.J., Wolery, M., Doyle, P.M., & Belanger, S. (1988). Comparison of constant time delay and system of least prompts in teaching sight word reading to students with moderate mental retardation. *Education and Treatment in Mental Retardation, 23*(2), 117–128.

Godby, S., Gast, D.L., & Wolery, M. (1987). A comparison of time delay and system of least prompts in teaching object identification. *Research in Developmental Disabilities, 8*, 283–305.

Goetz, L., Gee, K., & Sailor, W. (1983). Crossmodal transfer of stimulus control: Preparing students with severe multiple disabilities for audiological assessment. *Journal of The Association for Persons with Severe Handicaps, 8*(4), 3–13.

Halle, J.W. (1982). Teaching functional language to the handicapped: An integrative model of natural environment teaching techniques. *Journal of The Association for Persons with Severe Handicaps, 7*, 29–37.

Halle, J.W., Baer, D.M., & Spradlin, J.E. (1981). Teachers' generalized use of delay as a stimulus control procedure to increase language use in handicapped children. *Journal of Applied Behavior Analysis, 14*, 389–409.

Handen, B.L., & Zane, T. (1987). Delayed prompting: A review of procedural variations and results. *Research in Developmental Disabilities, 8*, 307–330.

Hinerman, P.S., Jenson, W.R., Walker, G.R., & Petersen, P.B. (1982). Positive practice overcorrection combined with additional procedures to teach signed words to an autistic child. *Journal of Autism and Developmental Disorders, 12*(3), 253–263.

Kleinert, H.L., & Gast, D.L. (1982). Teaching a multihandicapped adult manual signs using a constant time delay procedure. *Journal of The Association for the Severely Handicapped, 6*(4), 25–32.

Lancioni, G.E. (1983). Using pictorial representations as communication means with low-functioning children. *Journal of Autism and Developmental Disorders, 13*(1), 87–105.

Lancioni, G.E., & Smeets, P.M. (1986). Procedures and parameters of errorless discrimination training with developmentally impaired individuals. *International Review of Research in Mental Retardation, 14*, 135–164.

McDonnell, J. (1987). The effects of time delay and increasing prompt hierarchy strategies on the acquisition of purchasing skills by students with severe handicaps. *Journal of The Association for Persons with Severe Handicaps, 12*(3), 227–236.

Michael, J. (1985). Two kinds of verbal behavior plus a possible third. *Analysis of Verbal Behavior, 3*, 2–5.

O'Brien, F. (1978). An error-free, quick and enjoyed strategy for teaching multiple discriminations to severely delayed students. *Mental Retardation, 16,* 291–294.

Oliver, C.B., & Halle, J.W. (1982). Language training in the everyday environment: Teaching functional sign language use to a retarded child. *Journal of The Association for the Severely Handicapped, 8*(3), 50–62.

Rincover, A. (1978). Variables affecting stimulus fading and discriminative responding in psychotic children. *Journal of Abnormal Psychology, 87,* 541–533.

Sailor, W., & Guess, D. (1983). *Severely handicapped students: An instructional design.* Boston: Houghton Mifflin.

Schoen, S.F. (1986). Assistance procedures to facilitate the transfer of stimulus control: Review and analysis. *Education and Training of the Mentally Retarded, 21,* 62–74.

Schreibman, L. (1975). Effects of within-stimulus and extra-stimulus prompting on discrimination learning in autistic children. *Journal of Applied Behavior Analysis, 8*(1), 91–112.

Schreibman, L., & Charlop, M.H. (1981). S+ versus S− fading in prompting procedures with autistic children. *Journal of Experimental Child Psychology, 31,* 508–520.

Sidman, M., & Stoddard, L. (1967). The effectiveness of fading in programming a simultaneous form discrimination for retarded children. *Journal of the Experimental Analysis of Behavior, 10,* 3–15.

Smeets, P., Hoogeveen, F., Striefel, S., & Lancioni, G. (1985). Stimulus over-selectivity in TMR children: Establishing functional control of simultaneous multiple stimuli. *Analysis and Intervention in Developmental Disabilities, 5,* 247–267.

Snell, M.E. (1983). *Systematic instruction of the moderately and severely handicapped* (2nd ed.). Columbus, OH: Charles E. Merrill.

Striefel, S., & Owens, C. (1980). Transfer of stimulus control procedures: Applications to language acquisition training with the developmentally handicapped. *Behavior Research of Severe Disabilities, 1,* 307–331.

Terrace, H.S. (1963). Discrimination learning with and without "errors." *Journal of the Experimental Analysis of Behavior, 6,* 1–27.

Touchette, P.E. (1971). Transfer of stimulus control: Measuring the moment of transfer. *Journal of the Experimental Analysis of Behavior, 15,* 347–354.

Walsh, B., & Lamberts, F. (1979). Errorless discrimination and picture fading as techniques for teaching sight words to TMR students. *American Journal of Mental Deficiency, 83*(5), 473–479.

Wolery, M., Gast, D.L., Kirk, K., & Schuster, J. (1988). Fading extra-stimulus prompts with autistic children using time delay. *Education and Treatment of Children, 11*(1), 29–44.

10

Bringing Communicative Behavior under the Control of the Appropriate Stimuli

Joe Reichle and Jeff Sigafoos

A REPERTOIRE OF communicative behavior is most useful when it is under appropriate stimulus control. Stimulus control exists when responses of a given class occur in the presence of stimuli associated with reinforcement (i.e., discriminative stimuli) and do not occur or are less likely to occur in the presence of stimuli associated with no reinforcement. Behavior is under appropriate stimulus control when the discriminative stimuli controlling a particular class of behavior correspond to the stimuli that should control that behavior in the natural environment.

All communicative behavior involves discriminations. It is therefore important to understand the basic types of discriminative repertoires, procedures for establishing appropriate stimulus control, and common difficulties often encountered by interventionists in teaching discriminations.

DISCRIMINATIVE STIMULI

A discriminative stimulus is defined as an environmental event that sets the occasion for the reinforcement of a particular class of behavior. Certain people (e.g., doting grandparents) may have a history of catering to the learner's desires. Requests made in the presence of such people may frequently be granted, thus encouraging the learner to request in their presence. Over time these people become discriminative stimuli for the learner's requesting behavior. There are other people (e.g., strangers) who never or rarely reinforce requesting. The presence of strangers thus represents a discriminative stimulus for silence.

Intervention is often required to bring communicative behavior under the control of naturally occurring discriminative stimuli. Certain other stimuli should control nonresponding. Intervention may also be necessary to prevent irrelevant antecedents from controlling communicative behavior. For example, inability to remove the lid from a jar of pickles represents a natural discriminative stimulus for requesting assistance; in contrast, an easy to remove jar lid represents the discriminative stimulus to refrain from requesting assistance, and should prompt independent attempts to remove the lid. The color of the lid has no bearing on whether or not assistance is needed, and thus should not affect the learner's behavior. Initially, teachers may need to supplement intervention by providing instructional cues or prompts to ensure that the desired behavior occurs in the presence of the appropriate natural stimulus. Ultimately, the use of such instructional cues and prompts should be faded, leaving the behavior under the appropriate stimulus control of naturally occurring cues.

Differential reinforcement refers to the practice of delivering reinforcers when a behavior occurs in the presence of appropriate discriminative stimuli, but not when the behavior occurs in the presence of inappropriate stimuli. It is the basic mechanism through which a given form of nonverbal behavior (e.g., performing a task) is brought under the control of a spoken directive. For example, when told "sweep the floor," a learner may retrieve the broom and sweep the floor. Reinforcement is delivered after each step of the task is completed, or after the learner has met a prespecified criterion of performance. Over successive opportunities, the prompts are systematically faded until the spoken utterance "sweep the floor" causes the learner to perform the corresponding action.

A *stimulus class* refers to stimuli that exert similar control over a given class of responses. For example, both a soft drink can and a water bottle serve as discriminative stimuli in teaching a learner to request a drink.

A *response class* consists of all behaviors that are effective under a given set of stimulus conditions. For example, several different forms of responses (e.g., "Yes," "Juice, please,"

"Want") may be equally effective in requesting an offered item. Sometimes, however, a particular communicative situation controls different response forms that do not serve similar functions. At one time the offer of something to drink might control a request ("Yes, please"), whereas at another time the offer of something to drink might control a reject in ("No, thanks"). In this example, to the observer the two consecutive opportunities appear similar, but could probably be traced to the internal state of the person producing the utterance (e.g., how thirsty a person may be at a particular time).

Part of teaching a learner to discriminate among stimuli is establishing appropriate matches between various stimulus and response classes. A green light, for example, represents a stimulus class that may come to control a variety of responses. Members of this stimulus class often vary widely in terms of shape, size, intensity, color, location, and context. A discriminative repertoire is set up by establishing appropriate matches between various stimulus and response classes.

GENERAL CASE
INSTRUCTIONAL STRATEGIES

One goal of general case instructional strategies is to ensure that the full range of exemplars comprising a stimulus class come to control appropriate members of a corresponding response class. These strategies can thus be used to facilitate appropriate matches between samples and choices. Horner and his colleagues (Horner & McDonald, 1982; Horner, Sprague, & Wilcox, 1982; Sprague & Horner, 1984) have studied the effectiveness of general case instructional strategies for teaching a variety of functional skills to learners with moderate and severe disabilities. From that research, several basic tenets have been validated. Adherence to these principles, which are outlined below, may facilitate the acquisition of discriminative repertoires among learners with severe disabilities.

1. Define the Instructional Universe

A first task for the interventionist using general case strategies is to define the instructional universe (Horner, McDonnell, & Bellamy, 1986). The instructional universe can be thought of as the complete stimulus class relevant to a particular activity. In teaching a learner to request beverages, for example, the instructional universe may be defined as all beverage items available in the learner's home, school, work, and community settings. A different learner, in contrast, may prefer to drink only certain types of beverages. For this learner, the instructional universe may be defined as orange, apple, grape, cranberry, and grapefruit juices. As these two examples illustrate, the definition of an instructional universe depends upon characteristics of the learner's environment, characteristics of the learner (e.g., his or her preferences), and the nature of the skill to be taught.

2. Identify Teaching Exemplars

Once the instructional universe has been defined, representative members of this stimulus class are selected for instruction. At this step it is crucial to select multiple teaching exemplars that sample the range of variation found within the defined instructional universe (Horner et al. 1986). For example, in teaching a learner to request beverages, several items (e.g., a carton of orange juice, a bottle of water, a can of cola) might serve as teaching exemplars.

It is also crucial to select negative teaching exemplars, that is, items that do not belong to the instructional universe. In the presence of a negative exemplar, the learner is taught not to respond (Horner et al. 1986; Lee, 1988) or to make some other more appropriate response. A negative exemplar of that class of objects known as beverages might be a can of condensed milk. This negative exemplar shares many features with some positive exemplars of beverages (e.g., it comes in a can, has a liquid

form), but differs from other members of the class in that a speaker would not request condensed milk to quench his or her thirst. A range of exemplars must be chosen that adequately reflects the class of negative cases. While the learner is being taught to request beverages, he or she should also be taught that condensed milk, bottled gravy, and perhaps cartons of whipping cream are not items to be requested when thirsty.

3. Begin Instruction

The third step in a general case instruction format is to begin teaching learners to respond in the presence of the selected positive exemplars. Because of the large number of items in most classes of objects, learners are taught to request some subset of items that samples the range of diversity within the class. After the request has been established for this subset of exemplars, probes can be conducted using different (untrained) exemplars. If the positive exemplars included in the initial instruction adequately sample the range of diversity within the particular stimulus class, then appropriate responses often generalize to probe items. For example, after having been taught to request a *carton* of juice, a *bottle* of water, and a *can* of cola, learners are in a much better position to respond appropriately to a carton of *milk,* a bottle of *beer,* and a can of *high protein milk shake.*

In a similar manner, initial instruction on a range of negative exemplars may promote generalization of nonresponding to novel (untrained) negative exemplars. Horner et al. (1986) recommended that initial instruction include both ". . . maximally similar positive *and* negative exemplars. . . ." (p. 294).

In summary, general case instruction strategies have proved effective and efficient for teaching a variety of generalized and functional skills to learners with severe disabilities. Using the techniques outlined above, interventionists can design effective instruction to establish appropriate discriminative repertoires among learners with severe disabilities.

MATRIX TRAINING PROCEDURES

Matrix training represents a variation on the general case method that has been used to establish generalized discriminative repertoires. It is a powerful technology for achieving generalized performance (Goldstein, 1985; Karlan et al., 1982). Matrix training is a way of structuring what is taught so as to maximize the gain derived from each training effort. Suppose, for example, that the interventionist collects five objects (e.g., an orange, a box, a bottle, a book, a bag) and wants to teach a learner to perform five actions (e.g., give, put away, open, point to, pick up) with each object when given the appropriate instruction (e.g., "give

orange," "point to book," "open box"). Without a strategy to promote generalization it would be necessary to teach each action with each object. A total of 25 separate interventions would thus be required to cover each of the cells shown in Figure 1.

In a matrix approach, only those cells marked with an X are taught. By using such an approach a minimum of training is needed to establish each of the action–object sequences.

Although matrix training is presented here in the context of establishing generalized instruction following, the strategy is also applicable to developing appropriate stimulus control over expressive repertoires. At the two-symbol level, for example, a matrix approach could be used to teach learners to describe actions (e.g., push, pull, open, turn) performed with various objects (e.g., wagon, drawer, window, knob).

OBJECTS

ACTIONS	ORANGE	BOX	BOTTLE	BOOK	BAG
PICK UP	X	X			
POINT TO		X	X		
OPEN			X	X	
PUT AWAY				X	X
GIVE	X				X

Figure 1.   A matrix training approach for teaching following of generalized instructions.

RECEPTIVE DISCRIMINATION

Before a learner can discriminate among different verbal stimuli (e.g., instructions), at least two receptive discriminations must be established (i.e., the learner must be able to perform one behavior when given one instruction and another behavior when given a second instruction). This type of discrimination has often been called *receptive language,* and is said to involve the comprehension of speech. However, it is important to note that "comprehension of speech" can include comprehension of signs, gestures, and graphic symbols. Most of a listener's behavior involves discriminations of this sort (Vargas, 1988). A listener's receptive interpretation may depend upon the pragmatic intent of the speaker's prior communicative utterance. For example, when the speaker requests bread, the appropriate listener action may consist of bringing the speaker some bread. When the speaker comments on the fact that it is raining, the appropriate listener action may consist of acknowledging the response (e.g., "Yes, it is") and perhaps getting an umbrella.

EXPRESSIVE DISCRIMINATION

Another type of discriminative behavior is required to communicate effectively. In communicative expression, samples are typically objects or other nonverbal stimuli, and the matching choice involves the selection and production of a vocal, gestural, or graphic mode response. The relationship between sample and choices in communicative expression involves a referent object or event controlling a particular communicative response. For example, an appropriate response to seeing someone eating an apple would be to comment on, sign, or point to a line drawing of an apple. If the learner instead saw someone eating an orange, he or she would be reinforced for saying "orange," signing "orange," or pointing to a line drawing of an orange. Traditionally, expressive discriminations

have been taught within structured situations. The interventionist shows an object (e.g., a cup, a pencil), prompts the learner to produce the correct response, and reinforces correct responses. Less structured situations, such as incidental and mand-model procedures (see Chapter 8), have also been used to teach such discriminations. In either case, correct responses are differentially reinforced with respect to the presence or absence of the corresponding object. Similar discriminations can be established in requesting or rejecting, as well as with responses that provide information and a host of other pragmatic intents.

DISTINCTIONS BETWEEN RECEPTIVE AND EXPRESSIVE REPERTOIRES

A clear distinction between receptive and expressive repertoires is typically maintained in beginning an augmentative system of communication for learners with severe disabilities. The instructional environment may be arranged at one time to establish a particular receptive discrimination (e.g., appropriate responses to spoken, signed, or graphic instructions). At another time, the instructional environment may be arranged to establish a particular expressive discrimination (e.g., requesting an offered item). In the first case, the learner is taught to function in the role of a listener. In the second case, the learner is taught to function in the role of a speaker. This distinction between speaker and listener roles is extremely important.

There is substantial evidence demonstrating that listener and speaker repertoires are separate and distinct. Guess (1969) demonstrated that teaching learners to discriminate receptively between instructions such as "point to the cup" and "point to the cups" was not sufficient to ensure correct performance on a corresponding expressive task in which the learners were shown a single object or a pair of objects and asked, "What do you see?" Learners readily acquired the receptive discrimination, but failed to acquire expressive labels for pairs of objects. Given direct expressive training using imitation and differential reinforcement, however, correct expressive labels for pairs of items were acquired. The functional independence of receptive and expressive repertoires was further demonstrated in a third condition, in which the receptive repertoire was reversed by reinforcing pointing to the single object given a plural command and reinforcing pointing to pairs of objects given a singular command. Despite this manipulation, the "normal" (nonreversed) expressive repertoire remained unchanged. Acquisition and reversal of a receptive repertoire had no effect on a corresponding expressive repertoire. Other researchers have systematically replicated the lack of generalizations between receptive and expressive tasks (Guess & Baer, 1973; Lee, 1981; Siegel & Vogt, 1984). One implication of this research is that separate interventions may be required to establish expressive and receptive repertoires among learners with severe disabilities.

In the graphic mode the distinction between receptive and expressive communicative discriminations is less clear, highlighting the fact that these two repertoires are perhaps best viewed as different points along a continuum rather than as separate entities. For example, in the graphic mode, when the samples are real objects or events, the learner's responsibility is to select the matching graphic representation from an array. This task meets the conditions for an expressive discrimination. In contrast, when the samples are line drawings and the choices are real objects, the task is similar to a receptive discrimination.

INTERACTIONS BETWEEN RECEPTIVE AND EXPRESSIVE REPERTOIRES

A complete communicative exchange often includes aspects of both receptive and expressive repertoires. This can often be noted when the referent for a response is not present (e.g., a learner is asked, "Where is your coat?" when the coat is hanging in the next room). Producing a relevant reply would appear to require both an understanding of the question and the availability of an appropriate word, phrase, gesture, or symbol.

When exchanges of this sort involve learners using graphic modes of communication, there will no doubt be a certain amount of delay while the learner scans the available symbols to locate the correct selection. The original question must be remembered during this interval. Among learners with severe disabilities, inability to keep the original question in mind during such delays may seriously interfere with effective communication. Overcoming problems created by such delays is described later in this chapter.

ESTABLISHING DISCRIMINATIVE REPERTOIRES

Establishing Expressive Repertoires

Suppose that the interventionist's goal is to teach a leaner to say, sign, or select the symbol for "cookie" when he or she sees someone eating a cookie, and say, sign, or select the symbol for "hat" when he or she sees someone wearing a hat. That is, the goal is to teach the learner to discriminate between "cookie" and "hat." Initially, an errorless strategy might be used (Terrace, 1963). For example, the learner could be shown a cookie and immediately prompted to produce the corresponding response using whatever level of prompting is required. The interventionist might also elect to initiate each teaching opportunity by asking, "What is this?" as the object is displayed. One possible problem in doing so, however, may be that the learner will not spontaneously name the object unless specifically asked to do so.(See Chapter 8 on the problem of establishing spontaneity.)

At this point the response "cookie" may not necessarily be controlled by the object per se but rather by the response prompts used to recruit the behavior. It will, therefore, be necessary to implement fading procedures to eliminate the response prompts (see Chapter 9).

Even when a response is under appropriate stimulus control, the appropriate discriminative repertoire may not have been developed. If shown a hat, for example, the learner may still reply "cookie." Discrimination training must bring at least one other response under the stimulus control of the appropriate object. For example, the learner is shown a hat and prompted to produce "hat." Once the prompts are successfully faded, opportunities to name a cookie are interspersed with opportunities to name a hat. The discrimination is maintained by reinforcing the response "cookie" in the presence of a cookie and reinforcing the response "hat" in the presence of a hat. Each response is separately established in the presence of the corresponding object through prompting, reinforcement, and prompt-fading procedures. Once established, a discrimination between the two

behaviors is maintained through differential reinforcement.

Acquisition of such an initial discrimination may be facilitated by using very different stimuli (Lovaas, 1977). A cookie and a hat look very different. The corresponding response forms also differ greatly. The objects are also functionally distinct. These differences may facilitate teaching the initial discrimination.

Even though the use of very different stimuli, such as hats and cookies, may make it easier to establish a first discrimination, performance on a previously mastered discrimination will often deteriorate when another stimulus – response relation is taught. For example, when the response "hat" is introduced, it is reasonable to expect a temporary decline in accuracy on opportunities to name the previously mastered "cookie" (Lovaas, 1977). Figure 2 shows an example of this effect. Performance on the first response (i.e., "cookie") declines after intervention to establish the second response (i.e., "hat") is begun. Continued discrimination

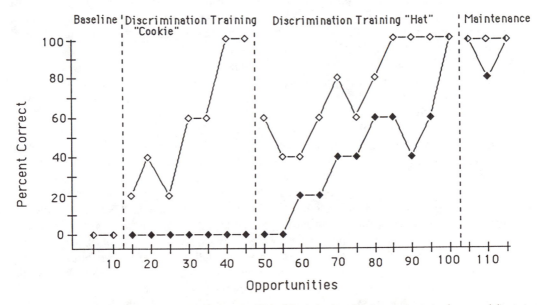

Figure 2. An example of the temporary disruption in an established discrimination when intervention to teach a second discrimination is first implemented. Filled-in diamonds show performance of "hat"; empty diamonds show performance on "cookie."

training is usually sufficient to recoup any such losses. In addition, as additional discriminations are introduced, the magnitude of such losses diminishes and they are generally recouped more quickly.

Communicative environments demand discriminations not only among very different stimuli, but also among stimuli that differ only minimally (Albin & Horner, 1988). Eventually, learners may need to be taught discriminations not only among objects such as hats and cookies, which look very different, but also among objects such as cookies and crackers, which may look very similar. The procedures used to teach difficult discriminations are the same as those used to teach easy discriminations. Early evidence tended to suggest that difficult discriminations were more readily established among learners with histories of intervention on easier discriminations (House & Zeaman, 1960). However, more recent research suggests that minimally different exemplars can be introduced relatively early in a discrimination procedure (Albin & Horner, 1988).

A successful discrimination training program will result in a learner who readily produces the correct word, sign, or symbol in the presence of the corresponding object or in situations in which that object is wanted or needed.

It is important to ensure that the basis of the discrimination is the object itself or the need to communicate about the object, rather than some irrelevant feature of the environment. Any feature of the environment present at the time of reinforcement could potentially come to control the response. For example, a learner who has been taught to sign "apple" when shown a red apple may also sign "apple" in the presence of any red object. A learner taught to stuff envelopes may do so only if the envelope is a standard size. This tendency for learners to allow irrelevant features of the environment to control discriminative behavior has been called *stimulus overselectivity*. It has been widely docu-

mented (Koegel & Schriebman, 1977; Koegel & Wilhelm, 1973; Lovaas, 1977).

To prevent irrelevant features from gaining control of a response, it is important to vary the irrelevant features systematically during discrimination training. For example, if the focus of intervention is to teach the learner to request both red and green apples, then the color of the apples presented should be systematically varied during intervention.

Establishing Receptive Repertoires

A similar intervention sequence can be used to establish receptive discriminative repertoires. First, the learner is taught to perform a single action (e.g., passing the salt to a peer when asked, "Pass the salt."). After establishing this initial response, however, it may still not be clear that the action is controlled by the actual form of the phrase. That is, it is possible that regardless of the content of the request, the learner will continue to pass the salt. It is also possible that the actual controlling stimulus is not the verbal stimulus but rather some other aspect of the environment. Young children, for example, are often credited with understanding speech when a gestural cue is actually suggesting the spoken instruction.

This point was dramatically illustrated in a study described by Dixon, Dixon, and Spradlin (1983). They taught adolescents with severe disabilities to follow a set of three explicit instructions. One learner who participated in their study was taught to sit in the hallway upon arrival each morning when told "Go sit hall." At 10:15 A.M., as the class was preparing for a snack, this learner was taught to respond appropriately to the command "Get cups." In preparation for lunch, the learner was taught to sit in the hallway when told "Go sit hall." It was hypothesized that correct performance could occur either because the learner understood the instructions or because of the contextual cues. To test this hypothesis, the learners were given instructions in contexts different from those under which they had been trained. At the 10:15 snacktime the learner was instructed to go sit in the hall instead of the usual "Get cups." If the learner responded by going to the hallway it would suggest that it was the instruction that was controlling the behavior. If, however, the learner continued to respond by retrieving cups, then it would be clear that it was the context and not the instructions that controlled the learner's actions. This latter type of contextually based responding was, in fact, often observed. While the instructions appeared to function as sort of a "go" signal to respond, the type of response the learners made often depended more on the context than on what was said. This kind of evidence highlights the importance of establishing discriminations among different forms of verbal stimuli in various contexts through general case instructional strategies.

After the learner has been taught to respond appropriately to one instruction, the next step is to teach him or her to respond appropriately to a second instruction. Two options are available. One is to teach the learner to perform the same action he or she performed initially but with a different object (e.g., passing the pepper). This option is roughly equivalent to the minimally different exemplar approach discussed earlier. A second option is to teach a completely different action (e.g., closing the window) or an unrelated action involving the same object (e.g., filling the salt dispenser).

The specific receptive discriminations taught are determined by the demands of the learner's environment. A learner working as a custodian in an office may, for example, need to be taught to empty the garbage, sweep the hall, or vacuum the rug when asked to do so. Family dining skills may require the learner to be taught to discriminate between "pass the salt" and "pass the milk."

A large number of such discriminations are required in day-to-day life at home, in school,

and on the job. Little progress could be made if each discrimination had to be taught directly. Needed, therefore, are intervention strategies that promote generalized instruction following or generalizations across different receptive discriminations. Ideally, it would be most beneficial for the learner to pass the salt not only when asked to "pass the salt," but also when asked, "Give me the salt," "Could I have the salt?", or simply "Salt, please." There are, then, variations in the forms verbal stimuli take even though the corresponding listener action is the same. The action of passing the salt should, therefore generalize to these variations in the form of the verbal stimulus. Such generalization can be facilitated by training loosely, that is, by incorporating variation into the instructional cues (Stokes & Baer, 1977). In addition, it would be beneficial for the learner taught to pass the salt to be capable of also passing pepper, milk, or salad. The response of *passing* should thus generalize to other objects. The matrix training approach described earlier is ideally suited for this type of generalization programming.

The vast majority of language intervention programs emphasize teaching learners with severe disabilities to understand single words in the presence of the objects and activities with which the words are associated. Unfortunately, many of the occasions that require appropriate receptive discriminations involve situations in which the referent objects are not present. For example, consider a learner seated in the living room of his home. The learner's mother says, "Hey, go get yourself a cookie." Consider what skills are called into play in this situation. First, assuming that the learners' receptive vocabulary is limited, he must separate the critical part of the message ("get" and "cookie") from the rest of the message. Additionally, he must be able to remember the instruction long enough to get the cookie.

Few intervention programs have been structured to examine the value of teaching the learner to act on major carriers of meaning that may be embedded in a longer utterance. Keogh and Reichle (1985) suggested that some learners might benefit from a program designed initially to emphasize the critical word in a longer utterance. The critical element of the instruction can initially be produced significantly louder than the remainder of the utterance. Across instructional opportunities, the loudness level is reduced systematically until the learner can identify critical messages carrying words contained in a longer utterance based on only natural stress and emphasis produced by the speaker. In a second application, the critical word of an instruction is placed at the end of a lengthier utterance (e.g., "Please go *get a cookie*."). Across instructional opportunities, the critical portions of the instruction are placed in less prominent positions (e.g., "Could you *get a cookie* right now?"). Teaching learners strategies to identify critical components in the range of utterances they are apt to encounter in community environments continues to be a critical area of scrutiny that has been addressed only in a very limited fashion.

Many learners may hear a message directed at them but fail to remember it long enough to use the information contained in it. This becomes a particularly important skill for persons with severe disabilities, because they are often unable to request clarification.

Virtually no empirical work has been done on the problem of remembering language. An intervention strategy that the authors have implemented is to increase systematically the amount of time between receipt of the instruction and the learner's ability to act on it. For example, initially a learner may be asked to get a Coke™ from a refrigerator located a few feet away in another room. Contingent on successful performance, the interventionist increases the distance between the learner and the location of the target item or activity. The strategy is designed to result in errorless performance.

Extending the amount of time between an instruction and the learner's opportunity to act presupposes acquisition of the required receptive discrimination. Initially, many learners may not respond appropriately to communication produced by others. Some learners may demonstrate the ability to match objects, however. Appropriate receptive discriminations might then be established by pairing the spoken word with the sample item (e.g., saying "Coke" as a bottle of Coke™ is displayed). Some learners will be able to match real objects to identical real objects. For example, a learner might be wearing red mittens. While shopping she may spot another shopper wearing identical mittens. She may then point to her mittens and then to the shopper's mittens. Next, the spoken words "spoon" and "fork" would be paired with the display of each sample. Finally, the samples would be reduced to only spoken words. A discrimination between "spoon" and "fork" is established once the learner succeeds at matching the spoken word to the real object.

TEACHING MATCHING-TO-SAMPLE

Both expressive and receptive are often established in the context of matching-to-sample tasks. A matching-to-sample repertoire, required for successful use of graphic mode systems, involves selecting a choice stimulus that matches a displayed sample. Matching requires establishing both simple and more conditional discriminations.

Teaching Simple Discriminations

A simple discrimination occurs when responses occur in the presence of one stimulus but not in the presence of others. For example, in teaching a generalized request, the learner may be taught to point to the "want" symbol when offered a variety of preferred objects. Later a second symbol may be added. Continued selection of the "want" symbol after the introduction of the second symbol would indicate that the learner could discriminate between the two symbols.

Keogh and Reichle (1985) described how such simple discriminations could be demonstrated using a differential reinforcement procedure. For example, a learner is presented with an array of two or more items. These items might consist of two graphic symbols or two real objects (e.g., a spoon and a fork). The learner is then asked to pick one. One item is arbitrarily designated as correct. Selecting the correct item is followed by delivery of a reinforcer. No reinforcement is delivered for selecting the incorrect symbol. As this differential reinforcement procedure continues there is an increased tendency for the learner to select only the "correct" item.

Figure 3 shows how such a simple discrimination might develop. Initially, the correct and the incorrect items are selected about equally often. With continued implementation of the differential reinforcement procedure, the number of correct responses increases steadily.

From session 5 on, the learner is clearly discriminating between the two choices.

Clearly, effective use of a graphic system of communication requires acquisition of such simple visual discriminations. Learners must be taught to distinguish among the symbols that comprise their system. Such simple discriminations are not sufficient for functional communication, however. To communicate, the learner must also be able to match symbols to referents in the environment.

Teaching Conditional Discriminations

Conditional discriminations can be established by implementing match-to-sample procedures. In a match-to-sample procedure, the learner is first presented with an array of two or more choices. For example, two line drawings (one of a spoon, the other a fork) can be placed in front of the learner, one to the right, the other to the left. The left and right placement of these

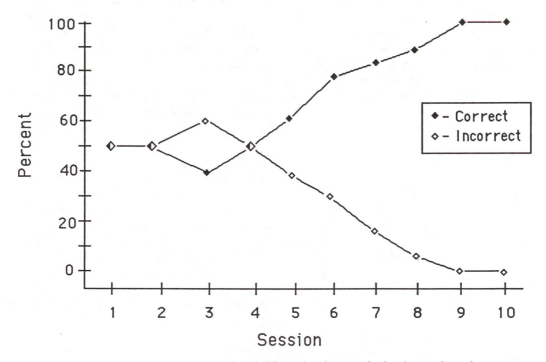

Figure 3.   Development of simple discrimination through differential reinforcement for the selection of one of two items.

choices is randomized across opportunities to prevent position-based responding from being reinforced. Next, the interventionist displays a sample that bears some relationship to one of the choices. After displaying the sample and perhaps requiring the learner to look at it, the learner is provided with an opportunity to match the symbol to the item in the environment. Such a match could signify a request (e.g., "I want a fork."), a simple provision of information (e.g., "There's a fork."), or a host of other communicative functions. Selecting the line drawing of a fork would be reinforced when a real fork was used as a sample, whereas selecting the line drawing of a spoon would be reinforced when a real spoon was displayed.

The conditional discriminations required in match-to-sample tasks often prove difficult to teach to learners with severe disabilities (Saunders & Spradlin, 1989). Some learners may have tremendous difficulty acquiring effective matching skills (Sidman & Stoddard, 1967; Keogh & Reichle, 1985). One reason for such failure may be that the typical trial-and-error procedures may not be the most efficient for establishing match-to-sample skills. (Stimulus control procedures that can be used to increase the effectiveness of intervention are described in Chapter 9.)

LEVELS OF VISUAL MATCHING

Keogh and Reichle (1985) described six levels of visual matching that depend on the relationship between samples and choices. These six levels fall within two major classes, identical and nonidentical matching tasks.

Identical Match-To-Sample Tasks

Tasks in which the choice and sample stimuli are the same in every respect are called *identical match-to-sample tasks*. For example, a learner might be taught to match a real red apple sample to a real red apple choice. At a more abstract level, the learner might be taught to match identical line drawings or identical photographs. Identical matching can thus occur at three levels: matching identical real objects, matching identical photographs, or matching identical line drawings. Because the learner's task is to select the choice stimulus that is identical to the sample, identical matching is similar to imitation.

Nonidentical Match-To-Sample Tasks

A nonidentical match-to-sample task involves the use of choice and sample stimuli that are not identical. For example, a learner might be taught to match a real object sample to a photograph or line drawing of that object. Learners participating in such a task are also performing a type of expressive discrimination similar to naming a displayed object. When the task is reversed, and the learner selects real object choices that match line drawing samples, the resulting repertoire is similar to a receptive discrimination. At another level the learner may match spoken words (e.g., "Find the spoon") to the corresponding real object or to a drawing of that object.

A variation of these two types of nonidentical match-to-sample tasks would involve matching real objects to different real objects. The learner might be taught to match a large red tennis shoe to a smaller red tennis shoe. In this example, the match is based upon a similarity of form (tennis shoe) and color (red). At the next level, the learner might be taught to match a red tennis shoe to a white tennis shoe. Matching here is based upon form alone. Other arrangements could be used to teach the learner to match a real black tennis shoe to a real black basketball shoe rather than a wingtip street shoe. Function may also serve as a basis for matching. For example, a learner might be taught to match a spoon to a fork, because both are eating utensils.

At a third level, a learner could be taught to match real objects to photographs of those same objects. A real spoon, for example, might be matched to a picture of the spoon.

Figure 4 shows the various levels of visual matching described by Keogh and Reichle (1985). This sequence can be used in two ways. In one, first identical objects, then identical photographs, and finally identical line drawings are matched. In the other, learners are initially taught to match nonidentical objects and then to comprehend object names. In this latter task, two objects are placed in front of the learner as choices. The teacher then randomly chooses one of the items and instructs the learner to select it. Progression through this sequence of matching tasks is designed to prepare the learner for effective use of a communication board or wallet to request objects or provide information.

Selecting Samples and Choices in a Matching Task

The ease with which a particular matching relationship is acquired may depend on the type of stimuli that serve as samples and choices in the task. A good example is provided by Brady and Saunders (1989), who taught object-to-symbol (i.e., abstract lexigrams) matching to an adult with severe mental retardation. Initially, this learner failed to match the object to the symbol when the lexigrams served as samples and the corresponding real objects served as choices. However, he readily acquired accurate levels of matching when the lexigrams were presented as the choices and the real objects were displayed as samples. Once acquired, accurate matching was maintained even when the sample and

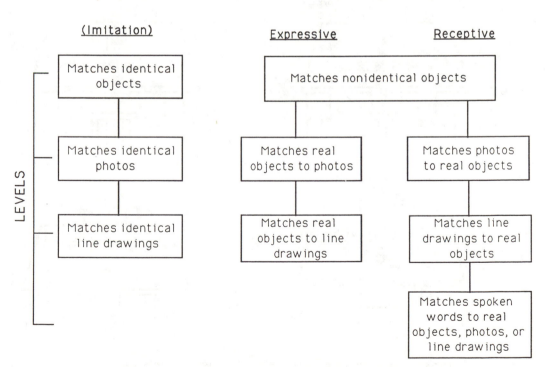

Figure 4.   Levels of visual matching. (Adapted from Keogh and Reichle, 1985.)

choices were again reversed to the configuration presented originally. These results highlight the importance of considering the different arrangements of samples and choices when teaching matching to learners with severe disabilities. Figure 5 shows four different arrangements of samples and choices that can be used in match-to-sample tasks.

The authors' experience, along with a growing body of literature, suggests that it may be best to use items among which the learner most readily discriminates as members of the choice array in the earliest phases of discrimination training. For example, assume that a learner readily discriminates among real objects but has more difficulty discriminating among graphic representations. There may be merit in organizing an initial matching task so that real objects

serve as the choices and the graphic representation serves as the sample (e.g., a learner is offered a product logo of ketchup and asked to locate the bottle from the array of other items in the refrigerator).

Generalized Matching-to-Sample

At some point after sufficient exposure to match-to-sample procedures, learners who have been taught to select the choice matching a displayed sample may come to match new samples without direct instruction. For example, a learner who has been taught to match identical spoons, forks, and cups may eventually come to match other identical objects without additional training. This is termed *generalized matching-to-sample*, or *reflexivity* (Sidman & Tailby, 1982). A similar phenomenon is frequently ob-

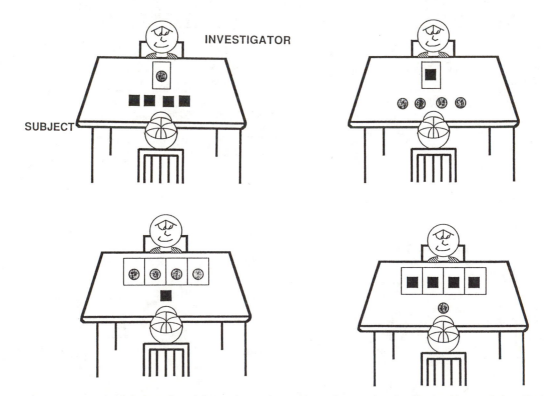

Figure 5.   Four arrangements of sample and choices that can be used in match-to-sample tasks. (Reprinted by permission of Kate Franklin.)

served when teaching imitative behaviors. At some point, learners become generalized imitators (Baer & Deguchi, 1985).

Generalized match-to-sample performance can also be observed at another level. For example, in the study by Brady and Saunders (1989), teaching a learner to match real object samples to lexigram choices resulted in the subsequent ability to match lexigram samples to real object choices. This reversibility of sample and choices is termed *symmetry*. Symmetric relationships may depend upon the sequence in which various levels of matching are taught.

ESTABLISHING CONDITIONAL USE OF NEWLY ACQUIRED COMMUNICATIVE REPERTOIRES

An interventionist's initial efforts involve getting newly established communicative behavior to occur more often. For example, after consuming a cookie, a learner may request "more cookie." During the initial phase of acquisition, repeated requests are apt to be honored in order to increase the probability that requests will continue to be made. Increasing the frequency with which requests occur is highly desirable, since the more frequently a behavior is produced, the more likely it is to be maintained. However, care must be taken to ensure that the increasing frequency of communicative actions occurs only in those situations in which the behavior is acceptable.

Most communicative behavior must be used conditionally. As discussed earlier in this chapter, there are situations in which communication should be used and situations in which the learner should refrain from communicating. Some conditional uses are setting specific. Other uses are person specific. Other conditions are even more subtle. For example, it may be acceptable for a learner to request a second cookie, but unacceptable for him or her to request a third. Figure 6 lists situations that commonly require conditional discriminations.

Type of Situation	Example
Setting-specific	Refrain from requesting something to drink during a concert until intermission.
Person-specific	Use signs when communicating with familiar persons, but use graphic symbols when communicating with unfamiliar persons in community sites.
Frequency of access	Request two or three cups of coffee in succession, but reject an offer for a fourth cup.
Task-specific	Request assistance with difficult tasks, but complete easy tasks independently.
Other ecological	Take a snack without requesting permission at home, but request a snack at a friend's house.

Figure 6.   Types of situations that require conditional discriminations.

Some situations require that the learner refrain from engaging in a particular communicative behavior. Other conditions require that a learner produce a competing response. For example, if a learner needs ketchup and sees some on the other side of the kitchen table, he should touch a symbol in his wallet or produce a sign requesting ketchup. If the ketchup bottle is sitting beside him, he should simply pick it up and refrain from engaging in a request.

Some ecological conditions support the unlimited use of newly established behavior. For example, at a baseball game, comments such as "let's go" can be made very frequently and still be perceived as socially appropriate. However, other communicative behaviors, such as repeatedly requesting a hot dog, may eventually become annoying to the listener. From a programmatic perspective, there are two alternatives that can result in the conditional use of a new communicative behavior. One option is to place conditions on when frequently performed behaviors can be performed. A second option is to place conditions on when a behavior can be performed at the outset of intervention.

When a learner is beginning to learn to communicate, he or she will encounter utterances that he or she will not understand. Learners with severe communicative deficits must be taught to communicate to their listener when they do not understand. In essence, after hearing an utterance from a communication partner, a learner must decide whether he or she has understood it, and then respond accordingly. If the learner has not understood the utterance, he or she must communicate that he or she has not understood.

There is growing evidence to suggest that some excess behavior may occur in response to utterances that are not understood. Prizant and Duchan (1981) reported that for some learners, verbal echolalic behavior is more apt to be produced following utterances from communication partners that were not understood. Teaching the learner to communicate his or her failure

to understand may thus reduce some socially motivated excess behavior.

Teaching learners to request clarification when an utterance has not been understood can be accomplished in at least two ways. First, the interventionist can provide only unclear messages, prompting the learner to request clarification during each instructional opportunity. The strategy here is to increase the frequency of requests for clarification (i.e., using a symbol "I don't understand") and then set up the conditional discrimination by presenting some messages that do not require clarification. A number of instructional opportunities to prompt the desired response can be arranged in a relatively brief period of time with this approach. However, it may prove difficult to prevent the learner from requesting clarification when easily understood messages are eventually introduced.

The second option involves establishing the conditional discrimination from the beginning of instruction. This could be arranged by including both clear and unclear messages on a random basis during the initial instructional opportunities. Because both positive (unclear messages) and negative (clear messages) exemplars are included, opportunities for establishing requests for clarification are dispersed over a longer period of time, thus possibly reducing the rate with which the response is acquired.

CIRCUMVENTING POTENTIAL DIFFICULTIES IN ESTABLISHING INITIAL DISCRIMINATIONS

Position-Biased Responding

A position bias occurs when selection of a choice stimulus is determined by its position (e.g., left, right) rather than by its relationship to the sample. In a typical two-choice match-to-sample task, for example, a learner may come always to select whichever choice is on the right, regardless of which of the two sample stimuli is displayed. This pattern of selection may persist because correct responses occasionally occur and are reinforced. Ultimately, the pattern needs to be broken if the match-to-sample relationship is to be established. Often the standard random placement of choice stimuli from trial to trial will be sufficient to prevent position-biased responding. When such patterns have been acquired, however, other more elaborate solutions may be needed.

One solution is to place a majority of the correct choices in the nonpreferred location during an intervention session (e.g., if the learner frequently selects the choice on the right, then a majority of correct choices are placed on the left). In order to receive reinforcement with the same frequency as before, the learner will need to begin selecting the choice on the left. Before randomizing the left/right placement of objects, a sufficient number of opportunities should be implemented to ensure that the position bias has been corrected.

Another solution is temporarily to employ more intrusive response prompts to recruit correct selections. After the learner has been prompted repeatedly to select the choice that matches a displayed sample, these prompts can be faded. During the time these more intrusive response prompts are used, it is important to ensure that the correct choice occurs in randomized locations.

A third solution is to teach learners first to look at the sample stimulus and then to scan the available choice array before making a selection. One way to do this is first to present only the sample, with the choices offered only after the learner has examined the sample. It is possible that many learners adopt systematic error patterns, such as position biases, because they lack the observing and scanning skills necessary for successful completion of match-to-sample tasks.

Position-biased response patterns can also develop in the vocal or gestural mode systems. For example, some learners may show a tendency to imitate the last word in a sentence. When

asked, "Do you want a cookie or an apple?" the learner may reveal a position bias by always repeating "apple." In this case the position bias may be eliminated by using a loudness fading procedure. Here the word "apple" is initially spoken very softly while the rest of the sentence is spoken at a normal volume. The low volume of the word "apple" may prevent the learner from repeating this word. Over successive opportunities the loudness with which this last word is spoken is gradually increased until the entire sentence is spoken at the same volume.

Another technique is to say the name of the more preferred item first. If the learner preferred apples over cookies, for example, the tendency to imitate the last word may be thwarted by placing "apple" further up in the question (e.g., "Do you want apples or cookies?").

In the gestural mode, a position bias could develop such that the learner imitated the last gesture produced by the interventionist. This pattern is similar to imitating the last word spoken. Similar procedures might, therefore, thwart this type of bias (i.e., the emphasis given to the last gesture in a sequence could initially be reduced and then gradually returned to a normal level). Gestures corresponding to more preferred items could also be embedded within a sequence rather than put at the end.

Item-Biased Responding

An item bias occurs when a learner consistently selects a particular choice stimulus regardless of what sample stimulus is shown. For example, in a two-choice matching task involving a spoon and a cup, the learner who always selects the cup is revealing an item bias. The same types of solutions offered for correcting position biases may work to correct an item bias. A majority of trials may involve the nonbiased item (e.g., a spoon is more often displayed as the sample), more intrusive response prompts can be temporarily added and then faded, or better observing and scanning skills can be taught. Sometimes an item bias may develop because the item selected represents the more preferred item. In these cases, item biases may be prevented by using the same type of reinforcer for all correct responses. Another option would be to ensure all items involved in discrimination training were equally preferred.

Another example of an item bias is the consistent use of a particular response form. The learner may, for example, consistently respond with a particular word or sign regardless of the demands of the situation. The similarity among various responses may promote the development of certain response patterns. Signs such as "eat" and "drink," for example, are similar in appearance, which may cause some learners to confuse the two symbols. Other learners might react to this situation by producing a cross between two similar signs. This type of bias may also develop in the vocal mode because of a similarity among words. In either case, when the bias develops gradually, people familiar with the learner may come to recognize the resulting response approximations. This can cause problems for learners when they are forced to produce a precise sign or gesture in order to communicate with someone unfamiliar with the poorly articulated form. Novice sign learners, for example, may be able to decipher only very well articulated signs. Hence, learners whose signs have become too sloppy may be unable to communicate with some potential communication partners. Sometimes this problem is compounded when gestures are taught to learners who may already exhibit stereotypic movements, such as hand flapping or arm waving. Listeners may find it extremely difficult to distinguish a legitimate communicative gesture from the existing stream of stereotypic movements.

OVERCOMING DELAYS IN COMMUNICATIVE OPPORTUNITIES

Graphic mode communication involves the selection of symbols that match some environ-mental stimulus. It is important for the interventionist to ensure that selection of symbols is determined by an appropriate environmental stimulus and not by some irrelevant feature of the task.

In more natural settings, graphic mode communicators will often experience a delay between presentation of a sample and the opportunity to select a symbol to communicate. Much of the learner's communicative episode will thus function more within a delayed match-to-sample paradigm as opposed to a standard match-to-sample task. A delay paradigm includes a period of time between display of a sample stimulus and availability of the choice stimuli. Such delays occur naturally for graphic mode system users because they must look away from the sample in order to locate the corresponding symbol in their board or wallet. For learners with several pages of symbols, such delays may be lengthy as pages are turned to locate the correct symbol. As such delays increase, selection of correct symbols may show a corresponding decline. Improving the learner's fluency in accessing available symbols may help mitigate any negative effects caused by such delays.

Another delay may occur between the time a learner makes a request, for example, and the ensuing opportunity to select the requested item. Suppose a learner requests a cookie and sometime later is offered a plate containing several snack items including the requested cookie. Under these conditions, it is perhaps not surprising that the learner may not actually select the item previously requested. Among learners with severe disabilities this lack of correspondence between requests and subsequent selections may become quite pervasive (Tetlie & Reichle, 1986). Fortunately, it has proved possible to improve correspondence between requests and selections by teaching learners to select only those items that match a prior request (Reichle, Sigafoos & Piché, 1989). Correspondence between requests and selections is not, of course, a issue relevant only to graphic-mode systems. Indeed, this and other potential problems (e.g., position bias, item bias) are just as much a source of difficulty when establishing discriminative repertoires in vocal and gestural modes. In fact, many learners who have been taught several utterances or gestures may produce their entire repertoire of signs at each opportunity to do so. This type of response pattern may develop because eventually the learner may produce the correct response and thus be reinforced. The outcome of such practices is that the learner is taught to randomly produce signs, utterances, gestures, or symbols until his or her repertoire has been exhausted. This pattern can be prevented by implementing a response-interruption and error-correction procedure. For example, as soon as an incorrect sign is produced or is about to occur, the interventionist interrupts the learner and prompts a correct response. Over successive opportunities those prompts can be faded. In addition, whenever a string of responses is produced, the interventionist would withhold reinforcement.

SCHEDULING COMMUNICATION INTERVENTION

Several options exist for scheduling intervention opportunities to teach initial discriminative repertoires. In a *massed-trial format,* a block of opportunities is implemented at one time. No other activities are performed between trials.

Early intervention programs relied heavily on massed-trial instructional formats (e.g., Guess, Sailor, & Baer, 1974; Lovaas, 1977). For learners who tend to acquire new skills slowly, a massed-trial format may be adopted for early phases of intervention. (Mulligan, Guess, Holvoet, & Brown, 1980).

Massed-trial instruction is often pitted against both distributed and spaced-trial formats as if the three represented mutually exclusive rivals. In a *distributed strategy,* intervention opportunities from separate programs are implemented be-

tween successive trials of the first program. For example, between two requesting episodes, the learner might receive an instructional opportunity designed to teach him or her a domestic skill (e.g., peeling an orange). The rationale behind a distributed-trial strategy is clearest when the two programs are functionally linked (e.g., a learner peels an orange after having requested it).

Spaced-trial formats involve a pause between successive intervention opportunities. For example, opportunities for requesting a snack might be separated by 5-minute breaks. Spaced formats spread intervention opportunities over a longer period of time, which may enable more opportunities to be implemented with learners prone to become satiated from the reinforcers being used.

Massed, distributed, and spaced formats are not incompatible. Massed trials can be spaced throughout the day. For example, four or five requesting episodes can be implemented during a mid-morning snack routine and then again during the evening. While there will almost certainly be intervening activities between the two snack times, intervention to teach requests implemented during these routines occurs at two points in the day. In contrast, between each of the four or five requesting opportunities, intervention trials from another program might be implemented. After requesting a cup of coffee, for example, the learner might be taught to initiate a conversation with a peer before another opportunity to request a cup of coffee is made available. This sequence is essentially a distributed-trial training format, but if two or three cups of coffee are made available for requesting, then the sequence could contain some elements of a massed-trial format.

Some activities readily lend themselves to massed-trial instruction. In teaching two learners to cooperate on a dishwashing task, for example, multiple opportunities exist for teaching one learner to request that the other "dry a dish." Each time the first learner finishes washing and rinsing a plate, he or she can be taught to instruct the peer to "dry this one." During a single dishwashing activity, 20 or more opportunities to teach this skill may arise.

Other activities, in contrast, may be better suited for distributed-trial instruction. For example, teaching a learner to request help in putting on a coat can be done only when the learner is about to go outdoors. Such opportunities are likely to arise three to four times a day.

SUMMARY

In order to communicate efficiently, a learner must be able to identify those situations that either provide opportunities or obligate him or her to produce communicative behavior. These situations constitute the discriminative stimuli for the production of communicative behavior. Responses to these discriminative stimuli consist of both communicative expression and communicative reception. Among learners with se-

vere disabilities, the ability to generalize from expression to reception may be limited or nonexistent. That is, the vocabulary that a learner produces may not be fully understood and vice versa. This phenomenon is important, since so many of our conversational interactions intertwine reception and expression. For example, one conversational participant asks, "Is it cold outside?" His or her partner may respond, "Yes." In doing so, the partner had to understand the phrase "Is it cold outside?" and produce the answer "yes." Although this book focuses, for the most part, on expressive repertoires, reception is also important.

The remainder of this chapter focused on intervention techniques that assist in maximizing 1) the discriminability of graphic and gestural symbols and 2) the degree to which symbols generalize to a variety of relevant discriminative stimuli. Finally, several error patterns that learners may produce in acquiring discriminations were examined.

REFERENCES

Albin, R.W., & Horner, R.H. (1988). Generalization with precision. In R.H. Horner, G. Dunlap, & R.L. Koegel (Eds.), *Generalization and maintenance: Life-style changes in applied settings* (pp. 99–120). Baltimore: Paul H. Brookes Publishing Co.

Baer, D.M., & Deguchi, H. (1985). Generalized imitation from a radical-behavioral viewpoint. In S. Reiss & R.R. Bootzin (Eds.), *Theoretical issues in behavior therapy* (pp. 179–217). New York: Academic Press.

Brady, N.C., & Saunders, K.J. (1989). *Some considerations in the effective teaching of object-to-symbol matching*. Unpublished manuscript.

Dixon, M.H., Dixon, L.S., & Spradlin, J.E. (1983). Analysis of individual differences of stimulus control among developmentally disabled children. In K.D. Gadow & I. Bialer (Eds.), *Advances in learning and behavioral disabilities* (pp. 85–110). Greenwich, CT: JAI Press.

Goldstein, H. (1985). Enhancing language generalization using matrix and stimulus equivalence training. In S. F. Warren & A. K. Rogers-Warren

(Eds.), *Teaching functional language* (pp. 225–249). Austin, TX: PRO-ED.

Guess, D. (1969). A functional analysis of receptive language and productive speech: Acquisition of the plural morpheme. *Journal of Applied Behavior Analysis, 2,* 55–64.

Guess, D., & Baer, D.M. (1973). An analysis of individual differences in generalization between receptive and productive language in retarded children. *Journal of Applied Behavior Analysis, 6,* 311–329.

Guess, D., Sailor, W., & Baer, D.M. (1974). To teach language to retarded children. In R.L. Schiefelbusch & L. Lloyd (Eds.), *Language perspectives: Acquisition, retardation, and intervention* (pp. 529–563). Baltimore: University Park Press.

Horner, R.H., & McDonald, R.S. (1982). A comparison of single instance and general case instruction in teaching a generalized vocational skill. *Journal of The Association for the Severely Handicapped, 7,* 7–20.

Horner, R.H., McDonnell, J.J., & Bellamy, G.T.

(1986). Teaching generalized skills: General case instruction in simulation and community settings. In R.H. Horner, L.H. Meyer, & H.D. Fredericks (Eds.), *Education of learners with severe handicaps: Exemplary service strategies* (pp. 289–314). Baltimore: Paul H. Brookes Publishing Co.

Horner, R.H., Sprague, J., & Wilcox, B. (1982). General case programming for community activities. In B. Wilcox & G.T. Bellamy (Eds.), *Design of high school programs for severely handicapped students* (pp. 51–89). Baltimore: Paul H. Brookes Publishing Co.

House, B.J., & Zeaman, D. (1960). Transfer of a discrimination from objects to patterns. *Journal of Experimental Psychology, 59,* 298–302.

Karlan, G.R., Brenn-White, B., Lentz, A., Hodur, P., Egger, D., & Frankoff, D. (1982). Establishing generalized, productive verb-noun phrase usage in a manual language system with moderately handicapped children. *Journal of Speech and Hearing Disorders, 47,* 31–42.

Keogh, W., & Reichle, J. (1985). Communication intervention for the "difficult-to-teach" severely handicapped. In S. Warren & A.K. Rogers-Warren (Eds.), *Teaching functional language* (pp. 157–194). Austin, TX: PRO-ED.

Koegel, R.L., & Schriebman, L. (1977). Teaching autistic children to respond to simultaneous multiple cues. *Journal of Experimental Child Psychology, 24,* 299–311.

Koegel, R.L., & Wilhelm, H. (1973). Selective responding to the components of multiple visual cues by autistic children. *Journal of Experimental Child Psychology, 15,* 442–453.

Lee, V.L. (1981). Prepositional phrases spoken and heard. *Journal of the Experimental Analysis of Behavior, 35,* 227–242.

Lee, V.L. (1988). *Beyond behaviorism.* Hillsdale, NJ: Lawrence Erlbaum Associates.

Lovaas, O.I. (1977). *The autistic child: Language development through behavior modification.* New York: Irvington.

Michael, J. (1985). Two kinds of verbal behavior plus a possible third. *Analysis of Verbal Behavior, 3,* 1–4.

Mulligan, M., Guess, D., Holvoet, J., & Brown, F. (1980). The individualized curriculum sequencing model (1): Implications from research on massed, distributed, or spaced trial training. *Journal of The Association for the Severely Handicapped, 5,* 325–336.

Prizant, B.M., & Duchan, J.F. (1981). The functions of immediate echolalia in autistic children. *Journal of Speech and Hearing Disorders, 46,* 241–249.

Reichle, J., Sigafoos, J., & Piché, L. (1989). Teaching an adolescent with blindness and severe disabilities: A correspondence between requesting and selecting preferred objects. *Journal of The Association for Persons with Severe Handicaps, 14,* 75–80.

Saunders, K.J., & Spradlin, J.E. (1989). Conditional discrimination in mentally retarded adults: The effects of training the component simple discriminations. *Journal of the Experimental Analysis of Behavior, 52,* 1–12.

Sidman, M., & Stoddard, L.T. (1967). The effectiveness of fading in programming a simultaneous form discrimination for retarded children. *Journal of the Experimental Analysis of Behavior, 10,* 3–15.

Sidman, M., & Tailby, W. (1982). Conditional discrimination vs. matching to sample: An expansion of the testing paradigm. *Journal of the Experimental Analysis of Behavior, 37,* 5–22.

Siegel, G.M., & Vogt, M.C. (1984). Pluralization instruction in comprehension and production. *Journal of Speech and Hearing Disorders, 49,* 128–135.

Skinner, B.F. (1957). *Verbal behavior.* New York: Appleton-Century-Crofts.

Sprague, J.R., & Horner, R.H. (1984). The effects of single instance, multiple instance, and general case training on generalized vending machine use by moderately and severely handicapped students. *Journal of Applied Behavior Analysis, 17,* 273–278.

Stokes, T.F., & Baer, D.M. (1977). An implicit technology of generalization. *Journal of Applied Behavior Analysis, 10,* 349–367.

Terrace, H.S. (1963). Discrimination learning with and without "errors." *Journal of the Experimental Analysis of Behavior, 6,* 1–27.

Tetlie, R., & Reichle, J. (1986). *The match between signed requests and objects selection in four learners with severe handicaps.* Unpublished master's thesis, University of Minnesota, Minneapolis.

Vargas, E.A. (1988). Verbally-governed and event-governed behavior. *Analysis of Verbal Behavior, 6,* 11–22.

11

Replacing Excess Behavior with an Initial Communicative Repertoire

L. Scott Doss and Joe Reichle

Excess behavior is behavior by a learner that results in self-injury or injury of others, causes damage to the physical environment, interferes with the acquisition of new skills, and/or socially isolates the learner. Self-injury, aggression, and property destruction are the most commonly reported forms of excess behavior (Morreau, 1985). Discovering effective methods for reducing excess behavior among people with severe disabilities remains a major focus of intervention and research.

A variety of strategies is used to replace excess behavior with more socially acceptable repertoires. Some of these are designed to support adaptive behavior in the short term, while others are designed to support adaptive behavior in the long term (O'Neill, Horner, Albin, Storey, & Sprague, 1989). A growing body of work suggests that communication instruction may be a useful component of an intervention protocol aimed at reducing excess behavior (Bird, Dores, Moniz, & Robinson, 1989; Carr & Durand, 1985a; Day, Rea, Schussler, Larsen,

& Johnson, 1988; Doss, 1988; Doss & Reichle, 1989; Durand, 1986; Durand & Carr, 1987; Durand & Crimmins, 1987; Horner & Budd, 1985; Smith, 1985).

This chapter examines the relationship between excess behavior and communication instruction. First, the functions served by excess behavior, the principles of reinforcement, and the roles of participants in social interactions are examined. Second, methods of assessment are reviewed. Third, issues to consider when determining if communication intervention is appropriate are examined. Fourth, techniques that can be used to teach communication to a learner who engages in excess behavior are examined. Finally, two examples of the process of assessment and intervention are presented.

FUNCTIONS OF EXCESS BEHAVIOR

Applied behavior analysis has traditionally distinguished between the social and nonsocial functions of excess behavior. This distinction is

important, because understanding the function
of the behavior can be useful in identifying reinforcers and the context in which communication
instruction should take place.

Nonsocial functions are functions that involve proprioceptive, visual, tactile, gustatory,
and auditory stimuli (Favell, McGimsey, &
Schell, 1982; Rincover & Devany, 1982). Examples include poking oneself in the eye to produce visual stimulation, scratching a mosquito
bite to relieve irritation, or stealing favorite food
items from others to produce gustatory satisfaction.

Social functions are functions that require the
mediation of others. Social functions include
gaining attention, gaining access to objects or
activities, or escaping or avoiding nonpreferred
situations (Carr & Durand, 1985; Durand &
Carr, 1987; Lovaas, Freitag, Gold, & Kassorla,
1965; Lovaas & Simmons, 1969; Weeks &
Gaylord-Ross, 1981). For example, a social
function is served when a learner pinches a
caregiver in order to escape after being told to
bathe.

Social and nonsocial functions are not mutually exclusive. An excess behavior may initially
serve a nonsocial function, but develop a social
function over time. Carr and McDowell (1980)
reported a case in which self-scratching initially
caused by an allergy developed a social function
over time, presumably because of the attention
received when the behavior occurred. Failure to
distinguish between social and nonsocial functions makes identification of reinforcers more
difficult. Behavioral chains may occur that
serve both social and nonsocial functions, complicating the design of intervention strategies.
For example, a learner may steal food because it
tastes good (i.e., serves a nonsocial function)
and strike others who discover him stealing
(i.e., serves a social function).

Complex relationships between the function
and form of the excess behavior may complicate
attempts to discover the behavior's function.
For example, learners may strike others or bite

themselves to escape a task, or hit to escape a
task and pinch to recruit attention (Carr & Durand, 1985; Durand, 1982; Heidorn & Jensen,
1984). Both assessment and program development are complicated if a learner engages in one
excess behavior to serve one function (e.g.,
self-injurious hand-to-head hitting when tasks
are presented) and another excess behavior to
serve a second function (e.g., striking another
person in order to procure a favorite beverage).
Another learner may produce the same excess
behaviors to serve different functions. In these
instances, assessment becomes complicated because additional information needs to be
gathered about when the different functions
come into effect. Program development becomes more complicated because intervention
protocols require different procedures to address
the various functions.

EFFECT OF POSITIVE AND
NEGATIVE REINFORCEMENT
ON EXCESS BEHAVIOR

The principles of positive and negative reinforcement are important in attempting to explain
why excess behavior occurs and in designing
interventions to replace excess behavior with
more socially acceptable behavior. These principles also provide the basis for a powerful
instructional technology to reduce excess behavior.

A learner may engage in socially unacceptable behavior because in the past the consequence of such behavior has been favorable
(i.e., attention, access to objects). In this instance, the behavior may be maintained by
positive reinforcement. Conversely, a learner
may engage in excess behavior because doing
so has usually resulted in a caregiver removing
an undesired task or activity. In this case the
behavior is maintained by negative reinforcement. An implication of this analysis is that
manipulating reinforcement contingencies will

change the likelihood that the behavior will occur.

ROLES OF SPEAKERS AND LISTENERS IN SOCIAL INTERACTIONS: THE INFLUENCE OF PRAGMATICS ON COMMUNICATION INSTRUCTION

Pragmatics is concerned with the communicative force of behavior in social interactions (Hart, 1981; Prutting, 1982). As discussed in Chapters 1 and 4, behavior that occurs in the presence of others has both *perlocutionary* properties (i.e., affects the listener's behavior) and *illocutionary* properties (i.e., reveals the intention of the speaker) (Prutting, 1982). Pragmatics thus stresses the function rather than the form of the communicative behavior (Goetz, Schuler, & Sailor, 1981). The function of the communicative response depends upon: 1) the immediacy of the consequence of the response, 2) the potentially reinforcing nature of the consequence, 3) the specificity of the consequence for the response, and 4) the naturalness of the response to the user's interaction with the environment (Goetz et al., 1981).

A learner who engages in excess behavior in the presence of others may be thought of as the speaker in a communication episode. For example, a learner who bites his hand when a teacher presents a nonpreferred activity may be communicating, "I don't like this activity. Withdraw it!" A learner who strikes a caregiver when little interaction is available may be communicating, "Hey, talk to me!" If such behavior influences what others do, the excess behavior and the subsequent actions performed by others represent a communication episode.

ASSESSING EXCESS BEHAVIORS

Assessment should examine the relative contributions of as many factors as possible. Table 1 summarizes the factors cited by O'Neill et al. (1989) and Bailey and Pyles (1989) as impor-

tant in evaluating excess behavior. Several of these factors are highlighted in the following sections.

Characterizing Excess Behaviors

Each of the excess behaviors a learner produces should be characterized. First, the nature of the behavior should be described. For example, does an aggressive learner simply push people away or does he close his fist and punch them in the face? Does a self-injurious learner continuously tap her chin with an open hand or does she poke her index finger up to the second knuckle into her eyes? Second, the frequency and the intensity of the excess behavior should be evaluated. Measuring intensity is more difficult than measuring frequency because of the subjectivity involved. Nonetheless, ratings (Thompson, 1985), injury reports filed by the agency, or permanent products (e.g., photographs of a learner who punches himself in the face) provide mechanisms by which intensity and changes in intensity may be measured.

Describing When and Where Excess Behaviors Occur

Specifying the circumstances under which excess behaviors occur serves two important purposes. First, the interventionist obtains clues about why the learner engages in the excess behavior. Second, this information may help determine the best times to implement interventions during the course of the day.

Any activities, peers, or caregivers that seem to lead to increased levels of excess behavior should be discussed with caregivers and, if necessary, pursued more systematically through direct observation.

Describing When and Where Excess Behaviors Do Not Occur

Meyer and Evans (1989) point out that assessment (interviews and direct observation) should also include specifying situations in which the excess behavior is *least* likely to occur. Identify-

Table 1.   Factors to consider in evaluating excess behaviors

What excess behaviors does the learner perform?

What is the topography, frequency, intensity, and duration of the excess behavior?

When is excess behavior most and least likely to occur?

Where is excess behavior most and least likely to occur?

With whom is excess behavior most and least likely to occur?

What activities are most and least likely to produce excess behavior?

Are there circumstances under which the excess behavior never occurs?

Could the excess behavior be related to any skill deficit?

How is excess behavior affected by presenting the learner with a difficult task?

How is excess behavior affected by interrupting the learner from a desired activity?

How is excess behavior affected by delivering a stern request, command, or reprimand?

How is excess behavior affected by changing the learner's routine?

How is excess behavior affected by ignoring the learner?

How is excess behavior affected by preventing the learner from obtaining a desired object?

Does the learner engage in excess behavior when no one else is present?

Do excess behaviors occur in a chain?

Could the excess behavior be caused by the side effect of medication?

Could the excess behavior be caused by a medical condition (e.g., asthma, allergies, rashes, sinus infections, seizures)?

Could the excess behavior be caused by physical discomfort (e.g., stomach ache, ear infection, dizziness, blurred vision)?

Could the excess behavior be caused by a deprivation condition (e.g., thirst, hunger, exhaustion)?

Does the behavior occur during certain seasons of the year?

What are the learner's sleep cycles?

What are the learner's eating routines and diet?

How predictable are the learner's daily activities?

Are the learner's daily activities boring and/or unpleasant, or does the learner value them?

How often does the learner get to make choices about activities, reinforcers, and so forth?

Does the excess behavior occur because the learner is bored or lonely?

Does the excess behavior provide self-stimulation?

How many people share the learner's environment?

How well trained are the staff dealing with the learner?

What is the quality of interactions between the learner and the staff?

How much physical effort is involved in the excess behavior?

Can the excess behavior cause serious tissue damage?

How often does the excess behavior result in a "payoff"?

How much of a delay is there between the excess behavior and the "payoff"?

Does the learner get attention as a result of the excess behavior?

How does the learner communicate (e.g., vocal speech, signs, gestures, communication boards)?

How consistently does the learner communicate in a particular mode?

Which communicative behaviors does the learner use to achieve which communicative functions?

Does the learner follow verbal requests or instructions? If so, to how many?

Does the learner respond to signed or gestural requests or instructions? If so, to how many?

How does the learner indicate "yes" and "no"?

What objects, activities, and people does the learner perceive favorably?

What functional alternative behavior does the learner know?

What socially appropriate behaviors does the learner perform that achieve the same ends achieved by the excess behaviors?

Adapted from O'Neill, Horner, Albin, Storey, and Sprague (1989) and Bailey and Pyles (1989).

ing times when excess behavior is unlikely may help to specify modifications to the environment that prevent or attenuate the excess behavior. The authors have worked with a learner who refused to ride the bus and often became disruptive when asked to do so. Caregivers were asked to indicate circumstances under which the individual complied with the request to ride a bus, and circumstances under which he refused to comply with the request, as well as the consequences in each of these situations.

Identifying Contributing Health Problems

A thorough medical assessment should be performed before designing behavioral techniques to reduce excess behavior. Gunsett, Mulick, Fernald, and Martin (1989) demonstrated that a number of behavior problems could be resolved by treating medical problems (e.g., impacted bowel, urinary tract infection). Observations by primary caregivers will often provide clues that health issues may be implicated in an excess behavior.

Intermittent, recurring physiological or medical conditions may exist that influence the likelihood of excess behavior (e.g., menstruation, otitis media, allergies). For example, a generally even tempered learner might become aggressive when asked to clean the living room if troubled by an ear infection; a usually well behaved person may solicit attention by banging her head when afflicted with hay fever. Such recurring physical conditions may create the impression that the excess behaviors occur randomly. Although the effects of intermittently recurring medical and physiological conditions on excess behavior have not been well documented, numerous anecdotal reports by parents, caregivers, and professionals argue against dismissing their importance.

Identifying Other Physiological Influences

As Table 1 indicates, other factors may influence excess behavior. Careful documentation may reveal that excess behavior is affected by insomnia or indigestion (Gardner, Cole, Davidson, & Karan, 1986). It may be possible to modify some of the conditions that tend to increase excess behavior. To establish a possible relationship between excess behavior and particular physiological conditions, detailed records of the circumstances surrounding the occurrence of such behavior must be maintained.

Identifying a Learner's Preferences

Every candidate for communication instruction should be assessed in order to determine which objects or activities he or she prefers, since expressing preferences (i.e., requesting preferred objects or activities, rejecting nonpreferred objects and activities, informing others about one's preferences) is the primary reason for communicating. (See Chapter 5 for a discussion of assessment of preferences.) Such an assessment should provide cues as to which objects or activities should be incorporated into a communication program. Knowledge of a learner's preferences allows the interventionist to reward prosocial, nonproblematic behavior with outcomes the learner values.

The assessment of reinforcers should also include the identification of the objects and activities that the learner finds undesirable. Often the presence of undesirable stimuli results in the production of excess behavior. Knowing what the learner finds unpleasant helps the interventionist design communication instruction that allows appropriate escape from such situations, identify hierarchies of desirable and undesirable objects and activities that may be used to help the learner make choices, and construct ecologically sound procedures that prevent excess behavior from occurring.

Describing the Degree to Which Excess Behaviors Pay Off

Documenting how the learner's excess behaviors are reinforced is emerging as a very important issue in assessment and intervention (Horner & Billingsley, 1988). The adoption of socially acceptable behavior to replace excess behavior depends on how well the new skills pay off for the learner under naturally occurring conditions. New skills will not be used if previously established excess behaviors are more effective in producing a desired outcome.

Billingsley and Neel (1985) taught learners with severe retardation to use signs to request food instead of grabbing it. After being taught to sign for desired food items, the learners persisted in grabbing desired food during maintenance and generalization probes. Only after procedures were implemented to interrupt grabbing did the learners begin regularly using signs to request food.

Horner and Billingsley (1988) identified three issues that must be addressed in developing efficient intervention procedures to replace socially motivated excess behavior. First, how efficiently and reliably do the socially inappropriate behaviors work to produce outcomes desired by the learner? Second, do any other behaviors that the learner performs achieve the desired outcomes? Finally, do competing behaviors occur in the presence of some very specific stimuli or in the presence of many general stimuli and situations? The new skill being taught must be as efficient as the excess behavior that the interventionist is attempting to replace. It may be that in order for the new skill to be acquired and used consistently, programmed consequences that delay or deny delivery of reinforcement for excess behavior may need to be implemented along with procedures that teach use of the communicative alternative.

Identifying Previous Attempts at Intervention

It is always useful to list previous attempts at intervention and, if possible, to indicate why each failed or partially succeeded. By examining previous efforts, the interventionist may recognize that a particular strategy is unlikely to work, or that a strategy that had previously failed could be modified and reattempted. In developing this list, the interventionist should record all previous efforts, including procedures that modified the ecology of the learner's environment (e.g., reducing demands, spending

more time with the learner, introducing more interesting activities).

Procedures for Gathering Information

Informal Interviews Talking with caregivers may be the most important assessment activity performed. Simply asking "Why do you think this learner does this?" may generate hypotheses to investigate (Meyer & Evans, 1989). Subsequent questions should seek to identify situations in which the excess behavior is least and most likely to occur (e.g., task demands, transitions, menstruation). Caregivers should be asked about the learner's likes and dislikes, idiosyncratic ways of communicating (e.g., self-injury or gestures), and social relationships with peers and caregivers. Determining which staff members like or dislike the learner may also be important, as this may illuminate additional problems to overcome in implementing intervention procedures (Meyer & Evans, 1989). The questions listed in Table 1 provide an excellent basis for the interview.

Structured Interviews and Checklists Structured interviews and checklists provide an opportunity to corroborate caregiver impressions and focus the subsequent use of direct observation methods. With the Motivation Assessment Scale, developed by Durand and Crimmins (1988), the respondent (i.e., family member or caregiver) indicates his or her level of agreement with four sets of items, each pertaining to potential influences on excess behavior. The four sets of questions pertain to requesting attention, requesting tangibles, escaping demands, and receiving sensory stimulation. The pattern of scores across the series may indicate a single motivation or multiple motivations for the excess behavior. Comparing the scores across sets of questions may indicate the relative importance of each motivation.

Structured interviews are useful in that they elicit information about a learner's excess behavior from people who are familiar with the learner. Interviews are also relatively easy to conduct. However, because they are designed for use in a variety of situations, they may not be very sensitive to circumstances specific to the learner being assessed. To obtain more detailed information about the conditions under which a particular learner's excess behavior occurs, more open-ended questioning and direct observation techniques should be considered.

Direct Observation Direct observation of excess behavior often involves measurement over several days (possibly much longer) and/or several situations. The suitability of direct observation depends upon the frequency, duration, and predictability of the excess behavior. Behaviors that occur infrequently and behaviors that are not very predictable are not generally amenable to direct observation. The primary advantage of direct observation is that it provides the basis for the design of effective interventions by identifying specific naturally occurring conditions (both antecedents and consequences) that influence excess behavior. Because the learner is observed across a range of provoking situations, a more comprehensive description of the situations that provoke excess behavior may be obtained. The primary disadvantage of direct observation is that it is both time consuming and labor intensive.

A-B-C Analyses Analyses of behavioral antecedents and their consequences, known as A-B-C analyses, may reveal factors that relate to the excess behavior. For example, an A-B-C analysis may indicate that for a particular learner, headbanging (the behavior) is usually associated with having to wait for lunch (the antecedent), and usually results in the delivery of lunch (the consequence). Another learner may strike a caregiver (the behavior) whenever asked to go to the toilet (the antecedent), and the behavior typically may be followed by a stern lecture from a supervisor (the consequence).

As noted earlier, Meyer and Evans (1989) suggest that A-B-C analyses should also include a specification of situations in which the excess behavior is least likely to occur. They reason

that identification of situations associated with a low probability of excess behavior may help to specify modifications to the environment that might prevent or attenuate excess behavior.

The occurrence of excess behavior across times of day and days of the week can be plotted on a grid (Touchette, MacDonald, & Langer, 1985). Caregivers fill out the grid by indicating whether a particular excess behavior occurs within a given time period. The completed grid may reveal whether excess behavior tends to cluster around certain times of day or certain days of the week. This may be very important because certain times or days may be correlated with specific activities (e.g., down time, task demands). The completed grid may also suggest good times for caregivers to implement interventions. Codes may be added to the grid to describe ongoing circumstances and to specify the intensity, frequency, and type of excess behavior.

An example of a completed grid is shown in Figure 1. The completed grid reveals a pattern that the interventionist must try to decipher. The data were collected during the day at the learner's place of employment over a 2-week period. They reveal that most of the excess behaviors occurred in the morning, immediately before lunchtime. This finding should prompt the interventionist to investigate what happens in the morning that does not happen in the afternoon.

Sometimes grids are used as the initial instrument of data collection, followed by the use of a form requiring much more specific information from the caregiver. For example, the completed grid may indicate that self-injurious headbanging usually occurs around 5:00 P.M. Use of A-B-C analysis between 4:00 P.M. and 6:00 P.M. could then help pinpoint the provocative aspects of the environment during that period. Unlike simple frequency counts, which provide very rough estimates of the problem (Romanczyk, 1986), data collection records generated through A-B-C analyses provide a more precise

Name: _Larry K._

Description of behavior(s) of interest:

throwing objects

Directions: At the end of each fifteen minute interval fill in the square indicating the appropriate time and date on the chart using the code given below.

no behaviors ☐　　　one time ◹　　　more than once ◼

8:30-8:45												
8:45-9:00												
9:00-9:15												
9:15-9:30												
9:30-9:45												
9:45-10:00												
10:00-10:15												
10:15-10:30												
10:30-10:45												
10:45-11:00												
11:00-11:15												
11:15-11:30												
11:30-11:45												
11:45-12:00												
12:00-12:15												
12:15-12:30												
12:30-12:45												
12:45-1:00												
1:00-1:15												
1:15-1:30												
1:30-1:45												
1:45-2:00												
2:00-2:15												
2:15-2:30												
2:30-2:45												
2:45-3:00												
Date	Aug 1	Aug 2	Aug 3	Aug 4	Aug 5	Aug 8	Aug 9	Aug 10	Aug 11	Aug 12		

Figure 1.　A completed grid for tracking behavioral problems.

estimate of behavior during provocative circumstances. As archival records, A-B-C analyses and/or grids may be directly compared to data collected after intervention begins.

Functional Analyses Analyses of functional relationships (i.e., the reinforcement contingencies that maintain behavior) have consisted of demonstrating that excess behavior is more likely to occur under certain conditions than others. Determining the different levels of excess behavior associated with various conditions is conceptually similar to A-B-C analyses. Unlike an A-B-C analysis, a functional analysis involves actively manipulating conditions in order to test hypotheses and draw inferences about the causes of excess behavior. For example, a condition with task demands may be compared to a condition with no demands.

Typically, functional analyses have used conditions that simulate naturally occurring provocative situations. However, such contrived situations may have little resemblance to the contexts typically encountered by learners (Donnellan &

LaVigna, 1986; Evans & Meyer, 1985). Table 2 summarizes the results of some of the research that has been performed on assessment of excess behavior through simulation.

It is possible that the more contrived the conditions of functional analyses are, the less useful any inferences about excess behavior under natural conditions may be. An alternative approach would, therefore, be to conduct the functional analyses in the natural environment, contrasting conditions that are typically assumed to provoke the excess behavior with conditions known to provoke little or no excess

Table 2. Methods by which different studies analyzed motivations of excess behavior

Motivation	Methodology	Study
Effect of attention	A condition in which the excess behavior resulted in obtaining attention was compared to one in which the absence of behavior resulted in attention.	Iwata, Dorsey, Slifer, Bauman, & Richman, 1982; Sturmey, Carlsen, Crisp, & Newton, 1988
	A condition in which relatively little adult attention was available was compared to one in which much attention was available.	Carr & Durrand, 1985; Durrand & Carr, 1987; Durrand & Crimmins, 1988
Effect of tangibles or activities controlled by attending adult	A condition in which the excess behavior resulted in the opportunity to perform various activities controlled by the attending adult was compared to a condition in which no such contingency was in effect.	Lovaas, Freitag, Gold, & Kassorla, 1965
	A condition in which preferred tangibles were freely available was compared to a condition in which the tangibles were visible but not available.	Durrand, 1986
Effect of task demands	A condition in which demands were delivered frequently was compared to one in which no demands were delivered.	Carr & Newsom, 1985; Carr, Newsom, & Binkoff, 1976; Carr, Newsom, & Binkoff, 1980; Durrand, 1982; Weeks & Gaylord-Ross, 1981
	A condition in which the task was difficult to perform was compared to one in which the task was easier to perform.	Carr & Durrand, 1985; Durrand, 1982; Durrand & Carr, 1987; Weeks & Gaylord-Ross, 1981
	A condition in which task demands and the contingent removal of the demands following the excess behavior were present was compared to one in which task demands were present but their contingent removal was not.	Durrand & Carr, 1987; Durrand & Crimmins, 1987
	A condition in which task demands and the contingent removal of the demands following the excess behavior were present was compared to one in which no task demands were present.	Iwata et al., 1982; Sturmey et al., 1988

behavior. In addition to helping determine the context of instruction, specification of both types of conditions may help identify ecological modifications that might reduce excess behavior.

Because functional analysis involves the deliberate provocation of excess behavior, it may not be appropriate for all learners. Whenever a functional analysis that is likely to provoke excess behavior is contemplated, care must be taken to ensure that the procedure is ethically acceptable. The need to identify and study specific provocative circumstances and the likelihood that important knowledge will be uncovered using functional analyses should be weighed against the seriousness of the behavior. The analysis and interpretation of data collected during direct observation should result in a better understanding of the learner's excess behavior. Analysis of the data should seek to categorize conditions encountered by the learner as provoking or not provoking excess behavior. For example, if the average level of excess behavior is high under certain circumstances and low under others, the interventionist can infer that the former circumstances are provocative and the latter are not. If there is significant overlap in rates of excess behaviors across conditions, the interventionist cannot conclude that one condition causes more excess behavior than another.

TEACHING COMMUNICATION TO LEARNERS WHO ENGAGE IN EXCESS BEHAVIOR

Determining When Communication Instruction is Warranted

Views differ on the relationship between excess behavior and communication. In their seminal article, Donnellan, Mirenda, Mesaros, and Fassbender (1984) suggest that any excess behavior that occurs in the presence of others may be thought of as communicative.

The view that every learner who engages in excess behavior in the presence of others is a candidate for communication instruction is unsatisfactory, since other types of interventions may be better suited for some behavior problems (Axelrod, 1987; Day et al., 1988; Favell, McGimsey, & Schell, 1982; Mace & Knight, 1986; Repp, Felce, & Barton, 1988; Rincover & Devany, 1982). Day, Johnson, and Schussler (1986) have suggested that communicative *intent* should be a prerequisite for communicative instruction. Limiting communication instruction to learners who demonstrate communicative intent is unsatisfactory, however, because of the difficulty of operationalizing "intent," particularly in the context of excess behavior that is not socially motivated.

An alternative to rigid adherence to either view is to consider whether there is reason to believe the unacceptable behavior can be replaced or supplanted by a functional communicative alternative, and whether the learner's preferences can be honored.

Carr and Durand (1985), Durand and Carr (1987), and Durand and Crimmins (1988) have demonstrated the successful replacement of socially motivated excess behavior by more conventional means of communication. Through instruction, learners were taught to solicit attention by asking the teacher for praise and to reduce the difficulty of a task by requesting assistance from the teacher.

Doss (1988) demonstrated that functional alternatives can replace excess behaviors when those behaviors serve nonsocial functions. He identified four adults with developmental disabilities who took food from peers during lunch. The participants were taught to use graphic symbols to request food items they had taken in the past. Although taking food from others during lunch was probably motivated by nonsocial factors (e.g., access to food), a functional communicative alternative was nonetheless taught. This application of communication instruction is noteworthy because it emphasizes that behavior that serves a nonsocial function may be replaced by teaching a communicative skill that facilitates access to the maintaining reinforcer.

Determining When the Learner's Preferences Can be Honored

Teaching a learner to communicate may serve no purpose if the learner's communications will not be acted upon. For example, consider a learner who engages in self-injurious behavior to avoid going to work. Teaching the learner to replace this excess behavior with a more socially acceptable behavior would not make sense, since the rejection could not be honored (Meyer & Evans, 1989). In this instance, it would be preferable to teach the learner that leaving home and going to work results in being allowed to have a cup of coffee before work. Alternatively, the ride to work might be assessed to determine how unsettling an effect it has on the learner. Steps could be taken to try to reduce the stressfulness of the trip if it were found to be upsetting to the learner.

Communication Intervention Strategies Aimed at Minimizing Excess Repertoires

The tactics of communication instruction change when a learner performs excess behavior. Excess behavior often competes with more appropriate alternative behaviors. For example, in order to avoid a nonpreferred activity, a learner may strike a caregiver before the caregiver can prompt the learner to use a symbol or gesture for rejection. Hitting the caregiver competes with using an appropriate and socially acceptable form of rejection. In this example, communication instruction will be most efficient if the target communicative behavior can be prompted before the excess behavior occurs. A variety of communication intervention strategies may be useful in teaching learners alternatives to their existing repertoires of socially unacceptable behavior.

First, the interventionist must identify opportunities for implementing communication interventions to establish a repertoire that will compete with the learner's existing repertoire of socially motivated excess behavior. Second, the interventionist must determine what form the new communicative behavior should take (e.g., gestures, symbols). Third, the interventionist must decide whether it is important to establish a level of participation before introducing a communicative utterance that can be used to take leave (e.g., the learner must participate in an activity before being allowed to play).

Identifying Opportunities for Replacing Excess Behavior with Communication Effective instruction may depend upon gradually and systematically introducing circumstances the learner finds provocative into his or her day. Often, service providers have already developed effective methods of preventing excess behavior from occurring. For example, caregivers in a residence may avoid putting demands upon a particular learner because of the certainty that he or she will start striking caregivers and peers when demands are made. The desirable aspect of these ecological modifications is that the level of the excess behavior is kept low. The undesirable outcome is that the learner has little chance to experience the opportunities that come with environmental demands, and is unable to pursue a more normal lifestyle (e.g., holding a job in the community).

The immediate outcome of beginning communication instruction with a learner may be to increase the likelihood of excess behavior. Therefore, instructional strategies may have to incorporate the gradual introduction of demands while simultaneously keeping the excess behavior at an acceptable level.

Determining the Form of the Communicative Alternative If a learner is motivated by escape and can be aggressive to people nearby, a communicative alternative that may be discerned from a distance (e.g., "stop" gesture) may be preferable. Graphic symbols require that the listener be fairly close to the speaker in order to be understood.

The explicitness of the vocabulary selected for instruction may be important if the excess behavior is motivated by a particular event. For example, a learner may always hit his head with his fist when he wants a chocolate chip cookie. Teaching a generalized "want" symbol may not be specific enough in this situation. Instead, an explicit "chocolate chip cookie" symbol would be more appropriate.

Establishing Participation in Activities Prior to Establishing Communicative Alternatives   Releasing a learner from a nonpreferred activity usually reduces the frequency or intensity of excess behavior. One approach to replacing excess behavior produced to escape or avoid involves establishing a generalized rejecting or leavetaking response that could be used frequently during the initial phase of intervention. For example, in an undesired work activity, the learner might come to a task for a brief interval and then communicate that he or she wishes to leave (reject the task). If the learner produces the leavetaking symbol or gesture, he or she is released.

Establishing that a socially acceptable communicative alternative will result in release from an undesirable task will increase the frequency of learner's use of the socially acceptable leavetaking response. Eventually, staff members will have to teach the learner that there are some conditions in which use of the communicative alternative cannot be honored. At this point, the frequency and intensity of the excess behavior may increase.

An alternative to the scenario described above occurs in the context of increasing the learner's participation in tasks. In vocational settings, for example, it may be helpful to create conditions under which a successful work history can be established. Once the work history is established, the interventionist can establish ways for the learner to control his or her release from a task. The primary difference between this intervention strategy and the one initially described is that in the latter strategy, the use of a rejecting/leavetaking response is taught conditionally from the moment that it is implemented. In the former strategy, attention is focused on establishing the frequent use of a rejecting/leavetaking response.

Determining the Importance of the Provoking Activity   Sometimes considerable thought goes into matching a learner to a specific job. However, in other instances, the learner is assigned to an activity because someone on the learner's program team thought it might be a "good idea." If there is no compelling program logic for the activity, or if it does not appear critical to the learner's ability to work and live more independently, it may be advisable to consider whether that activity should be continued. Often the easiest way to reduce excess behavior is to change the arrangement of the learner's work. This may mean assigning the learner a new job, or partially altering the learner's current job in an effort to disrupt possible setting variables that occasion the excess.

Determining What the Learner Does Well in the Activity   It is very important to identify learner behaviors that can be reinforced. The interventionist should determine the amount of time or the amount of work the learner can be expected to complete before engaging in excess behavior. The goal is to identify a behavior that can be reinforced. If the interventionist has an idea of how much the learner can be expected to do before engaging in excess behavior, steps can be taken gradually to shape more participation.

Determining Objects or Activities That the Learner Would Prefer During Breaktime   The interventionist needs to establish him- or herself as the deliverer of breaks as well as the deliverer of work.

Using a Safety Signal   Safety signals, discussed in Chapter 6, can be used to reduce excess behavior. For example, Ralph, a 42-year-old man with severe retardation, was learning to load vending machines. Immediately upon arrival of work, Ralph would lie down on the floor. So great was his distaste for his job that teaching him a socially acceptable way to request leave would have resulted in constant requests to avoid work. Ralph's interventionists thus first implemented a program to increase his participation in work. Upon arriving at work, Ralph was offered a small cup of coffee before he lay down on the floor. Once the routine of immediately lying down on the floor was eliminated, the presentation of the coffee was delayed until Ralph had moved in the direction of the vending machines. A safety signal ("coffee break soon") was then delivered just prior to the delivery of the coffee. Eventually, Ralph had to walk to the work station and engage in a small amount of work prior to the delivery of a safety signal and the ensuing break. Eventually, a leavetaking symbol was introduced just prior to the production of the safety signal. Touching a leavetaking symbol after the safety signal had been given resulted in a brief break with desired, but not highly preferred, reinforcers. During other occasions, if Ralph worked until the end of a regular work activity, the break was extended and highly preferred reinforcers were made available. Eventually, Ralph's excess behavior was extinguished, his productivity increased, and he learned to control the time of his breaks.

Teaching Self-Regulation with Schedule and Message Boards Some learners who engage in excess behavior may do so because they are confused by a world that appears random and unpredictable. Learners with severe developmental disabilities often do not determine their own activities. Because their schedules are imposed on them, they may be confused by transitions and disruptions of routine. Excess behavior that takes place during transitions between activities or as a result of a change in routine may simply reflect the learner's confusion. The learner's response to transitions between activities and to disruptions of his or her routine should be recorded as part of the assessment, particularly if caregivers report intolerance of schedule changes. The record should note whether transitions were from pleasant to pleasant situations, from unpleasant to pleasant situations, or from unpleasant to unpleasant situations. This information will assist the interventionist in determining whether transition per se or the reinforcing qualities of tasks involved in the transition motivate the excess behavior.

The organization of the learner's day should be scrutinized, since the problem may not be transitions or disruptions of routine, but rather the way in which activities are organized in relation to one another during the day. For example, a learner may be expected to work at a boring task for long periods without a break. Less desired activities may not be interspersed with more desired activities. If the learner is frazzled because of a lack of predictability in his or her daily routine, providing a schedule board or activity calendar (discussed in Chapter 14) may be helpful. A *schedule board* is an activity calendar that lists the activities scheduled for the learner over a specified period of time. A *message board* informs the learner of particular chores or duties that need to be performed. There is evidence to suggest that the likelihood of some excess behaviors can be diminished by providing learners with a concrete method by which to regulate their lives by making activities in which they are about to engage more predictable and controllable. Schedule and message boards provide learners with needed reminders about their routines and social obligations without requiring others in the environment to provide that regulation. (The range of procedures that can be implemented to teach the use of schedule and message boards is discussed in detail in Chapter 14.)

To see how a message board might be used to reduce excess behavior, consider the following example. Caregivers may report that a learner becomes extremely agitated (e.g., yells, refuses to work, grabs at peers and staff) whenever her schedule varies from normal. A schedule board could be used to inform this learner of such changes, so that changes in her routine would not be unexpected. In the initial phase of intervention, instruction may consist of directing her to a board containing a photograph of the next scheduled activity. The learner would then be taught to gather the materials for that activity, and would be reinforced for participating in that activity. Participating in the listed activity competes with the excess behavior typically displayed when things are different from what the learner expects. Photographs of highly reinforcing items may also be placed on the board from time to time, and paired with delivering the item to the learner when she approaches the container holding the item. The idea is to make approaching the board and participating in the activity listed a pleasant experience for the learner.

Determining the Quantity of Available Instructional Opportunities

When teaching the learner to request as a replacement for excess behavior, the number of learning opportunities should be maximized. Because requests are used to procure desirable objects or activities, a large number of instructional opportunities may help to make the learner's environment more positive. In contrast, rejecting opportunities result in at least slightly unpleasant intrusions on the learner in which some less desirable item or activity is thrust upon him or her. Repeated exposure to rejecting opportunities may provoke excess behavior. Thus, the interventionist must carefully consider the number of opportunities to implement within a short interval of time.

Avoiding Provoking Excess Behavior During Learning Opportunities

By reinforcing the alternative immediately after or during an episode of excess behavior, the

danger exists that the excess behavior will be inadvertently reinforced, even if the chain includes the appropriate communicative alternative. Once an excess behavior has been produced, the use of more intrusive techniques to neutralize emergent crises may neutralize the goal of communicative instruction, which was to reduce the frequency and intensity of the excess behavior in a nonintrusive and educative manner (Evans & Meyer, 1985).

Delivering Instructional Prompts

Once the interventionist has determined the social motivations for an excess behavior, defined the communicative replacement behavior, and projected the point at which communicative instruction will be implemented, he or she can focus on developing the instructional prompts to be used. In developing instructional prompts, it is important to avoid establishing a behavioral chain in which the learner produces an excess behavior and then is prompted to produce the competing socially acceptable communicative behavior. Several potentially useful tactics for prompting socially acceptable communicative behavior while minimizing excess behavior are described in this section.

Taking on the Least Provocative Situation First It may be desirable to begin teaching a socially acceptable rejecting response by taking on the learner's mildest form of excess behavior. Choosing the less provoking instances for implementing communicative instruction allows the replacement communicative behavior to be established in the absence of intense excess behavior. A potential drawback to this strategy is that a relatively narrow range of intervention opportunities may be selected. During the early phases of intervention, generalization of the new communicative alternative is compromised significantly. Thus, if this option is chosen, great care must be exercised in quickly moving to new situations once some instructional control is established.

Using Milder Excess Behaviors to Cue Communication Many learners produce milder excess behaviors immediately prior to producing more severe excessive behaviors. For example, one learner tended to whine in response to task demands. If whining were unsuccessful in obtaining release from the task, he would throw work materials. During the initial assessment, behaviors that tend to serve as precursors to excess behaviors should be identified. Contingent upon the production of these precursors, the interventionist could prompt a socially acceptable response, followed by the corresponding rewarding consequence. The purpose of this technique is thus to interrupt a chain that predictably leads to the excess behavior. The drawback to this technique is that a socially marginal behavior (whining, in this example) is strengthened. The interventionist should assess any potential negative effects that may result from strengthening a marginal behavior. Any significant disadvantages should be anticipated so that the response prompts may be delivered before any signs of the marginal excess behavior occur. This requires staff who are familiar with the array of objects and activities that provoke the learner. Additionally, staff must be in a position to act quickly in order to prompt a target communicative response at the first sign of a provoking situation.

Using Two-Person Prompting Sometimes this need for quick action may require two staff members to prompt the desired behavior. In a two-person prompting procedure, one instructor approaches the learner with the provocative stimulus and another instructor approaches the learner from a different direction and delivers a prompt before the learner can perform an excess behavior.

Taking Advantage of Behavioral Momentum Mace et al. (1988) and Singer, Singer, and Horner (1987) have demonstrated that linking high- and low-compliance requests can increase the rate of compliance in the latter.

For example, a learner may be unlikely to comply with a request to make his bed (a low-compliance situation) but very likely to show his radio when requested to do so (a high-compliance situation). Asking the learner to show his radio may increase the likelihood of him complying with the later request to make his bed, because it creates an immediate history of reinforcement for compliant behavior. An alternative explanation for increased compliance is that the interventionist may be establishing him- or herself as a discriminative stimulus for reinforcement by first showing the learner that he or she is a source of rewarding outcomes.

This finding can be applied to communication instruction. Reinforcing an appropriate communicative alternative immediately before presenting an opportunity in a provocative context may set the stage for the use of the communicative alternative. For example, consider a learner who strikes out to obtain a favorite beverage, but who has not been observed to do so to obtain cookies (which he or she also likes.) Creating an opportunity for the learner to request a cookie before requesting the beverage may increase the likelihood that the communicative alternative rather than the excess behavior is used when the beverage is presented.

Using Response Interruption The preceding techniques might not always work well. It may be difficult to predict when a learner will produce excess behavior. There are also learners so provoked by certain situations that they engage in the excess behavior immediately. Under these circumstances response interruption may be helpful.

Response interruption has been used with differential reinforcement techniques to reduce a variety of excess behaviors, including rapid eating (Lennox, Miltenberger, & Donnelly, 1987), self-injury (Azrin, Besalel, & Wisotzek, 1982; Slifer, Iwata, & Dorsey, 1984), and self-stimulation (Fellner, LaRoche, & Sulzer-Azaroff, 1984). Billingsley and Neel (1985) and Doss

(1988) used response interruption to prevent food stealing while teaching appropriate requesting.

In provocative situations that have been targeted for communication instruction, excess behavior may be interrupted for a short period of time. At the termination of the interruption, the instructor prompts the learner to produce the communicative alternative. The shorter the interval, the more likely the excess will be chained to the communicative alternative. However, longer intervals may limit the usefulness of the learning opportunity.

The possibility of reinforcing a chain of behavior that includes the excess behavior is a potential drawback of this strategy. Response interruption should be used only in conjunction with other techniques and only as a backup when other methods fail. The complications associated with using response interruption need to be explored for each learner.

HYPOTHETICAL CASE STUDIES

John at Work

John is a 22-year-old man with profound retardation. Until very recently he lived in a public institution. He now resides in a community group home. He does not talk, and uses no other formal communication system regularly. He has a history of pica, self-injurious head-banging and hitting and pinching others. Both self-injury and the aggression toward others are sometimes severe. John had undergone a complete physical examination just prior to meeting with the technical assistance team.

First, the technical assistance provider conducted informal interviews, including the Motivational Assessment Scale (Durand & Crimmins, 1988), with staff members who worked regularly with John, asking them to describe his excess behaviors and to hypothesize about why he performed them. From these informal interviews, it was determined that staff members believed John's excess behaviors were related to task demands.

Once an initial hypothesis had been formulated, staff members were asked to record when the behaviors occurred (during which activities), how often they occurred, and how consistently they occurred. An unusual feature of the data collection instrument was that it required staff members to give their perceptions, at the time the excess behavior occurred, of why John performed the behavior. This feature allowed further corroboration of the initial hypothesis. Since the data collection instrument was based upon partial interval time sampling (i.e., if the behavior occurred at any time during the interval, the form was marked) of fairly long intervals, it was easy for staff members to use. Figure 2 shows a completed data collection form from a single day. During the intervals in which self-injurious behavior (SIB) and aggression occurred, caregivers almost always attributed the motivation to rejecting tasks. Staff were asked to describe any times during the day when they rarely observed the targeted behaviors. Determining when behaviors were not performed was important in further testing the hypotheses used to predict the motivation of the excess behavior. For example, if instances could be found in which John did not engage in excess behaviors when task demands were made, the hypothesis would require further refinement.

Once there were sufficient data to confirm that John did engage in specific excess behaviors during tasks, staff members were asked to develop a list of activities that John encountered regularly. Based upon this list, the more detailed data collection form shown in Figure 3 was developed. This form requires much more attention by staff members, since it involves noting how long after a task is introduced a particular excess behavior is performed. The purpose of this form is to specify the circumstances under which communication instruction should occur. The instrument allows assessment of both the range of excess behaviors and the

Motivation

Behavior

Directions:
For each interval mark an "x" in the box
corresponding to the type of behavior
(aggression, SIB, pica) and the presumed
reasons for the behavior (reject tasks,
request attention, request tangibles, or unknown).

Interval	Aggression	SIB	PICA	Reject tasks	Request tangibles	Request attention	Unknown	Comments and initials of observer
8:30-8:45		X		X				J.H.
8:45-9:00		X		X				S.D.
9:00-9:15			X				X	S.D.
9:15-9:30	X			X				S.D.
9:30-9:45								S.D.
9:45-10:00								J.D
10:00-10:15		X		X				S.D
10:15-10:30		X		X				RM - bolted from table
10:30-10:45								RM
10:45-11:00		X					X	RM
11:00-11:15	X			X				RM
11:15-11:30			X				X	RM
11:30-11:45								RM
11:45-12:00		X		X				RM - bolted from table
12:00-12:15		X		X				RM - bolted from table
12:15-12:30								RM - at lunch
12:30-12:45	X			X				RM - at lunch
12:45-1:00		X		X				RM - at work - bolted
1:00-1:15		X		X				RM
1:15-1:30								J.H.
1:30-1:45		X		X				J.H. - bolted
1:45-2:00		X		X				J.H.
2:00-2:15	X	X		X				J.H. -- bolted
2:15-2:30								J.H.
2:30-2:45	X			X				J.H.
2:45-3:00		X					X	J.H.

Figure 2.   A data collection instrument for assessing excess behavior by combining elements of interval data collection and A-B-C recording.

relationship between particular behaviors and particular tasks.

An interesting feature of the instrument shown in Figure 3 is that it provides information on how long John engaged in an activity before he performed excess behavior. This interval was used as an estimate of activity aversiveness, with shorter latencies corresponding to greater

Directions: For each task, record:
1. Whether the learner engaged in aggressive behavior (A), self-injury (SIB), pica (P), or attempted to bolt (B)
2. How long the learner worked before engaging in the excess behavior
3. The date, the time, and your initials

Task	Excess behavior	Work time prior to excess	Date and time	Excess behavior	Work time prior to excess	Date and time
Fill washer	SIB , B	5 min.	3/15 1ᵒᵒ P.M.	SIB	7 min.	3/19 2ᵒᵒ P.M.
Remove clothes from dryer	0	12 min.	3/15 1⁴⁵ P.M.	SIB	11 min.	3/19 2⁴⁵ P.M.
Wipe tables	B	10 min.	3/15 10ᵒᵒ A.M.	0	7 min.	3/19 9⁵⁰ A.M.
Take out garbage	A, B, SIB	30 sec.	3/15 12³⁰ P.M.	A, SIB	1 min.	3/19 12³⁰ P.M.
Wipe van seats	0	19 min.	3/15 3ᵒᵒ P.M.	0	21 min.	3/19 3¹⁵ P.M.

Figure 3.   A data collection instrument for assessing the effects of task demands on excess behavior.

aversiveness. It thus suggests which activities should be the targets of intervention first. Knowing how long John worked at an activity before producing an excess behavior was also important for designing safety signal conditioning procedures.

Several recommendations resulted from this assessment. First, staff members were instructed to try to make nonpreferred tasks more pleasant by providing John with a reinforcer contingent upon the performance of acceptable work over a prespecified period of time. Second, staff members were advised to schedule more breaks for John. These two ecological modifications of the work environment, while not related to communication instruction per se, served to reduce the general aversiveness of the work situation for John. The third recommendation was that a leave-taking program be designed. The program recommended consisted of placing a symbol ("stop") next to John.

When John touched the symbol, the task was terminated. Wiping the van seats (a task John did not find aversive) and filling the washer (a task John found somewhat aversive) were chosen first for intervention. After a predetermined period of time a safety signal was offered. The "stop" symbol was made available just prior to the safety signal. Whenever John touched the "stop" symbol after the safety signal, staff members terminated the task. Intervention was directed at teaching John to refrain from touching the symbol in the absence of a safety signal. Eventually, John was differentially consequated by being rewarded with a significantly longer break when he refrained from using the leavetaking symbol and did not engage in excess behavior.

Mary at Home

Mary is a 35-year-old woman with severe disabilities who has lived in a small group home in the community for 2 years. She had previously lived in a public institution. Mary speaks, but is not intelligible to most listeners. She has hit her head with her hand since she was 4 years old. The intensity and frequency of the hitting had recently increased.

As with John, the first step was to conduct informal interviews with staff members of Mary's home who knew her well. From the beginning of the interviews it was apparent that staff members felt that Mary's problems were not based upon communication deficits alone. They reported that Mary's menstrual cycle seemed to be related to both the frequency and the intensity with which she hit herself. Mary had a very regular 28-day menstrual cycle, and staff members reported that her hitting increased markedly the week before she began to menstruate and then decreased during the week of menstruation. They also reported that she appeared to be in distress when her hitting behavior was at its peak.

Staff members agreed that Mary tended to engage in hitting more often when demands were placed upon her and during transitions from one activity to another. Even during times when her menstrual period was not approaching, she hit herself in the head when certain demands were placed on her and during certain transitions.

Staff members were asked to list specific demands and transitions that were a problem for Mary. Understanding when activities occur in relation to one another during the day was judged to be very important, especially with a learner like Mary who seems to experience behavior problems around certain activities and/or transitions.

At one point in the interviews, caregivers were asked to identify Mary's preferences. The original purpose of this activity was to identify preferred objects or activities that could be used to reinforce participation in household chores. The interventionist discovered that caregivers did not know what objects or activities Mary

liked. Not knowing what Mary liked made it difficult to determine if Mary was being reinforced for engaging in less preferred activities or for moving through difficult transitions between activities.

Figure 4 shows the average number of times per day that Mary hit herself during the 6-month period immediately preceding intervention. The one feature that stands out is the periodicity of the data, with an increase in hitting occurring every 4th week. To analyze this periodicity further, data were summarized from the previous 6 months. The average across all of the weeks except every 4th week was compared with the average for every 4th week, and the high and low values for each of these data sets were calculated in order to evaluate how much the sets overlapped. The average frequency of hitting for the first set was about 90 per day, with a range of 65–110. The average frequency of hitting for the second set was 150 per day, with a range of 90–260. The averages were substantially different, and there was relatively little overlap between the two sets. Thus, the summaries corroborated the impression gained from interviews with staff and visual examination of the data that the pattern of excess behavior was substantially different during Mary's menstrual period.

Staff who worked with Mary were advised to seek consultation with a gynecologist. Concur-

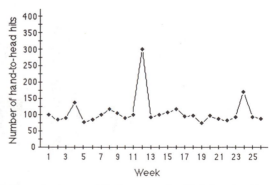

Figure 4. Average daily frequency of self-injurious hand-to-head hitting.

rently, the residence implemented a data collection system that was designed to evaluate suspected provocative and unprovocative conditions for Mary's hitting.

Figure 5 summarizes the frequency of hitting during particular activities over a 5-day period. Breaktime was included as a condition because staff members reported that Mary liked breaktime, a period during which she could sit quietly with no demands placed upon her. Breaktime thus served as a baseline condition. As Figure 5 indicates, hitting increased dramatically during transitions and during the nonpreferred work activity.

As a result of these assessment activities, Mary's preferences were identified and a variety of ecological modifications was proposed. Mary's schedule was made more predictable and was restructured to include frequent breaks, especially during activities she found unpleasant. Mary's schedule was made more predictable. Fourth, Mary was reinforced for successful transitions between activities. Steps were also taken to establish a picture schedule of activities. This increased the predictability of Mary's schedule. Photographs were used because one caregiver who knew her well suggested that she liked seeing herself in pictures. The consultant also advised that Mary be taught

the use of a gesture or symbol to escape appropriately from nonpreferred activities.

Mary saw a gynecologist and received a mild analgesic for menstrual discomfort. Mary's schedule was also altered slightly to include more frequent and slightly longer breaks during the week before her menstrual period.

SUMMARY

Excess behavior produced by learners with severe disabilities may often be motivated by attempts to communicate. This chapter has examined assessment and intervention strategies that can be implemented to replace socially motivated excess behavior with more socially acceptable communicative alternatives. Intervention will be most successful when the communicative behavior being taught closely matches the social motivation for the learner's excess repertoire. It is thus important that the range of provoking situations be carefully documented in assessment.

Efficient intervention procedures demand that the interventionist implement communication instruction proactively. Once the learner has produced serious excess behavior, it is very difficult to prompt a more socially acceptable com-

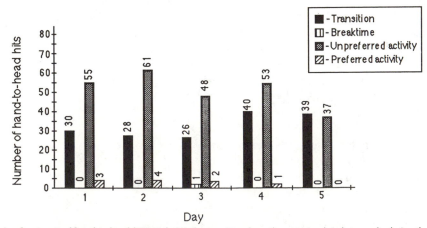

Figure 5. Average frequency of hand-to-head hitting during the transition from the morning break to work, during the morning break, during a preferred work activity, and during an unpreferred work activity.

municative alternative without reinforcing a chain of behavior that includes the excess behavior. Strategies for preempting excess behavior are only now being developed. As such strategies come to be implemented earlier and earlier, more dramatic results should emerge.

REFERENCES

Axelrod, S. (1987). Functional and structural analyses of behavior: Approaches leading to reduced use of punishment procedures? *Research in Developmental Disabilities, 8,* 165–178.

Azrin, N.H., Besalel, V.A., & Wisotzek, I.E. (1982). Treatment of self-injury by a reinforcement plus interruption procedure. *Analysis and Intervention in Developmental Disabilities, 2,* 105–113.

Bailey, J.S., & Pyles, D.A.M. (1989). In E. Cipani (Ed.), *The treatment of severe behavior disorders: Behavior analysis approaches* (pp. 85–107). Washington, DC: American Association on Mental Retardation.

Billingsley, F.F., & Neel, R.S. (1985). Competing behaviors and their effects on skill generalization and maintenance. *Analysis and Intervention in Developmental Disabilities, 5,* 357–372.

Bird, F., Dores, P.A., Moniz, D., & Robinson, J. (1989). Reducing severe aggressive and self-injurious behaviors with functional communication training. *American Journal on Mental Retardation, 94*(1), 37–48.

Carr, E.G., & Durand, V.M. (1985). Reducing behavior problems through functional communication training. *Journal of Applied Behavior Analysis, 18,* 111–126.

Carr, E.G., & McDowell, J.J. (1980). Social control of self-injurious behavior of organic etiology. *Behavior Therapy, 11,* 402–409.

Carr, E.G., & Newsom, C.D. (1985). Demand-related tantrums: Conceptualization and treatment. *Behavior Modification, 9*(4), 403–426.

Carr, E.G., Newsom, C.D., & Binkoff, J.A. (1976). Stimulus control of self-destructive behavior in a psychotic child. *Journal of Abnormal Child Psychology, 4*(2), 139–153.

Carr, E.G., Newsom, C.D., & Binkoff, J.A. (1980). Escape as a factor in the aggressive behavior of two retarded children. *Journal of Applied Behavior Analysis, 13,* 101–117.

Day, R.M., Johnson, W.L., & Schussler, N.G. (1986). Determining the communicative properties of self-injury: Research, assessment, and treatment implications. In K.D. Gadow (Ed.), *Advances in learning and behavioral disabilities* (Vol. 5, pp. 117–139). Greenwich, CT: JAI Press.

Day, R.M., Rea, J.A., Schussler, N.G., Larsen, S.E., & Johnson, W.L. (1988). A functionally based approach to the treatment of self-injurious behavior. *Behavior Modification, 12*(4), 565–589.

Donnellan, A.M., & LaVigna, G.W. (1986). *Alternatives to punishment: Solving behavior problems with non-aversive strategies.* New York: Irvington.

Donnellan, A.M., Mirenda, P.L., Mesaros, R.A., & Fassbender, L.L. (1984). Analyzing the communicative functions of aberrant behavior. *Journal of The Association for Persons with Severe Handicaps, 9*(3), 201–212.

Doss, L.S. (1988). *The effects of communication instruction on food stealing in adults with developmental disabilities.* Unpublished doctoral dissertation, University of Minnesota, Minneapolis.

Doss, L.S., & Reichle, J. (1989). Establishing communicative alternatives to the emission of socially motivated excess behavior: A review. *Journal of The Association for Persons with Severe Handicaps, 14,* 101–112.

Durand, V.M. (1982). Analysis and intervention of self-injurious behavior. *Journal of The Association for the Severely Handicapped, 7*(1), 44–53.

Durand, V.M. (1986). Self-injurious behavior as intentional communication. In K.D. Gadow (Ed.), *Advances in learning and behavioral disabilities* (Vol. 5, pp. 141–155). Greenwich, CT: JAI Press.

Durand, V.M., & Carr, E.G. (1987). Social influences on "self-stimulatory" behavior: Analysis and a treatment application. *Journal of Applied Behavior Analysis, 20,* 119–132.

Durand, V.M., & Crimmins, D.B. (1987). Assessment and treatment of psychotic speech in an autistic child. *Journal of Autism and Developmental Disorders, 17*(1), 17–28.

Durand, V.M., & Crimmins, D.B. (1988). Identifying the variables maintaining self-injurious behavior. *Journal of Autism and Developmental Disorders, 18*(1), 99–117.

Evans, I.M., & Meyer, L.H. (1985). *An educative approach to behavior problems: A practical decision model for interventions with severely handicapped learners.* Baltimore: Paul H. Brookes Publishing Co.

Favell, J.E., McGimsey, J.F., & Schell, R.M. (1982). Treatment of self-injury by providing alternate sensory activities. *Analysis and Intervention in Developmental Disabilities, 2,* 83–104.

Fellner, D.J., LaRoche, M., & Sulzer-Azaroff, B. (1984). The effects of adding interruption to differential reinforcement on targeted and novel self-stimulatory behaviors. *Journal of Behavior Therapy and Experimental Psychiatry, 15,* 315–321.

Gardner, W.I., Cole, C.L., Davidson, D. P., & Karan, O.C. (1986). Reducing aggression in individuals with developmental disabilities: An expanded stimulus control, assessment, and intervention model. *Education and Training of the Mentally Retarded, 21,* 3–12.

Goetz, L., Schuler, A., & Sailor, W. (1981). Functional competence as a factor in communication instruction. *Exceptional Education Quarterly, 2*(1), 51–60.

Gunsett, R.P., Mulick, J.A., Fernald, W.B., & Martin, J.L. (1989). Brief report: Indications for medical screening prior to behavioral programming for severely and profoundly mentally retarded clients. *Journal of Autism and Developmental Disorders, 19*(1), 167–172.

Hart, B. (1981). Pragmatics: How language is used. *Analysis and Intervention in Developmental Disabilities, 1,* 299–313.

Heidorn, S.D., & Jensen, C.C. (1984). Generalization and maintenance of the reduction of self-injurious behavior maintained by two types of reinforcement. *Behaviour Research and Therapy, 22,* 581–586.

Horner, R.H., & Billingsley, F.F. (1988). The effect of competing behavior on the generalization and maintenance of adaptive behavior in applied settings. In R.H. Horner, G. Dunlap, & R.L. Koegel (Eds.), *Generalization and maintenance: Lifestyle changes in applied settings* (pp. 197–220). Baltimore: Paul H. Brookes Publishing Co.

Horner, R.H., & Budd, C.M. (1985). Acquisition of manual sign use: Collateral reduction of maladaptive behavior, and factors limiting generalization. *Education and Training of the Mentally Retarded, 20,* 39–47.

Iwata, B.A., Dorsey, M.F., Slifer. K.J., Bauman, K.E., & Richman, G.S. (1982). Toward a functional analysis of self-injury. *Analysis and Intervention in Developmental Disabilities, 2,* 3–20.

Lennox, D.B., Miltenberger, R.G., & Donnelly, D.R. (1987). Response interruption and DRL for the reduction of rapid eating. *Journal of Applied Behavior Analysis, 20,* 279–284.

Lovaas, O.I., Freitag, G., Gold, V.J., & Kassorla, I.C. (1965). Experimental studies in childhood schizophrenia: Analysis of self-destructive behav-

ior. *Journal of Experimental Child Psychology, 2,* 67–84.

Lovaas, O.I., & Simmons, J.Q. (1969). Manipulation of self-destruction in three retarded children. *Journal of Applied Behavior Analysis, 2,* 143–157.

Mace, F.C., Hock, M.L., Lalli, J.S., West, B.J., Belfiore, P., Pinter, E., & Brown, D.K. (1988). Behavioral momentum in the treatment of noncompliance. *Journal of Applied Behavior Analysis, 21,* 123–141.

Mace, F.C., & Knight, D. (1986). Functional analysis and treatment of severe pica. *Journal of Applied Behavior Analysis, 19,* 411–416.

Meyer, L.H., & Evans, I.M. (1989). *Nonaversive intervention for behavior problems: A manual for home and community.* Baltimore: Paul H. Brookes Publishing Co.

Morreau, L.E. (1985). Assessing and managing problem behaviors. In K.C. Lakin & R.H. Bruininks (Eds.), *Strategies for achieving community integration of developmentally disabled citizens* (pp. 105–128). Baltimore: Paul H. Brookes Publishing Co.

O'Neill, R.E., Horner, R.H., Albin, R.W., Storey, K., & Sprague, J.R. (1989). *Functional analysis: A practical assessment guide.* Eugene: University of Oregon Press.

Prutting, C.A. (1982). Pragmatic and social competence. *Journal of Speech and Hearing Disorders, 47,* 123–134.

Repp, A.C., Felce, D., & Barton, L.E. (1988). Basing the treatment of stereotypic and self-injurious behaviors on hypotheses of their causes. *Journal of Applied Behavior Analysis, 21,* 281–289.

Rincover, A., & Devany, J. (1982). The application of sensory extinction procedures to self-injury. *Analysis and Intervention in Developmental Disabilities, 2,* 67–81.

Romanczyk, R.G. (1986). Self-injurious behavior: Conceptualization, assessment, and treatment. In K.D. Gadow (Ed.), *Advances in learning and behavioral disabilities* (Vol. 5, pp. 29–56). Greenwich, CT: JAI Press.

Singer, G.H.S., Singer, J., & Horner, R.H. (1987). Using pretask requests to increase the probability of compliance for students with severe disabilities. *Journal of The Association of Persons with Severe Handicaps, 12,* 287–291.

Slifer, K.J., Iwata, B.A., & Dorsey, M.F. (1984). Reduction of eye gouging using a response interruption procedure. *Journal of Behavior Therapy and Experimental Psychiatry, 15*(4), 369–375.

Smith, M.D. (1985). Managing the aggressive and self-injurious behavior of adults disabled by autism. *Journal of The Association for Persons with Severe Handicaps, 10*(4), 228–232.

Sturmey, P., Carlsen, A., Crisp, A.G., & Newton, J.T. (1988). A functional analysis of multiple aberrant responses: A refinement and extension of Iwata et al.'s (1982) methodology. *Journal of Mental Deficiency Research, 32*, 31–46.

Sulzer-Azaroff, B., & Mayer, G.R. (1986). *Achieving educational excellence using behavioral strategies.* New York: Holt, Rinehart, & Winston.

Thompson, T. (1985). *Maladaptive behavior scale (MABS).* Unpublished manuscript, University of Minnesota, Minneapolis.

Touchette, P.E., MacDonald, R.F., & Langer, S.N. (1985). A scatter plot for identifying stimulus control of problem behavior. *Journal of Applied Behavior Analysis, 18,* 343–351.

Weeks, M., & Gaylord-Ross, R. (1981). Task difficulty and aberrant behavior in severely handicapped students. *Journal of Applied Behavior Analysis, 14,* 449–463.

12

Accommodating Severe Physical Disabilities

Jennifer York and Gloria Weimann

MANY PEOPLE WHO require the use of augmentative or alternative communication systems have severe physical disabilities. Motor competencies directly affect the ability to communicate since a person must exert some control over body position and movement in order to communicate efficiently. The manner in which a person communicates can range, for example, from stiffening the body to indicate excitement to pointing to objects or symbols with a hand, foot, or eyes, to deflecting a switch connected to an attention getting buzzer or more sophisticated electronic communication aid. Efficient movement of the head, hands, and even the eyes depends on a stable and well-aligned body position from which to move (Bergen & Colangelo, 1982; Hardy, 1984; Ward, 1984). For example, if a person must use his or her arms for balance in order to remain in an upright sitting position, the arms cannot be used to point to a symbol on a communication board. It is thus crucial that the learner achieve a stable body position that provides a good view of the surrounding environment, and from which functional and efficient movements are possible. Specifically, the team of people that serves the learner must identify body positions that are stable, well-aligned, and comfortable, and body movements (e.g., pointing, eye gaze) that are reliable and accurate enough to be used for communication.

The purposes of this chapter are to provide an overview of the motor functioning of and difficulties encountered by people with severe physical disabilities, to discuss positioning as it relates to augmentative communication, and to discuss ways to improve body posture and movement in order to enable access to and use of an augmentative communication system.

NEUROMOTOR FUNCTION

The body system responsible for motor functioning is called the *neuromotor system*. It is comprised of the skeletal system, the muscular system, and the nervous system. The skeletal system is comprised of the bones and joints of the body that provide the structure to which muscles are attached. The muscular system is a very complex, interconnected, and multileveled arrangement of muscles. For example, muscles of the head and neck extend into the muscles of the upper trunk. Muscles in the upper trunk extend into the shoulder girdle muscles, which extend into the upper arm, then into the forearm and hand. Because of this interconnectedness, position and movement in one part of the body affect position and movement in other parts of the body. For example, before efficient use of the arm and hand is possible, the trunk and shoulder girdle must be appropriately aligned and stable. To see this, rest your right forearm in your lap. Place your left hand on the outside of your right shoulder. Now, try to lift your right forearm out of your lap without tensing up the muscles around your right shoulder. This is not possible.

The nervous system is made up of the central nervous system, consisting of the brain and spinal cord, and the peripheral nervous system, including the nerves extending from the central nervous system to the muscles. The nervous system is responsible for both sending messages out to muscles to contract or relax and for receiving sensory information about the position and movement of joints and muscles. Motor functioning is thus referred to more accurately as *sensori-motor* functioning (Bly, 1983). The sensation of movement is reinforced and begins to feel more efficient through repetition (Finnie, 1975). This is why after becoming proficient at a movement (e.g., throwing a ball), one can determine just by the feel of the movement if the movement has been made properly. The sensory feedback is integral to motor learning. We can, for example, tell the position of our body without looking (i.e., with eyes closed) because we get feedback from our joints and muscles about our current body position. This is an important concept to understand when working with people who have difficulty moving. As they spend hours each day positioned or moving in inefficient ways, they receive sensory feedback about their positions and movements. Be-

cause of this constant sensory feedback, undesirable positions and movements feel normal and become habitual. In order to acquire and maintain more efficient positions and movements, therefore, more efficient positions and patterns of movement must be experienced for sustained periods of time.

People with physical disabilities are often unable to coordinate input to different groups of muscles that surround a joint, an important function of the nervous system called "reciprocal innervation." For example, in order to bend (flex) the elbow, the muscles that bend the elbow must contract and concurrently, the muscles that extend the elbow must relax. In order to achieve efficient arm movement, certain muscles must remain relaxed while others contract. This type of coordination is often impaired in people with neuromotor dysfunction. For example, a person whose arms are held tightly in a bent position may not be able to relax the tension to allow straightening. Over time, the muscles actually become shorter.

The main functions of the neuromotor system are, then, to provide *postural control* and to allow *functional movement* for interaction with the environment (e.g., mobility, hand use for communication) (Ward, 1984). A basic understanding of the functioning of the neuromotor system is essential to understanding how and why body position and movement affect communication and participation in daily activities.

NEUROMOTOR DYSFUNCTION

Neuromotor dysfunction is caused by damage to the nervous system that results in impaired sensorimotor function. One of the most common causes of neuromotor dysfunction is cerebral palsy, a disorder of posture and movement that results from damage to the brain. Damage to the nervous system may result in abnormal muscle tone and reflex movement patterns that are obligatory and persist long after they should have been integrated (Levitt, 1982).

Abnormal Muscle Tone

Muscle tone refers to the degree of tension in a muscle. Currently, there is debate about the usefulness and accuracy of the traditional conceptualization of "muscle tone." Terms such as "postural tone" or "postural set" are considered more accurate descriptors (Ward, 1984). Here, however, the traditional references to hypotonicity, hypertonicity, and fluctuating tone are used, as they still prevail in practice.

For the body to maintain itself in an upright position and be able to move, there must be sufficient tension. However, too much tension will prevent the body from moving. Damage to the central nervous system may cause muscle tone to be hypotonic (insufficiently tense), hypertonic (excessively tense), or fluctuating (Levitt, 1982; Ward, 1984).

Hypotonicity refers to abnormally low muscle tone, and can result in a lack of joint stability, excessive range of motion, and the inability to maintain enough postural tone to remain upright against gravity. People with low tone frequently have a weak, floppy, or slumped appearance. They are also at risk for subluxation or dislocation of joints, because the joint surfaces are not as close together as normal, and because the lack of muscle tension permits range of joint motion beyond normal limits. In some situations, people with low tone will attempt to make up for the lack of joint stability by "fixing" (Bly, 1983). For example, in order to attain adequate stability around the shoulder joint to use the arm and hand, people with hypotonicity may raise their shoulders and lower their heads so that the shoulder and side of the head push against each other, resulting in greater, although atypical and potentially detrimental, stability. Over time, such abnormal fixing can result in shortening of the muscles, and limited range of motion around the joint. Limited range of joint motion impairs active movement and makes passive (assisted) movement difficult for caregivers.

Hypertonicity, or spasticity, refers to abnormally high muscle tone. Hypertonic muscles tend to rest in a shortened position, resulting in severe joint motion limitations and extreme difficulty in attempting to move. Most people with hypertonicity also tend to develop muscle imbalances. This means that certain sets of muscles tend to dominate, resulting in the maintenance of undesirable posturing of the total body. For example, some people tend to assume rigid, extended postures in which the lower extremities, spine, head, and neck are pushed backward. Such extreme postures indicate an imbalance of muscle tone and control. If prolonged, muscle imbalance can result in deformities.

Fluctuating muscle tone, or *athetosis,* refers to variations in muscle tone, usually from the extremes of very low to high tone. Movement is unsteady and uncoordinated and is sometimes extraneous, making the use of the arms extremely difficult.

While some people with central nervous system damage have predominantly hypotonic, hypertonic, or fluctuating muscle tone, both the type and degree of muscle tone can vary greatly within an individual. Differences between muscle tone during rest and muscle tone during movement or function can be extreme. Intervention strategies for achieving more efficient movement and posture will vary given the state of tension and control.

Interventions for people who have abnormal muscle tone that interferes with postural control and movement are designed to minimize the effects of abnormal tone by positioning, by facilitating active and controlled movement patterns, and by providing adequate stability (either manually or through the use of positioning equipment) so that movement is possible. Specific approaches to positioning and facilitating more efficient movement are discussed later in this chapter.

Persistent Reflexes

Reflexive movement patterns are a typical part of the sensorimotor progression of developing infants. Reflexive movement patterns provide the basis for development of voluntary muscle control. Much of the initial movement demonstrated by infants takes the form of reflex patterns involving the entire body. Over time, the infant develops greater intention and control of movement to accomplish specific functions, such as reaching for a toy or manipulating a spoon. Reflex patterns of movement become a problem when they persist beyond the point at which more sophisticated and voluntary muscle control should develop, and when they become obligatory, meaning that they almost always occur when any movement is attempted. In order for movement to be functional, the ability to isolate movement in one part of the body must be present. For example, the ability to reach with one hand is impaired if the entire body becomes tense and the head turns to the side, unable to maintain a midline orientation. Reflex patterns of movement typically involve the entire body to some extent, thus making more efficient and isolated functional movement impossible.

Traditionally, the term "reflex" has been used to describe particular recurring patterns of movement. Because there is often a range of variability in the actual movement patterns exhibited, practitioners now refer to "movement patterns or postures" instead of "reflexes." Traditional labeling of the movement patterns as "reflexes" has remained in isolated descriptions, such as those provided in the following section, which describes several of the most commonly observed reflex patterns of movement seen in people with neuromotor dysfunction (Ford, 1984; Levitt, 1982; Ward, 1984).

Galant Reflex   The Galant reflex is elicited by touching alongside the spine. This causes the muscles to shorten on the side stimulated, resulting in lateral curvature of the spine. This reflex is present at birth, but is normally integrated (i.e., replaced by a more sophisticated pattern) by 2 months of age. If it persists, the development of symmetrical trunk control in a seated position may be compromised. Asymmetrical positioning of the spine diminishes trunk stability and functional hand use. Eventually, scoliosis can develop. The effects of the Galant reflex can be counteracted by promoting and maintaining symmetrical positioning through handling procedures, use of therapeutic positioning equipment, and development of active muscle control.

Asymmetrical Tonic Neck Reflex   The asymmetrical tonic neck reflex (ATNR) is evoked by the turning of the head and results in an asymmetrical "fencer" posturing of the extremities and trunk. It is present at birth, and is usually integrated by 6 months of age. In the ATNR, the arms, legs, and trunk on the face side extend, and the arms, legs, and trunk on the skull side of the head flex. This posturing prevents symmetrical midline positioning and interferes with midline and hand-to-mouth use of the arms and midline orientation of the eyes. The focus of intervention in people dominated by ATNR posturing is to achieve and maintain midline orientation of the head, neck, and trunk through handling, development of active head control, and use of therapeutic positioning equipment.

Symmetrical Tonic Neck Reflex   The symmetrical tonic neck reflex (STNR) is evoked by moving the head forward into flexion or backward into extension. When the head moves forward into flexion, the arms flex and the legs extend. When the head falls back into extension, the arms extend and the legs flex. In infants without disabilities, this reflex posturing is seen at about 3 months and is integrated by 9 months as more active control in sitting is demonstrated. Persistence of this reflex prevents trunk rotation and lateral weight shifting, thereby interfering with reciprocal and unilateral use of the extremities. Intervention seeks to achieve and maintain a midline orientation of the head and neck by promoting better active control of head movement and by the use of appropriate therapeutic positioning.

Tonic Labyrinthine Reflex The tonic labyrinthine reflex (TLR) is elicited by the head position in space. When lying face down on the stomach (prone lying), the body responds by flexing or bending in toward the ground. The head/neck, arms, trunk, and hips all flex. When lying face up on the back (supine lying), the body responds by extending or pushing away from the ground. The head/neck, shoulders, trunk, and legs push backwards strongly. The tonic labyrinthine reflex is present at birth, and is usually integrated by 6 months of life. Persistent and obligatory posturing interferes with all sensorimotor development upward against gravity. Intervention focuses on avoiding positions that elicit this response pattern, and on developing active muscle control and use of therapeutic positioning equipment in order to achieve appropriate head position.

Supporting Reactions Supporting reactions, usually present until about 2 months of age, are elicited by holding the infant in a standing position, which results in a massive extension and inward turning of the legs to bear weight. Persistence interferes with a normal weight-bearing pattern, with control between extension and flexion of the joints in the legs, and with slight outward turning. Intervention is aimed at promoting controlled weight bearing through the legs with the ankle in flexion and the development of more active control through the pelvis and lower extremities.

POSITIONING AND HANDLING

Positioning and handling are the terms generally used to refer to the interventions designed to reduce the effects of abnormal muscle tone and persistent reflex patterns of movement, and to improve functional posture and movement.

Positioning is the process by which specific body parts, or the entire body, are manipulated and aligned so as to obtain the most desirable postures in which to maximize function. People without physical disabilities automatically position themselves to maximize efficiency and function. Functional positioning for people with physical disabilities is not a goal of intervention, but a means by which functional goals can be accomplished. For example, a goal might be for a learner to request a food item during snack time. In order to accomplish this goal, the learner would need to be positioned in a stable, upright position in the wheelchair so that efficient arm use (to point to the "want" symbol) was possible.

Handling refers to hands-on (i.e., direct contact) interaction with a person who has difficulty moving in order to achieve appropriate alignment and stability of body parts and to facilitate efficient movement. Handling procedures, therefore, can be considered a special type of physical assistance. When people have difficulty maintaining functional postures or executing efficient movements, team members, usually led by occupational and physical therapists, design interventions, referred to as positioning and handling procedures, to maximize participation in daily activities. Interventions are aimed at achieving well-aligned, usually symmetrical positions that promote function, and promoting efficient movement to participate in daily activities. Although positioning and handling are sometimes introduced separately, they are, in fact, complementary aspects of intervention. A number of principles should be kept in mind in designing positioning and handling interventions.

1. Use Yourself As a Reference

When deciding how best to position and move a person with a physical disability, it is helpful to analyze how a person without any physical disability is positioned and moves. Learn to use yourself as a reference (Campbell, 1986). If you were to perform the task demanded of the learner, how would you position yourself? What body position would you assume? How would your trunk be aligned? How would your head, arms, and legs be positioned? Assume the position, engage in the activity, analyze your posture and movement, and then use this information as one basis for determining effective postures and movements for your clients.

2. Employ Dynamic Forms of Assistance

There are two types of positioning, static and dynamic. *Static positioning* involves the use of equipment (e.g., a wheelchair with adaptations) to maintain the learner in a desirable position. When using equipment, the learner is usually supported externally in a relatively confined posture. This is referred to as static positioning because the supports do not automatically adjust as the learner requires more or less support to maintain the desired position at any moment in time. *Dynamic positioning* involves providing physical assistance for external support. For example, a caregiver may hold a child's trunk in a stable, vertical position so that the child can work at holding his or her head up independently. The support is dynamic in that as the learner is able to remain well-aligned independently, the person providing assistance lessens the degree of physical support. If the learner begins to lose control, the person providing dynamic support increases assistance for postural control. Dynamic support is highly desirable because it adjusts to the learner's ability to maintain postural control and maximizes the learner's active involvement. Essentially, dynamic assistance can be considered as a hands-on application of shaping and fading instructional procedures, described in greater detail in Chapter 9.

3. Use Key Points of Control

The concept of key points of control is useful in helping to decide where to provide assistance (Boehme, 1988; Finnie, 1975). Key points of control are those parts of the body from which joint position and muscle tension usually can be influenced most effectively. In general, these are proximal (i.e., close to the central part of the body) locations, such as the hips and pelvis and the shoulders. One reason that key points are proximal is that joint alignment and muscle tension in the proximal part of the body affects joint alignment and tension in more distal body parts (e.g., hands, fingers). Proximal stability and control are a necessary basis for distal control and function. Leverage and mechanical advantage are also offered by proximal points. When facilitating more efficient movement, it is important to consider that movement occurs in particular patterns involving multiple joints. That is, hand function is affected by simultaneous movement or patterning of the entire arm.

4. Keep in Mind That Repetition Facilitates Learning

Repetition of movement and prolonged periods of time in appropriate well aligned positions are important principles for intervention (Levitt, 1982). As efficient positions and movement are assumed and maintained, there is continual sensory feedback from the receptors in the muscles and in the joints about how it feels to be positioned and to move efficiently. This is necessary to counterbalance, at least to some degree, the continual sensory feedback about poor positioning and inefficient movement experienced by some people with physical disabilities. Team members, therefore, must strive to increase the amount of time that people with physical disabilities spend maintaining appropriate positions and moving efficiently, and decrease the amount of time spent maintaining maladaptive postures and engaging in inefficient movement.

5. "Normalize" Muscle Tone

Although it is unlikely that muscle tone can be made normal, efforts should be made to move in the direction of more normal and balanced tension in the muscles (Levitt, 1982). There must be adequate muscle tone to hold the body upright against gravity but not so much that movement is restricted. If a learner has excessive flexor tone resulting in rigid bending of the arms, for example, he or she will be unable to extend the arm to reach and point to a symbol on a communication board. Learning to provide physical assistance so as to normalize muscle tension and facilitate movement requires confidence obtained through considerable practice. Muscle tension can be reduced through firm, but rhythmic and gentle movement. Muscle tension is generally increased through quick, irregular movement and sometimes by bearing weight through the extremities, in standing, for example. With people with low muscle tone, great care must be taken to protect joints and not to allow movement into excessive ranges of motion. All members of the team who have frequent contact with a learner with physical disabilities should receive coaching from an occupational or physical therapist or other team member who has determined effective and safe handling procedures for that learner.

6.   Obtain a Stable Base of Support

Stability is required for mobility or function (Ward, 1984). Without the feet to stabilize the lower part of the body and the forearm to stabilize the upper part of the body, mobility and function are difficult. Two important points of stability are eliminated without the feet and forearms. The feet stabilize the lower part of the body and the trunk. The forearms stabilize the arms, shoulders, upper trunk, and wrists. Without these points of stability, the task of writing is much more difficult. Function and interaction thus depend critically on a stable base of support.

7.   Achieve Symmetry of Alignment

In general, symmetrical alignment of posture should be sought (Boehme, 1988; Ward, 1984). A symmetrical midline orientation provides the best view of the environment. In a seated position, the head/neck and trunk should be oriented to the midline of the body as opposed to asymmetrically oriented to one side or the other.

Asymmetrical postures tend to become habitual and can lead to inefficient alignment for function and to permanent deformity. Frequently, people with physical disabilities have muscle imbalance and have difficulty maintaining symmetrical upright positions, causing the body to slump to one side or the other. Prolonged asymmetrical posturing can result in deformity that diminishes functional movement, restricts the view of the environment, impinges on internal organs, and presents extreme difficulties for caregivers who provide assistance in dressing, eating, and other daily activities.

8.   Ensure That a Variety of Positions Is Assumed

In addition to improving function, positioning and handling interventions are intended to prevent debilitating deformities. Often deformities can be prevented by ensuring that the learner spends time in a variety of positions each day and by promoting active postural control (Bergen & Colangelo, 1982; Ward, 1984). By definition, body parts are aligned differently in different positions. In a seated position, for example, the hips, knees, and ankles are bent; in a prone position, the hips, knees, and ankles are straightened. As the body works to remain upright in various positions, different muscle groups need to work actively against gravity. The physical or occupational therapist can assist other team members in identifying appropriate positions to assume and maintain throughout the course of the day.

DESIGNING POSITIONING AND HANDLING INTERVENTIONS FOR COMMUNICATION

Positioning and handling procedures are an integral part of any augmentative communication system designed for people who have difficulty maintaining appropriate positions and moving efficiently (Campbell, 1989; MacNeela, 1987).

Physical and occupational therapists usually help to develop assessment and intervention procedures for people who have difficulty moving. Family members, service providers, and friends usually have the greatest knowledge of functional demands and opportunities experienced by the learner in the course of his or her daily activities. Knowledge of neuromotor functioning and of daily demands must be integrated in designing interventions. Together, team members establish individualized positioning and handling procedures to be implemented during specific daily activities.

Functional
Positioning for Communication

Most daily activities call for an upright position. In this position, the head is stable, and the eyes can scan the environment and make eye contact, two important aspects of communication. Many people with severe physical disabilities are unable to stand or walk, and spend most of the day seated upright in a wheelchair. Appropriate seated positioning, therefore, is a primary consideration for the team. All people with physical disabilities, however, should spend portions of their day in positions other than sitting, such as supported standing and lying. When designing a communication system, the team must consider the range of positions in which use of the system must be accommodated. Too often, systems are designed to accommodate only a seated position, rendering a learner without a means of communication during those portions of the day when he or she is not in a seated position.

Seated Positioning   Campbell (1989) provides a sound rationale for working to establish a stable and well-aligned seated position: 1) most people function better in an upright position than when lying; 2) too frequently, the only piece of adaptive positioning equipment available is a wheelchair; and 3) sitting is an age-appropriate position in school, community, and work settings. In the seated position, the hips, knees, and sometimes trunk are flexed (or bent). Use of other positions that counterbalance sitting, that is, positions in which the hips, knees, and trunk are extended, must also be integrated daily to prevent or reduce the severity of contractures and orthopedic deformities that can result from maintaining any position for a long period of time.

There is a definite order to achieving a well-aligned, stable seated position. Guidelines offered here are based on the work of various authors (Bergen & Colangelo, 1982; Fraser, Hensinger, & Phelps, 1987; MacNeela, 1987; Rainforth & York, 1987; Taylor, 1987; Trefler & Taylor, 1984). Appropriate positioning begins with the pelvis, which provides the base of support from which the lower extremities and the spine, head, and neck align. In order to maintain an appropriate position of the pelvis, the thighs, legs, and feet must be well aligned and stable also. After the lower part of the body (the pelvis and lower extremities) is positioned, the trunk, upper extremities, head, and neck are positioned. A checklist that can be used to guide seated positioning efforts is presented in Figure 1. Guidance from a learner's therapist or from a family member should be sought in developing specific strategies for assuming a well-aligned and supported seated position, since precautions must be taken in handling many people with severe physical disabilities and multiple handicaps. Some people react negatively to certain types of assistance. Some have bones that are very brittle and cannot withstand much external pressure. Others have deformities that preclude attempts to achieve a position considered desirable or normal.

As the team assesses the seated position, it is important to determine both whether the learner can assume and maintain a stable, well-aligned seated position independently, and how much assistance he or she will require. For example, some people may require assistance to assume a well-aligned seated position but once positioned can maintain the position independently. Others

PELVIS AND HIPS
_____ Hips flexed to 90°
_____ Pelvis tilted slightly forward
_____ Pelvis centered in the back edge of seat
_____ Pelvis not rotated forward on one side

THIGHS AND LEGS
_____ Thighs equal in length
_____ Thighs slightly abducted (apart)
_____ Knees flexed to 90°

FEET AND ANKLES
_____ Aligned directly below or slightly posterior to knees
_____ Ankles flexed to 90°
_____ Feet supported on footrest
_____ Heel and ball of feet bearing weight
_____ Feet and toes facing forward

TRUNK
_____ Symmetrical, not curved to the side
_____ Slight curve at low back
_____ Erect upper back, slight extension

SHOULDERS, ARMS, AND HANDS
_____ Relaxed, neutral position (not hunched up or hanging low)
_____ Upper arm flexed slightly forward
_____ Elbows flexed in midrange (about 90°)
_____ Forearms resting on tray to support arms and shoulders if necessary to maintain alignment
_____ Forearms neutral or rotated downward slightly
_____ Wrists neutral or slightly extended
_____ Hand relaxed, fingers and thumb opened

HEAD AND NECK
_____ Midline orientation
_____ Slight chin tuck (back of neck elongated)

Figure 1.   Checklist for assessing efficiency of seated position.

may require assistance both to assume and to maintain appropriate positions. One general approach to positioning assessment is outlined here.

1. Provide an opportunity for the learner independently to assume and maintain a seated position. Observe the movement patterns and resulting sitting posture to determine if there might be ways to improve the efficiency of movement and positioning.

2. If the learner is not able independently to assume a seated position, provide assistance while allowing the greatest degree of participation possible. The learner's participation can range from keeping the head relaxed and forward to preventing rigid extension when being assisted into the wheelchair to performing a standing pivot transfer with minimal assistance for balance.

3. If the learner is not able independently to maintain an appropriate seated position, use your hands firmly and smoothly to move the learner into a position that is stable and approximates better alignment. Begin by providing assistance at proximal body parts, beginning with the pelvis. The trunk and the legs align from the pelvis. Work your way out to more distal body parts. The checklist in Figure 1 is ordered in the sequence generally followed to align body parts. Use your hands to provide

dynamic support in order to determine whether individually designed positioning equipment might provide adequate support to maintain a more efficient alignment. In effect, your hands firmly and gently simulate the type of support that might be sought through use of equipment.

Other Positions   While people with physical disabilities spend major portions of their day in a seated position, other positions must be assumed in order to prevent the development of contractures and deformities (Bergen & Colengelo, 1982; Rainforth & York, 1987; Trefler & Taylor, 1984; Ward, 1984). Furthermore, movement in and out of a variety of postures, and time spent working in different positions promotes more active use of all body parts and muscle groups. Generally speaking, learners should spend time in at least three positions—seated, standing or kneeling in an upright weight-bearing position, and lying with the body elongated. Before determining which positions an individual should assume and maintain, and how to assist in this process, the physical or occupational therapist, orthopedist, or other team member with expertise in positioning and handling should be consulted, since there may be precautions and contraindications related to specific positions.

The same guidelines apply to helping a learner assume and maintain a functional position other than sitting. Stability and optimal alignment are necessary for mobility or function within any posture. The specific positioning procedures and equipment needs must be individualized. Advantages and disadvantages of specific positions are presented in Table 1.

Team members must actively plan effective means of communication within each of the positions assumed by an individual with physical disabilities. Because seated positioning may be the most frequently assumed position, augmentative communication systems are sometimes designed and implemented based only on this

position. Optimally, a learner would be able to use the same augmentative system in any position. Because hand use, as well as the ability to use a communication system, can change significantly across positions, a complementary communication system or strategy may be necessary. For example, a duplicate or somewhat modified system that is portable might be developed. Communication in a position other than sitting may require a change from a direct select mode to a scanning mode. In such a case, the learner may be taught to produce a vocalization or gesture, or to activate a switch in order to obtain a listener's attention. After doing so, the listener may need to menu the symbol options manually, whereupon the user would signal when the listener had arrived at the desired symbol (see Chapter 13).

In addition to ensuring access to a communication system in different positions, access is necessary during transitions also. Another consideration, therefore, relates to ambulatory people with physical disabilities, for whom portability and accessibility are important factors. In terms of portability, a communication device can be carried or it can be secured to the user. Carrying options include wallets, folders, binders, and books. Communication systems that are secured to the user include symbols or miniboards attached to the user's belt or on a retractable key holder. (See descriptions of these options in Chapter 1.) Because coordination and hand-use skills may be impaired, team members need to consider how the learner is to reach the communication system.

Functional Movement for Communication

Once appropriate positions are achieved, the way in which the learner will use the communication system is determined. A learner who is capable of varied and controlled movement can use direct select techniques. Direct select methods are preferred over scanning methods for several reasons. First, direct selection is usually

Table 1. Position options for learners with physical disabilities

Position	Advantages	Disadvantages
Prone	Normal resting position; requires no motor control; promotes trunk and hip extension	Possibility of suffocation; stimulates asymmetry if head turned to side; may stimulate flexor tone; functional activities limited
Supine	Normal resting position; requires little motor control; no danger of suffocation; symmetry can be maintained	May stimulate extensor tone; prolonged position inhibits respiration; possibility of aspiration; view ceiling; functional activities limited
Prone on elbows	Encourages head, arm, and trunk control; allows improved view	May stimulate flexor tone; may stimulate excessive extension; tiring position; limits hand use
Side-lying	Normal resting position; usually does not stimulate abnormal tone; improves alignment; brings hands together at midline	May require bulky equipment; sideward view; few functional activities; pressure on bony prominences (hips)
Sidesitting	Easy to assume from lying, hands and knees, kneeling; promotes trunk rotation, range of motion in hips and trunk if sides alternated	May reinforce asymmetry; may require one or both hands for support; difficult with tight hips or trunk
Indian or ring sitting	Wide base of support; symmetrical position; easier to free hands	Difficult transition to/from other positions; may reinforce flexed posture
Longsitting	May provide wide base of support; may prevent hamstring contractures	Impossible with tight hamstrings; may stimulate trunk flexion, flexor spasticity
Heel- or W-sitting	Easy transition to/from other positions; stable base of support; frees hands	Reinforces hip, knee, and ankle deformity; reduces reciprocal movement, weight shifting, and trunk rotation
Chair sitting— standard chair	Normal position and equipment; easy transition to/from other positions; minor adaptations can be added to improve position	May not provide adequate position for feet, trunk, hips; may be overused

(continued)

Table 1.   *(continued)*

Position	Advantages	Disadvantages
Chair sitting— bolster chair	Reduces scissoring at hips; may increase anterior pelvic tilt	Bulky equipment; difficult transition to/from other positions
Chair sitting— corner chair	Inhibits extensor tone in trunk and shoulders	May encourage excessive flexion; may rotate trunk and pelvis
Chair sitting— wheelchair	Allows for positioning and mobility simultaneously; adaptations can control most postural problems	Chairs may be expensive, complicated, easily mal-adjusted; may become overreliant on chair
Kneeling	Promotes trunk and hip control; improves hip joint; possible despite knee flexion contractures; stabilizes hip joint	May cause bursitis at knees
Standing prone	Promotes trunk and hip control; standing stabilizes hip joint; allows access to normal work surfaces (e.g., counters)	May stimulate flexor tone; may stimulate excessive extension; may need hands for support; requires bulky equipment
Standing supine	Promotes trunk and hip control; stabilizes hip joint; hands free for work; head supported	May stimulate extensor tone; may not reach work surfaces; requires bulky equipment
Standing upright	Promotes greater trunk and hip control and balance	May require bulky equipment

From Rainforth, B., and York, J. (1987). Handling and positioning. In F. P. Orelove and D. Sobsey, *Educating children with multiple handicaps: A transdisciplinary approach* (pp. 77–78). Baltimore: Paul H. Brookes Publishing Co.; reprinted by permission.

much faster than scanning. Perhaps more importantly, a scanning technique forces the learner to rely heavily on a communicative partner to menu choices. In essence, the learner is almost never in a position to initiate an interaction. When a learner has limited variety and control over movement, however, scanning methods may be the best option for communicating. To use scanning, the learner must have at least one reliable, accurate, voluntary movement. For learners who do not have such control, the team must decide which body movement the learner has the greatest potential for learning to control.

Direct Selection   The most common direct select method is pointing with the index finger. Pointing can also be done with a fisted hand or eyes, or by using an adaptation (e.g., T-bar, splint with a pointer, headstick, or light beam). In most situations, the team assesses hand use first, then proceeds to evaluate the efficiency of head movement, eye gaze, or other body parts for pointing. A checklist that can be used to guide assessment of direct select options is presented in Figure 2.

To determine if direct select communication is a viable option, the team must assess the

	Independent movement	Assisted movement	
		Requires preparation only	Requires manual guidance
RANGE OF DIRECTED REACH			
Top left	_____	_____	_____
Top center	_____	_____	_____
Top right	_____	_____	_____
Bottom left	_____	_____	_____
Bottom center	_____	_____	_____
Bottom right	_____	_____	_____
POINTING OPTIONS			
Index finger	_____	_____	_____
Middle finger	_____	_____	_____
Ring finger	_____	_____	_____
Little finger	_____	_____	_____
Thumb	_____	_____	_____
Eye	_____	_____	_____
Toe	_____	_____	_____
ADAPTATIONS			
Handheld pointer	_____	_____	_____
Headstick	_____	_____	_____
Light pointer	_____	_____	_____
Other	_____	_____	_____
Other	_____	_____	_____
Other	_____	_____	_____

Figure 2. Checklist for assessing a learner's direct select capabilities.

range and accuracy of various pointing methods. The ability of the learner to point independently and to point with physical assistance must be determined. Some learners are able to move with reasonable efficiency if provided with physical assistance before or during movement attempts. If this is the case, interventions to establish independent movement and to reduce the need for physical assistance could be designed and implemented. The general approach to evaluating direct select methods of pointing follows the same sequence presented for positioning. After an optimal position is assumed and maintained, the learner is provided with the opportunity independently to reach and point to various locations. This can be accomplished by asking the learner to point to specific targets or symbols located on a communication board display. Team members assess the learner's efficiency and range of movement in terms of speed, accuracy, and fatigue as he or she points to the various locations. If independent pointing requires considerable effort (as evidenced by the learner becoming very tense or haphazard), attempts are made to facilitate movement by providing and fading physical assistance at various points of the movement.

Physical assistance procedures can be used immediately prior to pointing attempts. These procedures are referred to as *preparatory handling*. Alternatively, physical assistance may be used throughout the time the learner attempts to move. These procedures are known as *guided movement*. The goal of implementing use of these procedures is to determine whether the learner could improve movement efficiency. If therapeutic handling is considered beneficial, the learner should be assisted in moving more efficiently throughout the day. As movement becomes more efficient, fading procedures are designed so that the need for physical assistance is decreased or eliminated. This is a very important part of the assessment process because learners with severe physical disabilities often have not had frequent, repetitive, and consistent opportunities to learn to demonstrate more controlled and efficient movement.

A variety of handling procedures can be employed in an attempt to increase movement efficiency. Preparatory handling procedures can include normalizing muscle tone and repeated practice. Normalizing muscle tone and facilitating repetitions of the desired movement pattern provide the opportunity for the learner to feel and actively participate in a more efficient movement pattern. Some learners are able to demonstrate efficient movement independently after such preparation. Other learners require ongoing or at least intermittent physical assistance. Some learners have great difficulty initiating movement but are able to move efficiently once the movement pattern has been initiated.

After the team assesses the learner's ability to point efficiently to numerous locations, the decision is made whether or not to pursue direct select communication options. If the learner's pointing skills are judged inadequate, the team can decide to design and implement interventions to improve pointing, resort to scanning options exclusively, or pursue direct select methods in some circumstances and scanning methods in others. If the learner has a history of involvement with systematically designed and implemented interventions and no functional gains have been made in pointing skills, scanning options should be pursued. The learner has not had the benefit of systematically designed and implemented interventions aimed at improving pointing efficiency, such interventions should be tried.

Systematically designed interventions involve the specific delineation of both instructor behaviors and learner outcomes. Systematically implemented and evaluated interventions require training and ongoing support of direct service providers about how to implement the procedures, numerous daily opportunities across a period of weeks, and ongoing data collection and analyses. Guidelines for specifying handling procedures and movement outcomes are outlined in Table 2.

Scanning   To engage in a scanning method of communication, the learner must demonstrate one discrete, reliable motor response.

Table 2.   Specifying handling procedures for learners and instructors

Learner behaviors
1. Specify location of learner (and equipment) in the environment.
2. Specify body position of learner.
3. Delineate desired movement response.
    a. Specify body part.
    b. Specify how movement should be initiated.
    c. Specify movement pattern desired.
    d. Specify how much force/power is to be exerted.
    e. Specify speed of movement.
    f. Specify efficiency/smoothness of movement.

Instructor behaviors
1. Specify location of instructor in relation to learner.
2. Specify body position of instructor.
3. Delineate physical assistance to be provided by instructor.
    a. Specify purpose of the assistance (stability, mobility, relaxation, facilitation).
    b. Specify where to touch/hold.
    c. Specify how firmly to touch/hold.
    d. Specify when during movement to provide assistance (initiation, midrange, completion).
    e. Specify how long to provide assistance (intermittent, maintained).
    f. Specify how long to wait for a response from learner.
    g. Specify how many "practice" movements should be performed.
    h. Specify what to do if the learner begins to move in an undesirable pattern.

Figure 3 provides a checklist to guide the process of identifying this response. A variety of body parts and response movements is shown. Any of the movements could be used to activate a switch if an electronic scanning communication aid were being considered. If a manual scanning option were being pursued, any of the movements that could be reliably discerned as a discrete response could be selected.

York, Hamre-Nietupski, and Nietupski (1985) describe a decision-making process for using microswitches. In an effort to guide the selection of a motor behavior (movement response) for activating a microswitch, they pose the following questions:

If a reliable motor behavior is demonstrated, is it desirable?

Is it atypical, or reinforcing potentially harmful movement patterns?

Is it stereotypic?

Can it be shaped into an appropriate and desirable motor behavior?

If no reliable motor behaviors are demonstrated, what is the motor behavior that has the greatest potential for being desired or enhanced?

	Independent movement	Assisted movement	
		Requires preparation only	Requires manual guidance
UPPER EXTREMITY			
Lift shoulder	———	———	———
Push out arm	———	———	———
Flex/extend elbow	———	———	———
Rotate forearm	———	———	———
Flex/extend wrist	———	———	———
Flex/extend fingers	———	———	———
Spread fingers	———	———	———
Move thumb	———	———	———
HEAD/NECK			
Turn/drop to side	———	———	———
Drop forward	———	———	———
Push back	———	———	———
FACE			
Open mouth	———	———	———
Move tongue	———	———	———
Raise eyebrows	———	———	———
TRUNK			
Bend forward	———	———	———
Lean to side	———	———	———
Bend backward	———	———	———
LOWER EXTREMITY			
Lift leg	———	———	———
Move leg to side	———	———	———
Flex/extend knee	———	———	———
Flex/extend ankle	———	———	———
Flex/extend toes	———	———	———

Figure 3.   Checklist for assessing a learner's scanning capabilities.

Identifying or shaping a reliable movement response that can be used efficiently for scanning purposes requires careful attention to both positioning and movement abilities. The team may choose to assess movement abilities in a variety of positions because positioning affects movement (Trefler, 1984).

The team should assess both independent and assisted movement. Assisted movement may involve preparatory handling (e.g., normalizing muscle tone, repeated practice) and/or physical guidance for all or parts of the movement. For example, a learner may become very tense when attempting to bend his or her arm. One reason for the tension may be lack of stability at the shoulder. If stability is provided externally by firmly holding around the shoulder, and the learner is assisted to initiate movement of the arm to reach, relatively controlled movement may be possible. It may be necessary to fade the physical assistance after several repetitions of assisted movement, or assistance may need to be maintained throughout the entire movement.

Numerous handling procedures can be implemented. It is important to evaluate assisted movement, because too frequently decisions are made that learners cannot demonstrate one reliable, discrete movement before a range of intervention options has been attempted. (For a detailed discussion of scanning, see Chapter 13.)

SUMMARY

People with severe physical disabilities who require augmentative communication systems present special challenges to service providers. Achieving stable and well-aligned positions is crucial if efficient communication is to be possible. In determining the best positions and most efficient methods of indicating (direct selection, versus scanning), team members should both observe independent movement and provide a variety of forms of physical assistance to determine the potential for improving efficient movement.

REFERENCES

Bergen, A.F., & Colangelo, C. (1982). *Positioning the client with central nervous system deficits: The wheelchair and other adapted equipment*. Valhalla, NY: Valhalla Rehabilitation Publications.

Bly, L. (1983). *The components of normal movement during the first year of life and abnormal motor development*. Chicago: Neuro-Developmental Treatment Association.

Boehme, R. (1988). *Improving upper body control: An approach to assessment and treatment of tonal dysfunction*. Tucson, AZ: Therapy Skill Builders.

Campbell, P. (1986). You are your own best reference. In R. Perske, A. Clifton, B.M. McClean, & J.I. Stein (Eds.), *Mealtimes for persons with severe handicaps* (pp. 32–34). Baltimore: Paul H. Brookes Publishing Co.

Campbell, P. (1989). Dysfunction in posture and movement in individuals with profound disabilities: Issues and practices. In F. Brown & D.H. Lehr (Eds.), *Persons with profound disabilities: Issues and practices* (pp. 163–189). Baltimore: Paul H. Brookes Publishing Co.

Finnie, N. (1975). *Handling the young cerebral palsied child at home* (2nd ed.). New York: E.P. Dutton.

Ford, F. (1984). Neuromotor dysfunction as it relates to therapeutic seating. In E. Trefler (Ed.), *Seating for children with cerebral palsy: A resource manual* (pp. 10–24). Memphis, TN: University of Tennessee, Rehabilitation Engineering Program.

Fraser, B.A., Hensinger, R.N., & Phelps, J.A. (1987). *Physical management of multiple handicaps*. Baltimore: Paul H. Brookes Publishing Co.

Hardy, S. (1984). Neuromotor development and its implications for therapeutic seating. In E. Trefler (Ed.), *Seating for children with cerebral palsy: A resource manual* (pp. 3–9). Memphis, TN: University of Tennessee, Rehabilitation Engineering Program.

Levitt, S. (1982). *Treatment of cerebral palsy and motor delay* (2nd ed.). Boston: Blackwell Scientific Publications.

MacNeela, J.C. (1987). An overview of therapeutic positioning for multiply-handicapped persons, including augmentative communication users. *Physical and Occupational Therapy in Pediatrics, 7*(2), 39–60.

Rainforth, B., & York, J. (1987). Positioning and handling. In F.P. Orelove & D. Sobsey (Eds.), *Educating children with multiple disabilities: A transdisciplinary approach* (pp. 67–101). Baltimore: Paul H. Brookes Publishing Co.

Taylor, S. (1987). Evaluating the client with physical disabilities for wheelchair seating. *American Journal of Occupational Therapy, 41*(11), 711–716.

Trefler, E. (Ed.). (1984). *Seating for children with cerebral palsy: A resource manual*. Memphis, TN: University of Tennessee, Rehabilitation Engineering Program.

Trefler, E., & Taylor, S. (1984). Decision making guidelines for seating and positioning children with cerebral palsy. In E. Trefler (Ed.), *Seating for children with cerebral palsy: A resource manual* (pp. 55–76). Memphis, TN: University of Tennessee, Rehabilitation Engineering Program.

Ward, D. (1984). *Positioning the handicapped child for function* (2nd ed.). Chicago: Phoenix Press.

York, J., Hamre-Nietupski, S., & Nietupski, J. (1985). A decision-making model for using microswitches. *Journal of The Association for Persons with Severe Handicaps, 10*(4), 214–223.

13

Teaching Scanning Selection Techniques

Laura Piché and Joe Reichle

Scanning is a multistep method of communication in which a listener provides a menu of available items to the learner, and the learner then signals which of the presented items he or she desires. Scanning may be an appropriate method of communication for several types of learners with severe disabilities. Learners who do not exhibit sufficient motor control efficiently to direct select (i.e., touch) items on a communication board frequently need to use a scanning selection technique. Scanning may also be appropriate as a back-up method of communication when direct selection is not possible. For example, when a specific vocabulary item is not available on a learner's communication board, a listener might need to list choices verbally or point to the available items, thus menuing response options for the learner, who would then signal when the desired option was menued.

This chapter examines scanning as a potential method of communication for learners with severe disabilities. Specifically, the following aspects of scanning are presented and reviewed: 1) teaching initial scanning selection skills, 2)

applications and intervention strategies for more advanced scanning techniques, 3) concurrent use of direct selection and scanning communication systems, and 4) applications of auditory scanning.

TEACHING INITIAL SCANNING

Teaching initial scanning skills involves the following steps: 1) selecting a signaling response, 2) learning to use the signaling response conditionally (i.e., to indicate the desired item), 3) learning to use the signaling response given an increasingly larger array of items, and 4) learning to use the signaling response in different types of arrays (i.e., horizontal and vertical).

Selecting a Signaling Response

The initial step of a program to teach a learner to participate in manual (nonelectronic) scanning requires selecting a response and teaching the learner to use it to signal the listener that a symbol that has been menued is desired. Some signals, such as vocalization, do not lend themselves to traditional response prompts that include gestural or physical guidance. The selection of a vocal signaling response almost always results in the use of a differential reinforcement procedure as the intervention strategy of choice. (See Chapter 10 for a discussion of differential reinforcement procedures.)

Careful thought should be given to the selection of a signaling response. Voluntary motor behaviors that are part of an existing repertoire of undesirable stereotypic behavior should not be selected as signals, since their use as a signal is likely to increase their occurrence. For example, a head shake or nod should not be selected as a signal for a learner who engages in stereotypic head weaving. A signal that a learner is able to produce but that he or she finds fatiguing should also be ruled out. For example, a signal that consists of a learner dropping his or her head may be satisfactory if the learner needs to make only one or two responses. However, in situations that call for several responses in a brief period of time, the learner may become

fatigued to the point where he or she is no longer able to respond accurately, or he or she may stop responding entirely. Signals that involve the controlled use of an undesired reflex or movement pattern that could be physically harmful over time should also be avoided (Campbell, 1989), as should socially unacceptable signals. The voluntary behavior selected for the signaling response should also lend itself to prompting. By selecting an eye blink as the signaling response, for example, the interventionist has no way of prompting the signal when the learner fails to produce it. Careful attention must be paid to all of these issues when a signaling response is being identified. A summary of these considerations is presented in Figure 1.

Using a Signal Conditionally

Initial scanning intervention can be thought of as occurring in three phases (Figure 2). Once an appropriate signaling response has been determined, the interventionist enters into the first

SIGNALING RESPONSE	POTENTIAL PROBLEM
A voluntary motor response that is part of an existing repertoire of undesirable stereotypic behavior	May increase the occurrence of the stereotypic behavior
A motor behavior the learner can produce occasionally	Learner may become fatigued when required to produce several responses in succession, rendering the signal inefficient
A motor behavior that involves controlled use of an undesired reflex or movement pattern	Could be physically harmful to the learner over time
A voluntary motor response that is socially unacceptable	Could have negative social repercussions
A voluntary motor response that does not lend itself to prompting (e.g., eye blink or vocalization)	Interventionist cannot prompt the response when the learner fails to produce the signal

Figure 1.   Potential problems associated with various signaling responses.

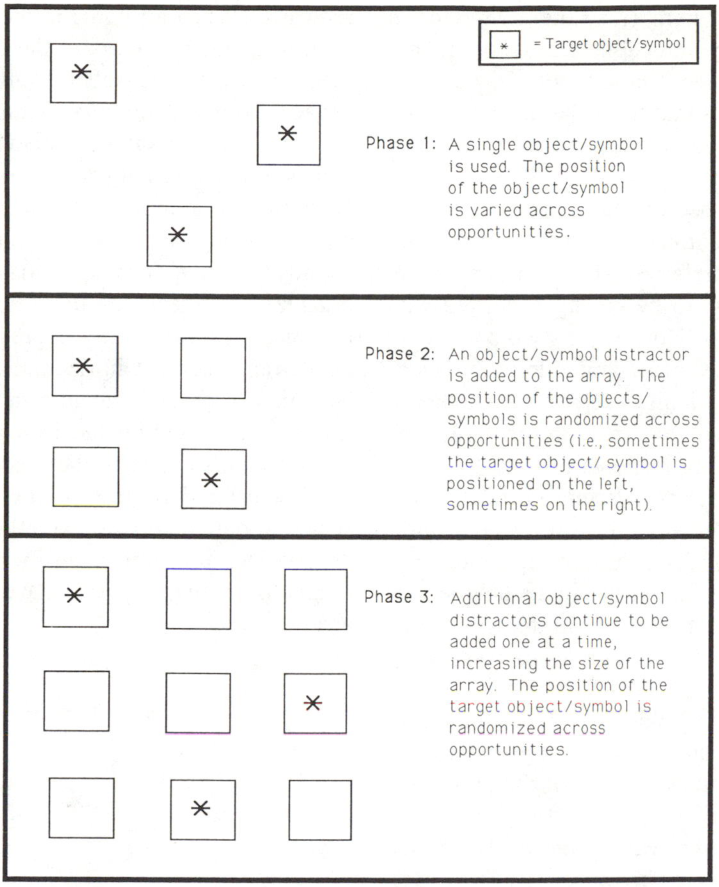

Figure 2. The phases of scanning intervention.

intervention phase. During this phase, the learner is taught to wait until the listener touches the desired object before producing the signaling response. At this stage, only one object is used and the position of the object is changed randomly across opportunities. When the learner is successfully waiting until the listener touches the desired object before producing the signaling response, the interventionist may consider adding items to the array of objects from which the learner may select the most desired (phase 2). In this phase, the interventionist's goal is to maintain the response under slightly more difficult circumstances.

Up to this point, the learner has not been taught to refrain from responding when the listener touches an item that is not desired. In phase 2, two items—a preferred item and a neutral item—are menued. The positions of the objects are randomized (i.e., sometimes the preferred item is on the learner's right, and sometimes it is on the learner's left). When the preferred item is on the learner's left, the situation is nearly the same as it was in phase 1. However, when the desired item is placed to the right of the nonpreferred item, the situation becomes very different. Frequently, the learner produces the signal as soon as the listener touches the first item (i.e., the nonpreferred item) in the array, indicating that he or she has not understood the meaning of selecting an item but rather believes that he or she need only produce the signal as soon as the interventionist touches any item.

During this phase of intervention, it will be important to randomize the position of the preferred and nonpreferred items. It may seem somewhat strange to be pairing a desired with an undesired item. However, if two potentially desired items were made available to the learner, it would be difficult to determine whether or not the learner had acquired the discriminative use of the signaling response.

Once the learner is selecting correctly from an array of two items, larger arrays can be introduced (phase 3). A learner participating in a linear, or sequential, scanning technique (the sequential menuing of available items) must be able to observe and refrain from responding while a number of items are menued. Some interventionists feel this is a disadvantage of scanning techniques. Vanderheiden (1984) writes that, "In essence, most of the time spent scanning is spent . . . pointing to wrong selections with the user waiting passively for the appropriate item to be presented" (p. 44). While there is no disputing this as a disadvantage of scanning, for some learners scanning is the only option available. Steps should thus be taken to increase the number of items within the array. In order to ensure that the learner is engaging in a discriminative response, the available choices are "seeded" with distractors, that is, items the learner does not prefer. If the learner selects nonpreferred items, either the interventionist has misjudged the learner's preferences or the learner is not using the scanning technique correctly.

Scanning with Vertical and Horizontal Arrays

Most methods of introducing linear scanning focus on presenting the array in a left to right sequence. When all items in the first row have been menued, the items in the second row are menued in the same left to right sequence. To engage in row-column scanning, the learner must begin to follow a presentation format that menus items in an up to down format within columns. To ensure that the learner can generalize a newly acquired scanning skills to a slightly different format, it may be helpful to organize some teaching opportunities in which the linear scanning array is presented in a vertical arrangement. A horizontal array should be used first in order to avoid establishing a position bias of selecting the nearest item (which many learners appear to be predisposed to do).

Figures 3 and 4 show a four-choice array presented in both a vertical and a horizontal array. To avoid establishing a position bias in scanning, some investigators have used circular arrays.

Figure 3.   A four-choice array presented in a vertical format.

Figure 4.   A four-choice array presented in a horizontal format.

Using Real Objects Rather Than Symbolic Representations

Whether real objects or symbolic representations are used will depend to a large degree on the learner's discrimination and matching skills.

Chapter 5 outlines an intervention strategy for teaching explicit requesting using a direct select technique that seeks to separate a product logo from the item itself, so that eventually the product logo is used to represent the item. This same strategy could be used in teaching scanning. In a two-choice array, a real object (e.g., a bag of potato chips) is paired with a symbol distractor (e.g., a symbol of a carrot, representing a nonpreferred object about which the learner will likely never communicate). The position of the items and the order in which they are menued is randomized: sometimes the potato chip logo is menued first, requiring the learner to produce the signal for requesting potato chips, and sometimes the symbol distractor is menued first, requiring the learner to wait until the potato chip logo is menued to signal the request. Over successive opportunities the potato chip bag gradually becomes flat. Once the learner correctly responds in the presence of the flattened potato chip bag, the size of the bag should be gradually reduced. This can be done in two ways. The size of the bag can be photocopied and gradually reduced until it is approximately the same size as the symbol distractor being used. Alternatively, the most salient features of the packaging can be identified and the bag can gradually be trimmed until only the product logo, which is approximately the same size as the symbol distractor, remains.

As the real objects are being shaped into symbolic representations, scanning should continue to be taught in the same manner it was when real objects were used.

CHOOSING BETWEEN DIRECT SELECTION AND SCANNING

Direct selection is often preferred over scanning because of its relative speed. However, in some cases a learner's upper extremity motor competence is such that it is difficult to compare the speed and efficiency of two techniques. A comparison is made particularly difficult with a very young learner or a learner who has severe cognitive disability since the learner may have to learn the scanning technique before the two techniques can be compared. The authors have made a practice of teaching scanning concurrent with direct selection with learners who appear to be at risk for failing to master direct selection. Concurrent implementation of direct select and scanning techniques is warranted in learners with progressive disabilities and in learners who use a mixed system. In learners who will experience progressive deterioration of the muscular or neuromuscular system, direct selection may be possible initially but may be too demanding as the disease progresses. Experience suggests that implementing an alternative selection technique before it is actually required helps in establishing its use.

Some learners may be able to direct select a particular quadrant on a communication board, but unable to specify an individual symbol. The listener would then begin menuing items in the designated quadrant. This application is observed most often among users of nonelectronic systems who may be candidates for an electronic aid that uses directed scanning (directed scanning is discussed later in this chapter).

To some degree, verbal mode users also use scanning techniques in certain communicative situations. For example, when a friend asks, "Do you want to go shopping, to a movie, or out to eat?" she has menued the available choices for the evening. You respond, "Shopping," which signals the desired activity. Given that verbal mode users often employ mixed mode techniques, it may be to an augmentative user's advantage to learn to participate in a scanning selection technique, thus enabling him or her to use a mixed mode system.

TEACHING VISUAL SCANNING TO A LEARNER WHO USES INFORMAL AUDITORY SCANNING

Sometimes learners comprehend an extensive array of spoken vocabulary, even though they cannot produce words in the vocal mode. If this is the case, the learner may already be participating in auditory scanning when he or she comes to the task of learning to scan using a communication board. For example, a learner might respond to auditory scanning (e.g., "Do you want to go to Hardee's? Burger King? McDonald's?") by allowing his head to drop forward to select an option. Because the learner is already engaging in a scanning technique, it would be relatively easy to teach him to scan graphic symbols on an electronic communication board. Initially the spoken choice for each symbol would be paired with the movement of a cursor across symbol choices. The learner's head would be connected to a switch that rested near his chin. Across opportunities, the verbal menuing would be faded using a constant time delay.

TEACHING VISUAL SCANNING TO A LEARNER WHO USES A DIRECT SELECT TECHNIQUE

Sometimes a learner has been taught a direct select method of communication but is able to use it only inefficiently. For example, the learner may use an unreliable signal, thus limiting him or her to communicating only with people who are familiar with the constraints of the response. In this instance, the interventionist might consider initiating a scanning program. There are ample instances during a learner's day that support the use of both scanning and direct select techniques. Some of these examples are outlined in Figure 5. Alternatively, particular vocabulary items could be assigned to particular modes to avoid duplication. However, since scanning generally requires greater learner effort than direct selection, it may be unnecessarily restrictive initially to assign a vocabulary item exclusively to a scanning technique. Instead, vocabulary should be taught using both direct select and scanning techniques.

Currently, the data are insufficient to support the adoption of any particular intervention strategy of concurrent implementation of direct select and scanning techniques. Chapter 3 describes procedures that may be used to identify a learner's communicative needs by scrutinizing the communicative demands of his or her environment. The same technique can be used to identify situations in which opportunities for direct selection and scanning can be introduced. One strategy the authors have used is to select particular activities that occur during the learner's day that tend easily to accommodate a scanning option. At mealtimes, for example, there

	Setting	Learner behavior	Listener behavior
Natural opportunities for scanning	Mealtime	Attempts to gain access to an object that is out of reach	
			Menus available objects by pointing to each object and saying, "Do you want this?"
		Produces signaling response when desired toy is menued	
	Toy store	Points to desired toy that is out of reach	
			Menus available toys in area asking, "This one?" as he or she points to each one
		Produces signaling response when desired candy is menued	
	Candy machine	Points to desired candy, but is unable to activate machine independently	
			Menus available candies by pointing to each one and asking, "Do you want Snickers™? Kit Kat™? Milky Way™?"
		Produces signaling response when desired candy is menued	
Natural opportunities for direct selection	Mealtime		Places food or beverage choices in front of learner (i.e., hamburger or hot dog; milk or juice)
		Reaches out and selects desired food or beverage	
	Soft drink machine		Asks, "What kind of drink are you going to get?" Helps put money in machine if required
		Reaches out and pushes the button for favorite soft drink	
	Recess		Gives choices of objects to play with during recess (e.g., ball or scooter board)
		Reaches out and touches or takes desired object	

Figure 5.   Some naturally occurring opportunities in which to engage in scanning and direct select techniques.

may be some foods or beverages that the learner will be able to obtain using direct selection (e.g., a glass of milk positioned in front of a learner can be obtained by reaching out and picking it up). However, there will likely be other foods the learner is interested in but is unable to reach or signal. These represent optimal occasions in which to implement a scanning technique. Consider, for example, a learner who loves ketchup, but does not have a sign or symbol with which to request it. At each meal a bottle of ketchup and a jar of mustard are placed on the table out of reach of the learner. The learner will likely try to reach for the bottle of ketchup, or will cry or vocalize to indicate that he or she wants something. At this point, the listener might say something like, "Oh, you want something. What do you want?" and begin menuing the condiments. Sometimes the ketchup would be menued first along with the verbal cue "Do you want ketchup?" At other times, the mustard would be menued first along with the verbal cue "Do you want mustard?"

It is not necessary to assign specific vocabulary items to either a direct select or a scanning system. There may be times when a vocabulary item assigned to a direct select system is ambiguous and requires the use of a scanning routine for clarification. For example, a learner may have a symbol for "soft drink" in his or her direct select repertoire. If at snack time a can of Diet Pepsi℠ is on the table and the learner requests a soft drink by touching the appropriate symbol, it is clear that he or she is requesting Diet Pepsi℠ since it is the only soft drink available. However, if the learner requests a soft drink while standing in front of a soft drink machine, it is not clear what kind of soft drink he or she wants. At this point, the use of a scanning technique would clarify the request. The listener would begin to menu the available items by pointing to the individual logos on the machine and saying, "Do you want Diet Pepsi℠, Dr. Pepper℠, Mountain Dew℠, or 7-Up℠?" The learner would produce his signaling response when the desired drink was menued. This example suggests that environmental conditions may be useful guides for suggesting when to use a direct selection versus a scanning technique.

MOVING
FROM LINEAR SCANNING
TO ROW-COLUMN SCANNING

In row-column scanning, the available rows are menued from top to bottom. The learner produces the signaling response when the row that contains the symbol he or she wishes to communicate is menued. As soon as the desired row has been selected, the items (columns) within that row are menued one at a time from left to right (see Chapter 1). Row-column scanning significantly increases scanning efficiency for most users. However, often, too little consideration is given to determining when a learner might derive greater benefit from a row-column technique over a linear scanning technique. Because linear scanning is relatively slow, it is important to have some method of determining at what point a row-column approach might be preferable.

Kulikowski (1986) introduced the term "pulse" to describe the amount of time it takes to menu any one item in a scanning array. The number of pulses can be used as at least a partial measure of the efficiency of a selection technique. For example, if in linear scanning a desired symbol is located four squares to the right of the first symbol, five pulses are required to select that symbol. With three symbols displayed in a linear scanning technique, it will take an average of two pulses to reach a symbol (assuming that all symbols are used equally often). Figure 6 shows two 10-symbol arrays. The upper array shows the number of pulses required to select a symbol within the array using linear scanning, the lower array shows the number of pulses required to select a symbol using row-column scanning. To determine if row-column scanning is more efficient than linear scanning, 1) count the number of pulses required to reach each of the symbols, 2) add the number of pulses across each symbol in the display, and 3) divide this number by the total number of symbols in the display.

Clearly, for 10 symbols, row-column scanning is more efficient than linear scanning. At what point does row-column scanning become the more efficient technique? Kulikowski (1986) computed the point at which efficiency is maximized in a row-column technique. Figure 7 compares the mean number of pulses required to select a symbol using each selection on technique given arrays of varying sizes. Row-column scanning becomes the more efficient selection technique when the symbol array contains more than six items. (All of the vocabulary are assumed to be used with equal frequency).

Linear Scanning

1	2	3	4	5
6	7	8	9	10

$$\frac{55 \text{ total pulses } (1+2+3+4+...+10)}{10 \text{ symbols}} = 5.5 \text{ pulses/symbol}$$

Row-Column Scanning

2	3	4	5	6
3	4	5	6	7

$$\frac{45 \text{ total pulses } (1+2+3+4+...+10)}{10 \text{ symbols}} = 4.5 \text{ pulses per symbol}$$

Figure 6. Number of pulses required to move through a 10-item array using linear scanning and row-column scanning.

The concept of pulses is also useful in suggesting the most efficient placement of symbols in the arrays of various scanning techniques. Figure 8 shows the number of pulses required to reach each symbol in a 25-item row-column and

SCANNING TECHNIQUE

SIZE OF ARRAY (in number of symbols)	LINEAR	ROW/COLUMN	DIRECTED
3	2	2.7	1
6	3.5	3.3	1.3
8	4.5	4.0	1.5
16	8.5	5.2	3.1
32	16.5	7.0	2.9
64	32.5	9.1	3.8

Figure 7. Mean number of pulses required to select a symbol using linear scanning, row-column scanning, and directed scanning given arrays of various sizes.

directed scanning array. From this figure, it becomes apparent that the efficiency of symbol placement in a row-column scanning array is maximized when symbols are placed along the diagonals of the array, moving out from the array's upper left corner. In a directed scanning array, efficiency of symbol placement is maximized when symbols are placed in a diamond shape that moves out from the center of the array.

Row-column scanning requires that a learner alter his or her communication technique in several important ways. First, he or she must learn to engage in a chain of signaling responses. That is, as the scanning cursor begins moving through the scanning array, the initial selection must be made when a response unit that corresponds to the row containing the desired choice has been menued. This initial response is then chained to the selecting strategy that the learner uses in order to engage in a linear scanning technique. In this respect, teaching the signaling response for row-column scanning is analogous to establishing a backward chain of behavior. In row-column scanning there is a need for keener visual scanning skills. In linear scanning, once the menuing of choices has been instigated, the learner could quickly glance across the row to see if he or she spots the desired symbol. If it is not there, the learner can relax until the cursor begins menuing a second row. Row-column scanning is far less forgiving to occasional lapses in attention. Because the cursor is traveling down a column, the learner must visually scan an entire row very quickly in search of the target symbol. This requirement results in relatively less "off" time for the learner.

Anticipatory Monitoring

Some learners who are somewhat more sophisticated in their scanning technique may locate the desired symbol before they activate the automated menuing on their electronic communication aid. Frequently, these learners must

Row-column scanning

2	3	4	5	6
3	4	5	6	7
4	5	6	7	8
5	6	7	8	9
6	7	8	9	10

Directed scanning

4	3	2	3	4
3	2	1	2	3
2	1	●	1	2
3	2	1	2	3
4	3	2	3	4

Figure 8.   Number of pulses required to reach each symbol in a 25-item row-column and directed scanning array.

compare the location of the menuing cursor and the symbol that they wish to select. This skill involves anticipatory monitoring. As used here, anticipatory monitoring refers to the learner's ability repeatedly to engage in visual localization that alternates between two objects that are far enough apart so that both cannot be viewed in the same visual field. Anticipatory monitoring can be viewed in infants during their first 6 months of life. An example of repeated visual localization occurs when a history is developed in which two hands swoop down from divergent angles in a game of "I'm gonna get you." Infants will readily move their gaze back and forth, focusing first on one hand, and then the other. In linear scanning, learners who have difficulty visually scanning tend to be those who respond late, after the cursor has moved one or more squares beyond the targeted symbol. Failing to scan visually results in a failure to plan where to initiate a signaling response. Consequently, signaling occurs after the cursor arrives at the desired symbol.

Cook and St. Lawrence (1986) described a computer-assisted visual training program that addressed teaching visual scanning skills. This program was implemented with a 6-year-old child with significant developmental delays. Intervention first focused on training the child to: 1) fixate her gaze, 2) scan the environment for

perception of a visual stimulus, and 3) track a moving stimulus. A personal computer linked to a projecting television was programmed to project a visual stimulus onto a white 4' x 4' screen. The child was instructed to say "all gone" when the visual stimulus disappeared from the screen. Cook and St. Lawrence reported a marked change in mean response time over baseline levels in all three areas targeted for intervention. "Both graphic display and statistical analysis confirmed the marked change which resulted from use of the computer-assisted training program and suggests that such a strategy may prove worthwhile with other handicapped children" (Cook & St. Lawrence, 1986, p. 55).

Establishing Row-Column Scanning

The technique selected to establish row-column scanning depends, in part, on the vocabulary selection strategy that was used in the initial phases of the learner's program. In Chapter 5, the spectrum of specificity of vocabulary was discussed. At one end of the spectrum a generalized requesting skill ("want") is established. At the other end of the spectrum an explicit requesting response (e.g., Diet Coke™) is established. Of course, a spectrum of options exists between these two extremes. For example, initial vocabulary items targeted for instruction often include "eat," "drink," "play," and "work." These vocabulary items are somewhat general, but are more explicit than "want." For some learners who will be using a scanning technique, it may be advantageous to begin teaching vocabulary at an intermediate level of specificity. This may be particularly advantageous for learners who will eventually use row-column scanning. These moderately specific symbols may eventually function as an indexing system for the learner beginning to use a row-column scanning technique.

Indexing systems are used in a wide variety of everyday applications. Subject dividers in notebooks, file folders with tabs, recipe files, and a Rolodex™ are but a few examples of products that typically use letter or word indexes. It may be possible to teach a learner to use an indexing strategy to acquire row-column scanning skills.

Initially, the same program described to establish linear scanning could be introduced, ensuring that on at least some occasions the symbol array would be presented in a vertical display, with the cursor moving from up to down rather than horizontally. As soon as the learner had acquired each of three to six semi-generalized symbols (e.g., "eat," "drink," "play," "work"), steps would be taken to teach the learner to engage in row-column scanning.

Figure 9 shows how the initial display might be arranged. In this example, "Diet Coke™" represents an explicit symbol that the learner will be taught to produce. This symbol would come to represent a special instance of requesting a drink. The logic for this program is identical to that presented in the description of program logic used to move a learner from generalized to explicit requesting using a direct selection technique (see Chapter 5).

Suppose, for example, that the learner wishes to request Diet Coke™. Prior to the introduction of this symbol, the learner would have scanned sequentially to the "drink" symbol. Even if a Diet Coke™ logo had been added to the array, the

Figure 9. An example of an initial display used to teach row-column scanning.

learner would likely continue to select the "drink" symbol. As soon as this response is selected voluntarily in a row-column technique, the cursor would immediately begin menuing each item within the "drink" row. When the scanning cursor arrives at the "Diet Coke™" symbol a response prompt would be delivered to select "Diet Coke™."

The most obvious advantage of an explicit requesting strategy is that it makes it easier for a listener to participate in an interaction with the learner. The learner can also gain experience using the augmentative communication system in a much wider range of situations. Additionally, the indexing strategy minimizes the need for intrusive response prompts during the earliest phase of instruction. A disadvantage is that use of the far left-hand column of a learner's display for an index takes up space. Where space constraints are binding, an index may not be a desirable alternative.

Before moving from linear scanning to row-column scanning, the learner must demonstrate that he or she can use such a system. One way of determining this is to have the learner participate in various games that use a row-column scanning technique. For example, Figure 10 presents a maze game appropriate for use with

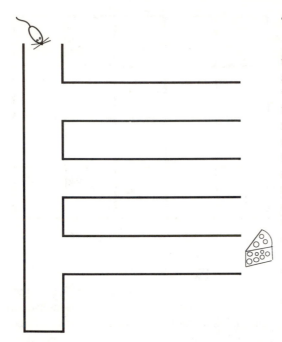

Figure 10.   A maze game that can be used to determine a learner's readiness to move from linear scanning to row-column scanning.

TEACHING DIRECTED SCANNING

In some respects, directed scanning can be thought of as a combination of direct selection and scanning techniques. In directed scanning, which is almost always an electronic application, the cursor begins in the middle of the array, rather than in the upper left corner of the array as in linear or row-column scanning (Figure 11). The cursor begins in the center of the display because this makes all symbols equidistant from the cursor, making it the most efficient scanning technique. The cursor is controlled by the learner's use of either a directional joystick or multiple switches.

It is extremely important to determine whether the learner is able to participate in the new scanning technique before the change is made. Games can be used to determine a learner's ability to move from row-column scanning to directed scanning. Many video games use directional joysticks. By observing a learner play such a game, the interventionist can judge whether the learner would likely be able to control a joystick to participate in directed scanning.

The concept of matrix training described in Chapter 10 is helpful to keep in mind when planning to teach directed scanning. In directed

an elementary school–age learner. The learner's task is to help the mouse find the cheese. The teacher moves the mouse to the first intersection and says, "Is the cheese down here?" He or she then moves the mouse to the second intersection and says, "Is the cheese down here?" He or she moves the mouse to the third intersection and says, "Is the cheese down here?" Here the learner should produce the signaling response. The position of the cheese should be changed each time the game is played. This same type of activity can easily be adapted for use with older children or adults by having the learner help a woman find the soft drinks in the aisles of a grocery store. By observing the learner participate in games such as these, the interventionist can determine whether the learner appears ready to make the switch to row-column scanning.

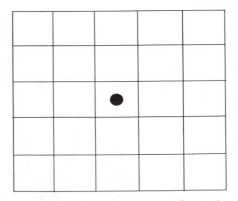

Figure 11.   An empty directed scanning array showing the starting position of the cursor.

scanning, intervention might be broken down into three main steps: 1) train in one direction, 2) train in the other direction, and 3) probe for generalization.

In Figure 12, the upper right quadrant has been selected for beginning instruction. The first step in teaching directed scanning is to select a direction in which to teach first. The interventionist begins by teaching a learner to move the cursor in a particular direction, say, rightward. Once the learner has been taught to scan to symbols positioned on a particular line and is able to do so consistently, the interventionist probes to determine whether the learner is able to move the cursor upward. If the learner is not able to do so, intervention could begin to focus on teaching the learner to scan upward to symbols positioned along the "up" line (see Figure 12).

As intervention in rightward and upward scanning is being completed, the interventionist should determine whether the learner is able to combine upward and rightward cursor move-

ments to enable him or her to select other symbols in the array. To do this, generalization probes should be conducted periodically throughout the course of the intervention. Possible sites for the placement of symbols for the generalization probes are indicated in Figure 12. In other to reach any of these symbol positions, a learner must combine upward and rightward cursor movements. For example, to reach a symbol positioned in the site indicated by "X_1," a learner would have to move two pulses to the right and two pulses up (or two pulses up and two pulses right).

The learner's performance on the generalization probes will dictate the course of the remaining intervention procedures. For example, if a learner failed to demonstrate generalization of cursor control to symbols in the positions indicated in Figure 12, the next target for intervention might be to teach the learner to scan to symbols located along the diagonal line of the upper right quadrant, as in Figure 13. While

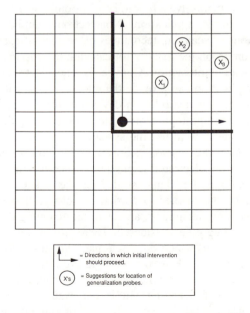

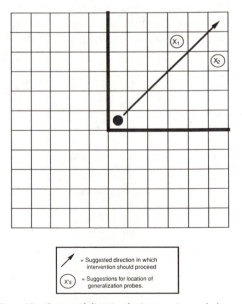

Figure 12. A directed scanning array indicating initial intervention strategies.

Figure 13. Suggested direction for intervention and placement of generalization probes once intervention has been completed in the "up" and "right" directions.

conducting intervention along the diagonal, it is important to continue to implement generalization probes using symbols positioned in untrained sites within the upper right quadrant. Intervention would continue in the upper right quadrant of the directed scanning array until a learner began to demonstrate generalization.

When the learner begins to demonstrate generalization within the upper right quadrant, probes should be implemented at various positions in the remaining three quadrants. For example, since intervention has already occurred in upward and rightward cursor movement, likely positions for generalization probes would be downward and leftward, since movement of the cursor downward and leftward is most similar to upward and rightward movement. Likewise, as intervention has already occurred with symbols positioned along the diagonal of the upper right quadrant, another area in which to conduct generalization probes would be along the diagonal in the lower left quadrant, since the movements required to reach those symbols are most similar to those already trained in the upper right quadrant (Figure 14). If a learner demonstrates generalization of the ability to move the cursor downward, leftward, and in the di-

rection of the lower left corner, additional generalization probes should be conducted to ensure that the learner is able to move the cursor to symbols located anywhere within the directed scanning array.

If a learner fails to generalize the ability to control the cursor downward, leftward, and in the direction of the lower left corner, the intervention previously described for the upper right quadrant should be replicated in the lower left quadrant. When the learner begins to demonstrate the ability to direct the cursor's movement to symbols in untrained locations within the lower left quadrant, generalization probes should be conducted at various locations within the remaining two quadrants.

MOVING FROM NONELECTRONIC TO ELECTRONIC SCANNING

With the exception of directed scanning, the techniques and intervention strategies described lend themselves to either electronic or nonelectronic application. Nonelectronic applications of scanning techniques place a significant burden on the listener for carrying the communicative interaction. Conversely a nonelectronic application can provide the interventionist with far greater flexibility in designing stimulus and response prompts required to begin teaching the learner how to use the system.

Generally speaking, instruction should begin with nonelectronic techniques. Once the interventionist has demonstrated that he or she can teach the learner to participate in a particular scanning technique, an electronic scanning device might be considered. There are several instances in which an electronic communication aid can be advantageous. One primary advantage of an electronic scanning aid over a nonelectronic scanning aid is the availability of voice output. A word, phrase, or sentence is programmed for each symbol in the array.

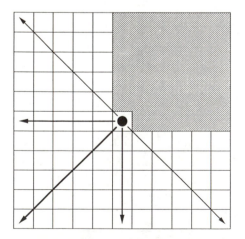

Figure 14.   Suggested directions for intervention once a learner begins to demonstrate generalization in the upper-right quadrant of a directed scanning array.

When the learner makes his or her selection, the message corresponding to the symbol is "spoken" by the device. With voice output, a learner is able to communicate a message to someone who is not directly attending to him or her, or to someone standing across the room. It also enables a learner to interact with peers who are not familiar with symbols, but who comprehend spoken language.

A second advantage of an electronic scanning device is that it allows the learner to communicate with naive listeners. Nonelectronic (manual) scanning places heavy demands on the listener, who must essentially carry the conversation. The listener must speak during his or her turn, then interpret the message produced by the learner and provide voice output for that message. In order to interpret the learner's message, the listener must understand how the learner's communication system works. This suggests that a learner using a manual scanning system would be able to communicate only with those people familiar with that particular system. A naive listener, such as a clerk at a fast food restaurant, would thus be unable to participate in a communicative exchange with the learner.

A third advantage of an electronic scanning aid is that a phrase, sentence, or even group of sentences can be represented by one symbol in the array. That is, the leaner may need to select only one symbol to produce a complete utterance. For example, a learner eating lunch at McDonald's need only select the McDonald's symbol on the scanning aid to produce an utterance that states, "I would like a cheeseburger, an order of French fries, and a chocolate shake."

Several considerations must be addressed in selecting an electronic scanning system. The interventionist must determine the type of switch to be used, its location, and the way in which it will be used to operate the system. Each of these issues is described in the sections that follow.

Selecting and Placing the Switch

York, Nietupski, and Hamre-Nietupski (1985) outlined a decision-making process for using switches that broke the process into the following components: 1) determine the learner's position for the activity, 2) select the motor behavior for activating the switch, 3) determine the type of switch to be used, 4) determine instructional procedures to be used, and 5) develop a strategy for data collection.

Determining the Learner's Position   As discussed in Chapter 12, body position affects movement and is therefore of critical importance when designing an electronic scanning system. York et al. (1985) identified several factors that need to be considered.

1. Ability to see peers, materials, and the instructor while activating the switch (e.g., if a learner had to drop his or her head forward to activate the switch, he or she would no longer be able to see the scanning system)
2. Proximity to the device being operated (i.e., is the learner close enough to the system to allow for optimal visual discrimination between symbols in the scanning array?)
3. Ability to perform desirable and efficient motor behavior
4. Ability to use the switch in alternative therapeutic positions (e.g., a position other than sitting) for learners who require a variety of positioning options throughout the day

Because a learner who is using a scanning system may activate the switch several hundred times per day, it is vital to select a position that allows for relaxed, controlled motor movements.

Selecting a Motor Movement   The considerations relevant to selecting a voluntary motor behavior with which to activate the switch are identical to those relevant to selecting a signaling response for use during initial scanning

training (see pages 258–259). Whenever possible, a motor response that is similar to the
signaling response should be selected. For example, if a learner has been tipping his or her
head to the left as a signaling response, it is
desirable for the learner to do so when activating a switch to engage the scanning device.

Selecting a Switch   Hundreds of types of
switches are available commercially. Several
different types of switches were examined in
Chapter 1. York et al. (1985) suggest several
factors to consider to ensure a good match between the learner and the switch selected. These
factors include the following:

1. How strong and accurate is the motor
    movement selected (i.e., how large does
    the response area of the switch have to be?
    How sensitive is the switch to touch,
    movement, sound, breath?).
2. Is the learner able to sustain contact with
    the switch? (Some types of switches re-
    quire more than fleeting contact for
    activation.)
3. Does the learner require some type of sen-
    sory feedback to indicate the switch has
    been activated? (Some types of switches
    provide auditory, tactile/kinesthetic, or vi-
    sual feedback that indicates activation has
    occurred).
4. Are there special mounting considerations?
    (Some types of switches are particularly
    difficult to mount.)
5. Is the optimal switch presently available?

Selecting a Switch Control Method   Once
an efficient body position, motor response, type
of switch, and placement of the switch have
been determined, the interventionist must decide how the switch will be used to signal the
scanning system. Blackstone (1989) outlined
three methods of switch control: automatic, inverse, and step/element. Each of these methods
is examined in the sections that follow.

Automatic Method   Probably the most
common method of switch control in electronic
scanning is the automatic method. A learner

engaging in linear scanning activates the switch
to initiate the cursor's movement through the
symbol array. This activates the menuing of the
symbols. The cursor continues to move through
the symbol array automatically until the learner
activates the switch again to select the symbol
currently being menued.

For a learner engaging in row-column scanning, the procedure is essentially the same. A
learner activates the switch to begin the cursor's
menuing of the rows in the symbol array. When
the cursor menus the row containing the desired
symbol, the learner activates the switch to select this row. This initiates the cursor's menuing
of the individual symbols (columns) in that row.
When the cursor menus the desired symbol, the
learner activates the switch a third time to select
that symbol.

There are some potential disadvantages of
using the automatic method. One disadvantage
is that some learners are unable to activate their
switch before the cursor begins menuing a different row or symbol. For some learners, this
can be extremely frustrating. Two possible solutions for learners who frequently "miss" their
desired row or symbol involve: 1) using two
switches, one to back the cursor up to the desired symbol and 2) using an alternative method
of switch control.

Inverse Method   As the name implies, the
inverse method is the operational opposite of
the automatic method. Using the inverse method, a learner engaged in linear scanning activates the switch to initiate menuing of the symbol array. To continue menuing, the learner
must maintain pressure on the switch (i.e., the
switch must be kept in an "on" position). As
long as the learner maintains the switch in an
"on" position, the cursor menus the available
symbols. When the desired symbol is menued,
the learner deactivates the switch (by ceasing to
exert pressure), indicating selection of that
symbol.

The methodology is essentially the same for a
learner using a row-column scanning system.
The learner activates and maintains the switch

in an "on" position, initiating menuing of the rows. When the desired row is menued the learner deactivates the switch, thus selecting the desired row. The learner then reactivates the switch and maintains it in an "on" position, thus initiating the menuing of the individual symbols in the selected row. When the desired symbol is menued, the learner deactivates the switch to indicate selection of that symbol.

The inverse method may be a desirable alternative for some learners. However, for others, the requirements of maintaining the switch in an "on" position for extended periods of time may prove too fatiguing.

Step/Element Method The step/element method is used primarily with linear scanning systems. A learner activates the switch to advance the cursor forward one pulse. When the learner stops advancing the cursor and pauses for a predetermined length of time, the electronic device selects the symbol currently menued. Sometimes two switches are used, one to move the cursor, and one to indicate symbol selection.

The step/element method is typically used with learners engaging in linear scanning who have a fairly small symbol array, or with learners who frequently "miss" their symbol. For learners with large arrays the system is often too fatiguing. Consider, for example, a learner with an array of 20 symbols. To request a cookie, the eighteenth symbol in the array, the learner would have to activate the switch 18 times.

TEACHING AUDITORY SCANNING

Auditory scanning represents an alternative where visual scanning is not a viable option (i.e., with learners with visual impairments). In auditory scanning, the choices are menued verbally rather than visually. Learners who may benefit from an auditory scanning technique are learners with limited motor control, reasonably good comprehension skills, and visual impairment. Auditory scanning may enable such learners to participate more fully in and exert more control over their environments.

Auditory scanning has been criticized as being inefficient. In a study conducted by Fried-Oken (1989), 96 adults were presented with three sets of 40 sentences. Each sentence contained five to seven syllables. One set of sentences was presented visually (shown on a monitor screen), a second set of sentences was presented visually and auditorially (shown on a monitor screen and presented simultaneously through a speech synthesizer), and a third set of sentences was presented auditorily (presented only through a speech synthesizer). Presentation of the sentence sets was conducted in such a way as to simulate visual scanning, visual-auditory scanning, and auditory scanning techniques. After presentation of each set of 40 sentences, learners were administered a sentence recognition test. They were instructed to activate a "yes" switch if they had seen and/or heard the sentences before, and to activate a "no" switch if the sentences were not familiar to them. Fried-Oken's results indicated that response accuracy was highest for the visual and visual-auditory scanning conditions, the auditory scanning condition producing "significantly more errors" (p. 68).

Three factors may account for the discrepancy in response accuracy between the visual and visual-auditory scanning conditions on the one hand and the auditory condition on the other. In the visual and visual-auditory conditions, the entire message is displayed on the screen for a given period of time, whereas in the auditory condition, the message cannot be processed as a whole since each component of the auditory stimulus is separated from the preceding one. A second factor may relate to the intelligibility of the auditory stimuli as produced on one of three speech synthesizers used (DECtalk™, VotraxPSS™, and ECHO PC™). The speech synthesizers yielded mean percent of correct responses that ranged from 78.93 to 82.23. A third factor may be related to the learners' lack of familiarity with auditory scanning.

Auditory scanning requires a certain level of memory skills since the available choices must be recalled and compared in the absence of any permanent display. Sometimes learners fall into the habit of using an "order of mention" selection strategy, in which they always select the last item named. Several instructional strategies are available to help learners overcome this problem. The first strategy involves pairing nondesired with desired items. This strategy is identical to that described for use in teaching a direct selection technique. In this application, the interventionist always presents the desired item first in the offered array and the undesired item last. Once the learner begins to alter his or her response strategy, the order is randomized, that is, the desired item is sometimes presented first and sometimes presented last. Sometimes this strategy alone is insufficient. A second strategy involves adding a loudness cue. The preferred item is menued first, using a particularly loud voice; the less preferred item is menued second, using a very soft voice. Across instructional opportunities, the volumes are tempered until the preferred and the unpreferred items are menued identically. These strategies can be used either alone or in combination with one another.

The research comparing visual, visual-auditory, and auditory scanning techniques has used sentences as the stimulus items. By keeping the array of choices small (two or three), and by using single words or short phrases rather than sentences, auditory scanning may represent a functional option for some learners.

SUMMARY

This chapter described procedures that may be used to establish a scanning selection technique for learners who are unable to use direct select techniques alone. A variety of scanning techniques, including linear, row-column, and directed scanning, was examined; decision strategies that lead to a successful match between a learner and a switch were reviewed; and scanning method options available to learners who rely on communication aids were examined.

Teaching learners to use scanning selection techniques is in its infancy. Few studies have systematically examined best practices in selecting or teaching scanning techniques. There is thus a critical need for empirical work in this area.

REFERENCES

Blackstone, S. (1989). Visual scanning: What's it all about? *Augmentative Communication News, 2*(4), 1–8.

Campbell, P. (1989). Dysfunction in posture and movement in individuals with profound disabilities. In F. Brown & D.H. Lehr (Eds.), *Persons with profound disabilities: Issues and practices* (pp. 163–189). Baltimore: Paul H. Brookes Publishing Co.

Cook, D.J., & St. Lawrence, J.S. (1986). Computer-assisted visual training with a developmentally-delayed child: Clinical report of a new technology. *Child and Family Behavior Therapy, 8*(2), 45–56.

Fried-Oken, M. (1989). *Sentence recognition for auditory and visual scanning techniques in electronic communication devices.* Paper presented at 12th annual RESNA Conference, New Orleans.

Kulikowski, S. (1986). *Scanning data types in nonvocal communication.* Paper presented at Closing the Gap Conference, Minneapolis.

Vanderheiden, G. (1984). High and low technology approaches in the development of communication systems for severely physically handicapped persons. *Exceptional Education Quarterly, 4*(4), 40–56.

York, J., Nietupski, J., & Hamre-Nietupski, S. (1985). A decision-making process for using microswitches. *Journal of The Association for Persons with Severe Handicaps, 10*(4), 214–223.

14

Using Graphic Organization Aids to Promote Independent Functioning

L. Scott Doss and Joe Reichle

SELF-REGULATION IS THE ability to adopt a set of rules about using information to guide action. Generally, self-regulation depends upon the ability to understand and use language (Whitman, 1990). Thus, reduced language skills, a characteristic of people with developmental disabilities, lead to diminished self-regulation. The graphic applications described in this chapter may allow learners who do not understand language well to regulate their behavior.

USING GRAPHIC SYSTEMS TO AID SELF-REGULATION

Some important routines occur every day at approximately the same time and are cued naturally. For example, the person who prepares a meal calls, "Dinner is ready," to cue listeners to come to the table. Additional cues may include the aroma of cooking dinner, the placing of platters of food on the table, or the movement of housemates toward the kitchen. Other routines, such as washing and drying clothes, occur less often and less predictably. The range of redundant environmental cues may also be narrower.

Most people require reminders to participate in at least some aspects of their daily schedules. For example, many people use date books to remind themselves of things they need to do. Lists, such as grocery store lists, are also often used. In creating lists, most people use traditional orthography. Unfortunately, few people with severe disabilities use traditional orthography competently. A number of studies have investigated the use of graphic prompts to teach and maintain participation in a variety of activities. Applications have included: 1) teaching cooking skills (Johnson & Cuvo, 1981; Martin, Rusch, James, Decker, & Trtol, 1982; Robinson-Wilson, 1977), 2) establishing and maintaining vocational skills (Berg & Wacker, 1989; Connis, 1979; Lancioni, Smeets, & Oliva, 1984; Sowers, Rusch, Connis, & Cummings, 1980; Wacker & Berg, 1983, 1984; Wilson,

Schepis, & Mason-Main, 1987) and 3) establishing and maintaining a variety of self-help and community survival skills (Frank, Wacker, Berg, & McMahon, 1985; Horner, Albin, & Ralph, 1986; McDonnell, 1987; Spellman, De-Briere, Jarboe, Campbell, & Harris, 1978; Thinesen & Bryan, 1981). An interesting specialized application of graphic systems is the use of tactile symbols to establish and maintain vocational performance in persons with sensory impairments (Berg & Wacker, 1989; Lancioni et al., 1984).

Teaching Meal Preparation

There may be a number of situations involving meal preparation in which the learner can successfully complete an activity through the use of graphic prompts (Johnson & Cuvo, 1981; Martin et al., 1982; Robinson-Wilson, 1977; Spellman et al., 1978). Picture recipes consist of a series of drawings or photographs depicting the task-analyzed sequence of activities required to prepare a meal (Figure 1). The learner examines each picture and performs the action depicted. In some applications the learner moves through steps given in the pictures in a prescribed sequence, performing the required action before progressing to the next step. In other applications, following a particular sequence is less important.

For example, Robinson-Wilson (1977) taught three adults with severe disabilities to prepare selected food items (e.g., Jello, hot dogs, and chocolate bars) using pictures drawn on 5″ x 8″ cards. The cards were joined together by two rings at the top of the recipe card booklet. During each session of instruction the participant was expected to perform each step in the recipe independently. The instructor provided assistance only after the participant had performed a step incorrectly. The participant was required to follow the exact sequence of steps listed in the recipe booklet only when a particular sequence was essential for successful preparation of the item. Robinson-Wilson (1977) reported that learners were able to prepare all

three recipes as a result of implementing the instructional program.

Establishing and Maintaining Vocational Skills

A variety of vocational skills has been taught successfully using graphic systems. These include complex vocational tasks (Wacker & Berg, 1983), independent job performance (Berg & Wacker, 1989; Wilson et al., 1987), job sequences (Connis, 1979; Wacker & Berg, 1984) time management (Sowers et al., 1980), and tool manipulation (Lancioni et al., 1984).

Wilson et al. (1987) used picture prompts to increase independent work performance at a restaurant by a man with severe disabilities. An assessment conducted at the beginning of the study indicated that he required frequent verbal prompts in order to perform the steps of the tasks involved in his job. For each task a book was constructed that consisted of photographs showing the participant performing each step of the task.

During the first phase of intervention, the instructor introduced each page in sequence, explained the relationship of the picture to the step, and modeled correct performance on the step. When the cues in the work environment matched the photograph, the instructor modeled marking an "X" in a box on the relevant page of the book. Finally, the participant was prompted to imitate the instructor's behavior. During the second phase of instruction, the participant was told to use his book to complete the assigned task. He progressed through the task until he made an error or failed to initiate the next step. Correct performance was praised intermittently and incorrect performance was corrected. Finally, the instructor was faded from the work environment, with the owners of the restaurant assuming responsibility for supervising the learner. Results indicated that use of the picture books reduced to nearly zero the number of prompts required to recruit correct performance by the participant.

Figure 1.   A picture recipe. (From Spellman, C., DeBriere, T., Jarboe, D., Campbell, S., & Harris, S. [1978]. Pictorial instruction: Training daily living skills. In M. Snell (Ed.), *Systematic instruction of the moderately and severely handicapped*. Columbus, OH: Charles E. Merrill; reprinted by permission.)

Establishing and Maintaining
Self-Help and Community Skills

Graphic aids have been used to establish and
maintain a variety of self-help and community
survival skills, including grooming (Thinesen &
Bryan, 1981), shopping (Horner et al., 1986;
McDonnell, 1987; Spellman et al., 1978),
scheduling and guiding the completion of
household chores (Spellman et al., 1978), and
using microcomputers (Frank et al., 1985).
Thinesen and Bryan (1981) taught three men
with moderate disabilities to initiate and maintain morning grooming routines using sequentially presented picture prompts. The pictures
were arranged on plastic pages in photograph
albums with eight pages per album. Each page
contained three photos depicting the grooming
routine and a picture of an edible reinforcer.
The participant was required to turn the pages of
the album to move through the grooming routine.

During intervention, each participant was
told to inform the instructor when he or she was
finished with the task. Although they had not
been instructed to do so, the learners began
completing the entire sequence before approaching the instructor to be checked. In the
final step of intervention the photos of reinforcers were removed sequentially, from the front
of the album to the back. Once a photo was
removed from the album, the participant no
longer received edible reinforcement for that
step. If performance deteriorated, the most recently removed photo of a reinforcer was rein-
stated.

Picture prompts have also been used to teach
other self-help skills. Spellman et al. (1978)
used picture prompts to teach people with developmental disabilities to do housekeeping
chores and to remind them to perform particular
chores (Figure 2). The first page of the book
showed the objects necessary to complete the
task. For example, the first page of the book for
sweeping with a broom showed a broom, a dust

pan, and a wastebasket. The learner was required to point to the pictured object; go to the
storage location for the object, which was also
marked with picture prompts; and use a matching-to-sample strategy to locate the needed object. The remaining pages of the chore book
consisted of pictures depicting the actions
needed to complete the chore (i.e., sweeping
the floor with the broom, sweeping the dust into
the dust pan, and emptying the dust pan into the
wastebasket).

Horner et al. (1986) taught six learners with
developmental disabilities to shop at convenience stores using color photographs of 10
items glued to notecards and housed in a three-
ring binder. During the first phase of instruction, the learner was taught to match items in a
grocery cart to the pictures in the shopping
book. Once the learner was able to match each
of the 10 items to the corresponding picture,
regardless of the order in which the item-picture
matches were requested by the instructor, the
second phase of instruction was initiated. During this phase, the instructor presented the
learner with an empty grocery cart and the picture prompt book opened to the picture of one of
the 10 items. The instructor led the learner to
the shelf containing the item, pointed to the
picture, and told the learner that this was the
item for purchase.

Some of these instructional opportunities involved nonmatches, that is, sometimes the instructor asked the participant if the picture
matched an item on the shelf that did not match
the picture. The nonmatching item could either
be very different from the appropriate match
(e.g., a picture of a hamburger matched to a
container of milk) or marginally different (e.g.,
a picture of a can of Coke™ matched to a can of
7-up™). The purpose of these negative examples was to teach the participant to reject items
that did not match pictures in the shopping
book. Results indicated that correct matching of
pictures to items in the shelves improved when
the negative examples used during instruction

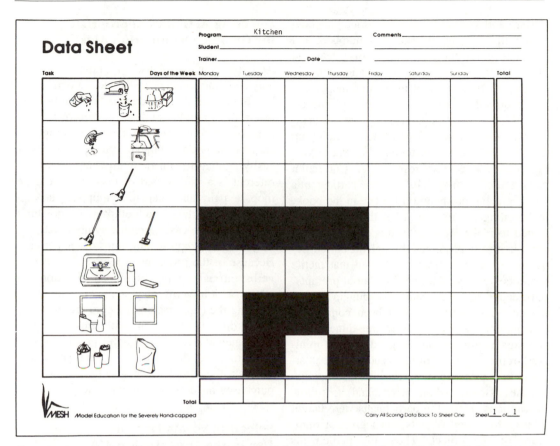

Figure 2. A graphic aid used to schedule and guide the completion of household tasks. (From Spellman, C., DeBriere, T., Jarboe, D., Campbell, S., & Harris, S. [1978]. Pictorial instruction: Training daily living skills. In M. Snell (Ed.), *Systematic instruction of the moderately and severely handicapped*. Columbus, OH: Charles E. Merrill; reprinted by permission.)

were minimally different from positive examples. When maximally different negative examples were used, generalization probes demonstrated less competent performance by the participants.

Establishing and Maintaining Performance with Tactile or Three-Dimensional Symbols

Use of graphic systems to promote independent performance is not limited to the use of photographs and drawings. There is also evidence that systems that use tactile or three-dimensional symbols may also be effective (Berg & Wacker, 1989; Lancioni et al., 1984). Rowland and Schweigert (1989) define symbols that can be used with people with multisensory impairments as being: 1) *permanent,* requiring only to be recognized by the learner; 2) *manipulatable,* allowing the learner to hold the symbol, give it to a receiver, or place it next to the referent; 3) *tactually discriminable;* and 4) *iconic,* making few demands on the learner's representational skills.

Berg and Wacker (1989) used dried glue covered with sand in the shape of numbers and letters to guide the performance of a deaf and blind student in a series of vocational tasks. During the first phase of instruction the learner was required to touch a sand-covered cue attached to a page, find a matching cue from two alternatives placed in front of her, and pick up the item behind the matching cue. Praise was provided for correct responding. Correction consisted of signing "No" into the participant's hand, placing her hand on the cue in the book, and signing "Want same?" If the learner continued to make errors after this correction, she was physically prompted through the correct sequence of steps. Results indicated that tactile prompts were as effective as pictorial prompts, but needed to be repeated to maintain performance once instruction had been completed.

Lancioni et al. (1984) used three-dimensional stimulus configurations (e.g., dolls and miniature representations of tools such as wheelbarrows) to assist three adolescents with severe disabilities (two of whom were blind) to follow instructions. First, the participants were taught to take full-sized objects when given a miniature of the object. Then, the participants learned to perform actions depicted by the objects (e.g., the doll standing behind the wheelbarrow). Rowland and Schweigart (1989) also describe "concrete calendars" and "activity shelves," which use three-dimensional objects as symbols. In these applications objects or parts of objects associated with activities (e.g., a crushed soda can for can crushing) are used to prompt the learner.

DEVELOPING GRAPHIC ORGANIZATION AIDS

Before designing an organization aid, the interventionist must consider which activities lend themselves to the use of graphic prompts, which vocabulary should be taught, and which components of the aid should be included. These issues are examined in the following sections.

Selecting Activities Appropriate for Graphic Organization Aids

Activities for which use of graphic prompts may be helpful include tasks that are performed less often than daily, and tasks that can be analyzed into a number of discrete steps (e.g., certain household chores, shopping, grooming, vocational activities). Graphic prompts are most easily applied to situations in which the object referent is a critical part of instruction (e.g., a mop, a pail, and soap in a mopping task; a toothbrush, a glass, and toothpaste for brushing teeth). In these cases, graphic symbols may be very useful in representing steps of the activity. Because of the problems in representing action verbs through graphic symbols, situations in which action verbs play a major role (e.g., twisting the cap, cracking an egg) are probably more difficult to teach with this approach (Spellman et al., 1978). Graphic prompting systems may be designed for listing household chores to be completed or selecting items to be purchased at the store, among others.

Selecting Vocabulary for Use in the Organization Aid

Once an activity has been selected, it is analyzed to determine which vocabulary items need to be represented. In part, the choice of vocabulary will depend on the purposes of the aid within the activity. For example, a reminder list for doing chores in the home must include graphic representations of the relevant chores; a reminder list for shopping must contain graphic representations of the items that need to be purchased. In contrast, an organization aid to be used to direct the learner to perform a series of steps within a task should include vocabulary items that represent the steps of the task and the materials needed to perform the task. For example, an aid for toothbrushing might include drawings of a toothbrush, a glass, and toothpaste, and photographs of the learner performing each of the steps in the task. The analysis should also include interviews with caregivers about whether the items or activities to be represented are preferred, neutral, or nonpreferred by the learner. Including neutral and nonpreferred activities or items in the vocabulary promotes generalized use of the aid. The symbols chosen must also accommodate the learner's sensory or motoric impairments. There may also be an advantage to using some symbols that the learner has acquired previously. For example, a learner may know how to request a soft drink using a graphic symbol; the same learner may now learn to use the symbol as a prompt to buy a soft drink when shopping. Thus, previously acquired vocabulary should be considered in developing the aid.

Designing the Components of the Aid

Organization aids may be used to represent steps within a task, to guide action within a task, or as elements of a reminder list. When used as a reminder list, the elements comprising the list may be collected over a relatively long period of time and the list may be used by the learner in a variety of locations. For example, a shopping list can be created over the course of the week and brought from home to the store.

Components of a Shopping List   Organization aids that use graphic symbols may be comprised of several components. For example, a system for constructing a shopping list may include a device for placing symbols corresponding to items that need to be purchased (e.g., a board with self-adhesive material for attaching symbols), a location for storing symbols when they are not in use on the shopping list (e.g., a small box that the learner can easily reach), and a device for transporting symbols from home to the store and back (e.g., a communication wallet). One way of constructing an organization aid for shopping lists is to adapt a magnetic bulletin board. A strip of self-adhesive material can be attached to the board and to the symbols so that they can easily be attached to the board. Symbols should be stored near the refrigerator door so that the learner can

easily place the symbols on the magnetized board list. For example, symbols might be stored in 3″ x 5″ file box kept on the shelf next to the refrigerator. During shopping the learner must transport symbols from one location to another (e.g., from the magnetized board at home to the store). The authors have found it useful for learners to carry symbols in a wallet with a Velcro™ strip affixed to the inner face of the wallet. The Velcro™-backed symbols are transferred from the shopping list to the wallet immediately before leaving on the shopping excursion. The interventionist may approach the learner and say, "It's time to go shopping," while pointing at the list on the refrigerator door. The interventionist may then prompt the learner to take the symbols from the list one by one, and place them in the wallet. Once at the store, the learner will match the symbols to items on the shelves.

Components of a "To Do" List   A three-ring binder containing pictures of the various steps of a household chore and the materials needed to perform them can be used to remind a learner what needs to be done. Matching symbols are placed beside the objects needed for the chore (e.g., a picture of a broom is placed in front of the broom closet). This system does not require a device for transporting the symbols, since its use is likely to be limited to one location.

An aid for doing chores is likely to have a board that is prominently displayed in an area the learner approaches often. If one of the purposes of the aid is to remind the learner to do a chore, there may be pictures of each chore. If the purpose of the aid is to promote independent performance, the chore may have a notebook with the materials associated with the chore as well as each of the steps necessary to complete the chore depicted by photographs. In addition, matching photographs of the materials can be attached to their storage locations so that the learner can match the photographs of the materials to the photographs in the notebook when gathering materials to perform the chore.

TEACHING THE LEARNER
TO USE THE ORGANIZATION AID

Certain guidelines govern teaching learners with severe disabilities to use organizational aids:

1. Chores represented in the organization aid should be varied.
2. Effective cues for prompting use of the aid by the learner should be selected.
3. Strategies to teach the discriminations implicit in use of the organization aid should be developed.
4. The routine involving use of the organization aid should be task analyzed.

Varying the Objects
or Activities Represented

To promote generalized use of the organization aid, a variety of chores and items should be represented. Building variation into the aid from the start will teach the learner to attend to the logos and symbols on the aid, and to refrain from simply memorizing a chain of actions to perform a single chore or purchase a single item. For example, if a learner purchases only one item on each shopping trip, he or she may come to associate going to a store with the purchase of a particular item. The learner thus need not consult the (one-item) shopping list. Rather than attending to the shopping list, the learner has simply memorized a chain of events (go to store, select item, pay, leave). Thus, in beginning a program to teach the use of a shopping list, it is important to vary the item or items that are being purchased across shopping trips.

Some required tasks or activities or non-preferred or neutral items that the learner must purchase (e.g., toilet paper) should be included from the start. By including only vocabulary associated with optional activities or preferred items during initial instruction, the learner may come to see the list as involving only optional activities or preferred items. This will sharply reduce the number of contexts in which use of the list will be functional.

Preferred items or activities should also be included during initial instruction on use of the aid. If only mandatory activities or unpreferred items are included as vocabulary, it may be very difficult to motivate the learner to use the aid. In particular, when constructing reminder lists for shopping, the learner's preferences should be considered an integral aspect of selecting initial vocabulary. Over a series of excursions a shopping lexicon should be developed based upon the stable preferences expressed by the learner for particular items. For example, if the learner always purchases diet cola of a certain brand, a symbol associated with that brand (i.e., a product logo) should be included in the lexicon for shopping lists. Over time the lexicon will come to reflect items normally purchased during excursions to the supermarket.

Selecting Cues to Prompt
Functional Use of the Organization Aid

In designing graphic organization aids for completing chores such as doing laundry, cleaning the bathroom, or vacuuming the carpet, care must be taken to provide cues that effectively direct the learner to a symbol display while promoting the greatest degree of independence possible (Spellman et al., 1978). For example, an organization aid for completing chores may include a signal to remind the learner to check the aid. If the learner is dependent on someone to remind him or her to monitor the aid, its purpose will be significantly compromised.

A number of natural cues are available. The authors have used an inexpensive digital watch with an alarm. This alarm can be set to go off for 15 seconds 1 hour after the learner arrives home. Initially, a more intrusive prompt (e.g., physical guidance) may be paired with the alarm to direct the learner through the steps of checking the organization aid. The more intrusive prompts could then be faded as the learner begins to move through the sequence independently.

Functional use of shopping lists may require additional cues to initiate the use of an organization aid. Items are added to a shopping list as their supplies are exhausted. In order to use a graphic shopping list, a learner may need to recognize the difference between "used up" and "not used up," and place symbols next to items on the list that have been used up. Several strategies may be necessary to guide the learner to place a symbol on the reminder list. Sometimes the learner may find that an item is empty when attempting to use it (e.g., an empty peanut butter jar). In these instances, the learner may be prompted to remove the corresponding symbol from storage and place it on the list. More stable, predictable cues may be provided by searching for "used up" items on a regular schedule (e.g., immediately before shopping trips).

Teaching the Discriminations Required to Use Organization Aids

A variety of discriminations may be required of the learner in order to use an organization aid successfully. First, the learner must discriminate among the symbols used in the aid. Second, the learner must be able to match the symbol with the object or activity being represented. Third, the learner must discriminate when and where the aid should be used. Each application requires somewhat unique discriminations depending upon the purpose of the system. Basic instructional strategies to teach the learner to discriminate among symbols are discussed in Chapter 10. For example, when compiling a list of items that need to be purchased, the learner must discriminate between items that are "used up" and items that are "not used up." During the course of a week certain products are more apt to be used up and need to be purchased during a trip to the store. As soon as a used up item is discovered, the learner's attention should be called to the empty container. The critical natural cue for the learner is the empty container.

In one strategy to teach the discrimination between "used up" and "not used up," the learner is rewarded for bringing the empty container to the attention of the instructor by being given the opportunity to consume some of the "used up" item or some other preferred reinforcer. For example, after showing an empty cola can to the instructor, the learner could be prompted to transfer the appropriate symbol from the storage location to the reminder list, and then be provided with a small amount of a desired item. Presenting a container of an item that was not "used up" would not be reinforced. Over successive opportunities, the learner can be taught to match the empty can with the cola logo on the shopping list.

As the learner becomes more proficient at identifying used up items and matching them to the appropriate logos, reinforcement would be provided on only some correct opportunities. The emphasis during this stage of instruction is on reducing how often the learner is provided with preferred tangible reinforcers for correct performance.

Another strategy is to schedule regular times during which the learner is to check storage areas of the home for used up items. The instructor could fill the storage areas with both empty and full containers. When the learner identifies an empty container, the instructor could escort him or her to the location where the product logos are kept; assist him or her in matching the empty container to the appropriate logo, moving to the reminder list, and placing the logo on the list; and then providing appropriate reinforcement.

Over time, prompts to the learner to initiate the sequence could be transferred to more natural cues. One more natural cue for transferring symbols from the storage location to the reminder list is the presence of the used up product on the pantry shelf. Natural cues for transferring symbols from the reminder list to the wallet might be a particular day of the week and time of the day (e.g., every Tuesday at 4:30 in the afternoon). Whatever the specific natural cue, instruction should be directed toward transferring control of the learner's performance of the routine from prompts delivered by the instructor to more naturally occurring cues.

Other uses of organization aids (e.g., daily schedules, reminder lists for chores) require discriminations peculiar to the particular application. For example, when using a reminder list for chores, the learner may be required to discriminate between a clean floor and a dirty floor (Spellman et al., 1978). The interventionist must consider the discriminations implicit in a particular application of organization aids and develop strategies to teach those discriminations.

Horner et al. (1986) demonstrated that when students with severe disabilities are taught to discriminate between items that match symbols in their lists and items that do not, they are better able to perform this task after instruction is completed. The results of Horner et al. (1986) suggest that learning opportunities should be included in which the symbol does not match the referent item when teaching the use of the reminder list for shopping to an individual with severe disabilities. This analysis also applies to "used up" versus "not used up" as well as other applications of organization aids. This strategy is an example of general case instruction because it samples the range of possible circumstances the learner will encounter when using the organization aid. (General case instruction is described in more detail in Chapter 8.)

Task Analyzing
Components of an Activity

The various steps of the routine must be specified in order to teach the use of an organization aid. When organizational aids are used to direct actions within the task (i.e., the steps involved in mopping the floor), the task analysis also provides the basis for pictorial representation of the task.

Task Analyzing Use of a Shopping List   To use a shopping list, a learner typically moves to the file box (or other storage location) containing logos and selects the logo that corresponds to the empty product container. The logo is then affixed to a magnetized board (or other display device) that is housed in a convenient location (e.g., on the refrigerator door). When it is time to go shopping, the symbols are transferred from the reminder list to the wallet (or other device for transporting symbols from the list to the store). When the learner finds an empty container, he or she is supposed to move to the storage location, gain access to the storage location, match the empty container to the appropriate symbol, and transfer the symbol to the reminder list.

As the time nears to go shopping, the learner is directed to go to the list and transfer the symbols to a single page of a communication wallet that has been equipped with a self-adhesive strip to house symbols representing items to be purchased. This activity also consists of a series of subtasks. The instructor may initiate the transfer activity with a statement such as "Time to go to the store!" The learner must then remove the wallet from his or her pocket, open the wallet to the appropriate page, transfer the symbols from the list to a designated location within the wallet, and return the wallet to his or her pocket.

Upon arrival at the store, the learner can be instructed to remove the wallet from his or her pocket and open the wallet to the page housing the shopping list. Subsequently, the learner can be taught to follow a standard sequence of moving through the store matching items pictured on the shopping list to items on the store shelf. Upon locating an item, the learner removes it from the shelf and places it in the shopping cart (Horner et al., 1986; McDonnell, 1987).

After the shopping trip has been completed and the learner has returned home, the learner can help put the products away in order to gain practice matching products to storage locations. The last step of this task is removing the symbols from the wallet and replacing them in the file box for future use. Storing purchased products may be facilitated by attaching product labels to the appropriate locations. The empty grocery bag could serve as the learner's cue to take the communication wallet to the file box, open the wallet, remove the symbols from the wallet, and place them in the file box. During initial phases of instruction, praise and corrective feedback could be given after the learner completes each of the substeps.

Task Analyzing Other Organization Aids Task analyses should be conducted for other organization aids as well. For example, the task analysis for using an aid to promote timely and effective floor mopping would include elements that first identified the circumstances that would naturally lead to mopping the floor (e.g., a dirty floor). Once the learner knows he or she is to mop the floor, the learner could be directed to the shelf containing the picture books corresponding to various household chores, including mopping. An organizational aid could be constructed that reminds the learner that it is time to mop the floor. In this use of the aid, the task analysis would include establishing cues to prompt the learner to check the aid. In this application, the "to mop" symbol is used to remind the learner that it is his or her turn to mop the floor, not to direct the learner within the mopping task.

The mopping organization aid might contain pictures of actions to take to complete the chore. One picture might show the learner at the storage location for the needed items (e.g., the mop, the pail, the floor detergent), the next picture might show the learner putting detergent in the pail, the next might show the learner running water from a faucet into the pail, and so forth. The teaching strategy would consist of reinforcing the learner for turning the pages in the book, and performing actions that correspond to those indicated in the pictures.

Reinforcing Correct Use of Organization Aids

Reinforcing the correct use of the organization aid is important because the components of the aid may not be reinforcing by themselves. Using the organization aid entails changing the pragmatic function of the vocabulary item used (e.g., changing from a request for diet cola to use of the diet cola logo for directing purchasing by the learner), which should be reinforced by the interventionist. Reinforcement is also important in teaching the discriminations involved in functional use of the organization aid.

During the initial phase of instruction the interventionist may find that verbal praise is not a sufficiently powerful motivator for the learner. In this circumstance, preferred edible or potable reinforcers may be required to motivate the learner to perform the subtasks.

A strategy that the authors have used to facilitate use of organization aids involves the establishment of an intermittent reinforcer delivered contingent upon the learner monitoring the aid. For example, on some occasions, when the designated signal (e.g., a beeper on a watch) is given and the learner moves to the aid, the learner will discover a product logo representing a favorite beverage or preferred activity affixed to the list. Contingent upon delivering this logo to the interventionist, the learner will receive the reinforcer. The authors' experience suggests that use of this strategy tends to result in the learner becoming increasingly independent in monitoring the aid, and tends to facilitate fading the prompts that were originally required to ensure that the learner moved to the aid.

Shifting Pragmatic Use of a Previously Acquired Symbol

Moving from the use of a symbol as a request to the use of the same symbol to perform a slightly different pragmatic function can create difficulties. Consider, for example, a learner who knows how to request diet cola at home and needs to locate the item during a shopping trip. A history may have developed that at home the learner is immediately reinforced with diet cola when he or she selects a diet cola symbol. In contrast, in the grocery store, the learner is not permitted to drink the cola immediately after selecting it. Learners may become upset upon being informed that they must wait until returning home before consuming the beverage.

There are long-term and short-term solutions to this problem. One option is to teach the learner to shop for items that do not represent strong reinforcers (e.g., tissue, dish detergent). This strategy merely postpones the problem and compromises the functionality of the organizational aid. Moreover, the exclusive selection of items of neutral interest may result in an unmotivated learner. A long-term solution involves attempting systematically to delay the delivery of the reinforcer contingent on a correct shopping selection. Most convenience or grocery stores have a soft drink vending machine. After the learner has shopped successfully for a soft drink, the interventionist says, "Let's go get a cola." At this point the learner goes to the vending machine and purchases a cola, which he or she may sip during the remainder of the shopping trip. Across opportunities, the amount of time between the successful shopping selection and the offer of a cola is lengthened in two ways. First, the time between the product selection and the offer by the interventionist is gradually increased across successive opportunities. Second, items are added to the shopping list so that the soft drink is purchased after increasingly long periods of work.

A variation of this reinforcement delay strategy involves providing more immediate access to smaller amounts of a reinforcer. Over opportunities the learner may come to choose the smaller reinforcer because its delivery is immediate (Ragotzy, Blakely, & Poling, 1988). This principle could be applied to many situations involving shopping for preferred reinforcers. For example, the learner could purchase potato chips, a highly preferred item. Contingent upon correct performance, the instructor could offer the choice between a single potato chip deliv-

ered relatively quickly and a small bag of potato chips to be delivered after a longer period of time. The study by Ragotzy et al. (1988) indicates that over a series of opportunities the learner will come to choose the smaller reinforcer rather than the larger reinforcer because of the delay in delivery associated with the larger reinforcer.

Of course, some learners will not wait for the instructor to present the offer to purchase the soft drink and will initiate a request immediately after the soft drink has been selected from the store shelf. Under these circumstances, the learner can be taught to wait for a short period following the request for the reinforcer. For example, when the learner requests a cola, the interventionist can say, "Hang on," or "In a bit." (This procedure is discussed in Chapter 11 in the section on the use of a safety signal.) The interventionist waits briefly and then provides the requested item. Across opportunities, the amount of time the interventionist waits is gradually increased. The initial delay used in this procedure is determined by the amount of time that can be added between shopping selection and delivery of reinforcers without socially unacceptable behavior occurring.

Each of these strategies requires time to work. Certain learners will not tolerate delay, and will become upset when the delivery of reinforcers is delayed. For such learners a short-term solution is to think in terms of providing relatively immediate reinforcement for correct performance. For example, as soon as the learner who likes diet cola (and who will not tolerate delay of reinforcement) removes the diet cola from the store shelf, he or she should be escorted to a vending machine and allowed to purchase a drink. Since this kind of immediate reinforcement is not natural (i.e., we do not typically rush to a vending machine after selecting our grocery items) this procedure is intrusive. The interventionist must simultaneously be working with the learner to establish tolerance of delayed reinforcement using the long-term strategies described above.

Correspondence between Symbol Selections and Learner's Actions

A calendar of the learner's daily routine may be useful in helping the learner recall his or her day. This is important for enhancing the learner's conversational skills, since a substantial portion of conversations involve recounting events that have occurred within the daily routine. Representing the events of the day graphically may serve to prime the learner for a similar routine the following day. A graphic representation of the events of the day may also serve as the basis for teaching the learner to use a chronological list as a memory aid. For example, suppose that a learner tends to complete the first two activities in his or her daily routine but forget the third. Such a learner could be taught to monitor a daily activity calendar and to cross off activities from the calendar as they are completed. In this way, the learner would have only to consult the daily activity calendar to determine what was expected next. At some later point in the day, the activity calendar might also be used in response to the question "What did you do today?" Thus, a daily calendar may serve: 1) as a reminder of activities the learner is required to perform, 2) as a daily organizer, and 3) as a tool for interacting with others about what the learner has been doing.

An important feature of teaching the use of a simple activity calendar involves ensuring that the learner links his or her actions to symbols representing the events of the day. Placing symbols on a calendar will be of little functional significance unless the learner follows the planned schedule. Persons with severe disabilities often have difficulty establishing a correspondence between their actions and their communicative behavior. That is, what the learner says he or she will do often fails to correspond to what the learner actually does unless special attention is given.

Preschool children often experience difficulty responding to both types of questions. Children may be reinforced inadvertently with positive attention for inaccurate reports of their involvement in various activities. This can lead to increased reporting of fabrications (Baer, Williams, Osnes, & Stokes, 1984; Guevremont, Osnes, & Stokes, 1986). De Freitas Ribeiro (1989) investigated this type of behavior in preschool children and found that reinforcing children's self-reports of toy play led to increased reports of toy play that had not actually occurred. Reinforcement of reports of play that had occurred resulted in increased correspondence between reported and actual play.

Once a learner has had an opportunity to use a calendar of regularly occurring daily events, it is possible to teach the learner to use the calendar as a mnemonic device to ensure correspondence between his or her actions and some aspects of his or her communicative behavior about those actions.

SUMMARY

In this chapter we have described an important application of graphic symbols that are part of a learner's augmentative communication system that goes beyond interpersonal communication. The uses described in this chapter relate directly to the establishment of strategies that the learner can use to more efficiently regulate and monitor him- or herself to achieve more normalized participation in a range of community environments with a minimum of intrusive prompts by other individuals.

REFERENCES

Baer, R., Williams, J., Osnes, P., & Stokes, T. (1984). Delayed reinforcement as an indiscriminable contingency in verbal/nonverbal correspondence training. *Journal of Applied Behavior Analysis, 17,* 429–440.

Berg, W.K., & Wacker, D.P. (1989). Evaluation of tactile prompts with a student who is deaf, blind, and mentally retarded. *Journal of Applied Behavior Analysis, 22*(1), 93–99.

Connis, R.T. (1979). The effects of sequential pictorial cues, self-recording, and praise on the job task sequencing of retarded adults. *Journal of Applied Behavior Analysis, 12*(3), 355–361.

De Freitas Ribeiro, A. (1989). Correspondence in children's self-report: Tacting and manding aspects. *Journal of the Experimental Analysis of Behavior, 51,* 361–367.

Frank, A.R., Wacker, D.P., Berg, W.K., & McMahon, C.M. (1985). Teaching selected microcomputer skills to retarded students via picture prompts. *Journal of Applied Behavior Analysis, 18*(2), 179–185.

Guevremont, D., Osnes, P., & Stokes, T. (1986). Preparation for effective self-regulation: The development of generalized verbal control. *Journal of Applied Behavior Analysis, 19,* 99–104.

Horner, R.H., Albin, R.W., & Ralph, G. (1986). Generalization with precision: The role of negative teaching examples in the instruction of generalized grocery item selection. *Journal of The Association for Persons with Severe Handicaps, 11*(4), 300–308.

Israel, A., & Brown, M. (1977). Correspondence training prior to verbal training and control of nonverbal behavior via control of verbal behavior. *Journal of Applied Behavior Analysis, 10,* 333–338.

Johnson, B.F., & Cuvo, A.J. (1981). Teaching mentally retarded adults to cook. *Behavior Modification, 5*(2), 187–202.

Lancioni, G.E., Smeets, P.M., & Oliva, D.S. (1984). Teaching severely handicapped adolescents to follow instructions conveyed by means of three-dimensional stimulus configurations. *Applied Research in Mental Retardation, 5,* 107–123.

Martin, J., Rusch, F., James, V., Decker, P., & Trtol, K. (1982). The use of picture cues to establish self-control in the preparation of complex meals by mentally retarded adults. *Applied Research in Mental Retardation, 3,* 105–119.

McDonnell, J. (1987). The effects of time delay and increasing prompt hierarchy strategies on the acquisition of purchasing skills by students with severe handicaps. *Journal of The Association for Persons with Severe Handicaps, 12*(3), 227–236.

Ragotzy, S.P., Blakely, E., & Poling, A. (1988). Self-control in mentally retarded adolescents:

Choice as a function of amount and delay of reinforcement. *Journal of the Experimental Analysis of Behavior, 49,* 191–199.

Risley, T., & Hart, B. (1968). Developing a correspondence between the nonverbal and verbal behavior of preschool children. *Journal of Applied Behavior Analysis, 1,* 267–281.

Robinson-Wilson, M.A. (1977). Picture recipe cards as an approach to teaching severely and profoundly retarded adults to cook. *Education and Training of the Mentally Retarded, 12,* 69–73.

Rowland, C., & Schweigert, P. (1989). Tangible symbols: Symbolic communication for individuals with multisensory impairments. *Augmentative and Alternative Communication, 5*(4), 226–234.

Sowers, J., Rusch, F.R., Connis, R.T., & Cummings, L.E. (1980). Teaching mentally retarded adults to time-manage in a vocational setting. *Journal of Applied Behavior Analysis, 13*(1), 119–128.

Spellman, C., DeBriere, T., Jarboe, D., Campbell, S., & Harris, S. (1978). Pictorial instruction: Training daily living skills. In M. Snell (Ed.), *Systematic instruction of the moderately and severely handicapped* (pp. 391–411). Columbus, OH: Charles E. Merrill Publishing Co.

Thinesen, P.J., & Bryan, A.J. (1981). The use of sequential pictorial cues in the initiation and maintenance of grooming behaviors with mentally retarded adults. *Mental Retardation, 19*(5), 247–250.

Wacker, D.P., & Berg, W.K. (1983). Effects of picture prompts on the acquisition of complex vocational tasks by mentally retarded adolescents. *Journal of Applied Behavior Analysis, 16*(4), 417–433.

Wacker, D.P., & Berg, W.K. (1984). Training adolescents with severe handicaps to set up job tasks independently using picture prompts. *Analysis and Intervention in Developmental Disabilities, 4,* 353–365.

Whitman, T.L. (1990). Self-regulation and mental retardation. *American Journal on Mental Retardation, 94*(4), 347–362.

Wilson, P.G., Schepis, M.M., & Mason-Main, M. (1987). In vivo use of picture prompt training to increase independent work at a restaurant. *Journal of The Association for Persons with Severe Handicaps, 12*(2), 145–150.

Index